The First
American Frontier

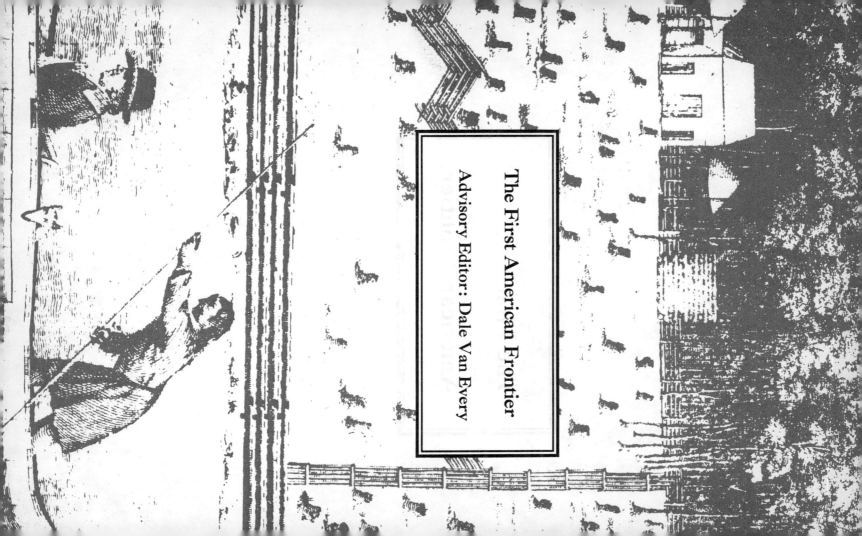

The First American Frontier

Advisory Editor: Dale Van Every

A History of an Expedition Against Fort Duquesne in 1755; Under Major-General Edward Braddock

Winthrop Sargent, Editor

Arno Press & The New York Times

[1971, 1855]

Reprint Edition 1971 by Arno Press Inc.

Reprinted from a copy in
The State Historical Society of Wisconsin Library

LC # 73-146420
ISBN 0-405-02884-9

The First American Frontier
ISBN for complete set: 0-405-02820-2

See last pages of this volume for titles.

Manufactured in the United States of America

Publications

OF THE

Historical Society of Pennsylvania.

BRADDOCK'S EXPEDITION:

A MONOGRAPH.

Affin que les honnorables emprises & nobles auentures & faicts d'armes, par les guerres de France & d'Angleterre, soient notablemēt enregistrez & mis en memoire perpetuel, parquoy les preux ayent exēple d'eux encourager en bien faisant, ie vueil traicter & recorder Histoire de grand' louange.——On dit, & il est vray, que tous edifices sont massonnez & ouurez de plusieurs sortes de pierres, & toutes grosses riuieres sont faictes & rassemblees de plusieurs surgeons. Aussi les sciences sont extraictes & compilees de plusieurs Clercs: & ce, que l'on sçait l'autre l'ignore. Non pourtant rien n'est, qui ne soit sceu, ou loing ou pres.——Les Cronicques de Messire Jean Froissart: Prol:

Paul Weber. Pinxt.　　　Engraved at J.M. Butler's establishment, 84 Chestnut St.　　　A.W. Graham. Sculp.

BRADDOCK'S BATTLE FIELD.

THE

HISTORY

OF

AN EXPEDITION

AGAINST

FORT DU QUESNE,

IN 1755;

UNDER

MAJOR-GENERAL EDWARD BRADDOCK,

GENERALISSIMO OF H. B. M. FORCES IN AMERICA.

EDITED

FROM THE ORIGINAL MANUSCRIPTS

BY

WINTHROP SARGENT, M. A.,

MEMBER OF THE HISTORICAL SOCIETY OF PENNSYLVANIA.

PHILADELPHIA:
LIPPINCOTT, GRAMBO & CO.,
FOR THE
HISTORICAL SOCIETY OF PENNSYLVANIA.
1855.

On the 13th of February, 1854, the Historical Society of Pennsylvania established a Publication Fund; by the terms of which any person whatever, on the payment of twenty dollars, becomes entitled to receive a copy of all of its future publications during the term of his life. The money thus received is invested on a special trust, and the interest alone is applied to purposes of publication. It already amounts to four thousand dollars. The present volume is the first fruit of this undertaking, and it is proposed to follow it with others of a like character. It is proper to add, that considerable aid is derived from the Society itself, and from the anticipated sale of the works thus produced.

TO

JOSEPH R. INGERSOLL;

THROUGH WHOSE PUBLIC SPIRIT

THE MATTER WHICH FORMS ITS BASIS WAS PROCURED:

THIS VOLUME

IS RESPECTFULLY DEDICATED.

CONTENTS.

ILLUSTRATIONS.

PREFACE.

DURING the term of Mr. J. R. Ingersoll's official residence at London, he procured, for the Historical Society of Pennsylvania, copies of the three journals which constitute the basis of this volume. A few months since, these were committed by the Society to the hands of the editor, with a request to prepare therefrom such a work as he now has the honour to lay before it and the public.

It is a matter of reasonable surprise, that the narrative of what Mr. Sparks has justly styled "one of the most remarkable events in American history," has never before been formally and circumstantially related. Perhaps the secret rests in the fact that much of the original material necessary to such an undertaking has hitherto slumbered in undisturbed repose, its very existence almost forgotten, upon the shelves of State-Paper Offices and public libraries in various parts of the world.

(xi)

A sketch of the combat, brief, but admirably exact, is given by the distinguished author before cited in the Appendix to the second volume of the Writings of Washington; and other notices, incidental and of less value, are to be found in numerous historical works. There are also two obscure and obsolete contemporaneous pamphlets, professing to give an account of Braddock's defeat, which, although not so rare as to be unknown to Rich, are hardly possessed of sufficient worth to save them from the limbo of Ariosto. The first of these is "A Letter to a Friend; giving a concise but just Account, according to the Advices hitherto received, of the Ohio Defeat," &c. (Boston, printed; Bristol, reprinted, 1755; 8vo., pp. 30.) The second, to which the editor has had access only since the body of his volume was stereotyped, is entitled "The Expedition of Major-General Edward Braddock to Virginia, with the two Regiments of Hacket and Dunbar. Being Extracts of Letters from an Officer in one of those Regiments to his Friend in London," &c. (London, 1755; 8vo., pp. 29.) This seems to be a mere catch-penny production, made up, perhaps, from the reports of some ignorant camp-follower. The privations and insubordination of the army, and the paltry and despicable character of the colonists and their country form the burthen of his strain. The only facts he relates concerning the expedition that we do not find elsewhere, are that the General was somewhat of a *bon vivant*, and had with him "two good Cooks who could make an excellent Ragout out of a pair of Boots, had they but Materials to toss them up with;" and that the soldiers, for lack of ovens, were compelled to bake their maize bread in holes in the ground.

Of a very different value are the copies of the French official reports of the action of the 9th of July, 1755, so kindly placed at the editor's disposal by Mr. Sparks; to whom the Society is also indebted for the use of the copper-plate from which the plan of the battle-field is taken. To Mr. Neville B. Craig, of Pittsburg, it is under like obligations for the plate of Braddock's route; and to Mr. Paul Weber, of Philadelphia, for the drawing of the wood-cut of Braddock's grave, and for the elegant original landscape painting engraved as a frontispiece to this volume. To these gentlemen, and to Mr. John Jordan, junior, of Philadelphia, the Rev. Mr. Francis-Orpen Morris, of Nunburnholme Rectory, Yorkshire, England, Dr. William M. Darlington, of Pittsburg, and Mr. Edward D. Ingraham, of Philadelphia, both the Society and the editor must confess their obligations. To Mr. Ingersoll and Mr. Buchanan, the late and present Ministers to England, and to Mr. Townsend Ward, the Librarian of the Society, acknowledgments are also due for the valuable assistance they have, in various ways, rendered him.

So far as regards the manner in which the editor has accomplished his task, he has only to say that, within the limits prescribed him, he has carefully endeavored to fulfil his duty. The Introductory Memoir was considered, by those whose views he felt called upon to regard, desirable to bring clearly before the reader's mind the origin and ulterior causes of this campaign; which was, in fact, but the prologue to the Seven Years' War. An Appendix is also added, in which will be found much matter bearing more or less directly upon the subject in hand. It may be objected that the notes abound too much in "matter needless, of importless burthen;" yet in such a place, it is submitted that no unimportant part of an editor's duty consists in elucidating neglected facts; nor should he spare to dwell upon the personal history of the obscurest name upon the roll:

——— il figlio
Del tale, ed il nipote del cotale
Nato per madre della tale.

INTRODUCTORY MEMOIR.

On the night of the 30th of April, 1748, the preliminaries of what was boldly asserted to be a definitive and lasting peace, were signed by the diplomatic representatives of England, Holland, and France, at the city of Aix-la-Chapelle. Exhausted by the fatigues of a long, harassing, and unsatisfactory struggle, the two great parties in this arrangement embraced, if not eagerly, at least without reluctance, a scheme which would give to each an opportunity to extricate itself from any unprofitable enterprise or dangerous dilemma in which it had become involved, and to prepare, at leisure, plans for a future and more successful war. "Never," says Lord Mahon, "never, perhaps, did any war, after so many great events, and so large a loss of blood and treasure, end in replacing the nations engaged in it in nearly the same situation as they held at first." The Earl of Chesterfield — the only man in the British Cabinet possessed of sufficient energy and capacity to have directed more successfully hostile measures, or to have procured more advantageous terms of peace —

(15)

had been compelled to withdraw from power six months before : and to the ignorant or feeble hands which continued to hold the reins of government, much of the future, as well as the then existing blunders in the policy of the Crown — at least, so far as America was concerned — may safely be attributed.[1]

Certainly, no one versed in the political secrets of the day could, by any possibility, have believed that this peace was to be a lasting one. It was deficient in every element of coherence. Nothing was settled by the treaty : conquests all over the world were to be mutually restored ; some trifling shiftings of territorial proprietorship on the part of the Italian and other minor princes engaged in the war were agreed upon ; a few other articles, relative to European affairs, of little or no consequence in proportion to the cost at which they were effected, were inserted ; and the treaty of Utrecht, as well as all former treaties, confirmed in existence. In short, matters were essentially placed *in statu quo ante bellum*, at a cost to England of £110,000,000. But there were two circumstances, connected with the treaty of Aix-la-Chapelle, galling in the last degree to British pride and British interest : these were the surrender of Cape Breton to its former possessors, and the delivery of hostages until that was done. Accordingly, whilst the Earl of Sussex and Lord Cathcart

---

[1] II. Hist. of Eng from Peace of Utrecht, &c., 290. So keenly was their disgrace felt by the English, that Charles Edward himself, then residing at Paris, could not view it without indignation. "If ever I ascend the throne of my ancestors," he exclaimed, "Europe shall see me use my utmost endeavors to force France, in her turn, to send hostages to England."

awaited, at Paris, in easy but dishonourable captivity, the tardy messengers whose return should announce that once more the lilies were planted upon the bastions of Louisbourg, there glowed in the breast of every true Briton the burning embers of mortified vanity, the but half-smothered lust of fierce revenge. From the throng of Hanoverian favorites around their alienigenate king, down to the hardy New England fisherman who trimmed his light sail as he glided within sight of that apple of the American eye, curses both loud and deep were vented against the degrading terms they had submitted to. They had suffered not only disgrace and dishonor, but infinite loss; and they anxiously awaited the hour of vengeance. That hour was not fated to be long delayed.

It has been observed, that the treaty of 1748 left England in a state of mind but too ready to seize, with avidity, upon the first pretext for bettering its condition, and restoring to itself those rights which it had unjustly perilled in that compact. Unfortunately for the peace of humanity, circumstances not so weak as to be considered mere pretexts, soon presented themselves, to provoke a renewal of the strife. It is, perhaps, not very expedient to go back to the ultimate causes of the war, and tracing their progress, event by event, finally, after the fashion of an inverted pyramid, taper this narrative down to the story of the single battle by which its epiphany was signalized. But a few brief comments upon the immediate and most glaring inducements to a contest so important in its conduct, so momentous in its results, may not be out of place.

2

If ever there was a just cause of war, England had it in 1755. By the treaty of October, 1748, (Art. III.,) that of Utrecht (1713), and numerous others, were recognised and confirmed in all their parts; save, of course, such as might be modified by the pact in question—and were formally constituted its basis. By the treaty of Utrecht (Art. XII.,) "all Nova Scotia or Acadia, with its ancient limits, and all its dependencies, was ceded to the crown of Great Britain;"[1] and, furthermore, it was provided (Art. XV.,) that "the subjects of France, inhabitants of Canada and elsewhere, should not disturb or molest in any manner whatever the five Indian nations which are subject to Great Britain, nor its other American allies." These articles were certainly incorporated into the treaty of Aix-la-Chapelle; but with neither stipulation were the French willing to comply. The last clause would evidently always

---

[1] "Dominus Rex Christianissimus eodum quae pacis praesentis Ratihabitationes commutabuntur die, Dominae Reginae Magnae Britanniae literas, tabulasve solenne et authenticas tradendas curabit, quarum vigore, insulam Sancti Christophori, per subditos Britannicos sigillatim dehinc possidendam; Novam Scotiam quoque, sive Acadiam totam, limitibus suis antiquis comprehensam, ut et portus Portus Regii urbem, nunc Annapolin regiam dictam, cæteraque omnia in istis regionibus quae ab iisdem terris et insulis pendent, unacum earundarum insularum, terrarum et locorum dominio, proprietate, possessione, et quocunque jure sive per pacta, sive alio modo quaesito, quod Rex Christianissimus, corona Galliæ, aut ejusdem subditi quicunque ad dictas insulas, terras et loca, eorumque incolas, hactenus habuerunt, Reginæ Magnæ Britanniæ, ejusdemque coronae in perpetuum cedi constabit et transferri, prout eadem omnia nunc cedit ac transfert Rex Christianissimus; idque tam amplis modo et formâ ut Regis Christianissimi subditis in dictis maribus, sinubus, aliisque locis ad littora Novæ Scotiæ, en nempe quae Eurum respiciunt, intra triginta leucas, incipiendo ab insula, vulgo Sablé dicta, eaque inclusa et Africum versus pergendo omni picatura in posterium interdicatur." Vide also Mem. des Comm. de S. M. T. C., &c.

open to Great Britain a *casus belli*; for it was impossible for a year at a time to pass by without some troubles between the Iroquois and their Canadian neighbors; and in such cases each party, on the showing of the other, is inevitably the aggressor. But the provision respecting Nova Scotia was widely different. The restoration of Louisbourg, as matters then stood, was a point of equal importance to the settlers in Canada and the colonists of New England. Under its ancient lords, this nursing-mother of privateers would be powerful alike to preserve the French, and to destroy the English trade and fisheries in that part of the world. The annoyance, therefore, of the New England people was extreme and well founded; and at their earnest representations, the Home Government was finally instigated to adopt the only practical method left of peaceably dissipating the dangers with which they were threatened by the constantly increasing power and malignity of the French. The armed occupation and settlement of the province of Nova Scotia, till then unnoticed or disregarded by the Ministry, became now a subject of consideration. In the spring of 1748, and during that and the ensuing year, several thousand colonists were sent thither by the government, at an expense of £70,000, and the town of Halifax was founded. But the French, who had hitherto evaded or disingenuously dallied with their obligations to yield up the peninsula — English there, and constantly increasing their own strength by reinforcements — now openly resisted, under M. de la Corne, the progress of their rivals. Thus commenced that scene of constant dissension and strife which ensued between the original settlers, scattered over the land, and the subjects of the crown to which it lawfully pertained; whose melancholy termination was that enforced expatriation which posterity has consecrated to sorrow in the pages of Evangeline. That the Court of Versailles, through its subordinate officers, promoted and encouraged the sturdy denial of British sovereignty by these loyal-hearted Acadians, cannot at this day be doubted or denied; but the result of such a course was as fatal to the fair fame of the conquerors, as to the happiness of the conquered.

Nor did the French government confine itself to an unavowed but well-supported resistance to the progress of Anglo-American power in the north only. Thirty years before, its grand scheme for uniting its colonies, from the Gulf of Mexico to the Bay of Fundy, by a chain of posts along the Mississippi, the Ohio, and the Lakes, had begun to be tangibly developed: ever bent upon the fulfilment of these cherished ideas, already its encroaching grasp was extended, with many ramifications, from Canada to the Lower Mississippi. In 1731, Crown Point was unlawfully erected by the French within the limits of the Five Nations, and of New York: Niagara had been seized on in 1720. In truth, their policy seemed both rational and feasible. During a large portion of the year, the natural outlets of Canada were effectually sealed by the angry elements: supplies of troops or provisions—in fact, almost every intercourse whatever with Europe—were utterly shut out from its ports. The facility of water communication between Canada and New Orleans, by the lakes and rivers of the West would, if made properly available, not only facilitate the secure transmission of supplies, but would inevitably throw the whole peltry trade of those regions into the hands of the French. It is no wonder, then, that they were desirous of procuring so manifest an advantage; but, unhappily for themselves, they grasped at too much, and lost the whole. Like the dog in the fable, they sacrificed not only the hoped-for gain, but all their present good, in the endeavor.[1]

To have opened a communication between their widely-separated establishments, by the way of the western lakes and the Illinois, would have been a comparatively safe, and by far the wiser mode of procedure for the French, under the circumstances of their position. So far as its ostensible objects were concerned, it would have perfectly answered the purpose, and the trade it would secure would have been prodigious: nor could the English, everything considered, have made any very effectual opposition. But to adopt this route would have left too wide a margin for British enterprise. The warlike tribes seated between the Illinois and the Alleghanies — the broad lands watered by the Muskingum, the Scioto, and other kindred streams, by whose marge arose the bark lodges of the Shawanoes and the Delawares — the gloomy forests, where

Beneath the shade of melancholy boughs,

---

[1] That the designs of the French were perfectly comprehended in the English colonies, is abundantly proved by Gov. Shirley's letter to Gov. Hamilton, of March 4th, 1754, printed in the Minutes of the Provincial Council of Pennsylvania, Vol. VI., p. 16.   And see also I. Entick, 105, and *The Contest in America between Great Britain and France.* (Lond. 1757.)

the Six Nations wandered on their distant hunting-parties — these would have still remained open to the visits — subjected to the influence of their hated rivals. The notion of occupying the head-waters of the Ohio, and of planting a line of forts from Lake Erie, by the Le Bœuf, to the Alleghany, and thence down the Ohio to the Mississippi, was a more dangerous but a more fascinating vision. Its execution would probably be fraught with much hazard, but its results, if successful, were too precious to suffer the powers that were to resist the temptation. Out of the nettle danger they hoped to pluck the flower safety ; and, at one time, it really seemed as though all their anticipations were to have been crowned with success. But the wisdom of Almighty Providence had ordered the event otherwise.

In an evil hour, then, for themselves, the French decided to persevere in the latter plan. While the Appallachian chain, it was thought, would serve at the same time as a bulwark against the British colonies, and as a well-marked and palpable boundary between the two nations, the whole body of the Western Indians would be thrown completely under their control. Already game had begun to be scarce, or to disappear utterly, east of the mountains, and the best furs were to be found upon the further side. With forts and trading-houses once established in their midst, it would not be difficult to prevent the savages from supplying the English dealers, or receiving in turn their commodities. The peltry traffic, so profitable to European commerce, had already to be pursued on the frontiers ; and it was not probable that the Indians would go thither to seek no better market than they could find at home. The certain consequences, too, of thus virtually monopolizing the right to buy and sell with the savages, would be to secure, beyond a peradventure, their services against the English, in any difficulty that might occur. There is nothing the American aborigine learns more quickly than to abandon his rude native weapons of the chase—the bow or the flint-headed spear—for the fusil and gunpowder of the whites; and having become thus dependent on his neighbors for the means of subsistence, it has never been found difficult to point out other and less innocent employ-ment for his arms. By thus building up a mighty power behind the English settlements, they would not only be in a position to terribly annoy, if not to entirely overcome them, in the event of war, but also to clog and embarrass their prosperity during time of peace. A very great staple of that commerce which made America so valuable to Great Britain being utterly destroyed, its domestic increase, its foreign influence, would be materially affected. The agricultural productions of the colonies would likewise be touched; for, with the constant necessity, through an imminent danger, there must likewise be the constant presence of a portion of the population in arms; and thus the tobacco plantations and the fields of maize would miss a master's hand, and yield a diminished crop. It is unne-cessary to consider here how many millions of money were yearly employed at this period in the trade between the mother country and her colonies—to how many thousands of souls it gave a support: nothing can be more evident than that such an attack upon the productiveness of the one must at once affect their value to the other, and thus render them, day by day, less important, and less self-capable of preservation. In short, as was well said in the House of Commons, the French held the colonies within their range of posts as in the two ends of a net, which, if tightened by degrees, would get them all into the body of it, and then drown them in the sea.[1]

It will be recollected, that for a long period the unde-fined western limits of the two English colonies of Penn-sylvania and Virginia had occasioned much controversy, and had induced considerable ill-feeling between those provinces. Their claims were conflicting; and no autho-rized power had yet reconciled their demands, and assigned to each sovereignty final and determinate territorial bounds. So long, therefore, as the question remained open, and the precise confines of either province unestablished, it was impossible for settlers to know from which government they could procure a good title. For this reason, chiefly, the lands lying west of the Alleghanies, and upon the streams which unite to form the Ohio, had remained unvisited by any other Englishmen than the few traders who found their annual profit in selling to the savages in the neighborhood of their homes. To perplex matters still more, the associates known as the Ohio Company obtained, in 1749, a vague grant from the crown, vesting in them vast but undefined tracts of land bordering on, if not actually embracing, the very territory in dispute between

---

[1] I. Entick, 126.

Virginia and Pennsylvania.[1] All these circumstances combined to render more easy of execution the manoeuvres of the French in regard to the occupation of the forks of the Ohio, and they were availed of without delay. The history of their first settlement in that vicinity; of the unsuccessful mission of Washington to procure their departure; of the consequent collision that ensued between the two parties; and the English defeat at Fort Necessity; are prominent passages in history. It is from these occurrences that we are to date the original conception, the organization and execution, and the disastrous results, of the expedition commanded by Major-General Braddock.

It is very true, that at the period in question both colonies claimed that the lands comprehended within the forks of the Ohio were included in their patents: yet, nevertheless, nothing can be more certain than that it rightfully appertained to neither Pennsylvania nor Virginia. The original patent, from James I. to the London and Plymouth Companies, which was relied upon by Virginia, had been legally overturned on a *quo warranto* in 1623; and the tacit acquiescence of those companies in the grant of Maryland to Lord Baltimore by Charles I., in 1632, was considered to have barred their right to open the case anew, after the interval of an hundred years. The charter from the crown to William Penn, in 1681, would appear to cover the whole

[1] Perhaps the influence with the ministry of John Sargent, Thomas Walpole, and the other associates of the Ohio Company, whose prospects were entirely subverted by the presence of the French, may have contributed more powerfully than any other cause to the expedition against Fort Du Quesne.

territory in dispute; but, hitherto, the proprietaries, to whom alone belonged the power of purchasing the soil from the Indians, had not come to any terms with their dusky neighbors. The land, in fact, belonged absolutely to its savage inhabitants; and the utmost the province of Pennsylvania could claim was the exclusive right of purchasing it from them. Nor had the French any better title: perhaps, if the comity of Christian nations were to be taken into the account, none so good. Thus, whatever it might be alleged, neither crown had as yet any right to the country west of the Alleghanies. But that was of small consideration: a block-house once established, and a garrison maintained there on some specious pretext; a judicious distribution of red ochre, gewgaws, fire-arms, and rum; and it would be easy enough to get an absolute title from the Indians.[1] This was the end of the French, who were not disposed to admit any English pretensions that conflicted with their own interests. When, therefore, in 1752, on the first alarm of the threatened invasion of these regions, the Penns instructed their Lieutenant-Governor to lend all aid in his power to Governor Dinwiddie of Virginia, in the erection of a fortress that might thwart their designs, it was also provided that no rights of the proprietaries

[1] Horace Walpole sneeringly dwells on the methods by which England and France seated themselves in America. "They enslaved, or assisted the wretched nations to butcher one another," says he, "instructed them in the use of fire-arms, brandy, and the New Testament, and at last, by scattered extension of forts and colonies, they have met to quarrel for the boundaries of empires, of which they can neither use nor occupy a twentieth part of the included territory." (I. Mem. Geo. II., 343.) But "we do not massacre," he adds, "we are such good Christians as only to cheat!" (III. Corresp. 136.)

should be prejudiced thereby. Two years later, when there was actual likelihood of such a fortress being erected, and Dinwiddie had issued his proclamation, granting away two hundred thousand acres of the soil upon part of which Pittsburg now stands, a correspondence ensued between the two governments, in which that of Virginia, while denying the fact of the forks of the Ohio being within the jurisdiction of Pennsylvania, very honestly conceded that if on investigation this should prove to be the case, the rights of that colony should not be at all impaired.[1]

Previously, however, to the actual occupation of this region, the French had been gradually strengthening their hands, and drawing closer their lines in that quarter. Their scattered posts upon the Mississippi, though few in number and wide apart, gave them the command of that stream; and they had already a fortified establishment upon the Ohio, at the mouth of the Wabash river. In 1745, the Marquis de la Galissonière was appointed Governor-General of Canada. Penetrated at once with the immense advantage that would result from an arrangement that should not only open the communication of Canada with the mother country during those seasons when all its natural outlets were closed by ice and frost, but would likewise restrain and cripple the English colonies upon the continent, he spared no toil to mature and

[1] Minutes of Provincial Council of Pennsylvania, Vol. VI, pp. 4, 8. I. Olden Time, 436. I am happy in joining my testimony with that of Mr. Francis Parkman (Conspiracy of Pontiac, 87.), as to the extreme value of Mr. Craig's labors in regard to the earlier settlements beyond the Alleghanies. So far, in particular, as relates to Western Pennsylvania, his collections are worthy of much praise.

put into shape the needful elements of its organization. It was he who, in 1748, despatched Bienville de Celoron, with three hundred men, on a tour of inspection along the Alleghany and the Ohio, depositing in various quarters leaden plates on which were inscribed a memorial of his master's title to those countries, and warning the English traders whom he encountered, that henceforth they were prohibited from visiting the Indians there.[1] In 1750, by command of his successor, the Marquis de la Jonquière, harsher measures were resorted to. A body of troops under Joncaire visited the Ohio country, seizing the property and persons of such English traders as they found there. The former they confiscated; the latter they sent prisoners to France.[2] These scenes were the commencement of a tedious and unresulting diplomatic correspondence between the Earl of Albemarle, His Britannic Majesty's Ambassador at the Court of Versailles, and the

---

[1] Olden Time, 238, 268, 270, 289. II. Histoire du Canada, par F. X. Garneau, 192. Craig's Hist. of Pittsburg, 20.

[2] Vide Lord Albemarle's letter to Lord Holdernesse, respecting the case of John Patton, Luke Irwin, and Thomas Bourke. I. Entick, 45. The Marquis de la Jonquière arrived in Canada in August, 1749; and acting under positive instructions from his court, faithfully pursued the policy of his predecessor in regard to shutting out the English from the Ohio. Descended of a Catalonian family, he was born in Languedoc, in 1696; and died at Quebec, May 17th, 1752. He was a man of superb presence and undaunted resolution; but, withal, prone to avarice. His whole career gave abundant evidence of his courage and soldier-like bravery: but the world ridiculed the passion that induced him, on his dying bed, to begrudge the cost of wax candles while his coffers were overflowing with millions of money. He enjoyed little peace towards the conclusion of his life, by occasion of his efforts to suppress the order of Jesuits in his government; and, indeed, this dispute is supposed to have shortened his days. II. Garneau, liv. viii, c. 3.

French authorities, which was prolonged without intermission upon either side of St. George's channel, until the capture of the Alcide and the Lis, by Boscawen's fleet, compelled the Duc de Mirepoix to demand his passport, and war was openly waged.[1]

In 1752, arrived in Canada, (to which government he had been appointed by the King on the recommendation of M. de la Galissonière), the Marquis de Duquesne de Menneville, a name destined to become indelibly impressed upon the history of that land whence the golden lilies of his nation, though watered by the best blood alike of friend and foe, were so soon to be extirpated. All of his antecedents that can be mentioned here are that he was a captain in the royal marine, and born of the blood of Abraham Duquesne, the famous admiral of Louis XIV.

---

[1] Roland-Michel Barrin, Marquis de la Galissonière, and a Lieutenant-General in the French service, was one of the ablest men of his time. As a scholar, a soldier, a statesman, his merit was deservedly esteemed. Born at Rochefort, Nov. 11, 1693, he entered the navy in 1710, in which he served with distinction until he was appointed to Canada. In that colony, his conduct was eminently conducive to the best interests of both the King and his people. The Swedish traveller, Du Kalm, bears abundant testimony to his scientific acquirements; while even his meagre appearance and deformed person added to his influence over the savages. "He must have a mighty soul," they said; "since, with such a base body, our Great Father has sent him such a distance to command us." De la Galissonière did not remain in America long enough to carry out the course he had begun: he returned to France in 1749, where he was placed at the head of the department of nautical charts. He is best known in English history by his affair with the unfortunate Byng, in 1756, which resulted in the judicial murder of that excellent officer, in order thereby to screen the criminal derelictions of his superiors. He died at Nemours, Oct. 26, 1756, full of glory and honour, and loudly regretted by Louis XV, who was so sensible of his worth, that he had reserved for him the baton of a Marshal of France. Biog. Univ. (ed. 1816), Vol. XVI, p. 367.

His abilities were good; and during his brief career he acquitted himself thoroughly of the duties of his position; but the haughtiness of his character, and the lack of affability in his manners, prevented his ever attaining any great degree of popularity with the Canadians. Nevertheless, he seems to have been possessed of some singularly generous dispositions. In October, 1754, an English woman, nineteen years of age, arrived in Philadelphia from Quebec. Twelve years before, while yet almost an infant, she had been captured by the savages, and by them sold as a slave in Canada. In new scenes and the lapse of time, the names of her parents, the very place of her birth, had entirely passed from her memory; but she still clung to the sounds of the tongue of her native land, and dreamed of the day when she should be reunited to her unknown kindred. By some chance, her pitiful story reached the Governor's ears; and, full of compassion, he at once purchased her freedom and furnished her with the means of returning to the British colonies. There she wandered from city to city, vainly publishing her narration, and seeking to discover those joys of kindred and of home that she had never known. An act of this kind should, at any season, reflect credit upon the performer; but considering its particular occasion, when war was plainly looming in the horizon, to liberate and restore in this manner a person abundantly qualified to reveal, so much of the local secrets of Quebec, must clothe the character of M. de Duquesne with the attribute of magnanimity, as well as of generosity.[1]

1754, however, he demanded his recall by the government, in order to return to the naval service, and to encounter the enemy upon a more familiar element. It will be sufficient in this place to add, that his instructions while in Canada, in regard to the Ohio, were of a piece with those of La Jonquière and Galissonière, and that he faithfully obeyed them.[1] In January, 1753, four traders on

[1] II. Garneau, liv. viii., c. 3. I have been not a little indebted to this valuable work (2nd ed. Quebec, 1852 : three vols. 8vo.), which, indeed, is the best history extant of Canada from the earliest period to the present time. In particular, I have occasionally found notices of the history of individuals that I know not where else to look for. It is to be hoped that the new edition of the *Biographie Universelle*, now being published at Paris by Didot, will, in respect to the lives of French worthies, at least, be more particular than that which it is designed to supplant. It is unjust to the past age, that the names of such men as Duquesne, Dumas and Contrecœur, should be consigned to oblivion. Thus we are left in ignorance of the period of Duquesne's death, and of all save a single circumstance in his later career. In 1758, M. Duquesne, being in France, was appointed to the command of all the forces, sea and land, in North America. In March he sailed from Toulon, in command of a small squadron, which, however, was utterly discomfited by the English. His own ship, the Foudroyant, of 84 guns and one thousand men, was engaged, after a long chase in which their comrades had been almost lost sight of, by the Monmouth, Captain Gardiner, of 64 guns and 470 men. Captain Gardiner had served under the murdered Byng in the Mediterranean, and the combat was a compulsory one with him. On the eve of sailing on this cruise, whence he was never to return, he mentioned to his friends that there was something which weighed heavily on his soul; that Lord A—— had recently said to him, that he was one of the men who had brought disgrace upon the nation; and he was convinced that in this very voyage he should have an opportunity of testifying to his lordship the rate at which he estimated the national honor. As his ship was going into action, he made a brief address to his crew: "That ship must be taken: she looks to be above our match, but Englishmen are not to mind that; nor will I quit her while this ship can swim, or I have a soul left alive!" Accordingly, he closed with the Foudroyant, and lay on her quarter within pistol-shot for several hours, till her flag came down. Shot through the head, and death inevitable, he still

the Kantucqui river, near the Ohio, were captured by a party of Caughnawagas, or French Indians from Canada, who divided their goods, to the value of several hundred pounds, among themselves. This was undoubtedly done in pursuance of instructions from Quebec. The captives were carried as slaves to Canada, where they remained until the summer of the succeeding year; their new lords refusing to suffer them to be ransomed under the price of a negro slave for each. The province of Pennsylvania at last, however, succeeded in purchasing their freedom for the sum of seventy-five pounds sterling; a rate which gave such umbrage to Onoraguiete, the chief sachem of the tribe, that he wrote a furious letter to the Indian Commissioner, declaring that for the future he should cause all prisoners to be murdered, since no higher ransom was to be paid for them.[1]

It was under the administration of Duquesne that the first steps were taken towards an armed occupation of the Ohio. It must not be forgotten, in referring to these proceedings, that so far as involved his duty to the King his master, and his interpretation of that sovereign's rights, his conduct was perfectly justifiable throughout. Though neither power possessed the least claim in justice to that territory, France as well as England had not hesitated

retained comprehension enough to say to his first-lieutenant, that "the last favor he could ask of him was, never to give up the ship!" That gentleman pledged himself that he never would; and nailing the flag to the staff, he stood by it during the contest with a brace of pistols, resolved to slay the first man, friend or foe, who approached to pull it down. A more gallant or hardly-contested sea-fight than that of the Monmouth and Foudroyant was never fought.

[1] Penn. Gazette, No. 1338. VI. Col. Rec., 129.

during many years to refer to it as their absolute inheritance, and virtually to utterly ignore any title in its original occupants to the sovereignty of the soil. No treaty with the Indians inhabiting it had ever been made, by which, even for the poor pittance of a few strings of beads or barrels of whiskey, they had ceded it to the stranger. It is true that the French assured them that their only object was to found trading-posts; that they had no idea of cutting down the woods, and tilling the fields, after the fashion of the English.[1] The savage was not to be thus gulled; and he viewed their first encroachments with as great repugnance as he did the more flagrant advances of the British, who boldly penetrated into the most secret recesses of his hunting-grounds, laying out the lines of a future settlement without the least form of a purchase from its outraged inhabitants.[2] Nevertheless, regardless of the Indian title, the King of France had, so early as 1712, granted the district watered by the river Wabash in his

[1] Shortly before quitting his government, Duquesne held a secret conference with the deputies of the Six Nations, at Montreal, in which he reproached them with their willingness to surrender the control of the Ohio to the English rather than to the French. "Are you ignorant," said he, "of the difference between the King of France and the English? Look at the forts which the King has built; you will find that under the very shadow of their walls, the beasts of the forest are hunted and slain; that they are, in fact, fixed in the places most frequented by you merely to gratify more conveniently your necessities. The English, on the contrary, no sooner occupy a post, than the woods fall before their hand — the earth is subjected to cultivation — the game disappears — and your people are speedily reduced to combat with starvation." In this speech, as M. Garneau well observes, the Marquis has accurately stated the progress of the two civilizations.

[2] II. Sparks's Washington, 434.   II. Garneau, 201.

letters patent creating the colony of Louisiana; and following the explorations of La Salle in 1679, had furthermore added all the streams flowing into the Mississippi that were known to this discoverer. This liberality was well matched by some of the English patents, which were bounded by the Atlantic ocean on the east, and on the west by the Pacific. It costs little to a monarch to be generous in this style; and no pope or king in Europe was backward in thus gratifying the importunities of his subjects. But when a nation undertakes to enforce such grants of a foreign soil, it behooves it to sagely consider whether, in so doing, the interests of its neighbor may not be threatened. This was precisely the case here: the English, whose claim was, where both were bad, no better than that of the French, saw, or thought they saw, in its fulfilment, the ruin of all that they then lawfully and actually held, and with wisdom resolved to oppose such a consummation.[1]

---

[1] Governor Shirley of Massachusetts, whose opinion on such points must have weighed greatly with the people, frankly declared, in his letter to Governor Hamilton of Pennsylvania (March 4th, 1754), that the language of King James the First, in the patents of the London and Plymouth Companies, was "the only rule for the English Governors to judge of the limits of the colonies under their respective governments, in all disputes with the French Governors concerning the extent of his Majestie's territories upon this Continent, except in cases where the original limits declared in these Letters Patent may be altered by treaty or other agreement between the two Crowns; and those Patents extend the English territories within the 32d and 48th degrees of northerly latitude, quite across this Continent, viz.: from the Atlantic Ocean to the South Sea; and I can't find that these eastern or western limits have been abridged by any treaty." Vide Penn. Col. Rec., Vol. VI., p. 16. Mr. Shirley had lately been acting at Paris as one of the British Commission to define the boundaries of Acadia and New England.

Strong in all the resources of civil and military centralization, the government of Canada moved with a resolution and celerity that, for the time, set at defiance the efforts of their slow-footed and divided adversaries. By the end of 1753, a connected line of forts existed, extending from Montreal to what is now called French creek, in Pennsylvania, but which was named by the French the Rivière aux Bœufs, on account of the numbers of buffalo that were found in its vicinity.[1] The nationality of its first European settlers soon caused it to receive another title. It was to this fort that in December, 1753, Major Washington repaired on a fruitless mission from the Governor of Virginia, to warn the trespassers to retire; and here it was that he observed the extensive preparations they had made for still further encroachments in the ensuing spring.[2] Fifty birchen canoes, and one hundred and seventy of pine, were, at that early stage of the winter, drawn up on the shore, ready for the opening of the streams; and numerous others were in progress of completion. In these the troops were to be floated down Le Bœuf and the Alleghany, on their way to the Ohio. For though but some six or seven hundred, of the expedition of two thousand men who had been sent in the preceding autumn to erect these posts, remained in garrison there during the winter, it was already settled that a large body was to arrive in the spring for the further operations alluded to.

The private scandal of the place and period attributed the building of these establishments and their dark train of consequent calamities to the same cause as had since

[1] II. Sparks's Washington, 436.   [2] Ibid, 442.

long before the day of Helen of Troy, according to Flaccus, brought about the waste of human life and the overthrow of mighty empires. M. Pouchot, an officer of rank in Canada, does not scruple to insinuate that the new governor, shortly after his arrival in Quebec, became involved in an intrigue with a beautiful woman, the wife of a resident of that place. M. Bigot, who had recently passed from the Intendancy of Louisbourg to that of Canada, had in like manner contracted a liaison with a Madame Péan, the wife of the *aide-major* of the city. Bigot being thus at the head of the commissary department of the colony, it was an easy affair for the Governor and himself to arrange a plan by which the willing husbands of the ladies in question should be detached from an inconvenient vicinity to their partners. Accordingly, it was decided to give them lucrative employments in an expedition which, it was gravely whispered, was concocted for the express purpose of placing these gentlemen at a considerable distance from home; and to Péan was assigned the command of the forces which were marched in 1753. The forts then built were furnished with numerous and expensive magazines of merchandise and provisions; a precaution necessary enough under the circumstances of their position, but which, in the manner in which the business was managed, must have afforded endless opportunities for the acquirement of ill-gotten gains. Together with the proper provisions and stores, all sorts of goods, always expensive, but here utterly useless, were purchased in the name of Louis XV., and sent, for his service, into the wilderness. Stuffs of silk and velvet, ladies' slippers and damask shoes, silk stockings, and the costly wines of Spain, figure largely in the category, and enable us to conceive how it came about that the French colonies cost the nation so much and returned it so little.[1] In fact, it would seem that the colonial stewards of the king were not unfrequently but too wont to look upon their office in no other light than as a source of revenue to themselves; and when, like Uriah the Hittite, the lords and masters of these new Bath-shebas were sent down to the host, they doubtless felt no compunction in making their absence as remunerative to themselves as possible. From Pouchot's position and character, it is not unjust to admit the truth of the facts upon which he bases his conclusions: but ignorant as, from the very nature of his subordinate rank, he must have been of the state arrangements and politic designs of the former governors and the Court of Versailles, it is easy to perceive how erroneous were his inferences. It may be true enough that the husband of each fair Evadne was

---

[1] In 1753, the exports of Canada amounted to but £68,000; its imports were £208,000, of which a great portion was on the government account, and did not enter into the ordinary channels of trade. The exports of the English provinces during the same year were £1,486,000; their imports, £983,000. In 1755, the Canadian imports were 5,203,272 livres; its exports but 1,515,730. And while the population of British America was 1,200,000 souls, that of all Canada, Cape Breton, and Louisiana, could not have exceeded 80,000. The policy of sustaining such a colony at such a cost was thus doubted by the most brilliant if not the profoundest writer of the day. "Le Canada coûtait beaucoup et rapportait très peu. Si la dixième partie de l'argent englouti dans cette colonie avait été employé à défricher nos terres incultes en France, on aurait fait un gain considérable; mais on avait voulu soutenir le Canada, et on à perdu cent années de peines avec tout l'argent prodigués sans retour. Pour comble de malheur on accusait des plus horrible brigandages presque tous ceux qui étaient employés au nom du Roi dans cette malheureuse colonie."—*Voltaire.*

named to a high command in the new expedition, but nothing can be more absurd than to imagine that to procure their absence was the primary motive to its undertaking.[1]

It must not be supposed that the detachment ordered to Lake Erie and the new forts by Duquesne consisted entirely of regular troops. There were, at that time, probably not more than one thousand regular soldiers in all Canada. But an exceedingly well-organised militia, and the hardy, active, semi-Indian class, half-trappers, half-traders, who dwelt on the outskirts of French civilization, furnished material for any enterprise involving war or adventure. Woodsmen by education, full of courage and vivacity by birth, they formed an admirable band for such ends as they were now engaged in. To this day, the *coureurs des bois* are of the primest favorites of the Indians, with whom they intermarry and assimilate, and at whom they "never laugh;" they were, therefore, just the men

---

[1] *Mémoires sur la Dernière Guerre de l'Amérique Septentrionale, par M. Pouchot.* (*Yverdon*, 1781,) Vol. I., p. 8. These two volumes contain much curious and authentic information respecting the subject to which they relate. The author was born at Grenoble, in 1712, and at the age of twenty-two was an officer in the regiment of Béarn. His talents as an engineer, cultivated under such masters as Vauban and Cohorn, early pointed him out to favourable notice, and in season he acquired a captaincy in that regiment, and was created a knight of St. Louis. He came to America on the breaking out of the war of 1755, and gained much honor by the part he took therein, particularly in the defence of Forts Niagara and Levis, where he was in command. He was slain in Corsica, 8th May, 1769, during the warfare between the French and the natives of the island His memoirs, prepared by himself for publication, did not see the light for several years after his death. They are accompanied with explanatory notes, apparently by a well-informed hand. My opinion of their value is confirmed by that of M. Garneau.

required for a business that must depend for success mainly on the good-will of the savages.[1]

Returning to Williamsburgh from his bootless errand on the 16th of January, 1754, Washington made his report to the Governor of Virginia; when it was instantly resolved, in compliance with the King's directions, to fit out an expedition which should proceed with all haste to the confluence of the Alleghany and the Monongahela, where the Ohio Company had already commenced to build a fortified trading-house, and there to erect such works as might, for the season, prevent any further enterprise on the part of the French. For this object, the Assembly of Virginia voted the sum of £10,000, and the party was put under the control of Colonel Joshua Frey, who, dying on the 31st of May, was succeeded in office by Washington, the second in command. His instructions were to capture, kill, or destroy all persons who should endeavor to impede his operations. Aid was also requested from the neighboring provinces; but none seems to have reached Virginia in time; and she is thus entitled to the honor of having single-handed first entered the lists against France, to struggle for the mastery of the continent.[2]

---

[1] Schoolcraft: Red Races of America, 134.

[2] Mr. Wheeler, in his recent History of North Carolina (Vol. I., p. 46), states that in compliance with Gov. Dinwiddie's request, the president of that province "issued his proclamation for the legislature to assemble at Wilmington on the 19th February, 1754; who met and appropriated £1000 to the raising and paying such troops as might be raised to send to the aid of Virginia. Col. James Innes of New Hanover marched at the head of a detachment, and joined the troops raised by Virginia and Maryland. But there being no provision made by Virginia for supplies or conveniences, the expedition was countermanded, and Col. Innes returned with his men to

The little army with which the beginning of all this was to be accomplished, was to consist of but four hundred men. In January, 1754, William Trent was commissioned to enlist one hundred; he succeeded in raising but seventy, with whom he instantly marched for the Ohio: the remaining three hundred were not raised so soon. They were furnished with ten cannon and eighty barrels of powder; and would, it was hoped, have succeeded in throwing up a couple of forts before the arrival of the French. If that were found impossible, Governor Dinwiddie looked to their attacking and destroying the enemy by a *coup de main*.[1]

In the meanwhile, however, the French had not been idle. Nearly a year before, in the spring of 1753, they had built, at Presqu'Isle on Lake Erie, a strong fort of chestnut logs, fifteen feet high, and one hundred and twenty feet square, with a block-house on each side.

---

[1] The cannon sent towards the Ohio were four-pounders, selected from thirty pieces presented by the King to his colony of Virginia. They went from Alexandria to Will's Creek, and thence in wagons. Small arms and accoutrements were also provided by Dinwiddie; with thirty tents and six months' provision of flour, pork, and beef. The uniform was a red coat and breeches; and a half-pint of rum *per diem* was allowed each man. The pay was as follows: To a colonel, 15s. *per diem*—to a lieutenant-colonel, 12s. 6d.; a major, 10s.; a captain, 8s.; a lieutenant, 4s.; an ensign, 3s. The privates received 8d. *per diem* and a pistole bounty. Vide Dinwiddie's letter, in VI. Penn. Col. Rec., 6.

North Carolina." Besides these North Carolina troops, three of the King's Independent Companies, two from New York and one from Carolina, had been ordered to Virginia. As they were paid by the King, but retained in the colonies for local protection, it was usual for the provinces to contribute to their victualling expenses on any extraordinary service in which they might be employed; which Virginia, on this occasion, refused to do. II. Penn. Archives, 169.

Leaving a strong garrison here, they marched to the Rivière aux Bœufs, where they erected another fort, and that at Presqu'-Isle. Here garrisons were maintained during the winter of 1753–4, and here strong reinforcements from Canada were directed to rendezvous in the spring of 1754, fully prepared to march to and occupy the head of the Ohio.[1] For this purpose, a corps of some 800 Canadians, under M. Marin, had been carefully raised and accoutred. Every man was amply provided with the needful equipments, while to each of the officers, naively observes an old chronicler in his enumeration of the good cheer provided for the detachment, was allotted a bottle of wine every day, two gallons of brandy a month, and food in proportion.[2] Being thus prepared, M. de Contrecœur (who succeeded in the command at French creek to

[1] VI. Col. Rec., 10. It is possible that the French had some sort of an establishment at Presqu'-Isle so early as 1749; the ruins of the fort of 1753 are still perceptible within the limits of the town of Erie. It was provided with bastions, a well and a ditch; and was the head-quarters of communication between Canada and the Ohio. Thirteen miles distant was the fort *de la Rivière aux Bœufs*, on the spot where now stands the village of Waterford (Erie county, Penn.). A small lake, and a stream rising from it to fall into French Creek, still preserve the memory of the long-vanished buffalo, which once fed on its fertile meadows. The last post on the route to the Ohio was on the Alleghany at the mouth of French Creek (where now is the village of Franklin), and was called Venango, being a corruption of *In-nun-gah*, the name by which the Senecas knew the latter stream. Its ruins are still to be seen. It was 400 feet square, with embankments which are yet eight feet in height, and furnished with four bastions, a large block-house, a stockade, and a ditch seven feet deep, and fifteen feet wide, fed through a subterraneous channel of fifty yards by a neighboring rivulet. See Day's Hist. Col. Penn., 312, 642.

[2] I. Pouchot, 10.

Legardeur de St. Pierre, the one-eyed old warrior who had received Washington), set out betimes in the spring of 1754. On the 17th of April, at the head of from five hundred to a thousand men, with eighteen pieces of artillery, he appeared before the incomplete and defenceless works which occupied the spot where now stands the great city of Pittsburgh. Ensign Ward, with his forty-one men, was in no condition to resist such a force. Without a struggle he was compelled to reluctantly abandon his post to the enemy, and was suffered to retire unmolested to his own country. The French set at once about the strengthening and perfection of their conquest. Under the directions of Mercier,[1] a captain in the artillery, new works were added and the former made more complete: till, by the middle of May, 1754, it was placed in a position to defy any force that could then be brought against it. Its breast-works were probably calculated to resist such small field-pieces as those which Washington had with him, as

[1] On the fall of Fort Necessity, M. le Chevalier de Mercier went back to Canada, whence he was presently sent to France with an account of the campaign on the Ohio. Here his advice was much regarded at Versailles; and in 1755, he returned with Vaudreuil and Dieskau to America. His counsels were received by the latter with implicit faith, and eventually influenced Dieskau to measures which ended in his utter defeat at Lake George, 8th Sept., 1755. In August, 1756, he directed with great skill the works with which M. de Montcalm besieged Oswego, and on the surrender of that place, according to Pouchot, secreted to his own use a large share of the public property. In March, 1757, he was sent by M. de Vaudreuil to demand the surrender of Fort William-Henry, but received a peremptory denial from Major Eyres, its governor. (Vide Pouchot and Mante.) This first architect of Fort Du Quesne seems to have been an accomplished officer, but a leech on the public purse. He was probably one of that large tribe of locusts who went to Canada determined to make a fortune quocunque modo.

they were made in part, at least, of earth, and were two fathoms in thickness at the base.[1] A force of some eight hundred or a thousand men garrisoned the post, officered by such men as Laforce, Drouillon, de Villiers, Jumonville, Chauvignerie, de Longueil, and many others, whose names were war-cries along the border; and from Contrecoeur, who commanded the whole, it now for the first time received its title of Fort Du Quesne.[2]

Washington was at Will's Creek when the tidings reached him of Ward's discomfiture; and acting promptly, on the same principle which had governed his mind in originally urging the very measure that was thus defeated, he was resolved to proceed to the mouth of the Red-stone Creek, and there to erect a fortification under whose shelter he should await such things as time might bring forth. With his scanty force, it was impossible to think of the re-investment of Fort Du Quesne and its new garrison until the arrival of the reinforcements which were constantly expected; but he wished to be as near to the French as he possibly could get, and this spot offered too many advantages to be passed over. By tedious marches, and suffering under the greatest deprivations of food, raiment, and stores, he had arrived at the Great Meadow, when, on the 28th May, he encountered a detachment of thirty-five men under M. de Jumonville, sent out from Fort Du Quesne as ambassadors, as was alleged by M. de Contrecoeur, to warn him to withdraw. Considering all that we can learn of the characters of the two French

---

[1] II. Sparks's Washington, 19.

[2] De Contrecoeur's summons to Ensign Ward is given at large in VI. Penn. Col. Rec., p. 29.

officers, and the circumstances of their position, it is to be regretted that there seems some cause to believe the truth of this story. Contrecœur's treatment of Ward had not been in anywise treacherous or unmanly : his demeanor on other occasions seems to have been creditable and fair ; and it is difficult to believe that he would have wilfully put his hand to a deliberate falsehood, to be echoed not only by all his brother officers, but throughout France and Europe. But, granting the doubtful story that Jumonville was entrusted with such a commission, he bore about him no reason to inspire Washington with the prescience of the fact. An ambassador with thirty-five armed men at his heels in an enemy's country, with the army of his friends behind, his foe in front, and the shouts and clamor of victory still ringing through the air, was an anomalous character on that stage ; and we humbly conceive that it was perfectly fair and just in Washington to defeat and destroy his party in any manner of lawful war. Certainly, no sane Englishman could have doubted Jumonville's object was other than to gain scalps or intelligence : probably it partook as much or more of the nature of both as of that of a formal embassy. The strength of his party, and the impressions entertained of its designs by the Indians who were cognizant of its departure and brought the intelligence to the Americans — impressions, the justice of which was confirmed by the recorded testimony of officers of his own nation — these facts abundantly warranted Washington in treating him as an enemy in arms.[1] Washington could not

---

[1] I. Pouchot, 14. Since both the French and the English have published their own stories, it is but fair to give the Indian version of this affair.

but remember that Contrecœur had but a few weeks before, by dint of superior power, ejected Ward from Fort Du Quesne (the first scene, by the way, of overt hostility in the long and bloody drama that was about to be enacted); and even at this day there is little reason to believe that he would have hesitated for one moment in the commission of any act which he supposed came within the line of his duty and the service of the King. Be this as it may, however, Washington, on the 24th of May, received notice from a friendly Indian that a secret expedition had started from Fort Du Quesne two days before, with intent to strike the first English they might see. Thus forewarned, he engaged them on the 28th, when Jumonville was slain in a manner too often detailed to need repetition here. [1] In

---

[1] At a council held at Philadelphia, in December, 1754, Scarroyaddy their leader pointedly dwelt on the efforts Jumonville had previously made to seduce him from the English (whom he was on the way to join), and how he rewarded these insidious overtures by at once informing Washington of their whereabouts, and aiding in the combat by way, as he told Washington, of "a little bloodying the edge of the hatchet." John Davison, the interpreter, who was also in the battle, added that "there were but eight Indians, who did most of the execution that was done. Coll. Washington and the Half-King differed much in judgment, and on the Colonel's refusing to take his advice, the English and Indians separated. Afterwards the Indians discovered the French in an hollow, and hid themselves, lying on their bellies behind a hill; afterwards they discovered Coll. Washington on the opposite side of the hollow in the gray of the morning, and when the English fired, which they did in great confusion, the Indians came out of their cover and closed with the French, and killed them with their tomahawks, on which the French surrendered." VI. Col. Rec., 195.

[1] Adam Stephen of Virginia, who served with distinction under Braddock and in the war of the Revolution, gives a contemporaneous and interesting notice of this skirmish, which seems to have escaped the notice of the historian. On May 10th, Capt. Stephen was detached with a reconnoitring party towards Fort Du Quesne, whence, his vicinity being discovered,

detailing this event to his Court, M. de Duquesne gave his own version of the affair, the correctness of which was ever denied by the English, and questioned by officers of even his own army. Insomuch as he was taken by surprise, the French insisted that Jumonville's death was not only a base act, but a cowardly assassination; and for years, even down to our own times, their authors have continued to misrepresent the occurrence, and to do an injustice to him who was incapable of acting unjustly to another. Chief among them was M. Thomas, an accomplished *littérateur* of the day, and a member of the Academy, who, in 1759, published his *Jumonville*, a lengthy poem in four cantos, in which he not only painted the death of that soldier in the most tragic colors, but traces all the subsequent misfortunes of the English to that unpardonable act. His unseen shade is made to stand beside Washington on the ramparts of Fort Necessity, freezing his blood with supernatural fear, and calling into life poetic serpents to hiss and gnaw within his breast; or gliding through the

---

Jumonville was despatched against him. Stephen fell back before his superior foe till he rejoined Washington, who, at 11 o'clock at night, through a heavily-pouring rain, went forth with forty men to the attack. The French were lodged in bark cabins about five miles from Washington's position; but so dark was the night, and so bewildering the storm, that it was not until four the next morning that they drew near the enemy. Here it was found not only that seven men were lost on the journey, but that their pieces and ammunition were so wet as to be in a measure useless. They therefore charged the French with fixed bayonets, receiving their fire as they advanced, and not returning it till they were at close quarters. Stephen adds, that three Indian men and two boys came up with the English during the battle; and that he himself made the first prisoner, capturing the Ensign M. Drouillon, "a pert fellow." Penn. Gaz, No. 1343.

lines of his brethren, points at his bleeding wounds yet unrevenged,

——— "and cries aloud—to battle!"

Pursued thus by the inevitable sword of an avenging Nemesis, the woes of the British during the next five years—the heavy visitation of what the poet is pleased to consider retributive justice, is finely given; "*O malheureux Anglais!*" he exclaims; "Oh, wretched people!"

Je vois, dans ses projets, votre audace trompée,
Des flots de votre sang l'Amérique trempée.
Bradhoc, de vos complots sinistre exécuteur,
Des traités et des lois sacrilège infracteur,
Qui devait, en guidant vos troupes conjurées,
Au char de l'Angleterre enchaîner nos contrées,
Sur des monceaux de morts, percé de mille coups,
Exhale ses fureurs et son ame en courroux.

O triste Virginie! O malheureux rivages!
Je vois vos champs en proie à des monstres sauvages;
Je vois, dans leur berceaux, vos enfans massacrés,
De vos vieillards sanglants les membres déchirés,
Vos remparts et vos toits dévorés par les flammes,
La massue écraser vos filles et vos femmes,
Et, dans leur flancs ouverts, leur fruit infortunes,
Condamnés à périr avant que d'être nés.
Votre sang n'éteint pas l'ardeur que les dévore:
Sur vos corps déchirés et palpitants encore,
Je les vois étendus, de carnage souillés,
Arracher vos chevaux de vos fronts dépouillés;
Et fiers de ce fardeau, dans leur mains triomphantes,
Montrer à leurs enfants ces dépouilles fumantes.
Quels que soient les forfaits que nous aient outragés,
Anglais, peut-être, hélas, sommes-nous trop venges!¹

¹ Oeuvres Comp. de Thomas (par M. Saint-Surin), tom. V., p. 47. Mr Sparks (II. Writings of Washington, p. 447), has gone at length into the question of the death of Jumonville and has thoroughly cleared up the

A terrified soldier, escaping the fate of his fellows, returned to the fort with the sad tidings of Jumonville's discomfiture; and a council of war, to deliberate on what

clouds that in some minds had obscured the morning brightness of Washington's fame. He does not notice, however, M. Pouchot's version of the affair, which is too significant to be passed over here. This writer says that Jumonville was sent with a letter summoning the English commander to retire. Being taken by surprise, and finding the enemy's strength so much superior to his own, he endeavored to show them the despatch of which he was the bearer; but they, unwilling to compromise themselves by a parley, poured in a volley, slaying Jumonville and some others. The remainder were made prisoners. (Pouchot, Vol. I., p. 14.) His editor, it is true, adds a note of dissent to the insinuation that Jumonville had any hostile intentions; but the evidence of a brother officer, whose ideas were derived from personal communications with those who were present at the fort at the time, must be received with some deference. It is a little curious, that while the French made so much capital out of this occurrence, their version of its nature was very little considered in England. M. Thomas, for instance, opens his preface with the declaration that his theme is "l'assassinat de M. de Jumonville en Amérique, et la vengeance de ce meurtre." During fourteen years after the event, its mere mention had not reached the ears of one of the greatest political gossips of the period in London. In July, 1763, Horace Walpole had never heard of it, and was only then in possession of the news, through the intervention of Voltaire, who had made it a subject of national reproach in his letters. (V. Walpole's Correspondence, p. 212, ed. Lond. 1840.) It is due to a French historian, however, to add that there is an impartial account of the affair from the pen of M. Garneau. After considering the statements of either side, he says — "Il est probable qu'il y a du vrai dans les deux versions; mais que l'attaque fut si précipitée qu'on ne put rien démêler. Washington n'avançait qu'en tremblant tant il avait peur d'être surpris, et il voulait tout prévenir même en courant le risque de combattre des fantômes. Ce n'est que de cette manière qu'on peut expliquer pourquoi Washington avec des forces si supérieures montra une si grande ardeur pour surprendre Jumonville au point du jour comme si c'eût été un ennemi fort à craindre? Au reste la mort de Jumonville n'amena pas la guerre, car déjà elle était résolue, mais elle la précipita." (II. Hist. du Can., 202.) The historical statements of M. Thomas's work are ridiculously false: the only fact it contains is that Jumonville was really dead.

next should be done, was instantly assembled by Contre-cœur. Here the opinions of all were given in writing. The fiery Coulon-Villiers (known for his prowess as *Le Grand Villiers*), burning to avenge after the fashion of the savages his brother's death, was for violent and vindictive measures: the more safe and moderate advice of M. de Mercier prevailed.[1] The desire professed on this occasion, to avoid everything which might be construed into an indefensible violation of the letter of the Treaty of Utrecht, when its spirit and meaning were already infringed by his very presence on the ground, shows how clearly the Frenchman anticipated the approaching war; and his anxiety to preserve, if not peace, at least appearances with the world. Villiers, with some six hundred men, was despatched to meet Washington, and Mercier accompanied him as second in command.[2] On the 29th of June, Washington, who was then at Gist's plantation, received intelligence of their advance; and his council of war resolved to await the attack at that spot. Entrenchments were at once undertaken; two detached parties under Captains Lewis and Polson were recalled; and an express sent to the Great Meadows to summon Captain Mackay, with the Independent Company from South Carolina. Mackay marched into camp that night, and the next morning Lewis and Polson came in. Apprised now of the 30th

---

[1] I. Pouchot, 15.

[2] The accounts of their number vary from three to nine hundred men, besides Indians. Among the latter were many Delawares and others who had hitherto lived on terms of personal friendship with the English. Vide Min. Penn. Col. Council, Vol VI, p. 51.

of June·resolved, with one voice, to retreat to their former position at the Great Meadows. Two miserable teams and a few pack-horses being all their means of transporting their ammunition, the officers at once added their own steeds to the train; and, leaving half his baggage behind, Washington, for four pistoles, hired some of the soldiers to carry the remainder. For twelve weary miles over the Alleghanies did the Virginians drag with their own hands the seven swivels that formed their park; the Independents obstinately refusing to bear any share of the burthen, whether of drawing guns, carrying ammunition, or clearing the road. On the 1st of July, the party arrived at the Great Meadows in such a state of fatigue that, unless their stores were abandoned, it was absolutely necessary for them to pause there for a few days. They had a plenty of milch-cows for beef, but no salt to cure their meat, so it was not possible to lay in a stock of salt provisions; and as for bread, though they had been eight days without it, the convoy from the settlements brought but a few bags of flour, not more than enough for five days. But learning that the two Independent Companies of New York were arrived at Annapolis on the 20th of June, they concluded to make a stand here, in hope of receiving a speedy reinforcement. The spot selected for the works was well chosen; and to these rude defences was given the suggestive title of FORT NECESSITY. To Robert Stobo, a captain in the Virginia Regiment, the merit of being their contriver is attributable. The fort was a log breast-work 100 feet square, surrounded in part by a shallow ditch; and was commenced immediately on Washington's arrival. As day broke on the morning of the 3d of July, the near approaches of the enemy were proclaimed by some of their scouts shooting down an English sentry; and at 11 A.M., the whole force came in sight and invested the petty fortress. Expecting to be stormed, the Independents were posted in the ditch, the Virginians being drawn up within their lines, intending to retain their fire till it was certain to take effect. The enemy not adopting this course, however, but sheltering themselves among the trees that crowned a neighboring hill, the men were withdrawn to the cover of their works, and a dropping, desultory fire was kept up on either side during all the day. When night fell, and their ammunition (which only amounted to a handful of ball each, and powder in proportion), was nearly exhausted, the French repeatedly called a parley, which at last was listened to by the incredulous English; and a capitulation was speedily arranged.[1] To the besieged terms were proffered, not to be lightly rejected by men in their position: for two bags of flour and a little bacon now constituted all the provisions of 300 men; their guns were wet and foul, and there were but two screws in the party with which to clean them; and, to crown all, one-half the garrison was drunk. Yet even in this strait the capitulation produced by Captain Van Braam, who, being the only officer (save one who was wounded), that could speak French, was selected as his plenipotentiary, was considerably modified by Washington. The French stipulated for the surrender of the artillery and ammunition; the English insisted on

[1] MS. Gov. Sharpe's Corresp. in Md. Hist. Soc.

retaining the one and destroying the other; and even this was acquiesced in.[1] The cattle, etc., had already fallen into the enemy's hands. The articles of surrender, however, while they conceded all honors of war to the garrison, contained one awkward provision to which Washington unwittingly put his hand, in terms admitting that Jumonville's death was an assassination. This expression, by "the too great condescension of Van Braam," had been suffered to stand on the paper; and as his leader was compelled to take his oral version of their nature (for it was now nearly midnight, and the falling rain prevented a candle's burning more than a moment at a time), which substituted the word "death" for this odious phrase; it was not until afterwards that its real language was discovered.[2] In the meanwhile the negotiator, Captain Jacob Van Braam, together with Captain Stobo, both Virginian officers, were given up to the enemy as pledges of the faithful performance of the articles of surrender.[3]

[1] These guns, which were probably merely spiked and abandoned, were in later years bored out or otherwise restored to their former condition. For a long time they lay on the Great Meadows, useless and disregarded. After the Revolution, however, when bands of settlers commenced to travel towards the West, it was a favorite amusement to discharge these cannon: the Meadow being a usual halting-place. They were finally transported to Kentucky by some enterprising pioneers, and their subsequent fate is unknown.

[2] II. Sparks's Washington, 51, 456. Stobo's Memoirs, 17. Capt. Stephen's letter in Penn. Gaz., No. 1339. Col. Innes to Gov. Hamilton, VI. Col. Rec., 51: where also a correct copy of the capitulation will be found. II. Olden Time, 213.

[3] Robert Stobo was born at Glasgow, 1727, of respectable parentage, and was settled in Virginia as a merchant when the French troubles began in 1754. Dinwiddie giving him a company in Frey's regiment, he took an active part in Washington's campaign. It is not impossible he was one

On the following morning, the fourth of July, 1754, with drums beating and colors flying, the little garrison evacuated its feeble entrenchments, and sadly turned their faces homewards. Probably the memory of this day, whose return, twenty-one years after, was destined to open to him the gates of immortal fame, was for a season

of "those raw, surly, and tyrannical Scots, several of them mere boys from behind the counters of the factors here," with whom, according to Maury (Huguenot Family, 404), the governor filled the corps. As the stipulations for which he remained a hostage were not complied with, he was, with his brother the captain, Van Braam, sent from Du Quesne to Canada, but not before he had contrived to transmit a plan of its works to the English. His letters and drawings being found in Braddock's cabinet, excited no little odium against him. At last he escaped from captivity (whether with or without Van Braam is not certainly known to the writer), and after a series of romantic adventures, reached England. His Memoirs were there published, a reprint of which has lately been given at Pittsburg, by Mr. Neville Craig, to whose notes the preceding remarks are due. The only remaining feature in his story that has been discovered is the fact that on June 5th, 1760, he was made a captain in the 15th Foot (Amherst's Regiment), then serving in America; which position he held as late as 1765. He was an eccentric creature; an acquaintance of David Hume and a friend of Smollett, to whom he is said to have safe for the character of the immortal Lismahago. As for Van Braam, his career is still more obscure. Denounced as a traitor for his agency in the capitulation of Fort Necessity, it must not be forgotten that three weeks before the surrender, Washington (to whom he had served as interpreter on the mission of 1753), pronounced him "an experienced, good officer, and very worthy of the command he has enjoyed:" that he consented to going as a hostage to the French, with the certainty of his fraud being soon discovered by his own party, had he committed one; that he was detained rather as a prisoner than a hostage; and that he risked his life to return to the English. These facts do not exculpate him from the charge of imbecility, but they are inconsistent with the assumption of his deliberate treason. In 1770, too, it would appear that he claimed and obtained his share of the Virginia bounty lands, with Washington as Commissioner; and on 14th June, 1777, was made Major of the Third Battalion of the 60th Foot, or Royal Americans, then stationed in the West Indies.

marked in Washington's calendar as the blackest, the most melancholy epoch of his life. His visions of future fame in the service of his native land seemed to have received a dangerous, perhaps a fatal, downfall: nor could the reflections that its immediate memory must have adduced have been of a very cheering character. In spite of the stipulation of the French commander, the Indians hung on the skirts of his diminished band, plundering the baggage, and committing a hundred annoyances and mischiefs. The medical stores they entirely destroyed; thus cruelly aggravating the unhappy condition of the wretches, who, sick and wounded, and without a horse to assist them, were to traverse fifty miles of inhospitable forests, ere they could reach the nearest halting-place on Will's Creek. The number of savages, hitherto regarded as friendly to the colonies, whom he recognised enlisted under the standard of the enemy, was another source of regret. And so long as the French preserved their local superiority, he very well knew how little hope there was of these fickle people returning to their ancient friendships: nor was he blind to the unconcealed disgust at the result of the campaign of even those whose lot was immutably cast with the English.[1]

---

[1] The celebrated Seneca chief Thanacrishon (better known as the Half-King), complained bitterly to Conrad Weiser of Washington's conduct. "The Colonel," he said, "was a good-natured man, but had no experience; he took upon him to command the Indians as his slaves, and would have them every day upon the scout, and to attack the enemy by themselves, but would by no means take advice from the Indians. He lay in one place from one full moon to the other, without making any fortifications, except that little thing on the Meadow; whereas, had he taken advice, and built such fortifications as he (the Half-King) advised him, he might easily have beat off the French. But the French in the engagement acted like cowards,

And above all other annoyances, the discovery of the unenviable and unmerited position in which Van Braam's "evil intentions or negligence" had placed his character, must have stung him to the quick. With reason, then, on the morning of Washington's departure from Fort Necessity, dark visions swam before his eyes. He saw before but the frowning forests; behind, the scene of his own and his country's defeat. "At that moment," observes Mr. Bancroft, "in the whole valley of the Mississippi to its headsprings in the Alleghanies, no standard floated but that of France." Destroying, as he says, not only the cannon surrendered by the English, but also the smaller piece reserved by the garrison as a point of military etiquette, but which it was incompetent to drag away; and knocking in the heads of the liquor-casks, to prevent a savage debauch, "the Great Villiers" departed on the same day as his adversaries, but in an opposite direction.[1] Gracing his triumph with the Virginia standard, which in the confusion had been left at the fort, he turned his steps toward Du

and the English like fools."—*Enquiry into the Causes of the Alienation of the Delaware and Shawanese Indians*, &c. (Lond. 1759) p. 80. This volume, whose rarity is greater than even its value and importance, was the work of Charles Thomson, subsequently Secretary of the Congress; but in 1756, when he prepared his material, an usher in the Quaker grammar-school at Philadelphia. He writes in honest but bitter opposition to the Penns, on which account some allowances must be made in perusing his book. This Half-King, who was so free of his censure, was a pretty shrewd fellow. It was he who advised Ensign Ward, when summoned by M. de Contrecœur to surrender his post, to reply that his rank did not invest him with sufficient power so to do, and to desire a delay until his chief commander might arrive; a suggestion which, though ineffectual in practice, argues considerable astuteness on the part of its proposer. See II. Sparks's Washington, p. 7.

Quesne, where he arrived on the 7th of July; having destroyed all the English settlements on the way, and detaching also M. de la Chauvignerie for the same purpose. This circumstance in itself shows that the country had not utterly escaped the notice of colonists from the eastward, although it is more than probable that many of the houses so burned were trading-stations, or shelters recently erected for the convenience of some of Trent's or Washington's troops. On his journey, too, he encountered the place where his brother had fallen; and where mangled corpses, their skulls bare and bloody from the knife, still strewed the ground with shocking memorials of that scene of slaughter. A decent, if not a Christian burial, in earth best consecrated by the life-blood of a soldier, was bestowed upon their remains; and the grave of Jumonville is still shown to the curious traveller, who pauses, "by lonely contemplation led," to muse upon the spot where, like Philip's son, the future statesman and sage loosened the tangled web of policy with his sword; and invoking the *ultima ratio regum* to decide whether to a Guelf or a Bourbon North America should owe allegiance, the hands

---

1 In 1756, M. de Villiers took an active part in the capture of Oswego. (I. Garneau, 246: I. Pouchot, 71.) Till 1759, he would seem to have still been employed in that region, where he was one of the defenders and probably of the captives of Niagara: after which he is lost sight of. There were six brothers of the Villiers family killed in Canada during this war, fighting for France; each of whom was distinguished by some local surname. The seventh and last, also in the service, appears alone to have escaped. I. Forster's Bossu, 185. From the language of M. Thomas (Jumonv., ch. I.) we are at liberty to conjecture that they were natives of Old France.

of the Father of his Country were for the first time steeped in human blood.[1]

In the meantime, since their arrival in the spring the garrison under M. de Contrecoeur had experienced much privation and suffering. An expensive and abundant supply of provisions and stores had at an early day been despatched to this post from Canada, under a strong escort; but the difficulties incident on the portage at Niagara produced an unwelcome and unlooked-for delay. The want of horses and suitable equipages to transport them from the fort at Presqu'-Isle to the Ohio was also a great embarrassment. Four hundred of the party expired on the route, either from scurvy or from the fatigues of bearing all this burthen upon their shoulders. The provisions of the escort were soon expended, and the magazines intended for their comrades were put into requisition. Then their contents became known, and every one took freely from them such wares as pleased his fancy. The officers were clad in rich velvets, and drank to their fill of the rare wines with which, by the knavish connivance of the authorities with some unknown parties in interest, the detachment was charged. A scene of general waste and confusion ensued; and while the troops at Fort Du Quesne profited slightly enough by the costly engagements that had been criminally made for their benefit, the convoy which was to return to Canada arrived there brilliantly

[1] Journal of M. de Villiers: II. Olden Time, 213. Sharp's MS. Corresp. The whole French and Indian loss at Fort Necessity is stated here to have been but one cadet and two privates killed and seventeen dangerously wounded.

equipped, and with a report amply covering all their delinquencies.[1]

If the reception of the tidings of the compulsory evacuation of the Ohio territories by the English gave any satisfaction in France, the feeling was far otherwise in London. Unwelcome enough was this news to a country whose commercial prosperity was so largely identified with the success of its colonial system; nor were the witticisms of the young Comte d'Estaing (himself destined in time to direct heavy and successful blows against British dominion in America), sufficient to restore the good-humor of the people. "Pardieu, Messieurs," said he to the English courtiers, "ce seroit bien ridicule, de faire casser la tête à dix milles hommes pour quelques douzaines de chapeaux."[2] It was all very well to balance thus satirically the life of a man against the skin of a beaver; but the fur-trade on the Ohio, now lost to the English, was worth, though but in its infancy, no less than £40,000 a-year.[3] The privation of such a profit, not less than the manner in which it was lost, was eminently calculated to excite indignation; and ample details of the whole, forwarded to London by Governor Dinwiddie and others, speedily brought about the inception of those vigorous measures which it is the province of these pages in part to chronicle. In the month of August, 1754, the surrender of Fort Necessity and the conduct of its commander were freely commented on in the highest political circles. "The French have tied up the hands of an excellent fanfaron, a Major Washington,"

---

[1] I. Pouchot, 12.   [2] IV. Mahon's Letters of Chesterfield, 146.
[3] Penn. Gaz, No. 1344.

wrote Walpole, "whom they took, and engaged not to serve for a year."[1] In several places, the same writer repeats the anecdote of Washington's despatch on this occasion : "'I have heard the bullets whistle; and believe me there is something charming in the sound.' On hearing of this letter, the King said sensibly, 'He would not say so, if he had been used to hear many.'"[2] And the Duke of Cumberland avowed that "rather than lose one foot of ground in America, he would oppose the enemies of his country in that part of the world himself."[3] But the vacillating organization of the Ministry prevented, for a season, any fruit ripening from these warlike blossoms. The recent death of Henry Pelham, the only brother of the Duke of Newcastle, and an excellent cabinet minister, had occasioned a remodelling of that body; and for some months, so considerable and uncertain were their various alterations, there was nothing but change and inconsistency displayed in the conduct of the official and salaried advisers of the Crown. Newcastle, however, with his great fortune and enormous borough-interest, remained always at the head of affairs. Ambitious, but incapable, his combined ignorance and vanity cause him too often to appear in the memoirs of the period rather in the character of a ridiculous buffoon than that of a politic statesman; yet even to his understanding the necessity of a prompt movement was evident. Such was his natural imbecility,

[1] V. Walp. Corresp., 72.
[2] I. Walpole's Memoirs of George II., 346. Walpole to Sir H. Mann, V. Corresp., 71. And consult II. Sparks's Wash., 40.
[3] Penn: Gaz., No. 1342.

however, and his mean jealousy of all men in whom by any chance his imagination could foresee future rivals to himself, that a long and dangerous delay elapsed before anything like form and coherence was given to the proposed measures. Previously to considering these proceedings, nevertheless, and having now shown, in their natural course, the circumstances which had induced this crisis, it may not be amiss to dwell for a moment upon the position of affairs in those colonies for whose immediate protection so much treasure was to be lavished, so many lives spent.

The provinces most directly affected by the presence of the French upon the Ohio were those of Virginia and Pennsylvania. In the former, everything was ripe for war. Though its laws, forbidding the employment of the militia beyond their own confines, had prevented that body being called upon for the occupation of a region whose situation was well believed by many to be without its jurisdiction, this infant state had gallantly volunteered four hundred men for the undertaking, whose ill-success was crowned by the surrender of Fort Necessity. A martial spirit pervaded the land ; and the Governor was a man sagacious in his views and devoted to the interests of his nation.[1] With

---

[1] Very few colonial governors have obtained the popular verdict in their praise, and certainly Robert Dinwiddie was not one of that scanty number. His disputes with his Assembly in regard to his exaction of fees warranted by law but obsolete in practice, and his difficulties with Washington, have left an unpleasant impression of his character on the American mind. Yet he was an officer not unworthy of commendation. Remarkable integrity and vigilance in other employments, had procured him the government of Virginia ; and the records of the day show very clearly how untiring were his efforts to secure the colony from a foreign foe. A Scot by birth, he perhaps retained too many of the prejudices of that people ; but he was

the exception of the constant quarrels (incident almost to the very existence of a colony), on the subject of money between him and his Assembly, the people and their rulers were generally united and strong in their views of foreign policy, and, what was of even greater importance, were firmly bound together by the common ties of domestic associations.

The case was not similar in Pennsylvania. Its population at this period exceeded three hundred thousand souls; its products, almost exclusively agricultural, were sufficient to employ five hundred vessels, mostly owned in its capital, that annually bore away to other lands provisions sufficient to subsist one hundred thousand men.[1] The character of this population was, however, as various as its numbers. In the vicinity of Philadelphia, it is true, the descendants of the original Quaker settlers, with all their purity of morals and all the civilization that could have reasonably been expected to arise from their pacific tenets, still prevailed. But farther from the wealthier and more ancient settlements were to be found large establishments of Scotch-Irish and Germans, each strongly preserving the

---

not without their virtues: and as though in accordance with his armorial device — *ubi libertas, ibi patria* — he liberally aided in the protection and encouragement of knowledge and education, without which liberty so soon degenerates into license. The library of William and Mary College still preserves the evidences of his generosity; and Dinwiddie County, in the State of Virginia, perpetuates the memory of his name.

[1] I am aware that Mr. James S. Pringle, in a valuable paper read before the Historical Society of Pennsylvania in May, 1854, states the population of the province, in 1753, to have been but 250,000. Governor Morris, in March, 1755, computes it at the number above mentioned; though probably even his calculation was but conjectural. VI. Col. Rec., 336.

peculiar idiosyncrasies of their national origin. The Germans, in particular, clinging tenaciously together, are even to this day far from being undistinguishably absorbed in the mass of their fellow-citizens; but then, dwelling as it were aloof from other settlements, they formed a clearly-defined and distinct population. A description of the manner in which one of these settlements was formed may not be devoid of interest.

On Christmas-day, 1709, ten ships set sail from London for New York, freighted with some 4000 Protestant and expatriated Germans, who had been supported in London by the bounty of Queen Anne, and were now sent by that benevolent sovereign to seek new homes in a new world. On their arrival, they were soon dispersed over the whole province, many seating themselves at Schoharie upon lands which belonged to others. Discountenanced in their conduct by Governor Burnet, and embarrassed by the op-position of the lawful owners of the soil, they were finally induced, in 1723, to set forth once more on their wanderings. Like the Israelites of old, their spies had gone down before them and searched out the fatness of the land, and had brought back glowing accounts of the regions on the Swatara creek in Pennsylvania, and the parts adjacent. Cutting wagon-roads then from the Schoharie to the Susquehannah, they transported their effects through the unbroken forest, and in their rude canoes floated down the river to the mouth of Swatara creek; their herds following along the shore. Thus were founded the Swatara and Tulpehocking settle-ments. This was in the spring of 1723: it was not until 1732 that Thomas Penn purchased the country comprehending portions of Berks and Lebanon counties from the Indians; and, in the meanwhile, the settlements had continued to increase, not only against the will of the Proprietary, but to the annoyance and indignation of the savages, who beheld their hunting-grounds thus forcibly possessed by strangers.[1]

Intermingled with the rest at this time were numbers of English churchmen and Irish Catholics, all contributing to swell the mass of conflicting tongues and creeds that already was in itself sufficient to account for a certain degree of absence of mutual sympathy which so long seems to have prevailed among the people of Pennsylvania. In no manner did the exceeding difference of condition and feelings develope itself more plainly than in their intercourse with the Indians. By all the ties of their faith, as well as through their comparative freedom from the troubles incident on a near neighborhood with the red men, the influential Quakers were, as a general thing, persuaded of the propriety of treating them in the same honorable manner prescribed by the founder of the province and their own great apostle. With the frontier settlers, the case was otherwise. A hardy race, often of a temper too prone to inflict an injury, and always prompt to resent one, they were constantly, either in individual instances, or as a people, embroiled with their neighbors. Of the most important Indian tribes who were to be found about this period within the limits of Pennsylvania, and whose conduct and views would most materially influence the scattered remnants of other nations that still existed there, were the Delawares and the Shawanoes. The former had once been a powerful and a warlike tribe; but before the arrival of William Penn they were subdued by the Six Nations of the north, whose hunting-parties roamed at will, as feudal suzerains of old, through the whole region as far as the Ohio and the Chesapeake bay. They were compelled by their conquerors to put on petticoats, and acknowledge themselves women; terms so degrading that nothing but the extreme awe inspired by the prowess of the confederates of the lakes could have induced submission to — and they were not permitted in any way to exercise the privileges of an independent people. When, therefore, Penn, after purchasing from the Iroquois the land upon which he proposed establishing the seat of his budding empire, made furthermore a point of buying the same lands from their occupants and ancient masters, he acted towards the Delawares with a politic propriety not less just in the abstract than soothing and grateful to their pride. Henceforth the Delawares and the Quakers were as brothers; and the Shawanoes, an alien tribe supposed to have found their way thitherward from the everglades of Florida, participated in these sentiments. No land was to be occupied by the whites until it had been granted by the Proprietary; and the latter's title must rest upon a previous concession from the Indians.

But these halcyon days were not long to endure. As time wore on, and new settlers, impelled by adverse fortune or allured by the fertility of its soil, migrated to Pennsylvania from other shores, the rights of the Indian became more and more disregarded. His lands would be occupied by a stranger, destitute of the shadow of a title, the reverberations of whose gun or the baying of whose hounds would frighten off the game (the flocks and herds of the savage), into still deeper recesses of the forest; and his pride would receive a constant shock from the imperious bearing and, oftentimes, the brutal behaviour of the unlicensed and unwelcome guest. The proprietary government, it is true, sometimes endeavored to restrain its subjects within due bounds; but too frequently it was itself guilty of misconduct not less flagrant. It would too often connive at white settlements upon lands belonging to the aborigines; or worse still, engage in some disgraceful, dishonest swindle, by which the savage would be cheated out of his inheritance. By these means, it is not wonderful that his dispositions were gradually becoming hostile to the Europeans, and that his ancient confidence in their friendly professions was impaired. When, in 1741, that devoted New England philanthropist, John Sergeant, bore to the Shawanoes on the Susquehannah the tidings of salvation, they rejected with disdain his pious overtures. They had learned to hate the religion whose votaries corrupted their health, cheated them of their substance, and debauched their women.[1] And when the wiser and more foreseeing among them complained of the outrages they were subjected to by the traders, they met with but scanty redress. In 1727, the deputies of the Six Nations, who represented as well their own tribes as the subject Delawares, complained to Governor Gordon, at Philadelphia, of the traders who

---

[1] Hopkins's Mem. of Housatannuk Inds., p. 90. Thomson's Alienation, &c., p. 56.

came among them, getting all their skins at trifling prices. "They get so little for them, that they cannot live; and can scarce procure powder and shot to bring more. That the traders bring very little of these, but instead bring rum, which they sell very dear." They further urged that no more settlements should be made on the Susquehannah above Paxton; and that no more rum should be sold there to the Indians; and that none of the traders to the Ohio should be suffered to carry rum. To all which the Governor replied, that in regard to new settlements, as his people increased they must necessarily spread; and as to the traders — "they know it is the custom of all to buy as cheap and to sell as dear as they can, and that every man must be on his guard and make the best bargain he can: the English cheat the Indians, and the Indians cheat the English; and that they were at perfect liberty to destroy without compensation all the rum that was brought among them, as the provincial laws forbade it being carried thither."[1]   Perhaps the governors could not do any more than they did to restrain the excesses of the traders; but all that they did do was ineffectual; the abuse continued to operate, undiminished by time.[2]

---

[1] Thomson, p. 13.

[2] See the Governor's message in 1744: "I cannot but be apprehensive that the Indian trade, as it is now carried on, will involve us in some fatal quarrel with the Indians.   Our traders, in defiance of the law, carry spirituous liquors among them, and take the advantage of their inordinate appetite for it to cheat them of their skins and their wampum, which is their money, and often to debauch their wives into the bargain.   Is it to be wondered at then if, when they recover from their drunken fit, they should take some severe revenges?"—*Votes of Penn. Assembly*, Vol. III., p. 555.   These traders generally consisted, according to the report of the same legislature, in 1754, of the vilest of their own inhabitants, or of transported convicts from Great Britain and Ireland.

The result of the infamous Walking Treaty—as shameless a fraud as ever was perpetrated—had occasioned a great and natural discontent on the part of the unfortunates so unjustly and, as all will now concede, so illegally ousted from their homes. The story of this transaction is briefly as follows :

In 1686, as was alleged by the proprietaries and admitted by most of the Indians, Penn had purchased from the Delawares a tract of land comprehended within certain boundaries. The line was to begin at a certain spruce-tree on the river Delaware, above the mouth of Neshamony Creek : thence by a course west-north-west to the Neshamony : thence back into the woods as far as a man could walk in a day and a half; thence to the Delaware again, and so down to the place of beginning. No steps were taken to lay out this land until some sixty years afterward, when, upon mature consideration of the subject, it was decided by the proprietary to take formal possession of it. Accordingly, every preparation was made to secure as good a bargain as possible. A road was surveyed for the walk; expeditious means of crossing the intersecting streams were provided; and the swiftest pedestrians in the province were engaged to accomplish as great a distance as might be compassed within the time limited. This having been attained, the next point was to run the line to the Delaware; and here, whatever may be thought of the mode in which the first part of the business had been transacted, a glaring wrong was perpetrated by the government. In the original deed, a blank had been left for the direction which the proposed line should take : and as the topography of this country could not, in 1686, have been accurately known, this seems not unnatural. But now, by a foul advantage of this omission, it was resolved to run the line, not by the nearest course to the river, which would have been east-south-east, or parallel to that by which they set out, but by a north-east course for a hundred miles and more, till it struck the Delaware near the mouth of Lackawaxen Creek, far above Easton. A fortunate westerly bend in the channel enabled them to effect this, and to cover by their deed at least a million of acres, when, by a fairer computation, three hundred and fifty thousand should have confined their claim.[1]

Their best lands, and even their accustomed villages being invaded by this enormous fraud, the Indians on the Delaware evinced a decided inclination not to submit to it. To provide against any evil consequences on this head, a number of deputies from the Six Nations were, in 1742, invited to visit Philadelphia, nominally to transact public business of a mutual importance, but really to persuade them to overawe the Delawares into acquiescence in the chicanery that had been practised upon them. Accordingly, after having been conciliated with a few hundred pounds' worth of presents, they were requested to prevail on their cousins the Delawares to remove from the lands in the forks of the river, which, it was pretended, their fathers had sold and been paid for long before. The chiefs of this tribe being assembled in the council-chamber, were then earnestly addressed by the speaker of the Six Nations.

[1] Thomson, pp. 34 et seq. 70.

In homely but forcible phrase he reproached them with their misconduct. "They deserved," said he, "to be taken by the hair of their heads and shaken severely, till they recovered their senses and became sober. But how came you," he continued, "to take upon you to sell lands at all? *We* conquered you; *we* made women of you; you know you are women, and can no more sell land than women; nor is it fit you should have the power of selling lands, since you would abuse it. This land that you claim is gone through your guts: you have been furnished with clothes, meat, and drink by the goods paid you for it, and now you want it again, like children as you are! But what makes you sell lands in the dark? Did you ever tell us that you had sold this land? Did *we* ever receive any part, even the value of a pipe-shank, from you for it? * * For all these reasons, we charge you to remove instantly: we don't give you the liberty to think about it. You are women. Take the advice of a wise man, and remove immediately. You may return to the other side of Delaware, where you came from; but we do not know whether, considering how you have demeaned yourselves, you will be permitted to live there, or whether you have not swallowed that land down your throats as well as the land on this side. We therefore assign you two places to go, either to Wyomen or Shamokin. You may go to either of these places, and then we shall have you more under our eye, and shall see how you behave. Don't deliberate, but remove at once, and take this belt of wampum." Having thus satisfactorily closed all debate, the speaker summarily ejected "his cousins the Delawares" from the apartment.[1]

It was impossible for the Indians to disobey so potent a decree, and they removed as they were bidden. But the acquirement of their fields, so inexpensive at the beginning, in the end cost very dear. From that moment, they were ready to listen to the overtures of the French, and to contemplate with no great displeasure the discomfiture of both the Iroquois and the English. For it was not within the bounds of human endurance unmoved to see their wives and little ones starving by their side, and to feel themselves the sharp pangs of poverty and famine, while the whites were feasting on the fatness of their ancient inheritance. It is useless to tell a rudely-reasoning and famishing barbarian, or, for the matter of that, a sage philosopher in the same condition, as did the deputies of the Six Nations at Philadelphia, that he or his ancestors had long ago sold the millions of acres along the Delaware, which they once occupied; and had enjoyed the full benefit of the 'two guns, six stroud-water coats, six blankets, six duffel watch-coats, and four kettles,' that were said to have been paid to them by William Penn.[2] An undisciplined feeling of natural equity, stimulated perhaps by hunger, advised them that such a price, if the story of its ever having been paid at all were true, was a poor compensation for the abandonment of a region abounding at the time in game and yielding ready crops of maize and pumpkins, for their new and dreary homes. Conrad Weiser, that strange compound, to whom Indian

---

[1] Thomson, p. 45.

[2] Ibid, p. 19.

life and the Indian tongue were perhaps more familiar than English, gives a piteous account of their condition in the winter of 1737, when he passed from Tulpehocking in Pennsylvania on his way to New York. Scattered through the forests, they would fix their camps near a grove of sugar-maple trees, the juice of which constituted the only magazine of food upon which they could with any certainty rely. Here the children searched along the lowlands and the banks of streams for nuts and esculent roots,[1] or crowded weeping with their mothers around the traveller, in whose exhausted pouch yet remained a few crumbs of corn-meal. A handful of maize steeped in a pot of ash-lye to make a kind of soup, constituted to them a most luxurious but unwonted dish. In the meantime, the husbands and fathers of the party, disdaining to rob their families of the miserable pittance which preserved them from death though not from starving, would range for weeks at a time through all the region between the Shamokin and the upper waters of the Susquehannah in fruitless search of game. By day he scouted through the dense spruce-forests, beneath those evergreen boughs which the sun's rays rarely pierced; every sense painfully on the alert lest the tread of a deer or the distant flight of a mountain grouse should escape his observation; or lest, by a misstep, he should be cast headlong down some precipitous chasm, or slipping between treacherous logs, be chilled in the icy

---

[1] "The turkey-pea has a single stalk, grows to a height of eight or ten inches, and bears a small pod. It is found in rich, loose soils; appears among the first plants in the spring, and produces on the root small tubers of the size of a hazel-nut, on which the turkeys feed. The Indians are fond of, and collect them in considerable quantities."—*Hunter*, 425.

torrent of the dark, deep-flowing streams. Cold and hungry, he would lie down at nightfall crouched beneath a pile of boughs, the snow drifting the while in fierce wreaths about his sleeping form; and in the morning awake, stiff and cold, to find his fire still burning in the hole, two or three feet deep, that it had melted during the night in the snow. With returning light, the labors of the chase are resumed. In vain he threads the Dia-dachlu or Wandering River (as he named Lycoming Creek); its fords at this season waist deep, its current swift and powerful and icy cold; or the fierce Oscohu, mountain-born, flowing between fringing maples. Carefully avoiding the weird ravine which superstition invested with mysterious horrors as the home of the Otkon, an evil spirit who delighted in blood and was only to be appeased by magical sacrifices, he would shudderingly gaze from the brow of a distant hill at the skulls which, bleaching in the winter's storms, declared at once the extent of the demon's power and the place of his abode. Then turning to the north, he penetrates to the summit of the hill where, according to tradition, pumpkins, corn, and tobacco first grew there for the benefit of humanity; but only to find that they grew there no longer. Exhausted and weary, the poor wretch turns his face homewards, and with languid gait — sperans meliora — seeks his camp by the water-side; diverging perchance on the way to visit the beaver-dam at the confluence of the Towanda and Lycoming Creeks, where once within his own memory many pipes of tobacco had been smoked before "his grand-fathers the beavers." Now not a sign of their presence remained. To supply the insatiable maw of traffic, not only the males of the colony, but even the females, generally so sacred in the eyes of an Indian, had long since yielded up their skins; and the pool was silent and unbroken. With a sinking heart he invokes the Great Spirit to come to his relief lest he perish, or to give him a reason why he and his people should thus suffer; and in a vision of the night, "when deep sleep falleth on men, fear comes upon him and trembling which makes all his bones to shake." A spirit passes before his face, and he hears the words of the Manitou, pronouncing the doom of his race. Humbled in soul, but callous through long endurance, he returns empty-handed to his camp, happy if he finds there some benevolent stranger, differing from his color in being a Christian not only in name but in deed, who, as he divides his few remaining ounces of corn-bread with weeping, starving women and children, murmurs within himself blessings on His name "who hath made in His wisdom thistles to grow instead of barley in this land, and the owners thereof to lose their life."[1]

[1] There is not the least exaggeration in this sketch; every statement in it is literally true. Vide Weiser's Narrative of a journey in 1737, published in I. Coll. Penn. Hist. Soc., 17. In the revelation referred to, God declared to the Indians: *You inquire after the cause why game has become scarce. I will tell you. You kill it for the sake of the skins, which you give for strong liquor, and drown your senses and kill one another, and carry on a dreadful debauchery. Therefore have I driven the wild animals out of the country, for they are mine. If you will do good and cease from your sins, I will bring them back. If not, I will destroy you from off the earth.* Weiser asked if they put faith in this vision. "They answered, yes; some believed it would happen so: others also believed it, but gave themselves no concern about it. Time will show, said they, what is to happen to us. *Rum* will kill us, and leave the land clear for the Europeans without strife or purchase."

How changed was the Indian's condition since fifty years before! Then, save his own domestic broils, he had no enemies to contend with. Game was not slaughtered for the skin only, and food was therefore comparatively abundant. The twanging bow-string then answered all his purposes of destruction; the detonations of musketry had not yet broken the silence of his hunting-grounds and frightened off both bird and beast, and they were therefore easily accessible. Above all, rum, that scourge of the red race, was not familiar to his taste, and he was therefore independent. Cruel he was, and revengeful; and his social condition was marked with all those blemishes which almost prevent our regretting the means by which he has been destroyed in the reflection of the utter worthlessness of his existence to the rest of the world: but we must not forget that, so far as he was concerned, his lot was only injured by the approach of civilization. Now, he is vanished; passed away, with all his atrocious faults and noble virtues, from the memory of the land, like a hideous dream: then, he was its owner, its master, and was happy. The Indian has no original wants that civilization can gratify; no aspirations that barbarism cannot fulfil. His fields are tilled by the woman with whom he vouchsafes to share his couch; his lodge is raised upon poles hewed from the nearest forest, and covered with the spoils of the chase; his most glorious furniture is the scalps that dry in the smoke of his wigwam. His ornaments are arms, his pastime is war; his highest luxury consists in repletion. What to him are the rich marts of commerce, the narrow streets, the busy hum of crowded cities!

Coarse are his meals — the fortune of the chase;
Amidst the running stream he slakes his thirst;
Toils all the day, and at th' approach of night,
On the first friendly bank he throws him down,
Or rests his head upon a rock till morn:
Then rises fresh, pursues his wonted game;
And if, the following day, he chance to find
A new repast, or an untasted spring,
Blesses his stars, and thinks it luxury.

A glance, now, at the character and condition of the white settlers of those days, will not be out of place; and so different were they from the people of this generation, that the sketch may not be uninteresting. The diversity of national origin of the early population of Pennsylvania has already been noticed: there was a still greater difference in their intellectual and moral developments. Setting aside the shoals of convicts turned loose upon its borders from the English gaols, there were hundreds of other colonists arriving every year, whose presence, though necessary, perhaps, to the ultimate prosperity of the growing State, could not have been calculated to promote the immediate refinement and elevation of its character. In every colony there must be a class of settlers who shall there serve the same purpose as Linnæus beautifully attributes to the lichens and mosses of the physical world, when he aptly describes them as the bond-slaves of nature: they must form, upon the yet wild and unseated rock, the earliest soil from which, in time, the choicest of Nature's creations shall spring. Individuals must fall, and die, and be forgotten, as the leaves in the forest, their remains commingling with the mother earth, through long and tedious time, ere the solitude and gloom of the wilderness shall give place to the temples of luxury and civilization. Thus it is ever in this world; each man, each plant, each insect, living or dying, has a part to play, a place to fill. Change, eternal change, the imperishable secret of Nature, is the only immutable measure of all her laws.

It is not designed in this place to dwell upon the particular establishments that were from time to time made by English, Scotch-Irish, or Germans, in the various parts of the province; but a few words respecting their distinctive characters will be of service as tending to show the causes of the conduct and sentiment of the people under peculiar circumstances. In each of these classes were to be found men of education, intelligence, and virtue. The English naturally preponderated in characters of this stamp. The amiable, honest, benevolent followers of Penn, who flocked to the shores of the Delaware as to a haven of refuge, comprehended within their ranks a degree of mental and moral cultivation which would have reflected credit upon any people in the world; the wealth, too, of the province, and the control of the Assembly, were chiefly in their hands. Other English, of various denominations, were to be found, not inferior in station or capacity to the disciples of Fox; and although, at one time or another, the Presbyterians thought themselves neglected, or the churchmen took umbrage at the Quaker rule, yet, on the whole, we may safely conclude that there has rarely been an instance of religious power having been used with so much mildness. Certainly, had the societies of either the Church of England or the Westminster Assembly been in the position of the Quakers, there is no reason to believe they would have acted with a like tolerance to their fellow-citizens, while the poor Indian would have suffered terribly in the exchange.

The Scotch-Irish, as they were called, were emigrants from the northern part of the sister-kingdom, descendants of the Scottish colonies planted there by Cromwell. They were a hardy, brave, hot-headed race; excitable in temper, unrestrainable in passion, invincible in prejudice. Their hand opened as impetuously to a friend as it clenched against an enemy. They loathed the Pope as sincerely as they venerated Calvin or Knox; and they did not particularly respect the Quakers. If often rude and lawless, it was partly the fault of their position. They hated the Indian, while they despised him; and it does not seem, in their dealings with this race, as though there were any sentiments of honor or magnanimity in their bosoms that could hold way against the furious tide of passionate, blind resentment. Impatient of restraint, rebellious against anything that in their eyes bore the semblance of injustice, we find these men readiest among the ready on the battle-fields of the revolution. If they had faults, a lack of patriotism or of courage was not among the number.

We have already alluded to a lawless settlement of the Germans upon the Susquehannah; and indeed the province soon became a chosen harbor for these people, who appear to have migrated from Germany in very much the same sort as they do at this day. The wanderers were generally of the lower orders — peasants, mechanics, or sometimes small farmers or tradesmen. Selling their useless possessions at home, they would embark together in droves for the promised land. Many were so poor (and not of the Germans alone, but of all nations emigrating to America), that it was a very customary thing for a passenger to sell his or her labor for a term of years to the captain of the vessel as a payment for the passage. These inhabitants of the province. Thus as slaves, or servants for a fixed period, the unfortunate emigrants wore on their life of toil.

More fortunate were many who had not found a necessity of resort to this shift; but brought with them to the New World, if little pecuniary wealth, at least free limbs. These, adhering together in a foreign land, preserved their language and national characteristics for a surprisingly long period. Phlegmatic, parsimonious, industrious, and honest, their constant care was to accumulate wealth and to avoid disturbance. Being chiefly of the inferior classes at home, the first German settlers were not remarkable for any very elevated notions either in religion or politics; nor, indeed, is it a matter for surprise, that among all the frontier settlers (to whom, as a class, the remarks which are now being made are generally applicable), a higher value should be set on physical than on mental endowments; on skill in hunting, or the practical arts of daily life, and bravery in war, than on any polite accomplishments or taste in the fine arts.

Thus, many of the vulgar superstitions which had at one time held a place in the minds of the highest classes of the Old World, and which were still nourished among its peasantry, were transplanted to the wildernesses of America. Here, in the gloomy, silent shadows of a virgin forest, whose solitude was as yet uncheered by the murmurs of the honey-bee or the pleasant warbling of singing-birds — those invariable attendants upon the axe of the woodsman — the nightly howling of the dog, who bayed at the moon; the shrill, startling whoop of the owl, from some stridulous bough overhanging his camp-fire and bending to the evening breeze; the sinister croak of the raven, perched on the hollow oak, were notes of prophetic woe that filled the bosom of the pioneer with dismal forebodings.[1] In dreams, he foresaw the good or ill success of his undertakings; and after the fashion of the ancients, prosperity or misfortune would appear to him in the semblance of a female form. Over the low door of the German's cottage one would be sure to find nailed the horse-shoe, fatal to witches; and love-spells and barbarous charms against the dangers of the field were familiar to their lips. Absurd incantations were held in supreme repute as infallible remedies for hemorrhage, toothache, or the fatal battle-stroke; nor was a belief in witches and ghosts yet banished from the popular faith. The silver bullet, however, was rarely found necessary for the overthrow of a witch. The German who suspected his fire-place of being a resort for such characters, readily expelled them by burning alive a young dog or two therein. Nor did the black cat, that old companion of sorcery, escape

---

[1] Ante sinistra cavâ monuisset ab ilice cornix. — *Virgil.* The reader will call to mind Tully's veneration for the same omen. Non temere est quod corvus cantat mihi nunc ab læva manu. — Cic. de Divin. 1.

unscathed; but, earless and tailless, wandered through the neighborhood, a monument of the use to which its blood had been put in the treatment of St. Anthony's fire.[1]

But recently escaped from the galling oppression of their ancestral homes, the German settlers were as little disposed as able to yield a perfect obedience to the minor require-ments of laws of which they neither understood the lan-guage nor comprehended the objects; and from their own lips we learn how, as of old, when in Israel there was no king, every man did in those days what seemed good in his own eyes.[2] And if any reliance is to be placed upon the testimony of competent and intelligent witnesses, the earliest German colonists evinced, in the hour of necessity, a conduct which shows very clearly how vague was their comprehension of the new duties they had assumed. In 1753, Franklin, writing to Peter Collinson, declared that the Germans in Pennsylvania, being generally the most ignorant of their own countrymen, were perfectly intoxi-cated with the unwonted possession of a political power; which they exercised, even upon their own preachers, with equal bigotry and tyranny. Keeping apart from the Eng-lish, they preserved with tenacity the usages of their native land. Their conversation was carried on in Ger-man; their children were educated in ignorance of any

---

[1] I cite almost the very words of the intelligent and pious Joseph Dod-dridge, D.D.; a backwoodsman by birth, who lived and died among the people he taught. His *Notes of the Settlement, &c., of the Western Parts of Virginia and Pennsylvania* (Wellsburgh, Va., 1824), is one of the most interesting works we have upon the subject, and will be often referred to in this volume.

[2] Conrad Weiser, Coll. Penn. Hist. Soc., Vol. I., p. 3. Doddridge, pp. 23, 152, 166, &c.

other tongue; their books, their newspapers, their deeds and legal instruments even, were in German.

"The French," continues he, "who watch all advantages, are now themselves making a German settlement back of us in the Illinois country, and by means of these Germans they may in time come to a good understanding with ours; and, indeed, in the last war the Germans showed a general disposition that seemed to bode us no good. For, when the English, who were not Quakers, alarmed by the danger arising from the defenceless state of our country, entered unanimously into an association, and within this government and the lower counties raised, armed, and disciplined near ten thousand men, the Germans, except a very few in proportion to their number, refused to engage in it; giving out, one amongst another, and even in print, that if they were quiet the French, should they take the country, would not molest them; at the same time abusing the Philadelphians for fitting out privateers against the enemy; and representing the trouble, hazard, and expense of defending the province as a greater inconvenience than any that might be expected from a change of government." [1]

----

[1] Sparks's Franklin, Vol. VII., p. 71. In 1755, Franklin energetically addressed the British public in favor of excluding any more Germans from the colonies. "Since detachments of English from Britain sent to America," said he, "will have their places at home so soon supplied, and increase so largely here, why should the Palatine boors be suffered to swarm into our settlements, and by herding together establish their language and manners, to the exclusion of ours?" XXV. Gent. Mag., 485. That the intelligent and educated portion of the German population did not clearly comprehend and honestly conform to the requirements of their novel condition, is not insinuated: yet, even in 1754, when Henry Muhlen-

It is not with any desire to cast unmerited reproach upon the character of any people that these remarks are offered: the investigation has been made purely in a spirit of seeking after historical truth, where the student can never be considered at liberty to disregard the evidences that stare him in the face. But, after all, nothing that has been said is in conflict with the usual course of human nature. Many of the earliest settlers were doubtless in some respects better men than their descendants; but they were still far from being perfect. They were not less governed by circumstances than human beings usually are: their judgment was as likely to err, or be warped by passion. If the Quakers were sincere, pious, and benevolent, it does not follow that they should be willing to consent to what they conceived to be an unfair system of taxation: if the Germans were frugal and industrious, it does not necessarily involve the fact that they should wipe out in a moment from their minds the memory of the distant homes they had just left; or that they should enter, heart and soul, into the merits of a controversy in which they had no previous interest. It was natural enough, then, that they should be indisposed to peril their new-born independence and scanty fortunes in a quarrel between George and Louis; being utterly indifferent whether either succeeded, so long as they themselves might enjoy repose. But when they conceived it necessary and a number of the most influential and respected Germans in the province (men of pure hearts, unblemished lives, and pious souls), addressed themselves to Gov. Morris, loyally pledging their fidelity to the King, they admit that there were "a few ignorant, unmannerly people lately come amongst us," who entertained contrary sentiments. II. Penn. Arch., 201.

sary to fight, the Germans acted with ample spirit, as was abundantly testified in the war of the Revolution.

But while the masses of the people sought homes in regions yet unsettled, they generally kept the frontier lines considerably before them. Along the borders, however, was to be found a population consisting indifferently of the children of every nation, but uniting here in habits and customs peculiarly their own. Wherever a fertile bottom was spread along the banks of the stream, or a warm, sheltered champaign stretched beneath the covert of a range of hills, the steady, monotonous fall of the woodsman's axe would soon be heard through the long morning hours. Presently a dull crash would echo through the forest, as some monarch of the grove fell prostrate, to rise no more. Ere long, the circle of the sky would begin to expand above the spot, and the sunlight, for the first time during untold ages, bathe the earth beneath in a continuous flood of warmth and brightness. A deadening once made, a few acres of rustling corn would raise their heads and reveal their golden treasures to the autumnal wind; while all around, mute mourners at the scene, tall, ghostly trees, the springs of whose life had been destroyed by the girdling axe, exalted their phantom forms and stretched sadly forth their skeleton arms.[1] Vainly they yearned for the nymph,

---

[1] A *deadening*, in the rustic patois of Pennsylvania, signifies the effect produced on the trees by girdling, or cutting a ring about their trunks. The bark being thus completely severed, the sap ceases to communicate, and the tree loses all its foliage and soon dies. A *clearing*, according to the same authority, denotes a spot where the forest is cut down, and nothing but the stumps remain. The ghastly aspect of the former process would doubtless render it objectionable to the eyes of a landscape gardener; but

the tutelary divinity of their shade. Still deeper in the forest gloom, by some distant spring or lonely mountain tarn, the homeless Dryad bewailed the leafy shrine which she should see no more.

During the dull, dark days of early winter or approaching spring, the smoke of the consuming dead trees mounted slowly on the air and lost itself in the cold grey above. But when summer returned, the settler would find perhaps a score of like clearings going on around him; and as many evening fire-sides welcomed the return of autumn. It did not take long to build a house in those days. Logs were felled and hewed of the proper length, and arranged with friendly aid into the frame-work of a one-roomed log-cabin. A roof of puncheons, rudely shaped with the broad-axe, was placed upon it, and an outside chimney of stone and sticks, filled in with clay, adorned one end of the edifice. The interstices between the logs were then plastered up with mud and moss : a door, and an aperture for a window added, and, if the building were a luxurious one, a puncheon floor : and the house was done. A block or two served for stools ; a broad slab of timber for a table ; a rude frame-work for a couch. Here in one chamber would sleep all the family — men, women, and children, married or single, young or old : here was their kitchen ; here did they eat. In some more elegant establishments, a double-cabin, or even a loft, was to be found. A few wooden bowls and none such were probably to be found in the backwoods ; and the facility with which a tract could thus be prepared for agricultural purposes, was no small inducement to the settler. A good woodsman will soon deaden a number of acres, which by the next seed-time will be ready for cultivation.

trenchers, some spoons carved from a horn, a calabash and an iron pot, with two or three forks and knives, completed the simple furniture. China, or even ordinary delf-ware, was unknown in those times; a few pack-horses in their annual journey were the only means of communication with the sea-board. For food, the chief reliance was upon the product of the chase, the corn, pumpkins, and potatoes which were cultivated upon the little farm, and the invariable dish of pork. No settler was without his drove of swine; and "hog and hommony" is still a proverbial expression for western fare. Their cows yielded them milk; and corn-meal, either ground by hand or pounded in a wooden mortar, furnished their only bread. In times of scarcity, such as were of too frequent occurrence, when the granary was exhausted, the children were comforted with lean venison under the name of bread, till a new harvest should come around.

Nor was their costume less primitive than their diet. Petticoats and dresses of *linsey-woolsey* (a cloth, home-woven, of wool and flax) filled the wardrobe of the country maiden, innocent, save on state occasions, of superfluous shoes and stockings; while the men were clad in a coarse linsey or buckskin hunting-shirt, with breeches, leggins, and moccasins. Their cattle were of too much value living, to be slaughtered either for their flesh or their skins, and the hide of the wild deer, tanned by their own hands, was compelled to supply the place of leather. Hardy as they were, however, the first settlers suffered greatly from the inclemencies of the weather; against which neither their clothing nor their dwellings afforded a sufficient protection. The seasons were then far more severe than, even in the same country, they are at present. The summers were shorter, and more damp and cold; the winters earlier, and more stern. Rheumatic affections, and the usual train of disorders consequent upon exposure, were common afflictions; and doubtless owing to the extreme ignorance which prevailed in matters of medical science, there were very many lives needlessly sacrificed from a want of proper treatment.

But, after their own fashion, they were a happy race, these backwoodsmen. Reckless of future danger, unconscious of prospective woe, they lived very much in the present. Full of animal spirits, the blood coursing through their veins under spur of the excitement of a constant peril, that at bed or at board, at seed-time and in the harvest-field, was ever by their side, they embarked eagerly in every homely sport or rustic revelry. The most unartificial frolic was partaken of with a zest that would astonish the tranquil tastes of one bred among more civilized scenes. Athletic games—wrestling, running, or shooting at a mark—were the friendly arenas wherein each strove to bear away an honorable fame. The boys were taught to throw the tomahawk with unerring aim; to imitate the cries of the creatures of the forest with a fidelity that would deceive the most practised ear, or to properly wield a rifle. Other education they rarely had; for no school-house, for many long years to come, was destined to raise its low roof among them; no church, no clergyman taught them to think of higher aims. Sunday came, indeed, a day of rest for the weary, but a day of mirth and amusement to the young and gay; nor was it, with all, distinguished in even this extent from the other days of the week. Yet it must not be supposed that it found the people plunged in dishonorable vice or excessive immorality. On the contrary, they were perhaps less so than the inhabitants of many Christian cities. Profane they undoubtedly were; in their most ordinary conversation, "they clothed themselves with curses as with a garment," and, in the gust of passion, were careless of the destruction of limb or life. But lying and cheating were abhorred among them, and a coward was the scorn of the community. Their sons were brave and their daughters were virtuous. The loss of female chastity was a calamity that involved dishonor; and instances of its violation or seduction were of rare occurrence, and usually swiftly and bloodily revenged. Seldom was it for other cause than a family feud that a youthful couple found any impediment in the path to matrimony; and such dissensions were not likely to endure in a neighborhood bound together in a common danger. Indeed, the gaiety it produced was frequently a sufficient inducement for a young man, able to support her, to take unto himself a wife. Then the whole country-side would assemble at the bride's dwelling, and, with copious libations of whiskey, in which the happy pair set them the example, exhaust the night in merriment and sport. To the scraping of an old violin, four-handed reels or Virginia jigs would endure till morning dawned or the performer's strength failed him. As evening wore on, the blushing fair, with her lover by her side, would clamber up the ladder which led from the lower chamber, filled with a boisterous crowd, to the loft above, where the nuptial couch was spread; and at a later hour, a substantial meal of pork, cabbage, and whiskey would be served up to them in their privacy. Preposterous as all this appears at this day, it was then the custom of the country, and as such, honored in the observance.

The most important feature of a new settlement, was, however, its *Fort*. This was simply a place of resort for the people when the Indians were expected, and consisted of a range of contiguous log cabins, protected by a stockade and perhaps a blockhouse or two. It was chiefly in the summer and fall that the approach of the savage was to be dreaded; and at this season families in exposed positions were compelled to leave their farms and remove with their furniture to the fort. Parties of armed men would sally out by day, and in turn cultivate each plantation, with scouts at a distance to warn them of the presence of the foe. Every precaution that the swarthy warrior himself could adopt was resorted to by his no less wily antagonist. The earth beneath, the bushes around, the skies above, were carefully interrogated; and a broken twig, the impress of a moccasined foot upon the dewy sod, or a distant column of smoke faintly ascending to the heavens, were infallible "Indian signs" to the uneasy husband or father. Then women and children would be quickly brought within shelter; cattle and furniture placed in safety, and a few of the most adventurous spirits thrown out to observe or interrupt the progress of the suspected danger. But let the panic once spread, and the alarm of a general Indian onslaught along the frontiers get headway, and in a moment plantations and settlements were abandoned. The popular terror, like wildfire, communicating to every quarter, would crowd the inland towns with anxious, care-worn faces, and leave to the torch of the invader the scenes of their late prosperity. But occasions such as these, were, fortunately, not frequent; and when the snows of winter had begun to fall, and the improvident savage could no longer find sustenance in the fields tilled by his wife's hoe, he was conceived to have occupation enough in the quest of game and in endeavoring to avoid starvation; and all fear of an attack faded away. Then the settler, ensconced once more in his own cottage, would linger over the fire during the long winter evenings, framing articulate sounds in the wild wailings of the northern blast, that piled up the deep snow-drift against his wooden walls, or striving to decypher the phantasmagoria which played among the lingering embers. Perchance the fierce howl-ings of a distant wolf would call his thoughts to his own fold; and floundering through the snow, he would sally forth into the darkness to assure himself that his treasured herds were in safety. Shaking the white masses from his burly form, he would soon resume his station by the ample hearth, and

In social scenes of gay delight
Beguile the dreary winter night.

Some simple story of the chase, or a yet more thrilling tale of personal adventure, would arise. With open ears and busy hands the little family would gather around or within the roaring chimney; one boy mending the lock of a gun, another adjusting the barb of an arrow or the spring of a trap, and sighing for the day when he too might bear a rifle and be acknowledged a man—

> When young and old in circle
> Around the firebrands close;
> When the girls are weaving baskets
> And the lads are shaping bows:

the sire would, for the hundredth time perhaps, narrate to unwearied ears some ancient fable of far beyond sea: of knights and giants, and beauteous ladies ravished from their bowers ; or, with innumerable variations of incident, recite his valiant deeds who conquered Cormoran. Then, from some half-lit corner, where the flickering flame from the hearth (their only light), shaped monstrous, grotesque shadows on the irregular log-walls, the sound of female voices would rise ; and to the monotonous accompaniment of the unceasing shuttle, would be sung in low, subdued tones a ballad of "bold Robin Hood that merrye outlawe;" whose deeds furnished to these people the staple of their poetry. Little skill or art was necessary to please a willing ear :

> They chant their artless notes in simple guise ;
> They tune their hearts, by far the noblest aim :

and the cruelties of Barbara Allen, or the plaintive strains of 'Willow, willow, willow,' were enough to excite every emotion that these rough breasts could feel. Such ballads were naively enough, but not unaptly, styled 'love-songs about murder.'[1]

---

[1] Doddridge, from whom the above sketch is faithfully drawn, gives a singular description of the garb which the young men sometimes assumed

Such as has been described is a fair picture of the domestic scenery of the various portions of the land in the middle of the last century. On the one hand were the Anglo-Americans, eagerly pushing forward their borders, careless of the lowering brows or half-uttered threats of the Indians; on the other were savage tribes who had little love for the French, it is true, but whose dispositions were ripe for trouble with the English. So deeply rooted, indeed, was the lurking disaffection towards their ancient allies, that so early as 1744, the Iroquois had warned the Governor of Pennsylvania that in the event of another French war the Delawares and Shawanoes would inevitably be found in the ranks of the enemy. The latter had in fact for many years previously spared no pains to bring the Shawanoes into their interest.[1]

Nevertheless, the presence of the French upon the Ohio was exceedingly unwelcome to all the Indian nations. The Iroquois, as well as the Delawares and Shawanoes, made some overtures, in 1753, of removing by force of arms the party under M. de Contrecœur, after two separate messages had been vainly sent to persuade him to withdraw: and a

in times of Indian excitement. It consisted simply of a pair of moccasins, leggins that reached to the thigh, and a breech-cloth twisted through a belt so as to suffer a skirt some eight or nine inches broad to fall down before and behind. The body, embarrassed by perhaps as scanty clothing as has been worn since the days of Adam, was thus perfectly free for action. "The young warrior," continues the worthy divine, "instead of being abashed by this nudity, was proud of his Indian-like dress. In some few instances, I have seen them go into places of public worship in this dress. Their appearance, however, did not add much to the devotion of the young ladies."

[1] Votes of Penn. Assembly, Vol. III., p. 555. Thomson, pp. 55, 25.

deputation was despatched to Virginia and Pennsylvania to desire the countenance of those provinces in the anticipated troubles and to put matters on a right footing between all parties. At Carlisle they met the provincial commissioners, whom they urgently pressed to call back the whites already settled on the western side of the Alleghanies, where as yet the Indians had sold not a foot of land.[1] And though nothing came of this temper, which, if properly managed, might have been used to immense advantage by the English, yet it serves to show how powerfully old predilections and national traditions conspired to make these people still disposed to friendship with the English and hatred to the French. But, as has been well observed, the Indian is to a certain extent a venal character. The nature of his existence had by this time compelled him to look to the whites for powder and ball; for rum and tobacco; for blankets and vermilion. The simple weapons of other days were no longer sufficient to enable him to pursue successfully his prey. Unless he would starve, he must resort to the store-houses of the trader; and once there, soft words and flattering gifts would be very apt to bring his will into the control of the donor. The lustre of the benefaction last received seldom fails to obscure all that preceded it; and like a child with a new toy, he loses all appreciation of former favors in the contemplation of his present enjoyment. In this manner the French worked upon the savages who visited them at Fort Du Quesne. The needy warrior, who went empty-handed, would return

[1] Thomson, p. 73.

to his companions gratified with a new blanket, gun and ammunition, and flaunting in the unwonted attire of a laced coat and hat and a shirt streaming with ribbons. Then he would contrast the generosity of the French with the niggardliness of the English; and the event would be that his fellows would all hasten to participate in the precious harvest that awaited them.[1] The Canadian government certainly dealt with an open hand; in this respect possessing an immense advantage over its rivals, whose bounty, diluted through a dozen provinces, could never be brought to bear on a given point with the same efficacy that attended the operations of one centralized power.

What finally tended perhaps more than anything else to alienate the Indians of Western Pennsylvania from the people of that province was the injudicious conduct of the proprietary commissioners at the Congress of Albany, where, on the 19th of June, 1754, all the English colonies were

---

[1] The two Ohio journals of Post exhibit very strongly this feature of Indian character. In the one, just such a scene as is above described was enacted; poor Post himself being compelled to bear the odium of his employer's meanness. But by and by the tide changed; the stock at the fort perhaps ran low, and the bribes of the English told powerfully on the savages; and Post made a second journey to endeavor to detach them from the service of the enemy. Then he found the tables turned; nor could even the presence of the French captain restrain the expressions of contempt with which the chieftains spoke of him. "He has boasted much of his fighting," said they; "now let us see his fighting. We have often ventured our lives for him, and had scarcely a loaf of bread when we came to him, and now he thinks we should jump to serve him." It must not be forgotten that it was to the presents and kind words of the Quakers, who first set on foot these negotiations, that the merit of prevailing upon the Indians to leave unopposed General Forbes's route to Fort Du Quesne, and the consequent fall of that important post, are justly due.

actually or constructively represented,[1] and where the Six Nations were present to join in the deliberations concerning their common interests. In their warrant for convening this Congress, it is gratifying to observe how clearly some of the causes of Indian discontent were comprehended by the Lords of Trade; and how alive they were to the critical condition of the English interest. Smooth words and liberal gifts are recommended as a cure for past sorrows; and it was most imperatively urged that the allegations of fraudulent occupation of their land should be promptly and satisfactorily investigated. Liberal gifts, too, were sent from the Crown to buy the good-will of its dangerous allies.[2] On this occasion the Six Nations (claiming, it will be recollected, to be the absolute proprietors of the country in question, as well as protectors of their weaker nephews, the Delawares), made a forcible reply to the reproach by the Commissioners that the French had been permitted to build forts on the Ohio. Old Hendrick, that doughty Mohawk warrior (who the next year sealed with his life his devotion to the English by the pleasant waters of Horicon), answered that the conduct of the French had received no favor at their hands: "The Governor of Virginia and the Governor of Canada," said he, "are both

---

[1] Commissioners from all the New England colonies, from New York, Pennsylvania and Delaware, and Maryland, were in attendance; and Virginia and Carolina desired to be considered as present. II. Doc. Hist. N. Y., 330.

[2] VI. Col. Rec., 14. And see the proceedings of this conference, as preserved in the Johnson MSS., and published under the care of Dr. O'Callaghan in the second volume of the Documentary History of New York, p. 325.

quarrelling about lands which belong to us: and such a quarrel as this may end in our destruction. They fight who shall have the land. The Governors of Virginia and Pennsylvania have made paths through our country to trade and build houses, without acquainting us with it. They should first have asked our consent to build there, as was done when Oswego was built."[1]

This statement of the old Mohawk, like many other Indian speeches, was true but in part; and the commissioners, in turn, while they confessed that they ever had, and still acknowledged, the Ohio country to belong to the red men, reminded them that for thirty years traders from Pennsylvania had, without interruption, been in the custom of visiting the tribes dwelling there. All that was now intended, it was said, was to protect them in the free enjoyment of their own property, and to drive away the intruding Frenchman. By these speeches, and a judicious distribution of gifts, their savage ire was so far subdued, that ere the council closed some of the Six Nations were actually prevailed upon to sell to the proprietaries of Pennsylvania all the land in controversy! This fatal purchase, comprehending about 7,000,000 acres, was bounded on the north by a line to be drawn north-west by west from Shamokin, on the Susquehannah, to Lake Erie; on the east, by the Susquehannah; on the south and west, by the furthest limits of the province. It included not only the hunting-grounds of the Delawares, the Nanticokes, the Tuteloes, and other lesser tribes, but the very villages of the Shawanoes and Delawares, of the Ohio; who could not yet

[2] II. Doc. Hist. N. Y., p. 338.

have forgotten that, by precisely similar means, they had been driven hither from their former homes; and they now were to anticipate nothing less than the same fate. It is possible that there might have existed, in some age or country, a race base enough to submit to these degrading conditions; but no sane man could have anticipated such a tame surrender from the American savage. The tribes actually dwelling there were not consulted in the business. They had no deputies at the council to join in the sale; and the whole transaction was smuggled through in an unjust, underhanded manner. The chiefs of the Iroquois who conducted it were not authorized to act for their people in the premises; and, when it came to light, the negotiation was solemnly repudiated by the Grand Council of Onondaga.[1] All their discontents thus fanned into a flame, the Ohio Indians honorably determined to fight to the last in defence of their liberties; and in revenging this last and crowning outrage, to wipe away the well-remembered wrongs, real and fancied, which had rankled in their bosoms for years. For their own protection, the tribes on the Susquehannah formed a league, which was strengthened by daily accessions of straggling families, scattered, as chance or fancy dictated, along the brook-sides or under the edge of some forest-glade of that umbrose, scaturiginous land. At the head of this federacy was placed Tadeuskund, a Delaware chieftain, well known in border history; who, after dallying a space with either party, finally yielded to the pressure of the times, and

[1] Thomson, 77.

joined with his race in the warfare against the English.[1] What share the Iroquois had in bringing about this conjuncture, can never, it is probable, be with certainty known. Zeisberger, in Ettwein's narrative, it is true, openly charges the Six Nations with having secretly placed the hatchet in the hands of the Delawares, bidding them to strike; and afterwards turning treacherously against them for this very conduct.[2] But perhaps a just version of the affair would be to suppose that individual warriors of the Six Nations, acting on their own impulses (which in many instances were abundantly hostile to the English), egged on the Ohio Indians and the rest to a step which was never recommended by the confederates in their national capacity. Subsequently, the Iroquois reluctantly, but vigorously, entered into the measures of Sir William Johnson, and were of great service in the ensuing contest.

As ill-blood in the human system first discovers itself in

[1] Thomson, 84. Heckewelder's Hist. Account of Indian Nations, 301. The latter author would lead us to suppose that the Wyoming chief never actually took up arms; but Thomson, who knew him well, is explicit on this point; and in the political tract called the Plaindealer, No. III. (Phil., 1764), p. 14, is an undeniable instance of his prowess against the settlers of Northampton County. A memoir of Tadeuskund, the last sagamore of the Lenape, who remained east of the Alleghanies, whose consequence was so great as to win him the title of the "King of the Delawares," is given in Heckewelder, _ut sup._ He was burned in his lodge, in the spring of 1763. In the language of Uncas, that grandest of Cooper's portraitures, "he lingered to die by the rivers of his nation, whose streams fell into the sea. His eyes were on the rising, not on the setting sun."

[2] I. Bull. Hist. Soc. Penn., No. 3. The Rev. John Ettwein was a Moravian missionary for many years among the savages. He died a bishop of that church, at Bethlehem, Pennsylvania, in 1802, in the 73d year of his age. Rev. David Zeisberger was a devout brother of the same order, who went hand and soul with Heckewelder in his heroic labors.

eruptions and disorders, the malignity and unfriendly dispositions of the border tribes soon began to be manifested
in preparations for war, in casual rencontres, and other
sporadic acts of violence. Then, indeed, the proprietary
government, having unavailingly sought, with insufficient
means, to appease the ire of the foes whom hitherto it had
looked on almost as subjects, vainly having tempted
them to

> ———— Unthread the rude eye of rebellion,
> And welcome home again discarded Faith,

undertook, as to a court of last resort, to bring the delin-
quents before the tribunal of their lords, the Six Nations.
These, entering warmly into the merits of the case, peremp-
torily charged the Delawares to forthwith repent, while
yet there was time ; to lay aside their arms, and make
their peace for past offences : " Get sober," said they, in the
metaphorical manner of Indian speech ; " your actions
have been those of a drunken man." But the palmy days
of yore were gone, when the trembling Delaware stood
cowering, like a whipped hound, before the frown of an
Iroquois, and quaked to his inmost soul at the awful voice
of the undying fire. A blind, unhesitating submission to
the imperious, unreasonable mandates of the tribes that
had so long oppressed and insulted his nation, was no
longer written on his heart. He had resolved to throw off
the petticoat, and to again assume the proud rank of a
warrior of the once dreaded Lenni Lenape — ' a son of the
Great Unamis ' — among the children of the forest ;[1] and

---

[1] The true title of the gallant tribe whom we call the Delawares was
Lenni Lenape — " original people " — for they claimed to be of the pure,

to the words of the Iroquois, he returned scoff for scoff and scorn for scorn. "We are men," said the tribes on the Susquehannah to the deputies who had borne them the injurious behests of the Six Nations; "we are men and warriors. We will acknowledge no superiors upon earth. We are men, and are determined to be no longer ruled over by you as women. We are warriors, and are determined to cut off all the English save those that make their escape from us in ships. So say no more to us on that head, lest we make women of you as you have done of us."[1] Their day of serfdom had gone by; and from that time forth, the Delawares were once more an independent nation. Nothing could now be done with them by threats; but it was soon discovered that long habits of association still preserved their effect; and the friendly influence of the Six Nations being led to bear on them by Sir William Johnson, the best beloved of all the white men, they were eventually brought into measures of peace. To follow this theme further, would be to transcend the proper limits of our narrative. Suffice it to observe here, that many of the Iroquois themselves joined heart and hand in the original designs of the Delawares, and would never consent to come into the national views of their own people.

unmixed race, with which the earth was first populated, and would proudly boast, "We are the grandfathers of nations." The river whose banks was their chosen seat they named the *Lenapewihittuck*, or, "the rapid stream of the Lenape." And when the English renominated it in honor of Lord De la Warre, the people, with whose name its own was previously wedded, were still continued in the same connection. Heckewelder gives a most interesting account of the history of the Lenape.

[1] Thomson, 87.

Even while the Six Nations were openly at war with the French, many of their warriors were in arms at Fort Du Quesne against the English, and using all their influence to bring other Indians into the same views. When the Delawares began to waver in the hasty course they had adopted, we find these men using every argument to hold them firm; and it is curious to observe with what contemptuous indifference the lately subservient, "petticoated" Delaware had already begun to treat "their uncles the Iroquois." When Post brought overtures to Logstown, near Fort Du Quesne, the Delawares received him kindly; but one of the Iroquois who were there, an old Onondaga warrior, bitterly resented his presence. "I don't know this Swannock (or Englishman)," said he; "it may be that you know him. I, and the Shawanoes, and our fathers the French do not know him. I stand here," (stamping his foot), "as a man on his own ground. Therefore I, and the Shawanoes, and our fathers, don't like that a Swannock come on our ground." This allusion to the ancient claim of sovereignty by the Six Nations was too much for Delaware patience to endure, and one of them instantly rose and replied: "That man speaks not as a man: he endeavors to frighten us by saying that this is his ground. He dreams. He and his father have certainly drank too much liquor: they are drunk. Pray let them go to sleep till they are sober. You don't know what your own nation (the Iroquois), do at home; how much they have to say to the *Swannocks*. You are quite rotten: you stink. (*i. e.* Your sentiments are offensive.) You do nothing but smoke your pipe here. Go to sleep with your father, and when you are sober we will speak to you."[1]

Nevertheless, if they slew the English, it was not for love of the French. Equally jealous of both parties, all the savage desired was to see his old hunting-grounds unpolluted by the armies of the stranger, untrodden save by its native denizens; and so that this object was attained, the defeat of either or both would not seriously discompose him: to him, the success of either was a matter of as little importance—que le chien mange le loup ou que le loup mange le chien. With accurate perception, he gloomily dwelt on the idea that the permanent occupation of his lands was the real object of their controversy, and he bitterly vowed this should never be.[2]

But alas for the poor savage! Driven before the ever-onward surge of civilization, that may recede for a moment, but only to return with a mightier force, his shattered tribes—prostrated by the inherent defects in their own character and debilitated by Christian vices, their naturally ferocious tempers sharpened by the use of rum, the presence of poverty, and the memory of better days—have continued and shall continue to retire more and more westwardly, till already the scanty remnants of the people whose fathers are buried by the broad waters

---

[1] Thomson, p. 142.

[2] "D—n you," said Shamokin Daniel, a Delaware warrior on the Ohio, to the English, "why don't you and the French fight on the sea? You come here only to cheat the poor Indians and take their lands from them!" There was more of truth than of elegance in this pithy address, but it was echoed by his fellows: "The French say they are come only to defend us and our lands from the English, and the English say the same thing about the French; but the land is ours and not theirs." Thomson, 152.

of the Delaware, who daily gazed upon the Atlantic waves freshening in the light of the morning; now linger out a precarious life on the distant prairie whose face is wasted, as with fire, by the caravan of the emigrant; and pitch their lodges on declivities whose waters flow down into another ocean. Already with prophetic ear they hearken to the chafings of those billows which are the limit of an existence that has held a continent in its span: already they foresee the day when the wild cry of the sea-fowl, circling over the faint, murmuring waves of the ultimate Pacific, shall drown the parting sigh of the last of the Lenni Lenape!

Such then was the condition and disposition of Indian sentiment in Pennsylvania previous to and during the earlier stages of the war. We have seen how readily, in the summer of 1754, Major Washington had obtained the services of a large body of savages against the French: and we may judge from this fact alone how practicable it would have been to have enlisted them on the same side during the whole contest. It was impossible for a fight to come off at their very doors without their taking a share in it, on one side or another; and £10,000 well and liberally expended in presents at Fort Cumberland, with a fair-dealing or at least a plausible exposition of the designs of the English concerning their lands, would have bound all the Pennsylvania Indians in a common interest. Had such a consummation been effected, the scalp of every Frenchman on the Ohio would have been smoke-dried in the wigwams of Shamokin, or festooning the hoop-poles of Shenango, years before the British ensign was fated to be displayed upon the ramparts of Fort Du Quesne. But a different policy was unfortunately pursued, as will presently have to be noticed; and the bloody trophies which by hundreds graced the horrid triumph of the savage, were torn from the bodies of the English. In the meantime, let us resume the thread of our story.

When, in August, 1754, the tidings of the fall of Fort Necessity reached London, the exigencies of the case compelled the ministry to an energetic action. The affairs of the American colonies were at that time committed to the care of the Secretary of State for the Southern Province, assisted by the Board of Trade.[1] Since the days of Sir Robert Walpole, this Board had lingered out a supine, sinecure existence. The Secretary during all this period was the Duke of Newcastle, who, like the Old Man of the Sea in the Arabian tale, clinging about the neck of power with a tenacity that effectually prevented any policy but such as his own jealousy of merit or time-serving selfishness dictated, had hitherto carefully suppressed any indication of a desire on the part of his colleagues or subordinates to deserve the public approbation by the exercise of a capacity to promote the public good. The records of the Board of Trade were crowded with packages of remonstrances from the colonies, its tables were covered with bundles of unread representations and unnoticed memorials. It seems indeed to have existed for no other object than, in the language of Mr. Pitt, to register the edicts of one too powerful subject. Of the nature of American affairs, of the requirements and circumstances of the provinces he

[1] I. Walpole's Memoirs of George II., 343.

misruled with absolute sway, of their very geography he was ludicrously ignorant.[1] In the language of the great critic and satirist of the day, he was the strangest phenomenon that ever appeared in the political world. "A statesman without capacity, or the smallest tincture of human learning; a secretary who could not write; a financier who did not understand the multiplication-table; and the treasurer of a vast empire who never could balance accounts with his own butler." It is not surprising, then, that such a character should neglect or blunder through his duties, careless of the result so long as his own importance at court was not diminished. But fortunately for

---

[1] When General Ligonier hinted some defence to him for Annapolis, he replied with his evasive, lisping hum—"Annapolis, Annapolis! Oh! yes, Annapolis must be defended; to be sure, Annapolis should be defended—where is Annapolis?" (I. Walpole's Geo. II., 344). "He was generally laughed at," says Smollett, "as an ape in politics, whose office and influence served only to render his folly the more notorious." At the beginning of the war, he was once thrown into a vast fright by a story that 30,000 French had marched from Acadia to Cape Breton. "Where did they find transports?" was asked. "Transports!" cried he; "I tell you they marched by land." "By land to the island of Cape Breton!" "What, is Cape Breton an island? Are you sure of that?" And away he posted, with an "Egad! I will go directly, and tell the king that Cape Breton is an island!" The weaknesses of this man afforded an endless theme to the sarcasm of Smollett's muse. In another place, his manner of farewell to a general departing for America is exquisitely satired; "Pray, when does your Excellency sail? For God's sake have a care of your health, and eat stewed prunes on the passage—next to your own precious health, pray, your Excellency, take care of the Five Nations—our good friends, the Five Nations—the Toryrories, the Maccolmacks, the Out-of-the-ways, the Crickets, and the Kickshaws. Let 'em have plenty of blankets, and stinkibus, and wampum; and your Excellency won't fail to scour the kettle, and boil the chain, and bury the tree, and plant the hatchet, ha!" In Bubb Dodington's Diary (181-4), will be found other instances of the Duke's silliness.

Britain as well as America, the presidency of the Board of Trade was filled at this juncture by the Earl of Halifax, a man of parts and ambition, who was neither disposed to slumber on his post, nor to omit any opportunity of strengthening his own official power by enlarging the scope of his duties. We may fairly attribute to his energy the adoption in the cabinet of a resolution no longer tamely to submit to encroachments that, unless speedily checked, would inevitably turn all the channel of Indian trade from our borders, and immuring the colonies between the sea-board and the mountains, leave them to wither and perish, as a pool turned aside from its parent stream and enclosed with embankments, dries up beneath the rays of the sun.

Nevertheless, in the first steps taken by the ministry on this matter, Halifax was not consulted. The King had already held two councils upon American affairs, and instructions had been sent out to the provincial governors to repel any French encroachments force by force.[1] This policy had been decided upon; it was known how ingloriously its first practical workings under Washington had failed. Fired with the consciousness that vigorous measures to regain the ground thus lost must immediately ensue, Newcastle resolved to arrogate the entire merit and patronage of the plan to himself. Like the Athenian

---

[1] "It is His Majesty's command, that in case the subjects of any foreign prince should presume to make any encroachments in the limits of His Majesty's dominions, or to erect forts on his Majesty's lands, or to commit any other act of hostility; and should, upon a requisition made to them to desist from such proceedings, persist in them, they should draw forth the armed force of their provinces, and use their best endeavors to repel force by force." I. Entick, 111.

weaver, he would fain retain for his own glorification every part in which there was the least opportunity of gaining distinction, however incompetent he might be to fulfil it. Summoning to his secret counsels the Lord Chancellor Hardwicke and the Earl of Holdernesse, he endeavored in vain to fructify a conception which might subserve at once the public good and his private gain.

But natural incapacity, joined with talents which, though great, were transplanted for the occasion to an alien soil, could effect nothing. To organize military measures, military men must be consulted; to act with advantage in the colonies, some little knowledge of colonial affairs was required; and the Duke of Cumberland, the head of the army, and the Earl of Halifax, the best authority on plantation questions, were both studiously excluded from the deliberations of the triumvirate. Independent of any other reason of jealousy, it was evident that, in such an undertaking, the properest persons to direct its appointments were Cumberland and Halifax; and this was enough to alarm the Duke of Newcastle. His policy was to cook up, from the information of obscurer men, some scheme in which himself should shine the *magnus Apollo*, the dispenser of favor, and the sole original of reward. He first, therefore, summoned to his aid a Mr. Horatio Gates, a young English officer, who had recently served with reputation in America; and desired his advice.[1] Gates modestly

[1] Horatio Gates, afterwards so distinguished in American history, is said to have been the son of a respectable victualler in Kensington, and the godson of Horace Walpole. This latter circumstance may account for Walpole's knowledge of the details of the interview with Newcastle, which he certainly did not arrive at through the minister. Gates was born in

avowed his youth and inexperience; pleaded that he had seen nothing of America save the parts of Nova Scotia in which his regiment had been quartered, and his consequent incompetence to devise such an important operation. He professed his willingness to answer any questions that might be put to him; but he was too astute to be led into the enunciation of any grand system, the burthen of which he well knew would, in case of failure, break down his own shoulders, while all the praise of success would accrue to his superiors. In short, he utterly declined acting as he was desired. The trio next fell upon a Quaker gentleman, a Mr. Hanbury, whose connections were such that he happened to know a little about America, though nothing, probably, of warfare; and at his suggestion, Virginia was selected as the basis of operations, and it was determined to entrust the whole conduct of the business to Horatio Sharpe, Lord Baltimore's Lieutenant-Governor of Maryland. Though Sharpe was a lieutenant-colonel in the Royal Army,[1] he had never been engaged. But when the

1728. Soon after his return to England from Nova Scotia, he must have gone back to America; since we find him in command of the King's New York Independent Company under Braddock. It is believed these companies were formed of the regiments disbanded in 1748-9. Those stationed in Carolina were the remains of Oglethorpe's old regiment (Penn. Gaz., No. 1338); and it may be noticed here that while a part of his former command was thus posted in his vicinity, others followed Oglethorpe to his new colony, and became founders of the State of Georgia. The Independents do not seem to have had any field-officers; consequently, promotion must soon have lifted Gates from this sphere, since we find him, in 1759, acting as aide, with the rank of major, to Hopson, or his successor, Barrington, at the reduction of Martinico. In July, 1760, he was brigade-major, under Monckton, at Fort Pitt. (III. Shippen MSS., 392.)

[1] This grade (which, however, was local, and confined to the West Indies) Sharpe received July 5th, 1754. He held it so late as 1778.

contrivers of his promotion laid their plan before the king, it was accompanied with a declaration that he had served through the whole of the last war, and was well known to possess the good opinion of the Duke of Cumberland : "So good," replied the latter, "that if Sharpe had been consulted, I am sure he would have refused." In the mean while, however, his appointment was forwarded to him by the hands of Governor Arthur Dobbs, of North Carolina.[1] His instructions would seem to have contemplated nothing beyond the capture of Fort Du Quesne by a provincial force, although there was an intimation of a considerable body of regulars being shortly sent over from Great Britain. Proceeding at once to Williamsburg, he concerted with Dinwiddie and Dobbs his measures to effect the desired end. It was concluded to raise immediately 700 men, with whom, and the three Independent companies, the French fort should be attacked and reduced, ere reinforcements could be brought thither from Canada or Louisiana. This effected, that post and another which he thought it would be necessary to erect on a small island in the river, were to be held for the king. To garrison these and the fort at Will's Creek would require all his forces, and he concluded it would be useless for them to attempt anything further against the enemy on Le Boeuf and Lake Erie "without they be supported by such a body of troops from home as he dared not presume to hope for the direction of." But his enlistments went on slowly ; and at

---

[1] The governor, with his son, Captain Dobbs, had arrived at Hampton Roads, Oct. 1, 1754, in the Garland, after a stormy trip, in which the ship lost her main and mizzen-masts. They brought with them, also, £10,000 in specie for Virginia.

Will's Creek, where his men were to rendezvous, he learned that the French strength on the Ohio was much increased by the arrival of a number of Ottawas, Adirondacks, and Caughnawaga Indians; and he therefore abandoned all hope of striking an immediate blow.

As had been intimated to Sharpe, more effectual means were on the tapis; but he was not destined to control them. The most that his supporters could urge to the king in his favor was, that if not remarkably able, he was at least a very honest man. "A little less honesty," shrewdly replied the monarch, "and a little more ability, might, upon the present occasion, better serve our turn." It was decided to make, forthwith, a general movement; and for once Newcastle was compelled to yield to the counsels of abler men. At all events, it is certain that Cumberland's influence was eventually paramount in the formation of the scheme finally adopted.[1] Rather with a view, we may believe, to conciliate by a show of confidence, than to obtain the benefit of his advice, Newcastle sought to communicate the details of his plans to Mr. Pitt; but the disappointed statesman gave him a curt interruption: "Your Grace, I suppose, knows," said he, "that I have no capacity for these things; and therefore I do not desire to be informed about them."

While all these intrigues were going on, the ambassadors of the two powers — the Duc de Mirepoix and the Earl of

<hr>

[1] I. Walp. Geo. II., 347. MS. Sharpe's Corresp. VI. Col. Rec., 405, 177. Though Sharpe's views in regard to the campaign seem to have been very sagacious, yet it appears clearly, from this correspondence, that it was to his and Dinwiddie's suggestions that the royal order settling the comparative rank of provincial and regular officers was attributable — a step fraught with dangerous consequences to the best interests of the crown.

Albemarle, two very fine gentlemen, but sadly deficient in the qualifications necessary for the place and the moment —were frittering away their time in idle negotiations and empty professions of pacific intentions. Neither kingdom set the least practical store by these assurances, but busily went on arming for the steps they respectively purposed taking. Strong reinforcements were prepared in France for its American possessions, with instructions to hold, *à la main forte*, all they had hitherto acquired ; while, on the other hand, the English ministry ordered their governors to thrust out every intruder they found upon their back-lands, at whatever cost. Some anxiety was also manifested to enlist the services of the Indians ; who had, as was well known in London, relaxed in their friendship. From Virginia, Dinwiddie had written, in August, 1754, to the other colonies for aid in men and money to defend their common cause ; while to England he had applied for ordnance. This last demand was gratified by a present of two thousand stand of arms and accoutrements. Indeed, it was upon Virginia that the hopes of the crown chiefly reposed ; for Pennsylvania politics, as will presently be shown, were not such as to inspire much confidence in the military capacity of that wealthy province.

While the eloquent Whitfield, and other religious lecturers at Philadelphia, availed themselves of the presence of the enemy on their frontiers to lend an additional fervor to 'their exhortations,[1] the Cabinet of London were preparing more effective fulminations against the French. The Duke of Cumberland (who, whatever may have been his other demerits, was certainly possessed of a military capa-

---

[1] Penn. Gaz., No. 1341.

city) had been now called into the councils of the King; and, under his moulding hand, the preparations for an expedition whose destination was, as yet, kept secret from the public, began to assume some form and coherency. It was soon known, however, that two regiments of the line were designed for Virginia — the colony to which public attention had chiefly been attracted. Nothing was, as yet, said of their ulterior movements; and it was a perfectly reasonable thing for Great Britain to station so small a force in her plantations — a force which, according to Horace Walpole, was too insignificant to be of any service if the French intended to stand firm, but far too large to be exposed to the certain destruction of health and constitution of an American climate.[1] For the charges of this expedition, Parliament, on the 28th of November, 1754, voted the following sums:[2]

For two regiments of foot to be
  raised for North America; . . £40,350 15s.
For defraying the charges of the
  officers appointed to go with the
  forces commanded by General
  Braddock; . . . . . £7338 2s. 6d.
For defraying the charges of the
  officers appointed to attend the
  hospital for the expedition commanded by General Braddock; £1779 7s. 6d.
                             £49,468 5s.

[1] Letter to Sir H. Mann, Oct. 6, 1754. III. Walp. Corresp. (ed. Lond., 1840) 70.
[2] Univ. Mag, 1755.

Of the personal history of the gentleman to whom the command in Virginia had thus been entrusted, little or nothing more than what is contained in the public records of the period has, with unwearied care and research, been discovered to reward the student's curiosity. Before his name had become immortal in the scanty annals of the defeat and disgrace of British arms, Braddock had not done anything to earn himself a place in the chronicles of the times. Even the writers of memoirs, those gleaners in the fields of history, had not stooped to bind up such a poppy blossom in their sheaves: no "snapper up of unconsidered trifles" had sketched his biography. And so great, so horrible was the ignoscible disaster that crowned his existence, that only in vouchsafing him a soldier's death does it fall short of tragic perfection. Then, when the minds of men were exasperate with the thrill of national dishonor, for the first and last time does Braddock's name appear staining with its shameful characters the pages of history. Yet even the most bitter of those who sate in judgment on him, allow him certain merits. "Desperate in his fortune, brutal in his behavior, obstinate in his sentiments," says Walpole, "he was still intrepid and capable." Though a man of wit, his associations had probably not been such as to give him any place in the memorials of the literary characters of the day previous to his campaign in America; and perhaps for the very reason, that merely as an officer of the Guards and the élève of the Duke of Cumberland, he was well known to a certain portion of the court and city, and totally unknown to the rest of the world, his conduct finds no place in the social history of the period. Though a professed man of pleasure, it is not likely that the aristocratic doors of Boodle's or White's were opened to an Irish adventurer; yet even there he would hardly have come in contact with many of "the mob of gentlemen who write with ease." The few noble literati of the time—the Walpoles, the Selwyns, and the Herveys—do not seem to have had much personal acquaintance with him. It was at some place of lower resort that he pursued Fortune and staked his little means at gleek, passage, or the E O table. Still, even such were not the accustomed haunts of the garreteers of Grub-street or the *habitués* of the King's Coffee-House.[1] Thus, whether

Obliged by hunger—or request of friends—

the chronicler took his pen in hand, he was not often apt to find food for his meditations in the behavior of Brad-dock. It is in a letter of Mr. Shirley, his military secre-tary, written in all the confidence of friendship to Governor Morris, that the strongest picture of his charac-ter is to be found. Shirley was evidently, like all of his race, a man of ability and of ambition, and it was upon the observations of several months that his remarks were grounded. "We have a General," he says, "most judi-ciously chosen for being disqualified for the service he is in, in almost every respect. He may be brave, for aught I know, and he is honest in pecuniary matters." Benjamin Franklin, that sagacious and keen observer of human nature, sums up in a few words his opinion of Braddock's

---

[1] A place in Covent Garden Market, well known to houseless bards.

8

capacity. "This General was, I think, a brave man, and might probably have made a figure as a good officer in some European war. But he had too much self-confidence, too high an opinion of the validity of regular troops, too mean a one of both Americans and Indians."[1] Not dissimilar to this view is that of the English historian Entick, who, besides being a contemporary of Braddock, seems to have had access to very good sources of information in the preparation of his volumes. "It has also been hinted," says he, "that much of the disappointment in this expedition was owing to the General himself, in point of conduct. The plan was laid, and his instructions settled in such a manner, as to put him always on his guard against ambuscades, which were to be expected in a march through woods, deserts, and morasses. But this gentleman, placing all his success upon the single point of courage and discipline, behaved in that haughty, positive, and reserved way, that he soon disgusted the people over whom he was to command. His soldiers could not relish his severity in matters of discipline : and, not considering the nature of an American battle, he showed such contempt towards the Provincial forces, because they could not go through their exercise with the same dexterity and ability as a regiment of Guards in Hyde Park, that he drew upon himself their general resentment."[2]

From the confused and imperfect data that are obtainable at this day, it would seem that Braddock was an

[1] I. Sparks's Franklin, 160. VI. Col. Rec., 404. And Franklin's notion is followed by Lord Mahon. (IV. Hist. Eng., 69.)
[2] I. Entick, 143.

officer well versed in military science and tactics according to the system that then prevailed; a rigid martinet, utterly unforgiving to a neglect of duty; and a brave, unflinching soldier. It was never said during his life that he ever bade his men follow danger where he was not greedy to lead the way; and it will be seen in the course of these pages that he was as prompt himself to face perils and to encounter hardships as to exact a like readiness from those under his control. In short, his military character was precisely calculated to meet the approbation of the raiser of such a creature as the brutal Hawley; and, indeed, there were very many points of resemblance between these favorites: in the rebellion of 1745, the latter had even commanded the identical troops which Braddock now led. But Hawley proved himself in the field a braggart and a poltroon, and if his defeat at the rout of Falkirk was not as fatal in its consequences as that of the Monongahela, it was infinitely more ignominious to the general who with bloody rowels led a shameful flight. Braddock, whatever his defects, was too much of an Irishman ever to show the white feather. In private life, he was what would now be termed dissolute; he was prone to the debaucheries of his day and class, the bottle and the gaming-table; he was imperious, arrogant, and self-opinionated. But if dimmed by the vices of his profession, his character was also brightened by many of its virtues.

When or where Edward Braddock was born, there is no means of ascertaining. Dr. Goldsmith, with a poet's license, speaks of his family as one of the best in the kingdom,[1] and it is said to have been of Irish extraction;

---

[1] Goldsmith's Misc. Works, (ed. Prior, Lond. 1837), 294.

but even this is doubtful.[1] The name is certainly of Saxon, rather than Celtic or Erse, origin; and so, indeed, is it asserted, in a sort of monody, apparently by a friend, published immediately after his death, in which its derivation is said to be from two Saxon words, signifying Broad Oak.[2] It is possible his father or grandfather may have been one of those English adherents of William of Orange, who found, in Irish confiscated estates, the reward of their Protestant zeal; and this would, in a measure, account for the favor which some of the members of this family seem to have encountered at the hands of the House of Hanover. All that can now be discovered in this regard, however, is that, during the past century, with the exception of the father of the hero of this volume and his immediate posterity, there were none of the name who rose into public notice; and before and after that period, it is unknown in British history.[3] His father, who was also named Edward Braddock, must have been born about the middle of the seventeenth century, since we find him a lieutenant in the Coldstream Guards at least as early as 1684. In 1690, he was their senior captain; on the 1st

---

[1] The name, certainly, does not seem to appear at all in the Rotuli Hibernine, published by the Record Commission.

[2] Vide Appendix, No. V. The words Broad and Oak are of direct Saxon derivation.

[3] There was a Sergeant Braddock in General Forbes's army in 1758, and the name occasionally occurs among the lists of London bankrupts and traders that adorn the columns of Sylvanus Urban. But at present the Post-Office Directory shows that there is not one of that name resident in the 'royal city.' A highly respectable family in New Jersey, however, still bear, as I am told, the name of Braddock; and it likewise occurs in the Philadelphia and Pittsburg directories.

of October, 1702, he got his majority; and on the 10th of January, 1704, was appointed their lieutenant-colonel. He was gazetted a brigadier on the 1st of January, 1707, and a major-general on the 1st of January, 1709. In September, 1715, he retired from the service, and died at Bath, on the 15th of June, 1725.[1]

This "honest, brave old gentleman, who had experienced some undeserved hardships in life," is buried there, in the Abbey Church of St. Peter and St. Paul.[2] The old general must have been in at least comfortable circumstances, since he left to his two daughters the sum of £6000: to his only son, in all probability, a much larger amount descended. This son was the Edward Braddock with whom we have now to do. In the Appendix to this volume will be found the full particulars of the unhappy fate of one of the daughters, Fanny Braddock, who committed suicide at Bath on the 8th of September, 1731. Her sister, also unmarried, had died some years before. Mistress Fanny Braddock — as the fashion of the day styled all unmarried women — was a lady singularly gifted with attractions of person and of mind, and was, by her sister's death, in 1728–9, in possession of a competent fortune. But, yielding to an undisciplined impulse, she sacrificed the latter to relieve the necessities of the man whom she loved; and the former speedily lost their lustre in the eyes of the gay throng whose esteem she coveted. With-

---

[1] Gent. Mag. 1707–10. II. MacKinnon's Hist. Coldstreams; 453, 454, 464. III. Goldsmith's Misc. Works (Prior's ed., Lond. 1837), 294.

[2] I. Gent. Mag. (1731), 397. This seems to have been the fashionable place of sepulture for strangers: the reader will recollect Sir Lucius and his "I'm told there is very snug lying in the Abbey."

out a stain upon her honor, she at length sank into a condition of despair, and at the gaming-tables—then the frequent resort of ladies of fashion in England, as now on the
continent—she soon dissipated away the scanty remains
of her patrimony. Wearied of life, unable longer to endure
the painful contrast of her position as governess in the
family of a respectable tradesman with the brilliant place
she lately occupied, she resolved on self-destruction. During
the long night-watches in her lonely chamber, her mind
reverted to his infamy who had broken her heart and
squandered her fortune. To drive away these mournful
reveries, she took down a book and essayed to read. The
volume was the Orlando Furioso of Ariosto; and she
opened it at that passage of the ninth canto where Olympia
mourns the perfidy that had shut every avenue of hope
from her soul :

—— per lui toltomi il regno,
Per lui quei pochi beni, che restati
M'eran del viver mio soli sostegno
Per trarlo di prigione ho dissipati ;
Ne mi resta ora, in che più far disegno,
Se non d'andarmi io stessa in mano à porre
Di si crudel nimico, e lui disciorre.

The fatal similarity of fortune weighed upon her mind
and confirmed her in her unhappy resolve. With a firm
step and unwavering will, she passed through the portals
of the house of life, and in a moment more, was beyond
the reach of human sympathy or human censure.

Nothing could increase the feelings of disgust with which
the conduct of Edward Braddock, on this sad occasion,
must inspire the reader. That, through her levities or his

own misconduct, his affections should have been long since alienated from his sister, seems natural enough; but there must have been an inborn, consummate brutality, to guide the tongue which could frame no other expression of sorrow than "Poor Fanny! I always thought she would play till she would be forced to tuck herself up!"[1] No sensibility could exist in his heart who could, for the sake of a scurvy pun, jest upon the manner of a sister's death, and say that she had adopted this plan '*to tie herself up from cards!*'[2] Surely on this occasion Walpole was justified in terming Braddock "a very Iroquois in disposition!"

[1] III. Walp. Corresp., 142. Walpole tells us, that before making away with herself, she wrote, with her diamond, these lines (from Garth's Dispensary, Canto III.) upon her window-pane:

> To die is landing on some silent shore,
> Where billows never break, nor tempests roar:
> Ere well we feel the friendly stroke, 'tis o'er.
> The wise, through thought, th' insults of Death defy;
> The fools, through blest insensibility.
> 'Tis what the guilty fear, the pious crave;
> Sought by the wretch, and vanquished by the brave.
> It eases lovers, sets the captive free;
> And, though a tyrant, offers liberty.

The truth is, that, speaking twenty years after the event, the great letter-writer was led away by a similarity of sentiment and expression. The actual inscription was this:

> O, death! thou pleasing end to human woe!
> Thou cure for life! thou greatest good below!
> Still mayst thou fly the coward and the slave,
> And thy soft slumbers only bless the brave.

See I. Hone's Every-Day Book, p. 1279.

[2] XXXII. Gent. Mag., 542. *To tie one's self up from play*, was a cant phrase for incurring some obligation which should act as a restraint upon

There is another anecdote which does not any more tend to give one a very elevated conception of his character. It seems that his virtues, such as they were, had won the favor of a certain Mrs. Upton, on whose infamous wages he was not ashamed to live. By constant applications, he had kept this poor fool's exchequer so dry, that one day she frankly answered a demand for money by pulling out her purse with but twelve or fourteen shillings in it. With the keen eye of an experienced forager, Braddock saw cause to suspect this was not all its contents. "Let me see that!" he cried, and snatched it from her hand. In the other end he found five guineas. Coolly emptying all the money into his pocket, he tossed the empty purse into his mistress's lap. "Did you mean to cheat me?" cried he; and he turned his back upon the house to see her no more.[1] This shabby transaction was a subject of town-talk in the coffee-houses and lobbies of the day; and was cleverly seized by Fielding and brought upon the Drury Lane boards in 1732, in a witty but licentious play, called the Covent-Garden Tragedy. Captain Bilkum (by whom, it is said, Braddock was meant) is made to thus deny the consolations of "the humming bowl:"[2]

Oh! 'tis not in the power of punch to ease
My grief-stung soul, since Hecatissa's false;
Since she could hide a poor half-guinea from me!
Oh! had I searched her pockets ere I rose,
I had not left a single shilling in them!

Thus, there was an instance of the Duke of Bolton receiving a hundred guineas from Beau Nash on a contract to repay £10,000 if he should ever lose as much at one sitting; and the duke actually soon found occasion, at Newmarket, to comply with his bargain. (III. Goldsmith's Misc. Works, 281.)

gambling.

[1] III. Walp. Corresp., 142.

[2] A. I. sc 6.

If, indeed, the immortal satirist designed the whole of his character of Bilkum as a paraphrase of Braddock's, he could have held him but in the light of one of those hired ruffians whose office it is to awe into silence the poor cully whom their partners have robbed. This is going infinitely too far : an occasional solitary instance, such as has been cited, may have stained his reputation, but it was not a specimen of his general character. There were many better things in him than that : and perhaps it is pressing closely the limits of moderation to say that he kept his flight so near the ground that he could have stooped to such a scene of self-degradation. His faults were evidently considered by men of worth rather as foibles than vices : his intimacies were with persons of character and honor ; and in many respects he was worthy of their confidence, though his excesses must often have lost it. It was thus that he became embroiled with Colonel Gumley, an old comrade and friend, whose sister was married to Pulteney, Earl of Bath ; and a duel was the result. As they met on the ground, Gumley, knowing very well the state of his opponent's finances, coolly tossed him his purse. " Braddock," said he, " you are a poor dog ! Here, take my purse : if you kill me, you will have to run away ; and then you will not have a shilling to support you." His infuriated adversary was galled to madness by this new provocation ; he lost all command of his temper, and quickly saw his sword fly from his hand ; but he was still too proud to ask his life at the victor's hand.[1] Another duel between Braddock and Colonel Waller is recorded, fought with sword

---

[1] Ill. Walp. Corresp., 142.

and pistol in Hyde Park, on the 26th of May, 1718; but of its cause or consequences nothing can be traced.[1]

As may be judged from the date of his first commission, Edward Braddock must have been born towards the close of the seventeenth century. On the 11th of October, 1710, he entered the army with the rank of Ensign in the grenadier company of the Coldstream Guards; and on the 1st of August, 1716, was appointed a lieutenant.[2] In the columns of the Gentleman's Magazine his steps may be traced as follows:—On the 30th of October, 1734, Lieutenant Braddock was gazetted to a captain-lieutenancy.[3] On the 10th of February, 1736, he was appointed to a captaincy in the Second Regiment of Foot-Guards;[4] and on April 2nd, 1743, he had risen to the rank of a lieutenant-colonel in the line, and was further advanced to be the second major of this regiment.[5] At that period, as at present, the household troops were considered the choicest portions of the army, and a commission in their ranks could not be esteemed a light favor.

The Duke of Cumberland, the Captain-General of the British Army (a dignity in which the great Churchill and the good Ormond were his only predecessors), had been Colonel of the Second and was now in command of the First Regiment; and William Anne, Earl of Albemarle, was Colonel of the Second, or Coldstreams, to which Braddock was attached. It is more than probable, how-

[1] Origin and History of the Coldstream Guards, by Col. Daniel Mac-Kinnon. (Lond., 1833.) Vol. II, p. 473.
[2] II. MacKinnon's Coldstreams, 456, 472.
[3] IV. Gent. Mag., 628. II. MacKinnon, 476. [4] II. MacKinnon, 456.
[5] XIII. Gent. Mag., 219. II. MacKinnon, 477.

ever, that his father's position in the regiment may have facilitated the young ensign's entrance; and it may be worth noting that the total period of service in this regiment of father and son did not fall short of seventy years, during all which period the name of Edward Braddock appeared on its roster. Nor was there anything unusual in a lieutenant-colonel of the line accepting an inferior majority in the Guards, when a Field-Marshal was their colonel, and the commissioned officers of other regiments were taken from their rank and file.[1]

The recruiting standard of the regiment, it is true, was extraordinarily high: to be even a private in its ranks was not a privilege open to every subject of the crown, no matter how well he might by nature be qualified. No papist, no Scot or Irishman, no "vagabond," was suffered to be enlisted even as a private into this proud body; and the popular satire of the day shows what vulgar consequence was attributed to its non-commissioned officers.[2] One may form

[1] This was particularly the case in 1746, when no less than twenty-six privates of the Life Guards were commissioned as lieutenants or ensigns in other regiments, many of them on American stations. It is believed that the famous geographer Thomas Hutchins, the historian of Bouquet's expedition, on this occasion received his first commission as ensign in the King's South Carolina Independent Company. *Hist. Rec. of the Life Guards* (Lond. 1835), p. 154. These Records of the British Army, which have been more than once referred to, were commenced twenty years since by command of William IV., and are intended to comprise a particular history of every regiment. The few volumes hitherto published are as elegant as useful; and it is to be regretted that so laudable an enterprise should progress so slowly.

[2] Witness the case of poor Dick Ivy, in Smollett's inimitable tale; the poet whom not "disappointment, nor even damnation," could drive to despair. And yet he could not make his quarters good in the milk-woman's cellar in Petty France, but "was dislodged and driven up-stairs into the kennel by a corporal in the Second Regiment of Foot-Guards."

an idea of its arrogance when we find in the orderly-book of the Coldstreams a command to its men to behave civilly towards and not to laugh at or make game of the other troops, at a review by the King on the 26th of October, 1745.[1] Originally raised by Monk from the *élite* of Hesilrige's and Fenwick's parliamentary regiments, it took its name from its quarters at Coldstream, whence Monk marched it on New-Year's day, 1660, "to restore the monarchy and give peace to his distracted country." At the Restoration it was specially exempted by Parliament from the universal disbandment of the army, and was retained as a Guard by King Charles; and ever since that period it has continued to deserve and to enjoy a distinguished share of royal favor and public regard.[2] It would be an interesting task to trace the means by which a man destitute of all influence of family connection or prestige of great wealth — a mere Irish soldier of fortune, as by some he is termed — should have obtained and continued to retain through a long series of years such a desirable position. It may have been indeed that he purchased his promotions; but the cost of such a step was always enormous, and it is not likely that he should have had sufficient resources at his command.[3] It is to his merit

---

[1] II. MacKinnon, 341.

[2] It is believed that the only occasions upon which any considerable portion of this regiment was ever forced to ground its arms or surrender its colours were at Ostend, in 1745, and at Yorktown, in 1781 : on this last occasion the Guards either had no regimental flag, or it was secreted and never delivered.

[3] In 1720, the King fixed the price of a Lieutenant-Coloneley in the Coldstreams at £5000; a Major's commission cost £3600; a Captain's £2400; a Captain-Lieutenant's £1500; a Lieutenant's £900; an Ensign's £450. In 1766, these rates were about doubled; and at present the

and actual services that we are inclined to attribute his success. At the period of his appointment, a large portion of the Second Foot-Guards were with Marlborough in Flanders; and it is not improbable that thither the young soldier was sent to learn the first rudiments of the art of war. In March, 1713, the regiment was recalled to London, and on September 18th of the next year, Braddock's company was one of those which on his arrival received the first Elector of Hanover who reigned over England. In 1719, a part of the regiment took share in the Vigo expedition, and in 1742, its first battalion was sent to the Low Countries, and Braddock undoubtedly among them. At Dettingen, on the 16th of June, 1743, the Second Guards, commanded by the second Duke of Marlborough, behaved gloriously under the very eyes of the King and the Duke of Cumberland. At the famous battle of Fontenoy, fought on the 11th of May, 1745, between Marshal Saxe, with Louis XV. and the Grand Dauphin by his side, and the English and Dutch Allies, whose Captain-General was Cumberland, the Coldstreams again won great honor, losing in killed and wounded two hundred and forty men.

Every one knows what terrible slaughter took place on that memorable defeat, when the Irish Brigade fiercely swept away the thinned ranks of the British, and gratified, for the first time since the fall of James the Second, the feelings of triumphant revenge. But amid all the carnage

Lieutenant-Coloneley is worth £9000, and an Ensigncy £1200. (I. MacKinnon, 347.) The purchaser, however, must pass a previous examination to prove his competency, and the money, it is believed, goes to the retiring officer.

and confusion, the English Guards gained scarce less praise by their cool retreat than by their furious charges, sullenly moving off like a lion who, undismayed and almost disposed to turn again, grimly recedes into the darkness from the watch-fire of the hunters.[1] It was for his share in this day's bloody work, we may presume, that Braddock received, on the 27th of May, 1745, his promotion to be First-Major of his regiment,[2] and on the 21st of the next November, to be its Lieutenant-Colonel.[3] In the summer of 1745, he was with the Second in garrison at Ostend, whence in July he repaired to England to acquaint the Lords of the Regency with its condition, and thus probably escaped being present at its surrender on the 12th of August.[4] When Cumberland pursued Prince Charles's army from England in the winter of 1745-6, we know

---

[1] Perhaps history does not afford a more striking instance of undaunted courage, joined with the perfection of discipline, than was displayed by the Guards on this memorable day. They were ordered to attack the French Guards and the Swiss; who, in perfect confidence, awaited the onset. The English advanced, composed and steady as though on parade. As they drew near, their officers, armed with nothing but a light rattan, raised their hats to their adversaries, who politely returned the salute. "Gentlemen of the French Guards," cried Captain Lord Charles Hay, "fire, if you please." "Pardon, Monsieur!" replied they; "the French Guards never fire first: pray fire yourselves!" The order was given, and the French ranks were mowed down as ripe grain falls beneath the sickle. The English behaved throughout the conflict with the same steadiness; their officers in the heat of the fight with their canes turning the men's muskets to the right or the left as they seemed to require. (*Voltaire: Précis du Siècle de Louis XV.*, c. xv.) After nearly fifty years' service in such a regiment, no wonder that Braddock had formed exalted ideas of discipline.

[2] XV. Gent. Mag., 333.   I. MacKinnon, 373, II. ib. 473.
[3] XV. Gent. Mag., 668.   II. MacKinnon, 473.
[4] I. MacKinnon, 373.

that Braddock was actively employed under his command,[1] and probably shared in the butcherly glories of Culloden. In September, 1746, he commanded the battalions of the First and Second Guards which were embarked upon the secret expedition of Lestock and Sinclair against Quiberon and L'Orient; and in May, 1747, at the head of the second battalion of the Coldstreams, was ordered to Flanders, where the Allies, under the Prince of Orange, were ineffectually striving to raise the siege of Bergen-op-Zoom. He was quartered in the autumn at Bois-le-Duc; in the winter near Breda; and in July, 1748, after marching to Ruremonde and encamping at Grave, was cantoned at Eyndhoven, where Cumberland had fixed his head-quarters. Peace having been declared in January, 1749, the Coldstreams were once again stationed at London. As every company in this regiment has its own standard, it may be noted here that Braddock's ensign bore a star within a garter, with the union in the colour's dexter-corner; this device had first been adopted by Charles II. The badge was red.[2]

It is presumed that Lieutenant-Colonel Braddock conti- nued attached to the Coldstreams until 1753; making a total of forty-three years' service in that regiment. If we suppose his age when he was made ensign to have been about fifteen years, we may conclude him to have been at least sixty years of age and upwards when he was killed in America. But, notwithstanding his appointment as briga- dier-general on the 23d of April, 1746, he was now, through debt or other causes, compelled to seek a temporary exile

[1] I. MacKinnon, 381.

[2] Ibid, cc. 24, 25.

from England; and on the 17th of February, 1753, was nominated to the colonelcy of the Fourteenth Regiment of Foot, then stationed at Gibraltar.[1] Anxious to lose no time at home, he hastened to join his post, and set out at once to the Mediterranean; where his stay, though but temporary, was long enough to win the affections of a garrison rarely conspicuous for aught but violence and sedition.[2] During his absence, nevertheless, he was not forgotten by his patron and chief. On the 29th of March, 1754, he was gazetted a major-general;[3] and, on the 24th of the ensuing September, was appointed to the command of the troops to be sent to Virginia, and Generalissimo of all His Majesty's troops on the North American Continent.[4]

These are meagre details, it must be confessed; and nothing can be unacceptable that will tend to clothe their dry skeleton with even the semblance of vitality. It may not, then, be amiss to refer to a tradition (albeit, like most traditions, it be entitled to little credence) which insinuates that the secret of Braddock's advancement is, that he was a bold beggar—a sturdy tramp, so to speak—who, with an untiring pertinacity that would not take No! for an answer, was forever dunning the authorities for

---

[1] XXIII. Gent. Mag., 53.　II. Mackinnon, 473.

[2] Walpole erroneously asserts (III. Corresp., 145) that he had been Governor of Gibraltar; " where, with all his brutality, he made himself adored, and where scarce any governor was endured before." But this is so far from being true, that it does not appear that between 1749 and 1753 he ever officially even acted as commandant in the governor's absence (Drinkwater's Gibraltar, 23). He surely was never governor: martinet as he was, however, it is well to note this evidence of his popularity with his men.

[3] XXIV. Gent Mag., 191.

[4] Ibid, 530.

renewed means of obtaining money and distinction. To purchase at once relief from his importunities, and to promote the interests of the service, according to the same unreliable authority, he was selected for a distant command, the duties of which he was confidently esteemed capable of perfectly fulfilling, while its emoluments would be something prodigious. Thus, it will be noticed, the foul finger of scandal has soiled alike the reputations of the adverse chiefs Braddock and Duquesne; two characters opposite as the poles in life, but destined in their memories to an undying and indissoluble fraternity.

Such were the antecedents of the leader to whose hands the control of an expedition of such vital importance to the welfare of Great Britain and of America was committed. In the royal councils, the question had been thoroughly considered in all its bearings, and the most proper and feasible method of seizing the French forts and resuming possession of the wilderness they controlled was freely discussed. One voice — which we may well believe to have been that of the sagacious Halifax — earnestly opposed the whole notion of relying upon British regulars to accomplish these desired ends : well aware of the nature of the contest that would ensue, he was for employing, at the government's expense, a provincial force, which should be raised upon the spot, among men familiar with the Indian warfare and the Indian country. Had this plan been adopted, and a sufficient number of regular troops added to preserve discipline and to garrison the posts to be acquired, there can be little question of its having met with perfect success. The standing army of Great Britain was at that time singularly small, and still further reductions were in contemplation: in fact, when Braddock sailed, he left but three regiments in England; and so jealous was Newcastle lest Cumberland should have the filling up of commissions, that, in the very face of the coming storm, he would consent to no more being raised.[1] The rest of the army was scattered all over the world; and since the regular force was so incapable of enduring a heavy drain, one would have thought the idea of employing irregulars would have been highly acceptable. The king, likewise, had four Independent Companies quartered at New York, three in South Carolina, and one at Providence.[2] These were not ranked with the regular line, but were retained in America at the expense of Great Britain; and their services might have been most advantageously availed of in this crisis. The chief difficulty would have been the relative precedency of colonial and royal commissions; but even this might have been easily surmounted by making every officer receive his rank from the crown through the medium of a provincial authority; and the instances of Stanwix, Johnson, and Bouquet show what popularity might have attended the appointment of a commander not chosen from the regular ranks.

Meritorious as was this plan, it was utterly incomprehensible to the Duke of Cumberland, whose judgment was justly supreme in the cabinet on questions touching the

[1] I. Walpole's Mem. Geo. II., 382.
[2] Historical Memoirs of the late Duke of Cumberland, (Lond., 1767), 463.

art military. He was a person of fair capacity, of a thorough education in the German school of war — that school of discipline whose exponent was the great Frederick of Prussia — and was of the first rank in the service. He had heard a great deal, ten years before, of the value of irregulars: he had seen a whole empire trembling at the feet of a mere handful of undisciplined mountaineers; its armies blasted, its councils panic-struck, its rulers ripe for flight. With a ready wit he had taught his grenadiers to face and to foil this impetuous foe, and to turn the very secret of their success into failure and ruin. He naturally now thought that the barbarians of America were to be encountered as successfully in 1755 as those of Scotland in 1745: and through his intervention, no other resolution was adopted by the ministry than that of placing their chief trust in a regular force. To Cumberland properly belongs all the responsibility of the conception and organization of the executive portion of this enterprise, and the nomination of its leader.[1] And conceding the question of the expediency of his policy, and considering the lights the Duke seems to have possessed of the character of the war and the nature of the services expected from Braddock, it is not fair to say that the selection of the commander was an unwise choice. An enthusiast in the art of war, in which at an early age he had distinguished himself, the Duke exercised, or endeavored to exercise, an impartial regard to merit in his appointments; and we are particularly told, in regard to this one, that General

---

[1] I. Walp. Mem. Geo. II., 390. Mems. of Cumberland, 496.

Braddock's "courage and military discipline had recommended him as of ability for so great a trust."[1]

The scheme which Braddock was to carry into effect was a very comprehensive one; and embraced nothing less than the complete restoration of English power upon the American Continent.[2] As early as September, 1754, it was decided that two regiments of foot, the Forty-fourth, Colonel Sir Peter Halket, and the Forty-eighth, Colonel Thomas Dunbar, then stationed in Ireland, should form the stamina of the proposed expedition. These were at once to be sent to the colonies, where, having effected the objects immediately in view, they were to remain three years, to put the country and its people in a suitable posture of future defence.[3] It was intended that each of these regiments should embark five hundred strong, and that they should be recruited in America to a complement of seven hundred. Two other regiments of one thousand men each, to be commanded respectively by Sir William Pepperell and William Shirley, Esq., the Governor of the province of Massachusetts-Bay, were likewise to be raised at the King's cost in America, and abundant stores of

---

[1] I. Entick, 114. Smollett (Adv. of an Atom), says that Braddock was "an obscure officer, without conduct or experience, whom Cumberland selected for this service; not that he supposed him possessed of superior merit, but because no officer of distinction cared to engage in such a disagreeable expedition." He further intimates, too, an invincible aversion on the part of the Duke and his royal father to the employment of Indian allies as scouts. But it is the satirist, not the historian, who speaks: the whole volume is one continued tirade against every person in power during the Seven Years' War, from Pitt and Mansfield to Frederick of Prussia and the Empress-Queen.

[2] See Appendix, No. I.

[3] Penn. Gaz., No. 1365.

artillery, provisions, clothing, etc., were provided. In addition to these forces, which would at most make up but about thirty-five hundred men, the King's Independent Companies in America were to be under Braddock's command; and Royal Instructions had been sent to the different Governors, demanding not only the aid of the colonial troops, but the services of as many Indians as could be enlisted. What with regulars, militia, and savages, it was hoped that England would thus be able to bring from twelve to fifteen thousand men into the field. With these a simultaneous movement was if possible to be made against Forts Du Quesne, Niagara, and Crown Point; while Colonel Lawrence, who was stationed in Nova Scotia, was instructed to capture Beau-Séjour; all these places being, according to British views, unlawfully occupied by France. An English fleet, hovering on the coast, was to intercept all military supplies from the French, and thus prevent their adding any fresh strength to the posts in question.

On the 14th of November, His Majesty opened Parliament with a speech which, after the usual self-congratulatory remarks on the pacific relations still existing, announced his intention of improving the present advantages of a general peace to promote the commerce and protect the colonies in America. Parliament understood these words as they were meant, and straightway voted £4,000,000 for supplies; £1,000,000 of which was to increase the army and navy. The French representative, M. de Mirepoix, was not blind to this policy; but the object of his court was to stave off open hostilities, until it was thoroughly prepared for the conflict: and accordingly the duke kept couriers flying from London to Paris, and from Paris to London, while he vowed and protested his master's intentions to be utterly pacific. But both countries persevered, notwithstanding their mutual diplomatic tergiversations, in steadily arming for the fray.

In the mean time, the preparations for the campaign were carried on with vigor and activity. It was settled that the 44th and 48th regiments should continue on the Irish establishment despite their transportation to America; thus saddling its equivalent of the charges of the war on the sister kingdom, which, not being represented in the British parliament, was not called on to vote supplies. But their ranks being thinner than even in time of peace was customary, it was found necessary to recruit them by considerable drafts from other regiments, particularly from such as were then on duty in Ireland, unless stationed at Dublin. A regiment of ten companies should have counted seven hundred men at its musters : it was believed that these would have mounted up to five hundred each, leaving the additional two hundred to be engaged in America ; but the result showed a greater failure even than this. To supply this deficiency, prompt steps were taken. On October 29th, 1754, one hundred men were drafted from Lord Bury's regiment (the 20th) at Bristol, and as many more from Colonel Buckland's at Salisbury, who were at once ordered to Cork, whither Major-General Bligh had already repaired from Dublin to superintend the proceedings for embarcation.[1] Early in the same month, Sir Peter Halket had

<hr>

[1] Penn. Gazette, No. 1360, No. 1362.

picked up a few volunteers in London, and a sergeant and corporal of each company in the artillery were despatched to beat up recruits through the country.[1] In Ireland, four sergeants, four corporals, five drums and sixty-five privates of Lieutenant-General Bragg's regiment (the 28th), and the same number from that of Colonel Pole (the 10th), at Limerick, were drafted to Cork : and in the beginning of November drafts were also made from Lieutenant-General Anstruther's regiment (the 26th), and from the second battalion of the Royals, at Galway.[2] So odious was their destined service, however, that every effort of the officers could not restrain desertion. Many of the new drafts or enlistments, too, consisted of the worst class of men, who, had they not been in the army, would probably have been in Bridewell; and this did not tend to elevate the personal standard of the two regiments.

The preparations in the way of military stores, ordnance, etc., were also conducted upon an extensive scale. Till the close of October, the workmen at the Tower were busily employed in making artillery and ammunition wagons, and putting up cartridges for the expedition. Tents for eight thousand men, with marquees, drums, arms, accoutrements, &c., &c., as well as great quantities of ammunition, were shipped in the Thames for Cork.[3] Thither were also sent on the 9th of November twelve carriages with chests containing six hundred stand of arms from Dublin Castle. A number of army officers upon half-pay were recalled into service ; and on the 19th of October, orders were issued to the artillery for a captain, four ser-

---

[1] Penn. Gaz., No 1362.   [2] Ibid, No. 1367.   [3] Ibid No. 1360.

geants, and sixty bombardiers and matrosses to hold themselves in readiness to embark, at Woolwich for Virginia;[1] upon the 28th, Mr. Montresor was gazetted as Chief Engineer, and James Pitcher, Esq., was named Commissary of the Musters.[2] Several additional surgeons were also provided; and James Napier, Esq., Master Surgeon of the Hospitals in Flanders during the preceding war, was appointed Director of the Hospitals belonging to the forces on the American expedition.[3] On the 15th of October, Sir John St. Clair, Lieutenant-Colonel of Offarrell's regiment of foot (the 22nd), had already been gazetted as Deputy Quarter-Master-General for all the forces in America, to rank as a Colonel; who, with very little delay, hastened to Virginia to acquaint himself with the scene of his future duties.

Indeed, an unwonted energy reems at this time to have inspired the ministry. Not only were six thousand troops provided for the defence of the colonies at the cost of the crown, with an ample provision of the proper munitions of war;[4] but liberal supplies of money or its equivalent were granted to different provinces. To Virginia, for instance, were sent £10,000 in cash, with authority to draw for as much more; and Pennsylvania, for purposes of war, was furnished with six hundred firelocks (or muskets), with bayonets, cartouche-boxes, &c., three tons of musketballs, fifteen barrels of gunpowder, and five thousand flints.[5]

---

[1] A matross is an artillery soldier of a rank inferior to the bombardier or gunner.

[2] VI. Penn. Col. Rec., 303.

[3] II. Penn. Gaz., No. 1360, No. 1369.

[4] II. Penn. Archives, 293.

[5] Ibid, 300.

But all this unwonted display of vigor by a cabinet with whom ignorance and imbecility were the only stars that lighted the western horizon, was, *more suo*, destined to a rapid decline. During the ensuing three months exertion flagged, and nothing but delay and doubting appears to have characterized its proceedings. Upon the Sunday evening preceding the 12th of November, Braddock himself had arrived from France (on his route, we may suppose, from Gibraltar), at his house in Arlington Street, London; and on the same evening waited upon the King and the Captain-General. The latter had arrived but at 9 A. M. of that same day, and had barely taken possession of his winter apartments.[1] During his brief stay in the metropolis, Braddock had long and repeated interviews with the Duke, in which he received full and careful directions for his conduct; all of which, however, will be found repeated in the formal Letter of Instructions printed in the Appendix. On the Saturday before the 30th of November, he left Arlington Street for Portsmouth; whence he embarked for Cork on the Centurion, Commodore Keppel, to hasten and superintend the departure of the troops.[2] But, with all his impe-

---

[1] Penn. Gaz., No. 1362.

[2] The Hon. Augustus, second son of William Anne Keppel, 2d Earl of Albemarle, was born April 2d, 1725. He entered the navy as a midshipman at an early date, and received his first wound at the capture of Paita. He met with rapid promotion, and at Goree and in the battle off Belleisle distinguished himself for good conduct. In 1762, he was a commodore in the fleet sent out under Sir George Pocock to the Havannah. In consequence of grave charges brought against him by Sir Hugh Palliser, he was court-martialled for his conduct in the sea-fight near Ushant on the 27th of June, 1778; but was most honorably acquitted, while his accuser became the object of general opprobrium. So strong was the sympathy with Keppel, that Parliament went to the unusual length of voting him its thanks.

rious energy and impatience of delay, it was not until the 14th of January, 1755, that his object was effected. The transport-ships from England came in irregularly and slowly. On the 19th of November, the Seahorse, man-of-war, had arrived there for this service; and on the 21st, the Prince Frederick transport, Burton master, of five hundred tons, of and from London, with stores, &c., made its appearance at Cork to take in troops.[1] The Centurion followed close after, with most of the remaining transports and stores; and orders were at once issued for the men and baggage to be put on board. Still, there was a wearisome delay. Some transports, absolutely necessary to carry a portion of the expedition, which had duly sailed from England, were not yet arrived at the River Lee. A violent storm in the beginning of December had ravaged the coasts of Britain, and one vessel, with eight officers and sixty men on board, was lost off Falmouth.[2] The same gale had forced the Severn, Captain Rawlings, to put into Dartmouth, and the Molly, Captain Curling, to take refuge in Torbay.

Determined to wait no longer upon the tardy movements of the transports, Braddock, with his staff and a small part of the troops, returned to England in the Centurion and the sloop-of-war Cruizer, and on the 21st of December sailed from the Downs for Virginia; leaving the main

He had already (1763) been appointed Groom of the Bedchamber to the King; an office which he vacated in 1766. In 1782, he was made First Lord of the Admiralty; and in April of the same year, advanced to the peerage under the title of Viscount Keppel of Elvedon, in the County of Suffolk. He died in 1786, when his title became extinct.

[1] Penn. Gaz., No. 1368.   [2] Ill. Walp. Corresp., 88.

body of the fleet to follow at their earliest speed. On the 20th of February, 1755, Commodore Keppel's little squadron, consisting of his own vessel, the famous Centurion, the Norwich, Captain the Hon. Mr. Barrington, and the Syren, Captain Proby, cast anchor in Hampton Roads.[1] On board the Norwich were the General, Captain Robert Orme, one of his aides, and Mr. William Shirley, his military secretary; and the arrival of the transports was daily, if not hourly, expected. But the first intelligence that reached the Commodore's ears was a report that two French

[1] Not even the Victory, where Nelson died, was a more famous and favorite ship among British sailors than the old Centurion. In 1740, it was as her captain that Anson led his little squadron on their-venturous voyage to "put a girdle round about the earth." In 1749, we find Keppel in command. In 1755, when he hoisted his broad pennant as commodore of the Virginia fleet, William Mantell, Esq., was his captain. Towards the end of July, the Centurion, along with the Nightingale and the Syren, Captain Proby, sailed from Hampton Roads northwardly; and on the 4th of September, she was with Boscawen's fleet (Penn. Gaz., Nos. 1389, 1393). Though rated as of 400 men and 60 guns, she mounted now but 54. In 1759, she covered Wolfe's landing at Quebec; and it is a little odd, that at the moment the two future circumnavigators, Cook and Bougainville, armed on opposite sides, were present with the ship whose fame rested on its having performed the same feat. When she at last was broken up, her figurehead — a lion, so exquisitely carved in wood as to suggest the workmanship of Gibbons himself — was preserved to delight the eyes of the Greenwich pensioners. It is still preserved at their Hospital.

The Hon. Samuel Barrington, Captain of the Norwich, was the 5th son of John, first Viscount Barrington. He was born in 1729, and died an admiral of the white, and lieutenant-general of the marines, 6th August, 1800. His second-lieutenant on this Virginia voyage was the celebrated Adam Duncan of Lundie, who had sailed with Keppel in the Centurion as a midshipman since 1749. The Commodore, recognizing his merit, made a special point of obtaining his promotion on this occasion. In later years, the great victory of Camperdown, which gave Duncan a peerage, testified to the wisdom of Keppel's judgment.

men-of-war had lately been seen hovering along the coast; and, fearful lest they should insult the coming fleet, the Norwich and Syren were at once ordered to sea again to look out for the enemy.[1]

Braddock's long-expected arrival was hailed with a lively joy by the inhabitants of the colonies of Maryland, Virginia, and Pennsylvania; who certainly contemplated with enthusiasm the prospective discomfiture of the French; at the same time, perhaps, experiencing a secret satisfaction that the cost of the undertaking should mainly fall upon the mother country. Be that as it may, the expressions of popular pleasure on the occasion were neither circumscribed nor scanty; and to such gratulatory strains as these were the cisatlantic muses compelled to tune their unwonted lyres:[2]

Breathe, breathe, ye winds; rise, rise, ye gentle gales;
Swell the ship's canvass, and expand her sails!
Ye sea-green Nymphs, the royal vessel deign
To guide propitious o'er the liquid main:
Freighted with wealth, for noble ends designed,
(So willed great George, and so the Fates inclined.)
The ponderous Cannon o'er the surges sleep;
The flaming Muskets swim the raging deep;
The murd'rous Swords, conceal'd in scabbards, sail,
And pointed Bayonets partake the gale:
Ah! swiftly waft her to the longing shore;
In safety land her, and we ask no more!

Under convoy of two men-of-war, thirteen transports and three ordnance store-ships had left the Cove of Cork on the 14th of January, 1755; having on the last day taken on board £14,000 in specie.[3] The names of this little fleet were as follows:

---

[1] Penn. Gaz, No. 1368.   [2] Ibid, 1360.   [3] Ibid, No. 1371.

TRANSPORTS.

Anna, Captain Nevin;
Terrible, Captain Wright;
Osgood, Captain Crookshanks;
Concord, Captain Boynton;
Industry, Captain Miller;
Fishburn, Captain William Tipple;
Hallifax, Captain Terry;
Fame, Captain Judd;
London, Captain Brown;
Prince Frederick, Captain Burton;
Isabel and Mary, Captain Hall;
Molly, Captain John Curling;
Severn, Captain Jehosaphat Rawlings.

ORDNANCE STORE-SHIPS.

Whiting, Captain Johnson;
Nelly.
Newall, Captain Montgomery;

Parting company on the voyage, two transports, the Fishburn and the Osgood, each with one hundred men and officers on board, were on the 2nd of March the first to arrive at Hampton.[1] The General's original notion seems to have been to await here the presence of all the troops, cantoning them as they came in according to a plan of Sir John St. Clair's. But perceiving the objections to this arrangement, he left orders with the commodore at the port for each transport, as it should arrive, to take on board fresh provisions for the men, and to proceed at once up the Chesapeake to Alexandria or Belhaven (as it was indifferently styled) on the Potomac; while he himself hastened to Williamsburg to obtain an interview with Governor Dinwiddie. It would seem that there may have been some foundation for the rumor, that after conquering the French Braddock was to remain in this country as Governor of New York: but it was never alluded to in his intercourse with the colonies,[2] for the delays and difficulties of his

[1] Penn. Gaz., No. 1370.

[2] VI. Col. Rec., 286.

undertaking began already to be foreshadowed, and his mind was more than sufficiently occupied with what he had in hand. The transports came in slowly; it was not until the middle of March that the Severn arrived with the last company of the 48th regiment. Fortunately, despite their long and stormy passage, the health of the troops had continued good; but one man dying on the way. They were debarked at or hard by Alexandria, where they were for the present quartered. St. Clair had arranged an absurd plan for cantoning them in small divisions all over the country, which the General very wisely at once ignored.[1]

The sword was now drawn; it but remained to cast away the scabbard. In London, the wits of the court with profane levity cited Scripture for their purpose, and pretended to find in the inspirations of Ezekiel (ch. xxxv., 1–10), an assured prediction of the success of their arms in relation to the Ohio territories and Acadia. Punning on the words Mount Seir, Lord Chesterfield thus announced the prospective ruin of the French; "Moreover, the word of the Lord came unto me, saying, Son of man, set thy face against Mount Seir and prophesy against it, and say unto it, Thus saith the Lord God; Behold, O mount Seir, I am against thee, and I will stretch out my hand against thee, and I will make thee most desolate. * * Because thou hast said, These two nations and these two countries shall be mine, and we will possess it." Meanwhile, the pious Fontaine, secluded with his little flock in the western

---

[1] Braddock's Despatches, in II. Olden Time, 227. II. Penn. Arch., 286. II. Sparks's Washington, 68.

wilds of Virginia, lamented the turbulent times that had frustrated an expedition on the eve of departure for the exploration of the remotest sources of the Red River and the hardly-known Missouri, and the discovery of a water communication, through the heart of the continent, with the Pacific Ocean.[1]

It is here that the Journal of Mr. Orme commences; and in its pages the reader will find a lucid and particular account of the whole march. But since it is necessary to continue the history of the campaign upon a broader plan than that adopted by our Journalist, it will be endeavored to pass over as cursorily as possible, consistently with the preservation of the thread of the narrative, such circumstances as he has dwelt on at large, merely preserving a sufficient connection to admit the introduction of many collateral facts unknown to or unglanced at by him.

Upon the 10th of March, shortly after his arrival, the General had forwarded letters to the Governors of the different colonies to meet him in council at Annapolis in Maryland, early in April, and urging on them the establishment of a common fund to promote the common end of the protection of the English frontiers.[2] With the assistance of Sir John St. Clair, he next busied himself in organizing the basis and plan of the coming campaign. This officer had arrived in America about the 10th of January, 1755, in the ship-of-war Gibraltar, Captain Spry; and since had found active employment in acquainting himself with the nature and scene of his future duties.

[1] III. Walp. Corr., 110. Maury's Huguenot Fam., 391.
[2] VI. Col. Rec., 332.

Having procured from the Governors of Pennsylvania and Virginia, and from other sources, all the maps and information that were obtainable respecting the country through which the expedition was to pass, he proceeded in company with Governor Sharpe of Maryland upon a tour of inspection to Will's Creek. The fort here was garrisoned by Rutherford's and Clarke's Independent Companies of Foot, which, being ordered thither from New York by Governor Dinwiddie, had arrived in Hampton Roads in H. M. S. Centaur, Captain Dudley Digges, on the 8th of June, 1754.[1] On the 1st of September these troops were marched to Will's Creek, where they were joined by Captain Demerie's Independent Company from South Carolina; and on the 12th commenced erecting the works. On the 26th of January, 1755, Sir John and Governor Sharpe found the gallant fellows had built a sufficient fort, with several large magazines, and barracks for all the expected army. The latter were arranged in the manner of a fortified camp, flanking and flanked by the fort: ten four-pounders and some swivels constituted all their artillery. This post was called Fort Cumberland, in honor of the Captain-General. A company from Maryland had arrived there about the end of November, 1754, and remained through the winter quartered in huts they built for themselves. Later in the season the Virginia troops made their appearance. On his return, Sir John descended Will's Creek and the Potomac two hundred miles in an open canoe, till he reached Annapolis; whence he repaired to Williamsburg to await

_____

[1] These were the troops so anxiously looked for by Washington at Fort Necessity, in July, 1754.

the General's advent. He had inspected the Great Falls of the Potomac, and had no doubt that, by the aid of gunpowder, the rocks in the channel at that point might be removed to an extent sufficient to permit the passage of the flat-bottomed boats or batteaux in which the stores, etc., were to be transported to Fort Cumberland; and he employed a number of men upon that river to prepare the vessels. He also laid out a camp for the army at Watkin's Ferry, although no use was ever after made of it.[1] It was very unfortunate that Sir John had not with him an engineer or two to whom a portion of these duties might have been entrusted, leaving him leisure to occupy himself in other quarters where his presence was not less needed. Thus, the four hundred men who were to fill up the ranks of the 44th and 48th regiments to seven hundred each, were looked for by the Ministry to come from Pennsylvania.[2] This expectation was never fulfilled: so late as June 9th, 1755, we find Braddock writing to the Governor of that province, entreating him to use his efforts for this end, and offering a bounty of £3 sterling for each man.[3] The same colony was also relied upon to cut a road from a point on the Susquehannah, below the junction of the Juniata, to the Turkey Foot or forks of the Youghiogeny, by which flour and other stores might pass from Philadel-

---

[1] VI. Col. Rec., 299, 300.   Penn. Gaz., Nos. 1372, 1365, 1364.

[2] In October, 1754, Sir Thomas Robinson advised the Governor of Pennsylvania of the King's wish that he should have at least 3000 men enlisted from whom to fill up the ranks of the 44th and 48th regiments, as well as of Shirley's and Pepperell's. The mandate, however, had no legal force, and was never in the least degree complied with.   See VI. Col. Rec., 200.

[3] VI. Col. Rec., 423.

phia to the army. This road Sir John advised to be made along the ridges of the hills, so as to avoid the washing of the floods; and, in fact, made every suggestion for its plan that experience could prefer to his mind. The busy trade which to their shame the northern colonies at that particular period carried on with the French also arrested his attention; and on all these various topics, as well as in regard to a commissary whom he had sent to purchase a hundred wagon-loads of flour, he addressed the Governor of Pennsylvania.[1] Mr. Morris was anxious to do everything that St. Clair could ask, but his power was limited by the adjournment of his Assembly. Until it should vote supplies, he could raise no recruits nor cut any road; until it should declare the supplying of the French colonies with provisions illegal, he could not punish the offence. But such powers as he was vested with he freely used in this crisis. Pending the meeting of the Assembly, who were at once summoned to come together in Philadelphia, the Governor appointed commissioners to survey the country and report on the most proper route for the desired road;[2] and in consequence of a letter from Commodore Keppel, informing him that, by virtue of the King's command, he

[1] VI. Col. Rec., 301, 337. When the prospect of a war between the two countries was imminent, and the French in Canada were anxious to lay in a store of provisions, the commercial colonies of New York, Rhode Island, and Massachusetts hastened to supply them. Within three months of the first battle, no less than forty English vessels lay at one time in the harbor of Louisbourg. It is proper to say that Pennsylvania was not otherwise engaged in this traffic than in selling flour to the merchants of other colonies, who pursued it until stopped by the stringent enactments of their own legislatures.

[2] VI. Col. Rec., 318.

should in future seize all ships carrying provisions and stores to the French from Pennsylvania, he also issued his warrant to all the collectors and port-officers within his jurisdiction, forbidding them to suffer any vessel to pass outwards respecting whose destination there could be the least doubt.[1] By these means, much was effected towards promoting the wished-for end.

It was in the course of this correspondence with Sir John that the General first came into connection with Mr. Morris, to whom he had brought introductory letters from Lord Halifax and Thomas Penn, the Proprietary. On the 14th of January, Dinwiddie wrote to Morris to ascertain if six hundred thousand pounds of flour and a quantity of salted beef could be procured in Pennsylvania for the use of the expedition; promising to pay for it himself should that province refuse. After some hesitation, fourteen thousand bushels of wheat were voted to be delivered, in the shape of flour, immediately upon the arrival of the troops at the mouth of Conecocheague Creek; a large stream which flows to the Potomac through what is now Franklin County in Pennsylvania: this being a larger quantity than was asked, and entirely at the cost of Pennsylvania.[2] Sir John having become involved in this negotiation, Morris's reply was submitted to Braddock, who had just then arrived; and it elicited from the General a communication couched in no very gentle terms. After bitterly inveighing against the conduct of a legislature which, in full view of

[1] VI. Col. Rec., 319, 323.

[2] VI. Col. Rec., 297. II. Penn. Arch., 253. This flour was bought with part of the £5000 presently to be spoken of.

the King's goodness in sending a large force to rescue their country from the hands of the enemy, had done not a thing to subsist the troops or to facilitate their progress to the Ohio, he employs the following significant threat in relation to billeting his men for their winter-quarters:

"My Commission empowers me to settle the Winter as I shall think most proper. You may assure your Assembly I shall have Regard to the different Behaviour of the several Colonies, and shall regulate their Quarters accordingly, and that I will repair, by unpleasant Methods, what for the Character and Honour of the Assemblies I should be much happier to see cheerfully supplied."[1]

As not only all of the General's correspondence, but many historical accounts of these transactions, abound in violent aspersions of the patriotism of Pennsylvania on this occasion, it may be as well to give here an impartial statement of the facts of the case. It seems the emission of provincial paper money or bills had many years before attracted the attention of the Crown. A legalized currency of notes that soon became ragged and defaced, and for the redemption of which no assured fund was provided, was certainly calculated to injure the trader at a distance as well as the holder at home; and consequently, in 1740, instructions were forwarded to Governor Thomas, of Pennsylvania, that he should in future pass no law for creating paper money which did not contain a clause suspending its operation until it was confirmed by the King. The object of these regulations was to prevent any sudden emission of a fictitious currency, to be redeemed by posterity; and Sir

[1] Braddock's Letter of 28th Feb., 1755. VI. Col. Rec., 307.

Dudley Ryder, the most eminent counsel of his time, having been consulted on the question, had formally advised Mr. Hamilton (Mr. Morris's predecessor) that he and every other governor was fully bound by, and could not honorably nor safely violate them. This was one cause of discontent between the Assembly and the Governor; for the colony was not able to endure, or even to pay a very heavy direct tax; and the only mode in vogue of raising a large sum to meet an emergency was by an emission of bills. These the Crown was anxious to have redeemed in not more than five years, while the Assembly naturally preferred a longer day. Owing to the insuperable difficulty of any agreement upon a system of taxation in which the proprietary's unseated lands should pay their share with the rest of the province, the Assembly were now driven to a course which they perhaps hoped would place their Governor absolutely and finally in a false position. They resolved to issue £40,000 in paper money (£20,000 of which should be for purposes of defence), to be redeemed in twelve years; carefully excluding from the bill any clause of suspension. They hoped that the crisis would induce Mr. Morris to pass it into a law, and probably did not believe that any harm would come to him for so doing. But if he refused it, they would be in a position to charge him with the interruption of their efforts to serve the King. Of course, the Governor could not assent to such an act with the written opinion before him of the man who at that very moment was Chief Justice of England; and so he informed the Assembly. Warm bickerings at once broke out between them. The Governor laid all the con-

150 INTRODUCTORY MEMOIR.

sequence of the French invasion at the doors of the legislature; and the legislature, in return, not only refused to modify their bill, but even insinuated that there was no invasion at all; that whether the territory on which Fort Du Quesne was erected belonged to the English or the French crown, it apparently was not within the limits of Pennsylvania. And since the King, said they, who certainly was the best judge of the limits of his own dominions, had already directed his attention to this question, they declined taking any share in the business; more especially as there was no war existing, in their eyes, between England and France. Such was the satisfaction which they gave to the requirements of Sir Thomas Robinson.[1] Finding, however, that Mr. Morris was immovable, the Assembly resolved to borrow £5000 on its own credit, which was placed in the hands of a committee to be applied in defending the colony; and then suddenly adjourned without the Governor's approbation.

It is so much the fashion in this generation to regard

[1] VI. Col. Rec, 192, 233. XXV. Gent. Mag., 230, 243. There had been a general though a ridiculously absurd suspicion in Virginia, as well as Pennsylvania, that the story of French encroachments, &c, in the West was all a bugbear, gotten up by the Ohio Company in order to procure its occupation by the British, and so facilitate its own settlement. Thus Washington, who was interested in that concern, wrote, in 1757, to Lord Loudoun:

"It was not ascertained until too late that the French were on the Ohio; or rather, that we could be persuaded they came there with a design to invade His Majesty's dominions. Nay, after I was sent out in December, 1753, and brought undoubted testimony, even from themselves, of their avowed design, it was yet thought a fiction, and a scheme to promote the interest of a private company, even by some who had a concern in the government."—II. Sparks's Washington, 218.

every ante-revolutionary dispute between a governor and his assembly as a struggle between tyrannical oppression and popular rights, that it is with some diffidence an opinion is here ventured, that in this instance the legislature of Pennsylvania were altogether in the wrong. Setting aside all question of expediency or policy, their object plainly was to force the Governor to infringe the constitution. Failing this, they blindly persisted in a conduct which eventually drenched their borders in the blood of their own sons, and raised a spirit which in less than ten years tarnished the honor of the province, trampled on its laws, and threatened its integrity.[1] But it must be added that their errors were of the head, not of the heart; the tenor of their whole conduct compels the belief that they were honest and patriotic in their intentions, though sometimes very short-sighted. The censure which they received, often descending to sheer abuse, only tended, by a confidence of its injustice, to confirm them in the path they had adopted; and was quite as unmerited as that which their partizans liberally lavished on the Governor. The real secret of the trouble consisted in the refusal of the Penns to be taxed. Every effort of the province to circumvent or break down this odious and unjust distinction was as violent as it was vain, until public opinion compelled its abolition.

At this very moment, when their government had refused

---

[1] Allusion is here made to the Paxton riots, when a murderous array of frontiers-men marched on Philadelphia, threatening to repeat there the crimes they had already been guilty of at Lancaster. These shocking scenes would never have occurred, had the Ohio Indians been enlisted in time in the English interest.

to agree on any plan by which a provincial force could be raised in Pennsylvania to operate under Braddock against Fort Du Quesne, the men of Pennsylvania were enlisting by hundreds under the banners of Shirley and Pepperell, or carrying their services to Virginia or New York. In 1758, when affairs were better managed, the province raised 2700 troops for Forbes's army. But then, public matters on both sides of the Atlantic had taken a vastly different turn. In England, a Pitt had released the nation from the ministerial incubus by which it was oppressed; in Pennsylvania, the provincial levies were placed in every proper respect upon a level with the regulars; and a community, which for three-quarters of a century had existed without a militia law had at last (Nov. 1755), been prevailed upon to consent to a measure, which at least put it in the power of those who wished to learn how to defend their country.[1]

Unfortunately for himself, it was Braddock who was destined to reap this untoward harvest of popular discontent. Incapable of comprehending its origin, it was enough for him to know that it actually existed, and that, by soft words or wrathful, he could do very little with the legislature of Pennsylvania ; or, indeed, with that of any other colony. His temper naturally led him to take at once the most unkind, and frequently unfounded, views of their conduct. "Pennsylvania will do nothing," he wrote to Mr. Fox, the Secretary of War, "and furnisheth the French with whatever they have occasion for." And again he writes to Lord Halifax and to Sir Thomas

Robinson, one of the Secretaries of State: "I am very sorry that I am obliged to say that the inhabitants of these colonies in general have shown much negligence for His Majesty's service and their own interests. Nevertheless, they have not all equally deserved this censure; and particularly this province where I am (Virginia), ought not to be put in comparison with its neighbors, and may seem not to have merited these reproaches. * * I cannot sufficiently express my indignation against the provinces of Pennsylvania and Maryland, whose interest being alike concerned in the event of this expedition, and much more so than any other on this continent, refuse to contribute anything towards the project; and what they propose is made upon no other terms than such as are altogether contrary to the King's prerogatives and to the instructions he has sent their governors. * * I cannot but take the liberty to represent to you the necessity of laying a tax upon all His Majesty's dominions in America, agreeably to the result of council, for reimbursing the great sums that must be advanced for the service and interest of the colonies in this important crisis."[1] In what he insinuates respecting their connection with the French, Braddock was utterly wrong: in his allegations of a niggardly disposition on the part of the provincial Assemblies, he was perhaps

[1] II. Olden Time, 225, 232, 235. Before blaming *in toto cœlo* the rash judgment that dictated these intemperate counsels, it will be well to recollect that others besides Braddock (whether justly or not), were incensed beyond bounds by the conduct of Pennsylvania: "A people," said Washington, "who ought rather to be chastised for their insensibility to danger, and disregard of their sovereign's expectations." I. Sparks's Wash., 78. The suggestion of taxing America by Britain is perhaps one of the earliest on record.

not wholly incorrect. Virginia indeed had granted £20,000, Pennsylvania £5000, and North Carolina £8000 towards the common cause; and even Maryland seems to have voted £6000 — all, however, in their respective currencies, which were much less than sterling.[1] All of these sums were expended under their own directions. The contribution of South Carolina, amounting to £5714 5s. 8¼d. sterling, was all the American money that ever reached Braddock's hands. As for the funds raised north of the Delaware, they were very properly applied to ends more immediately local. The main cost of the expedition was compulsorily borne by Great Britain.

It is not surprising, then, that the General lost his equanimity in contemplating not only the unexpected deficiency in that supply of money which he had been taught to expect from the colonies, but also the first examples of that miserable, equivocating system of shuffling delay and petty economy which too often characterized their action. Thus, all the provisions that Dinwiddie was to have supplied were discovered, at the eleventh hour, to be not forthcoming; and new and hurried arrangements had to be entered into at a moment when everything of the sort should have been finally concluded. As the particulars of this transaction will be found at large in the ensuing text, however, it need not be further alluded to here. But with all the explosions of his temper, there were many instances in which the General manifested a spirit as wise as it was discriminating, doing equal honor to his head and his heart. Of these, was the manner in which he secured the services of Washington. The reader need hardly be reminded that in consequence of the King's order of November 12th, 1754, denying all precedence of rank to the colonial military in comparison with the bearers of commissions signed by himself or his American general-issimo, Washington, with a soldier's just feeling, had declined accepting any position in the troops raised by Virginia; and had, in fact, almost abandoned (with what reluctance may be conceived), every idea of serving his country in the field. No man could more perfectly appreciate the motives of such conduct than Braddock; and few could more delicately, while tacitly acknowledging their propriety, have fulfilled his duty of bringing to his sovereign's service such valuable aid. On the 2nd of March, he caused this letter to be addressed to Major Washington :—

"*Williamsburg, 2 March, 1755.*

"SIR :— The General having been informed that you expressed some desire to make the campaign, but that you declined it upon some disagreeableness that you thought might arise from the regulations of command, has ordered me to acquaint you that he will be very glad of your company in his family, by which all inconveniences of that kind will be obviated.

"I shall think myself very happy to form an acquaintance with a person so universally esteemed, and shall use every opportunity of assuring you how much I am, Sir, your most obedient servant,

"ROBERT ORME, *Aid-de-camp.*"

Washington's reply was couched in terms that evince clearly his gratification at this compliment. He had already addressed a congratulatory letter to the General on his safe arrival in this country; and he now ingenuously confesses that the laudable desire he possessed to serve, with his best abilities, his King and country, was not a little biased by what he calls selfish considerations. "To explain, sir," he continues, "I wish earnestly to obtain some knowledge in the military profession; and believing a more favorable opportunity cannot offer than to serve under a gentleman of General Braddock's abilities and experience, it does, you may reasonably suppose, not a little influence my choice." But domestic cares for a space prevented him from repairing to his post; and it was not until two months from this that he reported himself to the General at Frederick Town, in Maryland; his appointment, being proclaimed to the army on the 10th of May, 1755. In all this unavoidable delay, he had been treated with the greatest consideration; Captain Orme informing him that "the General orders me to give you his compliments, and to assure you his wishes are to make it agreeable to yourself and consistent with your affairs; and, therefore, he desires you will so settle your business at home as to join him at Will's Creek, if more convenient to you; and whenever you find it necessary to return, he begs you will look upon yourself as entirely master, and judge what is necessary to be done."[1] Indeed, throughout the campaign, the General's appreciation of this illustrious man goes far to soften the common impression of his brutality and haughti-

[1] II. Sparks's *Washington*, 68 *et seq.*

ness. Washington and Franklin were perhaps the only
two natives of America whom he distinguished with an
unstinted measure of approbation; and it certainly argues
no common character to have perceived in their dawning
the future meridian brightness of these glorious minds.
Washington never hesitated to express his convictions in
opposition to Braddock's. "From frequent breaches of
contract," he wrote,[1] "the General has lost all patience;
and, for want of that temper and moderation which should
be used by a man of sense upon these occasions, will, I
fear, represent us in a light we little deserve; for, instead
of blaming the individuals, as he ought, he charges all his
disappointments to the public supineness, and looks upon
the country, I believe, as void of honor and honesty. We
have frequent disputes on this head, which are maintained
with warmth on both sides — especially on his, as he is
incapable of arguing without it, or giving up any point he
asserts, be it ever so incompatible with reason or common
sense." While all will agree with Mr. Sparks that the
General had but too good grounds for complaint, it is pleasant to see how anxious he was to render justice to even
American merit, and to favor his Virginia aid-de-camp's
desires for promotion in the regular army of his sovereign.
Governor Dinwiddie, after the General's death, wrote home
to Sir Thomas Robinson, the Secretary of State, his convictions that Braddock, had he survived, would have
warmly recommended Washington to royal favor. And
he afterwards repeated the same thing to the Earl of Loudoun when that incapable nobleman came to America to

---

[1] Letter to W. Fairfax.   II. Sp. Wash., 177.

succeed Shirley in the chief command; strongly urging Washington's promotion in the regular establishment. "General Braddock had so high an esteem for his merit that he made him one of his aids-de-camp; and if he had survived, I believe he would have provided handsomely for him in the regulars," are part of Dinwiddie's words. And Washington himself says very strongly to Lord Loudoun, "With regard to myself, I cannot forbear adding that, had General Braddock survived his unfortunate defeat, I should have met with preferment agreeable to my wishes. I had his promise to that effect; and I believe that gentleman was too sincere and generous to make unmeaning offers where no favors were asked. General Shirley was not unkind in his promises, but he has gone to England."[1] These facts put a very different face upon a connection, honorable to both parties, which Lord Orford so falsely alludes to in his summing up of the Fort Necessity affair, when he says, "This brave braggart learned to blush for his rodomontade, and *desiring to serve General Braddock as aid-de-camp*, acquitted himself nobly!"[2] The insinuation that Washington sought for the post was, under the circumstances, as ungenerous as untrue.

Owing to a delay in Shirley's progress, the congress of the governors of five colonies met, on the 14th of April, at Alexandria, instead of Annapolis, where Braddock had expected them; when the plans for the summer's operations were fully developed and explained. This having been done (as will appear more fully in Captain Orme's Journal),

[1] II. Sparks's Washington, 97, 162, 229.
[2] I. Walp. Mem. Geo. II., 347.

Mr. Morris laid before the meeting the report of his road commissioners; who, in their portion of the embryo work, had succeeded beyond expectation. The document in question, moreover, presented a very characteristic specimen of the feelings with which those officers on whom the responsibility of failure would have to rest, had come to look upon the conduct of Pennsylvania. Sir John St. Clair had visited the commissioners with his warmest indignation, storming "like a Lyon Rampant," on account of the expedition having been so retarded by the delay of the road and the failure of the province to furnish provisions.[1]

[1] Shippen MSS., Vol. I. He threatened them "that instead of marching to the Ohio, he would in nine days march his army into Cumberland County (Penn.) to cut the Roads, press Horses, Wagons, &c.; that he would not suffer a Soldier to handle an Axe, but by Fire and Sword, oblige the Inhabitants to do it, and take away every Man that refused to the Ohio, as he had, yesterday, some of the Virginians; that he would kill all kind of Cattle and carry away the Horses, burn the Houses, &c.; and that if the French defeated them by the Delays of this Province he would with his Sword drawn pass through the Province and treat the Inhabitants as a parcel of Traitors to his Master; that he would to-morrow write to England by a Man-of-war; shake Mr. Penn's proprietaryship; and represent Pennsylvania as a disaffected province: that he would not stop to impress our Assembly; his hands were not tyed, and that We should find: ordering Us to take these Precautions and instantly publish them to our Governor and Assembly, telling Us he did not value anything they did or resolved, seeing they were dilatory and retarded the March of the Troops, and ——— an——— (as he phrased it) on this occasion; and told Us to go to the General, if We pleased, who would give us ten bad Words for one that he had given. * * He would do our Duty himself and never trust to Us; but we should dearly pay for it. To every sentence he solemnly swore, and desired we might believe him to be in earnest." The Shippen MSS. (consisting of the original papers, &c., of Edward and Joseph Shippen, Col. James Burd, and other members of a family that during the last century occupied a most distinguished position in Pennsylvania) are in the library of the Hist. Soc. of Penn. They contain a store of valuable information respecting

It was not difficult to present this transaction in its true light to the General, from whom St. Clair received a warm and severe reprimand for his officious violence.[1] The road, in the meanwhile, went on slowly enough. The Assembly, being sensible of the great advantage it would be to the province to have a direct communication with Fort Du Quesne, in time consented to its being made, and even projected another to Will's Creek; but the Governor, ascertaining that they were not disposed to expend a sum sufficient to half carry through both of these designs, contrived that the latter road should be abandoned in favor of that to the forks of Youghiogeny, which was of the most pressing importance.[2] But even the cost of this alone gave great offence, as it stood the province in £3000, while they were willing to spend but £800. As there were but about one hundred men employed, its progress was very tardy. Provisions were not regularly supplied them. The laborers, too, were kept in constant alarm of the enemy; no guard was allowed them by the province; and it was not until the end of June that the General detached from his own army Captain Hogg, with fifty men, for their protection. Advertisements, in English and German, for more workmen were vainly dispersed through the country.

So great was the necessity of opening a communication by which provisions could be sent to the army from Pennsylvania, that Braddock at first declared he would not advance beyond the place where it was to encounter his

[1] II. Penn. Arch., 317.

[2] Penn. Gaz., No. 1397.

the early history of the State, and an interesting correspondence with many of the chief characters in America.

own route, till it was made. "The general—the officers—the whole army place their account upon this road," wrote Richard Peters, the Secretary of the Province to the Commissioners. Finally, however, on the 17th of July, after they had once or twice been attacked by Indians and most of the party half frightened out of their senses, the chief commissioner, Mr. James Burd, received from Colonel Innes, at Fort Cumberland, notice of the General's defeat, and orders to retire without delay. Mr. Burd executed this movement with coolness and sagacity, leaving nothing behind him that he could possibly bring away, and indeed meriting by his conduct the praise which he subsequently received. It has been thought best thus to dispose, at one view, of the full history of this provincial road as connected with the campaign of 1755:[1] it is now necessary to return to the Congress of Alexandria.

What had ever induced the Ministry to select Virginia, instead of Pennsylvania, as the spot from which the expedition was to march, cannot be discovered; but the choice was a most unfortunate one. The former province could afford neither forage, provisions, wagons, nor cattle; in all of which the latter abounded. To be sure, the land carriage between the heads of navigation in the Potomac and the branches of the Ohio was less than a hundred miles; but this was a convenience of which Braddock could not avail himself. And it was computed at the time that had he landed at Philadelphia his march would have been shortened by six weeks, and £40,000 would have been

---

[1] Shippen MSS. *passim.*   II. Penn. Arch., 320, 345, 357, 363, 373. VI. Col. Rec., 433, 460, 466, 476.

saved in the cost of the expedition. Carlisle would have made an infinitely better frontier station than Will's Creek, being far more accessible from Philadelphia than Fort Cumberland was from Alexandria, and through a more productive and cultivated country: the distance from Fort Du Quesne was, however, much greater. This view is sufficiently proved from the fact that Forbes, in 1758, after full deliberation, judged it wiser to cut a new road through this province than to follow the path already opened by Braddock. The only motive, then, for the unhappy directions with which he was saddled must be believed to have been one publicly suggested in London at the time; namely, that to gratify a political favorite with a commission of 2½ *per cent.* on the funds sent to that country, Virginia was fixed upon for the debarcation of the troops.[1] The moment the General began to investigate the preparations made here for his subsistence, he perceived their utter deficiency. The twenty-five hundred horses, two hundred and fifty wagons, and eleven hundred beeves which were promised him from Maryland and Virginia, were not forthcoming: twenty wagons and two hundred horses were all that could be produced; and the provisions furnished by Maryland were on inspection discovered to be utterly worthless. Such disappointments as these were sufficient to inflame even a placable temper; and in the general failure, his wrath blindly vented itself upon the people of that province which abounded in all that he desired, yet from which he had received nothing. Fortunately, Governor

---

[1] Lewis Evans's Second Essay (Phil. 1756), p. 7. XXV. Gent. Mag., 378, 388. Hanbury was probably the person alluded to.

Shirley had insisted upon Franklin's accompanying him to the Congress at Annapolis, where he remained after its adjournment to establish a post-route between Will's Creek and Philadelphia. He found the leading officers of the army imbued with a fixed detestation of Pennsylvania, alleging that the province had refused them wagons, horses, and food itself at any price; had denied them a road from the camp to their back-settlements; and was even in secret correspondence with the French. Franklin could only reply that the Assembly had, before their arrival, granted £5000 to support the King's troops; that it was understood Virginia and Maryland were to furnish the wagons, etc., and that Pennsylvania did not know that more were wanted; and that a committee was at that very time surveying the ground to lay out a road. He added that it was a pity the expedition had not landed in Pennsylvania, where every farmer had his wagon. Catching at the hope held out in this conversation, Braddock at once asked him if he thought it possible still to procure horses and teams for the expedition in Pennsylvania; and if so, would he, at the General's cost, undertake to obtain a supply? To each part of this proposition Franklin cheerfully assented, and at once set about carrying the idea into execution in a manner not unworthy of his astute and usual worldly wisdom.[1] He caused a handbill to be printed and widely distributed through an extensive part of Pennsylvania, then comprehended but in three counties; in which, after an advertisement stating the terms upon which his natural

---

[1] II. Olden Time, 237. I. Sparks's Franklin, 183. VII. *ib.*, 96. II. Penn. Archives, 295.

son William Franklin or himself were desirous of hiring for the General fifteen hundred saddle or pack-horses, and one hundred and fifty wagons, each with a team of four horses, was published the following letter:—

"TO THE INHABITANTS OF THE COUNTIES OF LANCASTER, YORK, AND CUMBERLAND.

"*Friends and Countrymen:*

"BEING occasionally at the camp at *Frederic* a few days since, I found the General and Officers of the Army extreamly exasperated, on Account of their not being supply'd with Horses and Carriages, which had been expected from this Province as most able to furnish them; but thro' the Dissentions between our Governor and Assembly, Money had not been provided nor any Steps taken for that Purpose.

"It was proposed to send an armed Force immediately into these Counties, to seize as many of the best Carriages and Horses as should be wanted, and compel as many Persons into the Service as should be necessary to drive and take care of them.

"I apprehended that the Progress of a Body of Soldiers thro' these Counties on such an Occasion, especially considering the Temper they are in, and their Resentment against us, would be attended with many and great Inconveniences to the Inhabitants; and therefore more willingly undertook the Trouble of trying first what might be done by fair and equitable Means.

"The People of these back Counties have lately complained to the Assembly that a sufficient Currency was wanting: you have now an Opportunity of receiving and dividing among you a very considerable Sum; for if the Service of this Expedition should continue (as it's more than probable it will), for 120 Days, the Hire of these Wagons and Horses will amount to upwards of *Thirty Thousand Pounds*, which will be paid you in Silver and Gold of the King's Money.

"The service will be light and easy, for the Army will scarce march above 12 Miles per Day, and the Wagons and Baggage Horses, as they carry those things that are absolutely necessary to the Welfare of the Army, must march with the Army and no faster, and are, for the Army's sake, always plac'd where they can be most secure, whether on March or in Camp.

"If you really are, as I believe you are, good and loyal Subjects of His Majesty, you may now do a most acceptable Service, and make it easy to yourselves; for three or four such as cannot separately spare from the Business of their Plantations a Wagon and four Horses and a Driver, may do it together, one furnishing the Wagon, another one or two Horses, and another the Driver, and divide the Pay proportionably between you. But if you do not this Service to your King and Country voluntarily, when such good Pay and reasonable Terms are offered you, your Loyalty will be strongly suspected. The King's Business must be done; so many brave Troops, come so far for your Defence, must not stand idle thro' your Backwardness to do what may reasonably be expected from you; Wagons and Horses must be had; violent Measures will probably be used ; and you will be to seek for a Recompence where you can find it, and your Case perhaps be little pitied or regarded.

"I have no particular Interest in this Affair; as (except the Satisfaction of endeavoring to do Good and prevent Mischief), I shall have only my Labour for my Pains. If this Method of obtaining the Wagons and Horses is not like to succeed, I am oblig'd to send Word to the General in fourteen Days, and I suppose *Sir John St. Clair,* the Hussar, with a Body of Soldiers, will immediately enter the Province, of which I shall be sorry to hear, because

"*I am, very sincerely and truly,*

"*Your Friend and Well-wisher,*

"B. FRANKLIN."

Nothing could have better answered its purpose. St. Clair had actually, it is believed, served in a Hussar regiment abroad ; and usually wore a Hussar uniform on duty in America. Of a violent, impetuous temper, he had on more than one occasion threatened to dragoon the lukewarm inhabitants into activity ; and his character and profession forcibly recalling to the German farmers, who in great numbers occupied the back counties, the scenes they had witnessed at home, were artfully introduced by Franklin, and must have excited much amusement among Sir John's friends in camp. As for the English colonists, it was enough for them to be reminded that such things as a *Press* of private means for the benefit of the State still existed.[1] In a

---

[1] "I can but honor Franklin for y[e] last clause of his Advertisement."— W. Shirley to Morris. II. Penn. Arch. 311. Gov. Morris was instructed by the Crown to aid the army in impressing wagons, etc., if necessary : and

fortnight's space, the one hundred and fifty wagons and teams and two hundred and fifty-nine pack-horses were on their way to camp. In his letters to his government, the General expressed great satisfaction at Franklin's conduct in this business, which he characterized as "almost the first instance of integrity, address, and ability that he had met with in all these provinces." It is a pity it should be necessary to comment upon the difficulty which this matter afterwards brought upon its undertaker. Had Braddock lived, there would undoubtedly have arisen no trouble; but his death left his contractor involved in a debt of over £20,000, for which the owners of the property did not cease to importune him. Governor Shirley, it is true, relieved him of the greater part of this responsibility, with warm expressions of sensibility of his public services in "engaging those wagons without which General Braddock could not have proceeded;" but he left a portion of the accounts to be settled by Lord Loudoun, who, according to his usual habits, utterly neglected doing anything in the premises; and it is believed the patriotic postmaster was never wholly repaid. He very usefully employed Braddock's new-born partiality, however, in procuring the release of bought servants enlisted into the army, whose time belonged to their masters.[1]

we find his warrant for that purpose issued to the Sheriff of Philadelphia, in September, 1755. (*Ib.* 432.) And see VI. Col. Rec., 203.

[1] VII. Sparks's Franklin, 94, 138. See also Bouquet's testimony to his services on this occasion; *ib.* 262. As for the Earl of Loudoun, nothing could be juster than the comparison of his lordship to the figure of St. George over the door of a country inn, always on horseback, yet never going on!

Returning from the congress of Alexandria, each Governor sought his respective province, fondly imagining, perhaps, that the work was done and the fall of the French near at hand. This, at least, was the sentiment of the populace, who welcomed the prospect with noisy gratulation.[1] In the meanwhile, the General busied himself in getting the troops and stores advanced to Fort Cumberland, whence his march through a hostile wilderness, if not an enemy's country, was fairly to begin, and in concerting, with the different authorities, various measures of public convenience. Having fixed upon Winchester, Virginia, as the place to which his letters should be sent, he procured expresses to be laid by Pennsylvania and Maryland to that town.[2] Another object to which he devoted much attention was the obtaining of Indians to accompany his army. There is no point on which his conduct has been more misunderstood than this; he has always been looked upon as despising and refusing the services of the savages, and as actually repulsing their proffered aid: let us see what are the facts of the case.

Immediately upon the General's arrival in Virginia, he had spoken with Governor Dinwiddie in regard to this matter, and was given to understand that a large force of Catawba and Cherokee Indians, under the influence of his

[1] Thus Shirley, passing through New York, was encountered by a turn-out of the militia and a display of enthusiastic gentry, with whom he drank loyal healths and success to the King's arms; while "the doors, windows, balconies, and tops of the houses, being particularly decorated with red cloaks, &c., added," says the old chronicler, "no small beauty to the fame and diversion of the time." Penn. Gaz., No. 1376.

[2] Penn. Gaz., No. 1377. The mail-rider started from Philadelphia every Thursday morning after the 15th of May, 1755.

messengers, would presently arrive at Winchester, where they were to meet the Six Nations in council. The Catawbas alone would amount to one hundred and twenty warriors; and hopes of a considerable addition to this number might be based upon the management of the other tribes. The appointed time came, however, and brought with it no Indians. It would certainly seem that Dinwiddie was very much to blame in his whole conduct of this business. Other men, no better qualified than himself to judge, put no reliance whatever upon the Southern Indians promised him by Mr. Gist; and there can be no excuse for his utter neglect to send messengers with presents to the Ohio savages, which should have been his first care on receiving the funds from Great Britain. Taught by injurious experience, however, to depend no more upon the promises of colonial undertakers, Braddock, so soon as he began to suspect Dinwiddie's arrangements would fail him, addressed himself to the Governor of Pennsylvania. In his letter (April 15th, 1755), he states that he is told of a number of savages living within that province who formerly dwelt on the Ohio, who therefore were doubtless well acquainted with that region. Sensible of the value of such auxiliaries, he begged Mr. Morris to persuade their warriors to join his camp, and to advise him with what treatment he ought to greet them; desiring, too, that they should be informed he was on his way to remove the French, and to restore the country they occupied to its Indian proprietors, whose undisturbed enjoyment of it he was determined to protect. A week after, the Governor ordered George Croghan (who, with Conrad Weiser, had the virtual management of the colony's intercourse with the savages), to send belts of wampum to all the lake tribes, the Delawares, the Shawanoes, the Wyandottes, Twightwees (or Miamis), and Piankeshaws, inviting them to join the English without delay. As a matter of course, it was now too late for such messages to produce any good effect; and no good effect was produced. But in his immediate neighborhood at Aughquick, Croghan managed to collect a small party of Iroquois, whom he led to the camp. These were chiefly the same who had been with Washington at Fort Necessity and had retired with him to Virginia. After remaining there some time, they repaired to Aughquick, in Pennsylvania; where they, and their families (homeless, now, since their places on the Ohio were under the control of the French, whose blood they had shed) were supported during the winter of 1754–5 by that province. There were other Indians of the Six Nations who had in like manner left the Ohio, who, as well as these, were maintained by the public; the whole amounting to about three hundred souls. In April, 1755, however, the Assembly resolved to do nothing more for them; and, left to their own resources, the majority soon dispersed or went back to the French. On the night of the 30th of April, Croghan received the Governor's letter; on the 2d of May, he set out for Fort Cumberland, with his remaining Indians, to the number of about thirty or forty men and sixty women and children; it being impossible for the warriors to leave their families behind them with no means of support. When the General arrived at Will's Creek on the 10th of May, he found these people awaiting him; and, after the usual negotiations, they formally took up the hatchet against the French, and agreed to follow his fortunes. These were the hundred Indians of whom Franklin speaks, "who might have been of great use to his army as guides or scouts, if he had treated them kindly; but he slighted or neglected them, and they gradually left him." It is now a well-ascertained fact that forty or fifty, at the very most, were all the fighting men who joined Braddock; the lesser number, perhaps, being nearest the mark. Of these, but eight actually remained with him to the close; and for permitting the rest to leave him, Braddock is much to be blamed. Captain Orme, it is true, says that they departed, with a promise to return, under a pretence of placing their families in safety upon the Susquehannah; but their manager, Mr. Croghan, clearly explains this business. Colonel Innes, the Governor of Fort Cumberland, did not wish to have the destitute families of these people on his hands during the General's absence, and he accordingly persuaded him that he had best intimate to the warriors the propriety of taking them somewhere else. There thus being no provision for the entertainment of their children and wives whilst they were on the war-path, a majority of the savages were compelled to return to their late abode in Pennsylvania; the General retaining eight of them as scouts — a number which Innes assured him would be perfectly sufficient. At the same time, he seems to have labored under the misunderstanding that the remainder of the warriors would rejoin him on his march; which was far from being the case, albeit they were so anxious for war as to hang on to his array till he reached Dunbar's camp.[1] Certainly there is no reason to believe that Braddock was not desirous of the services of the savages, though perhaps he was not sufficiently versed in their nature to always employ the properest measures of securing them. Another reason he had for wishing the Indian women at once removed from the neighborhood of the troops, was the licentiousness their presence introduced into the camp. An eye-witness (Peters, the Secretary of Pennsylvania,) particularly states, that besides other causes of discontent at not being more frequently consulted with by the General, there were constant and high quarrels among the Indians on account of the amours of the royal officers with their squaws and the *largesses* the latter received. These gentlemen "were so scandalously fond" of their swarthy lovers, that an order was issued forbidding their admission into camp. And that Braddock's general deportment on the march was not courteous and polite, may readily be conceded. Such was the impression it produced, that the Indians with him sent belts to their Susquehannah friends, warning them to keep away from the army, lest they should be mistaken for allies of the French.[2]

[1] II. Penn. Arch., 290, 308, 316, 318, 321. VI. Col. Rec, 375, 397, 460. II. Olden Time, 238. I Sparks's Franklin, 189. And see Appendix, No. III. Full details of the conduct and position of the Indians who withdrew from the Ohio to Pennsylvania may be found in II. P. A., 259. VI. C. R., 130, 134, 140, 146, *et seq.* 189, 218, 257, 353, 398, 443.

[2] It is said that Braddock gave great offence to his Indians by forbidding them to take scalps, when, in fact, he published a reward of £5 to every soldier as well as Indian of his command for each scalp of an enemy. The sole authority for the story appears to have been John Shiekalamy, father

Thus, in the next month after his defeat we find them asserting to Mr. Morris that it was all caused by the pride and ignorance of that great general who came from England. "He is now dead," quoth Scarroyaddy their chief; "but he was a bad man when he was alive; he looked upon us as dogs, and would never hear anything that was said to him. We often endeavored to advise him and to tell him of the danger he was in with his soldiers; but he never appeared pleased with us; and that was the reason that a great many of our warriors left him and would not be under his command."[1] The reader has here three distinct versions of the secret of this savage exodus from the tents of the English: namely, Scarroyaddy's, Croghan's, and Braddock's own — from which he may select such a reason as best suits him. It is not difficult, however, to reconcile and to combine them all.[2]

[1] VI. C. R., 397, 589. II. P. A., 319.

[2] This chieftain, who played so active a part in Braddock's campaign, was an Oneida Indian, and one of the mixed band of various tribes of the Six Nations who lived, in 1754, near the Ohio. These people were used to choose from their number a ruler; and such for a time was Thanacharisson, the Half-King, who died at Aughquick in October, 1754, leaving his family very destitute. (VI. Col. Rec., 159, 184, 193. II. Penn. Arch., 178, 219.) In the Washington papers, and in the ensuing Journals, he is known by the name of Monacatootha, and it is well to note here that the two appellations apply to the same individual. (II. P. A., 114). As early as 1748, however, and almost universally in Pennsylvania, he was called Scarroyaddy, or perhaps more correctly, Skirooniatta. (II. P. A., 15. VI. C. R., 616.) In the winter of 1754-5, he was sent by his people to Onondaga, to obtain the views of the confederates on the expected troubles, and was about this time selected to succeed the Half-King. His services under

of Logan, whose speech is celebrated by Mr. Jefferson; an influential but discontented Delaware, who, early in July, 1755, reported this tale among his kindred, and shortly after took up arms for the French. Penn. Gaz., No. 1385.

With a single exception, these were all the Indians whom the General had any opportunity to secure. Between the 20th and the 27th of April, shortly after he had left Fort Cumberland, a few Delawares presented themselves to him, doubtless with no other view than to ascertain what terms they could obtain from him, and what were his chances of success. Whatever conclusion they came to, they never reappeared. The fact is, that the Indians were now in a state of high excitement and of bewildering doubt. There were of course among them predilections for one side or the other; but their wise men, whether of the French or the English faction, were not unwilling to stand neuter and let the two European nations "fight it out themselves, and

---

Braddock were fully acknowledged at Philadelphia in August, 1755: "You fought under General Braddock," said Gov. Morris, "and behaved with spirit and valor during the engagement. We should be wanting to ourselves not to make you our hearty acknowledgments for your fidelity and assistance. We see you consider yourselves as our flesh and blood, and fight for us as if we were of your own kindred." (VI. C. R., 524.) He ever continued a staunch ally to the English. In Sept. 1755, he headed a war-party from Shamokin against the French (VI. C. R., 616), and indeed the records of the period abound in evidences of his usefulness, being constantly employed in the quest of intelligence upon various missions, or the pursuit of the foe. In the last object, he must have been tolerably successful. In the Gent. Mag. for Sept. 1756 (Vol. XXVI., 414), is a fac-simile of his hieroglyphical memoirs, drawn by himself; by which it appears he had therefore slain with his own hands no less than seven, and captured eleven warriors; and had been present in thirty-one combats, the majority of which were doubtless of a very trifling nature. On his breast was tattooed a figure of a tomahawk, and that of a bow and arrow on each cheek. It will be seen how unluckily his son was killed during Braddock's march. In Dec. 1754, he had a wife and seven children with him at Augh-quick (II. P. A. 218), so there was still left him a numerous posterity. It only remains to add that he was not free from the inevitable failing of his race, and on occasion would, as Burns has it, be "fou for weeks thegither." (VII. C. R., 87.)

the more they destroy one another the better." But, if they were to be involved in the dispute, their anxiety was to discover which would be the winning side; and this was probably the errand of the Delawares. So little trouble had, however, been taken at the proper time by the provinces to convince them of their desire for their services, that the conclusion arrived at by those who were really well disposed towards the English was to endeavor to remain neutral. Thus, the Delawares and Shawanoes living at Kittaning, under Shingas and King Beaver and Captain Jacob, as well as those at Log's-Town, although both places were near to Fort Du Quesne, steadily resisted all the blandishments of the French to join with them against their enemy; until in April or May, 1755, a party of Canadian Indians visiting their towns, persuaded them to the measure. Of the war-party which was at once sent forth, it is not unlikely the Delawares who came to Braddock formed a part.[1] That this should have been the state of relations between the English and the savages, was a fact as censurable as unfortunate; but it was the inexcusable fault of none else than the authorities of the neighboring colonies, who utterly neglected to give them a single opportunity of selling their assistance, after their own national customs, and casting in their lot with the British. They looked for a belt to be sent them, and a supply of presents, ere they should engage in the war. The whole burthen and responsibility of doing what should long before his arrival have been done by Dinwiddie or Morris being thus cast upon a General who knew abso-

[1] VI. C. R., 343, 781. II. P. A. 318.

lutely nothing about the matter, it is no wonder it turned out a bungling failure.[1]

Even while at Will's Creek, the army was ill supplied with provisions; and what they had being chiefly salted, were far from acceptable or even wholesome to men just released from a long and tedious sea-voyage, where fresh food was out of the question. The tables of the officers themselves were scantily and meagerly furnished: very little fresh meat, and that generally half-spoiled, was to be found upon their boards; and butter (in a limited quantity), at the General's alone. The men and the inferior officers were actually in want of almost the necessaries of life. Franklin, in his autobiographical sketch, mentions that at Frederic-town, while supping with Colonel Dunbar, that gentleman expressed a strong concern for the condition of his subalterns, whose purses, never very deep, were now utterly drained by the exorbitant prices exacted for every sort of domestic stores needed for a long march through

---

[1] "Certainly," says Mr. Secretary Peters, on the 12th May, 1755, "some general meeting was necessary and expected by the Indians, that both they and we might see what number were for and what against the French encroachments; and in case it should have appeared a majority was on the side of the French, then it might have been prudent to have tried to bring the Indians over to a general neutrality—and it is the opinion of Mr. Weiser, our Indian interpreter, and my own, that this could have been effected, and would have saved the General an immense trouble, and the Crown an heavy expense." (II. P. A., 308.) Nor was this fact unperceived at the camp. On the 21st of May, Mr. W. Shirley thus writes: "I am not greatly acquainted myself with Indian Affairs, tho' enough to see that better measures with regard to 'em might and ought to have been taken; at least to the Southwᵈ. * * * Upon our Arrival at this Fort, we found Indian Affairs so ignorantly conducted by Col. Innes, to whom they were committed, that Novices as we were, we have taken 'em into our Managem'." (Ib. 321.)

the wilderness. On Franklin's return to Philadelphia, he interested the Assembly's Committee to apply a small portion of the £5000 in their hands to procuring camp-supplies for these gentlemen; and accordingly by a special detachment of horses from Lancaster a present of as many parcels was sent to twenty subalterns of the 48th regiment; each parcel, according to his own inventory, containing the following articles :—

6 lbs. loaf sugar.
6 " Muscovado do.
1 " green tea.
1 " Bohea do.
6 " ground coffee.
6 " chocolate.
½ chest best white biscuit.
½ lb. pepper.
1 quart white vinegar.
1 Gloucester cheese.
1 keg containing 20 lbs. good butter.
2 doz. old Madeira wine.
2 gallons Jamaica spirits.
1 bottle flour of mustard.
2 well-cured hams.
½ doz. dried tongues.
6 lbs. rice.
6 " raisins.

This little act of attention upon the then postmaster's part (the details of which may well be repeated here), was very kindly acknowledged by the recipients, and led the way for other and more substantial provision for the support of the army.[1] The three lower counties upon Dela-

[1] VI. Col. Rec., 397, 636. I. Sp. Fr., 188. "Colonel Dunbar writes in his letter of May the 13th concerning the present of Refreshments and carriage horses sent up for the subalterns : 'I am desired by all the gentlemen who the committee have been so good as to think of in so genteel a manner, to return them their hearty thanks;' and again, on the 21st of May—'Your kind present is now all arrived, and shall be equally divided to-morrow between Sir Peter Halket's subalterns and mine, which I apprehend will be agreeable to the Committee's intent. This I have made known to the officers of both Regiments, who unanimously desire me to return the generous Benefactors their most hearty thanks, to which be pleased to add mine, &c.;" and Sir Peter Halket, in his of the 23d of May, says, "The Officers of my Regiment are most sensible of the Favors conferred on the

ware (which now constitute the State of Delaware), although intimately allied with Pennsylvania and subjected to the same proprietaries and governor, at this period formed a distinct government from their more powerful sister. Whether it was that its inhabitants were less opinionated than those of his other colony or not, Mr. Morris seems to have possessed more influence over them than he could bring to bear in Philadelphia; and he stirred them up to forwarding to the camp a present of fifty fat oxen and one hundred sheep for the use of the army, as well as the following provisions for the General's own use:—

Twelve Hams.
Eight Cheeses.
Twenty-four flasks of Oil.
Ten loaves of Sugar.
One cask of Raisins.
A box of Spice and Currants.
A box of Pickles and Mustard.
Eight kegs of Biscuit.

Four kegs of Sturgeon.
One keg of Herrings.
Two chests of Lemons.
Two kegs of Spirits.
A cask of Vinegar.
A barrel of Potatoes.
Three tubs of Butter.

But it was not until late in the season that these welcome donations were despatched;[1] and in the mean time the progress of the expedition was fatally delayed at Will's Creek for the want of stores. Not less time than a month or six weeks, at the most moderate computation,

subalterns by your Assembly, who have made them so well-timed and handsome a present. At their request and Desire I return their thanks, and to the acknowledgments of the Officers beg leave to add nine, which you, I hope, will do me the favor for the whole to offer to the Assembly, and to assure them that we shall on every occasion do them the Justice due for so seasonable and well-judged an act of generosity.'"—*Assembly's Address*, 29th Sept. 1755.

[1] VI. Col. Rec., 408, 414. Penn. Gaz., No. 1380.

were thus consumed in awaiting the fulfilment of contracts for forage and food, which Braddock was obliged to make himself, in default of the proper and timely action of the colonies. It will be observed in season how dearly this shameful conduct was repaid; for, setting aside the loss to the crown of the whole cost of his undertaking, there is no doubt that a fortnight's earlier arrival on the Ohio would have given victory to his arms and peace to the borders of Pennsylvania, Virginia, and Maryland. In lieu of this, and in consequence of their own blind perversity, a desolating and ruinous war steeped for years their land in blood, and cost them eventually ten times as much as would originally have ensured their perfect security.

No longer relying at all upon the faith of colonial assemblies or colonial contractors, the General, in the beginning of May, set about procuring, on his own responsibility, as representing the Crown, the stores necessary for his march to Fort Du Quesne. On the 10th of May Captain Leslie, who had been appointed Assistant to Sir John St. Clair, was sent into Pennsylvania to purchase forage; and on the 24th, Mr. Morris was empowered to make further contracts for flour and cattle, or in default of any other provision, even salt fish, to support the troops after July, when their present magazines would become exhausted. Through the zealous coöperation of that energetic Governor, this business was fortunately carried through satisfactorily; else, to use Braddock's own language, he should inevitably have starved: for it was not until the stores procured by Captain Leslie reached Fort Cumberland that the army was able to move. Three precious months had already been consumed upon the two hundred miles that separated this place from Annapolis; and above one hundred and fifty yet remained to be overcome ere the host should reach the bourne of its desires.[1]

It is proper now to glance at the conduct of the ministry of France in this conjuncture, and to observe what preparations they had made to repel the advances of the English and to preserve their own encroachments. Although both governments had long persisted in positive declarations of their amicable intentions, neither was weak enough to place the least reliance upon assurances so thoroughly contradicted by the facts of their own conduct. Through its agents in France, England was never left uninformed of the extensive armaments that power was busily fitting out for its American possessions; while everything relative to Braddock's and Boscawen's instructions was known to the Cabinet of Versailles long before it was communicated to the public at home. One Florence Hennessey, an Irish physician, settled at London, was the spy employed. What were his sources of information is a mystery that has never been fathomed; but he assuredly had often access to the confidential secrets of the ministry, and was in possession of every detail of their foreign policy. Detected at last, he was convicted of high treason and sentenced to its doom; but, after several reprieves, was finally pardoned by George III. at the intercession of, and as a personal favor to, the French King. But being thus apprised in abundant season of the designs of Great Britain, their opponents hastened to take the precautions which were so necessary in the then condition of their own colonies; and ships and men were at once set in train for Quebec. The original force of 5000 militia, 600 Indians, and 400 regulars, which, in the year 1753, had been raised in New France for the occupation of the Ohio,[1] almost exhausted the strength of that province, and, its object being accomplished, was now entirely dissolved. Small but sufficient garrisons were maintained in the posts thus erected, and probably little alteration was made in their strength until the troubles of 1754. In February of that year, a very considerable number of French troops arrived in the Mississippi, some of whom were doubtless sent up to their western stations; while the Governor of Louisiana left no stone unturned to engage every savage within his influence in the general plan against the English.[2] When M. de Contrecœur first came upon Trent, in April, 1754, he probably had not more than from 750 to 1000 men with him; but his whole command had not yet arrived. By July, he was certainly strong enough to detach from 600 to 800 Indians, under M. de Villiers, against Fort Necessity; and at this period he probably had under him all the 2000 men which were designed for him by his superiors.[3] But when that victory was gained, and not an enemy remained within a hundred miles and more of his position, most of his troops were dismissed, and the fort remained, on the 25th of July, 1754, garrisoned by but 400 men, 200 of whom were workmen. M. de Mercier, the engineer by

[1] VI. Col. Rec., 20.
[2] Penn. Gaz., No. 1367.   II. Garneau, 201.   VI. Col. Rec., 32.
[3] II. Garneau, 201, 202.   VI. Col. Rec., 33, 37, 51.

whom the works were planned, had on that day departed with about 1000 men. For this, and for other information concerning the condition of the fort, we are indebted to the indefatigable patriotism of Captain Robert Stobo, of Frey's regiment; who, having been one of the hostages surrendered by Washington at Fort Necessity a few weeks before, was now confined a prisoner within its walls. Watching his opportunity, he made the opposite plan of Fort Du Quesne and forwarded it, as well as two letters describing its weaknesses, to his countrymen, by the hands of a friendly Indian.[1]

But a much fuller account is afforded in the Journal of one John M'Kinney, who, in February, 1756, was captured by the Indians and carried first thither and afterwards to Canada; whence he in a few months made his escape and returned, through Connecticut, to Pennsylvania. From a collation of these two narratives a tolerably clear idea of the nature and position of this slight but famous fortification may be formed.

Fort Du Quesne was situated on the east side of the Monongahela, on the tongue of land formed by the junction of that stream with the Alleghany. Though full of faults in its original construction, and small, it was built with immense labor, and it had "a great deal of very

---

[1] In a former note, reference to Mr. Lyman C. Draper's notices of Stobo and Van Braam (I. Olden Time, 369,) was unfortunately omitted. The curious reader may consult them with advantage. A copy of Stobo's drawing was probably made in the provinces before Braddock's departure, since we find an engraved plan of Fort Du Quesne published and for sale at London in August, 1755, immediately on the tidings of Braddock's misadventure. (XXV. Gent. Mag., 383.) It has vainly been sought to procure a copy of this engraving.

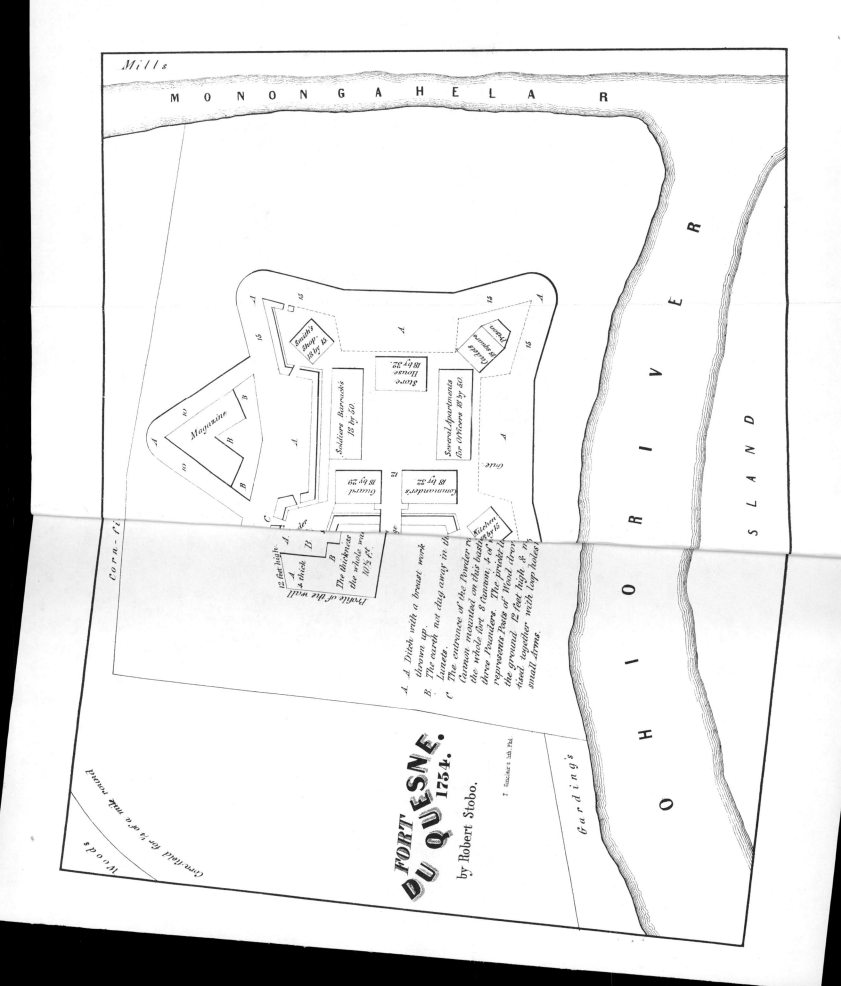

Mills

M O N O N G A H E L A   R

Smith's Shop. 18 by 15

Magazine

Soldiers Barracks 18 by 50.

Store House 18 by 32.

Cadets Apartment

Several Apartments for Officers 18 by 50

Guard 18 by 29

Commander's 18 by 32

Kitchen

Corn-field

Profile of the wall

12 feet high.

A 4 thick

The thickness the whole wa 10½ ft.

A. A Ditch with a breast work thrown up.

B. The earth not dug away in the Lunets.

C. The entrance of the Powder Ro
Cannon mounted on this bast
the whole fort 8 Cannon, 4 of
three Pounders. The pricks
represents Posts of Wood driv
the ground 12 feet high & n
ised together with loop holes
small Arms.

FORT
DU QUESNE.
1754.

by Robert Stobo.

T. Sinclair's lith. Phil.

Garding's

O H I O   R I V E R

I S L A N D

Woods

Corn-field for ¼ of a mile round

strong works collected into very little room."[1] By the doubtful evidences which we possess, its shape would seem to have been a parallelogram, its four sides facing very nearly to the points of the compass, but a bastion at each corner gave it a polygonal appearance. Its longest sides were fifty yards; its shorter, forty. The position of these bastions (which were fewer in number in Stobo's time than in M'Kinney's, and probably so continued till the summer of 1755,) may be seen by reference to the engraved plan. These were made of very large squared logs, to the height of twelve feet, and compactly filled in with earth to the depth of eight; thus leaving about four feet of ramparts to shelter the plateau. The sides of the fort nearest the rivers being comparatively protected by nature, were not furnished with bastions; but a strong stockade, twelve feet high, and made of logs a foot in diameter driven pile-wise into the ground, extended from bastion to bastion and completely enclosed the area. This stockade was ingeni-ously wattled crosswise with poles, after the fashion of basket-work, and loopholes, slanting downwards, were cut through them to enable the men to fire. At the distance of some four rods from these walls, as they may be called, a shallow ditch was dug completely environing them and protected by a second stockade, seven feet high, built in a manner similar to the first, and solidly embanked with earth. If we assume the proportions of Stobo's drawing to be correct, by a comparison of this work with the dimensions of the house marked "Soldiers' Barracks" on his plan, its extent will be found to be about seven hun-dred and seventy-five feet.

[1] II. Garneau, 216.   Bouquet in I. O. T., 184.

Two gates opened into the fort; the western from the water-side, and the eastern, about ten feet wide, from the land. Immediately between the eastern posterns was sunken a deep well, whose diameter was the width of the gate-way, and over which a drawbridge was placed that at night, or in time of danger, was drawn up with chains and levers; and these actually formed the gate. Both portals were strongly framed of squared logs; but the eastern gate opened on hinges, and had a wicket cut in it for ordinary use. Within the fort, and hard by the eastern gate, were placed the magazine and kitchen; the former, twenty feet wide by forty long, and but five feet high, was built of heavy, hewed timber, deeply sunk into the ground to almost its full altitude, and its roof plastered with a coating of potter's clay nearly four feet in thickness. By this means, it was comparatively secure from any missile save bombs or hot-shot thrown from the brow of the adjacent hills. It is to these precautions that we are indebted at this day for the solitary vestige of Old Fort Du Quesne that remains to us. Some workmen, in the summer of 1854—just about a century after Stobo wrote—being employed in making excavations for the Pennsylvania Railroad Company, brought to light this building, which alone, of all its comrades, had, from its peculiar formation, escaped as well the destroying hand of Time as the torch of its baffled creator, when, in 1758, he forever abandoned his beloved fortress and fled before the approach of Forbes. Leaves, dirt, and rubbish must soon have accumulated above its neglected roof. The storms of winter came, and the freshets of the spring; and ere long not a human being had reason to believe that beneath his feet stood, intact almost as on the day it was built, the Old French Magazine.[1]

Beside this, however, there were other buildings within the walls; heavy and substantial log-houses, such as the wants of the garrison might require. Two were store-houses or magazines; two others were barracks; a seventh was the commandant's residence; and lesser erections served for a guard-house and a prison. The backs of these were at but a yard's distance from the walls, which they aided greatly to strengthen; all the intervening space being filled in with earth. Their roofs, covered with boards sawed by hand upon the spot, were level at the eaves with the ramparts; nor were there any pickets or sharpened palisades crowning the walls. Had Braddock reached this place, it was St. Clair's proposition to erect a battery on the brow of the opposite hill, which perfectly commanded the fort, and thence, with hot shot, to set these buildings on fire, and so subdue the post. All their artillery consisted of eight cannon; one-half of them three, and the remainder four-pounders; five of which were mounted on the north-western bastion defending the Powder-Magazine. When Stobo wrote, M. de Contrecœur and a guard of five officers and forty men were all who lodged in the fort; bark cabins were erected around it for the rest of the garrison. Every preparation was made for their permanent comfort; and already kitchen-gardens upon the Alleghany and mills upon the Monongahela, and a vast corn-field, extending for

[1] In 1776, a slight inequality of the ground, a few graves, and the traces of its fosse above denoted the site of the fort: in 1831, a boat-yard was placed on the very spot: and at this day not a vestige of old Fort Du Quesne is visible save the lately-exposed magazine. (V. Haz. Reg, 191, VIII. *ib.* 192.

a quarter of a mile up either stream, furnished promise of future subsistence. The woods all around had been cut down, and hardly a stump remained within musket-shot to shelter the approach of a foe.[1]

Although the Canadian militia returning to their homes left but a small garrison of regulars to hold the fort towards the end of the summer of 1754, yet, if any reliance may be placed upon the reports which reached the English provinces, there was still a plenty of aid within call; no less than 2200 fresh troops being sent thitherward from Quebec during that season; and on the 25th of September 300 Caghnawagas or French Indians and a convoy of provisions from Quebec arrived.[2] Five days before, when Lieutenant Lyon with a flag of truce from Virginia and a fruitless proposition to exchange La Force (the officer captured at Jumonville's defeat), for Captain Stobo, visited Du Quesne, he found but one hundred men in the fort. But despite their scanty numbers, they were pursuing a most dangerous policy towards English interests by assiduously tempting the Indians of the Six Nations in the vicinity to forswear their ancient alliances; and sending their Caghnawagas among the Shawanoes and other western tribes to bring them into the interests of Canada. A number of savages had frequented the post ever since the capture of Fort Necessity, and among these numerous and valuable

[1] VIII. Hazard's Penn. Reg., 318. Stobo's Letters, VI. Col. Rec., 141, 161.

[2] II. P. A., 172, 177, 264. The Caghnawagas, according to Colden, were deserters from the Six Nations, who, settling in Canada under the auspices of that government, had, through continual accessions and their own natural increase, grown in time to become a powerful and warlike people.

presents were distributed. Through the medium of the Delawares, or perhaps more directly from Quebec and France, through the intercession of the spy Hennessey, they were in November advised of the expected reinforcements from England; and not comprehending a six months' delay in the enterprise, the French had hastened at once to reinforce Fort Du Quesne with eight additional cannon, and a plenty of stores. The garrison was also increased to 1100 men; and nearly 400 Indians, Adirondacks, Caghnawagas, and Ottawas, were sent thither from the confines of New France. The cost of maintaining such a force must have been enormous; and when the approach of winter, filling the ravines with snow, and making the mountains perfectly impassable, dissipated all apprehension of present disturbance, the great bulk of this army retraced its steps; and a garrison of perhaps not more than two hundred and fifty regular troops, under the veteran Contrecœur, was left behind.[1] About the same number were, however, stationed within call at Venango; and some allowance must be made for the neighboring savages, most of whom would probably, though not certainly, have sided with the French. The only Indians they could at this time with positive assurance rely upon were they who occupied the thirty or forty bark cabins that had grown up about the fort, or they who had come from Canada, and of whom very few remained through the winter. In April, 1755, there were scarce two hundred men, French and Indians, to garrison the place; and had Braddock then been in a condition to have struck, his success would have been

---

[1] "An experienced and courageous soldier," says Garneau, II, 216.

certain.[1] But by their scouting-parties, which were always ranging the mountains between the Ohio and the English settlements, they once more caught the alarm, and eagerly solicited reinforcements from Canada. The Marquis de Duquesne, however, though anxious enough to preserve a maiden fortress the works which bore his name, could not be easily brought to believe that it was yet seriously threatened, and constantly treated with contempt the rumors that during the past winter had from time to time reached his ears; pronouncing all the menaces and preparations of the enemy a mere fanfaronade — "un feu de paille." Thus, in the early spring of 1755, no steps had yet been taken in Canada for the relief of Fort Du Quesne.[2]

The conduct of the Court of St. James during this crisis was as little to be reconciled to a just notion of frankness and honorable dealing as that of its adversary. On the 15th of January — the very day after Braddock had sailed for Virginia — the Duc de Mirepoix proposed that each crown should prohibit all present hostilities, and that the matter of the Ohio territory should be left to an amicable adjustment; the destination and motive of the expedition which had just started being first pacifically explained. The ambassador could not at that very moment have been ignorant that his master was straining every nerve to throw such a force into Canada as would defy any attack; and they whom he addressed were well aware that he knew all

[1] VI. C. R., 162, 181. II. P. A., 213, 288. Penn. Gaz, Nos. 1379, 1383. VIII. Haz. Penn. Reg., 319.
[2] II. P. A., 288. And see Appendix, No. IV.

this. They, therefore, on the 22nd of the same month, furnished him with a Jesuitical reply, declaring that the only end of Braddock's mission was the defence and protection of the King's dominions in America, without any design to attack those of any other prince, or in any wise open the door to war; and that as to the Ohio country, the French must abandon and destroy all their settlements there, or, in other words, put matters in the condition they were in before the Treaty of Utrecht, before a friendly negotiation on that point could be thought of. In order to gain time, the French dallied with these propositions, at first disputing, and then making a show of accepting them: but the English in turn increased their demands to the extent of all they could hope to gain by force of arms: demands to which it was impossible for aught save the *ultima ratio regum* should justify Louis in yielding. Diplomacy thus kept up a feint of peace, until the tidings of Boscawen's success reached Europe; when triumph on the one hand and rage and disappointment on the other rent in twain the veil which shadowed the effigy of War.

In April, 1754, the most formidable armament that the kingdom could produce was gathered in the harbor of Brest. Twenty-two vessels of war, bearing the flags of two admirals, were there assembled to receive the troops destined for America. Six regiments whose names were known on almost every battle-field of Europe, were there arrayed for embarcation; the regiments of Artois, of Burgundy, of Guienne, of Languedoc, and of Béarn, and the famous regiment de la Reine; comprising fully 3000 men destined to find, beyond the stormy sea, a painful exile or a bloody grave. With them embarked the German Baron Dieskau, the favored pupil of Saxe, who was to command in chief the armies in America,[1] and the Marquis de Vaudreuil de Cavagnac, late Governor of Louisiana, and the second of his family to whom the government of Canada had been entrusted, who was to succeed M. de Duquesne. Perverse gales for a time prevented the squadron from proceeding to sea; but at 8 o'clock on the morning of the 3d of May the wind shifted to north-north-east, and the signal was at once given to weigh anchor and to set all sail.[2] At half-past ten the voyage commenced. On the 7th of May the Formidable, the flag-ship of M. de Macnamara, who had hitherto accompanied the squadron, shortened sail, and with his particular command he presently returned to France. A gun from the Entreprenant, at whose mast-head floated the pennant of M. Dubois de la Mothe, called the attention of the majority of the vessels. Stretching forward under a cloud of canvass, with a signal for the America-bound portion of the fleet to follow, the Entreprenant soon was lost beneath the verge to the anxious eyes not only of those who gazed from the receding galleries of the Formidable, but to the diligent espionage of half-a-dozen English frigates which had for weeks been lying in wait to watch the every movement of

---

[1] The high idea entertained of this officer's capacity may be seen in the rate at which the French paid his services. They gave him a salary of 12,000 livres as major-general; of 25,000 more as commander of the American expedition; and a retiring pension of 4000. Penn. Gaz., No. 1385.

[2] I. Pouchot, 25. M. Garneau fixes the date at the end of April; but Pouchot's journal of the voyage is so minute and interesting, that I prefer relying upon his statements.

the French. But any information they could carry would reach England too late to be of service, since Admiral Boscawen had already, on the 27th of April, set sail from Plymouth with instructions which, it may be confidently asserted, though probably merely verbal, assured him that if he should be able to thwart, at any price, the arrival of the French at Canada, he would render a welcome service to his King and Country. To this end he lay in wait for them among the misty vapors of the banks of Newfoundland: but the same cloudy column that concealed the attack, furthered the escape. He captured, indeed, the Alcide, of 64 guns and 500 men, commanded by M. Hocquart, and the Lis, pierced for 64 guns, but armed en flute for the transportation of troops, commanded by M. de Lorgerie; and he came very near catching the Entreprenant itself.[1] On board the ships captured, however, were Colonel de Rostaing (the second in command of the Canadian army), and several other officers of distinction, and eight companies of the regiments of Languedoc and la Reine. It has been alleged that Boscawen acted dishonorably in this transaction, pretending peace with the French ships till at half-pistol range he opened his fire upon them with grape and cannister; but this does not seem credible. The conduct of his employers was much more censurable, who had assured M. de Mirepoix that the admiral's orders were not to act upon the offensive, and that whatever might fall out, England would not begin the war. Such a mendacious tale could hardly impose even upon that polite minister;

[1] The Entreprenant was finally destroyed by the English at the capture of Louisbourg, 1758. Mante, 135.

and he rather vaguely replied "that the King his master would consider the first hostile gun fired at sea as a declaration of war." Lord Orford says that Newcastle, having nobody left at home undeceived, had diligently applied himself to humbug the ambassador; and succeeded. At all events, one thing turned out exactly as Mirepoix had predicted—Boscawen's trivial success was the signal for open hostilities. "Je ne pardonnerai pas les pirateries de cette insolente nation," exclaimed Louis XV.; and war was thenceforth inevitable.[1]

The safe arrival at Quebec of the rest of the fleet on the 19th of June and the succeeding days, increased the regular troops in Canada from 1000 to 3800 men. A militia of 8000 men was already in the field, or in garrison at the various forts. With all this numerous array, however, the Marquis de Duquesne was not at all aware of the dangers which environed the Ohio establishments, and left his government to his successor with the comfortable assurance that it was not possible for the English to traverse the Alleghanies in sufficient force to cause any uneasiness. The experienced and courageous commander of Fort Du Quesne was thus left to rely upon his own strength and the aid derivable, in an emergency, from the contiguous posts and such Canadians and savages as were always, in greater or less numbers, near at hand. Fortunately for him, though it was probably done with no idea of its imminent danger, at least 950 men had been sent in April from Canada to recruit the line of fortifications

[1] Capt. Richard Howe, afterwards the celebrated Admiral Earl Howe, chiefly distinguished himself in this action.

between Lake Erie and the forks of the Ohio.[1] And while every effort was made to obtain information of the intentions of their enemy, a strict watch was kept to prevent the betrayal of their own circumstances. One O'Conner, an English subaltern officer, was hanged as a spy at Quebec in the spring of 1755, and three others shared his fate; and on the 1st of May, two more British spies were executed.[2]

As little as possible has been said in this introductory sketch of the details of the march of the troops from their quarters in Alexandria to Will's Creek, since every particular on that head finds its most appropriate place in the ensuing Journals. But it may not be amiss to trace here, for the guidance of the reader, the exact line of route which they followed throughout the campaign. By St. Clair's advice, the army was to start from Alexandria in two divisions; one regiment and a portion of the stores to Winchester, Virginia, whence a new road was nearly completed to Fort Cumberland, and the other regiment, with the remainder, by way of Frederic, in Maryland. A portion of the stores were to be conveyed in part by water-carriage on the Potomac. Accordingly, on the 8th and 9th of April, the provincials and six companies of the 44th,

---

[1] I. Pouchot, 29. II. Garneau, 215. VI. Col. Rec., 411-12. Penn. Gaz., No. 1379.

[2] Penn. Gaz., Nos. 1394, 1396. XXV. Gent. Mag, 332. One of these inquisitive but unfortunate gentry had in his pocket a list of all the cannon cast at Quebec or imported thither since 1752, and of all the chief houses, the forts, magazines, &c., not only there, but on either side of the St. Lawrence to Montreal. Another was supplied with draughts of the batteries. These two were on the point of departure when they were suddenly arrested and hanged.

under Sir Peter Halket, set out for Winchester; Lieutenant-Colonel Gage and four companies remaining to escort
the artillery. On the 18th of April, the 48th, under
Colonel Dunbar, set out for Frederic, detaching a company
to the Conococheague to expedite the transmission of the
stores gathered there. Arriving at Frederic, however, it
was found there was no road through Maryland to Will's
Creek; and Dunbar accordingly was compelled, on the 1st
of May, to cross the Potomac at the mouth of the Conococheague, and strike the Winchester route. On the 5th, he
crossed the Little Cacapon; and on the 8th, was again ferried over the Potomac to Maryland from a spot, hard by
the mouth of Cacapon, which has since that day borne the
name of the Ferry Fields. Thence, along the river-side,
through Shawanoe Old Town, the dwelling-place of the
notorious Cresap, Dunbar passed through the Narrows at
the foot of Will's Mountain.[1] At high noon on the 10th
of May, while Halket's command was already encamped
at their common destination, the 48th was startled by the
passage of Braddock and his staff through their ranks, with
a body-guard of light-horse galloping on either side of his
travelling-chariot, in haste to reach Fort Cumberland.[2]
The troops saluted, the drums rolled out the Grenadier's
March, and the cortege passed by. An hour after, they
heard the booming of the artillery which welcomed the
General's arrival; and a little later, themselves encamped

[1] II. Olden Time, 541.
[2] He purchased this coach from Governor Sharpe, and left it at Cumberland during the rest of the march. Orme's Letter to Sharpe. (Sharpe's
MS. Corresp. in Maryland Hist. Soc.)

on the hillsides about that post. But in consequence of the difficulty of procuring teams, the artillery, &c., did not arrive until May the 20th.

The erection of Fort Cumberland and its strength have been already described. It stood upon the bank of Will's Creek, hard by its junction with the Potomac, on the site of the present town of Cumberland, and within what is now Alleghany County, Maryland.[1] Here had probably, in ancient days, been a Shawanoe village, and its Indian name, Cucucbetuc, is still preserved; and here, as we have seen, after a series of most distressing delays, Braddock at length succeeded in bringing together all his forces. As nearly as can be ascertained, these consisted as follows: The 44th and 48th regiments, originally 1000 strong, were increased by the Maryland and Virginia Levies to 1400 men. Of the remaining levies, about one hundred were formed by the General into two companies of Carpenters or Pioneers, each composed of thirty men, two sergeants, two subalterns, and a captain. The duty of these was to open the road and make the necessary repairs to the wagons, &c., on the route; and a few of the most experienced of the others were received into a company of Guides, composed of a captain, two aids, and ten men.[2] There was also a troop of provincial light-horse which he had procured to be formed, and which hitherto had served as his body-guard; and a detachment of thirty sailors, with some half-dozen officers, furnished by Commodore

[1] Cumberland is now a thriving town with about 7000 inhabitants. It is 179 miles west by north from Baltimore.

[2] II. Olden Time, 227.

Keppel to assist in rigging cordages, &c., should it be found necessary to build bridges on the way.[1] But the entire force which eventually marched from Fort Cumberland, as given by Captain Orme, consisted of 2037 men, out of a complement of 2100. To these must be added the Guides, the Light-horse, and the seamen; in all not exceeding one hundred, which, with the staff and the eight Indians, who remained with the General unto the end, will make a total of about 2150 souls. The usual train of non-militants who always accompany an army was not wanting here—women, who could not fight; Indians who would not; and wagoners who cut loose their horses and fled, to a man, at the first onset. Early in June, too, the well-known Captain Jack had repaired with his company to the camp and offered his services for the expedition. His merits as a

---

[1] The employment of *seamen* on this service seems to have caused a little natural surprise to those unacquainted with the circumstances of the case (II. O. T. 229); yet it was not a thing of unusual occurrence in America during this war. At Martinico and at Quebec they were employed to pull the guns. "An hundred or two of them, with ropes and pulleys, will do more than all your dray-horses in London." At Quebec, when Wolfe

"Fighting with the French
On the Heights of Abram,"

he found a number of jolly tars, who had been engaged in hauling up the cannon, meekly sliding into the ranks of his soldiery. As they were armed some with hangers, more with sticks, most not at all, he saw no advantage in permitting them to stay; and, despite their petitions, bade them retire. "God bless your honor!" they cried; "if we may not fight, at least let us stop and *see fair play between you and the French!*" Wolfe laughed at this droll request, and thanked them and sent them to their ships. But they were not disposed, after all their toil, to go away without a share in the battle; and lurking about till it actually begun, they took an active part in its perils and glories. See XXV. Gent. Mag., 130, 180.

guide and as an "Indian killer" were not unknown to Braddock, but the proffered services were coupled with some stipulations for freedom from the regular discipline of the army, and were rejected. This singular man was once a frontier-settler. Returning to his cabin one evening after a long day's chase, he found it a heap of smoking ruins, and the blackened corpses of his murdered family smouldering in its embers. From that fatal hour, he vowed never but with life to forgive the race who had wrought his woe, and to his dying hour he was the most dreaded enemy the Indians knew. In 1753, he held some commission under Governor Hamilton; and at this period, he was at the head of a party of bold woodsmen, clad, like himself, in Indian attire, and following very much the Indian mode of warfare. His home was in the Juniata country; but the celerity and extent of his movements caused his fame to reach from Fort Augusta to the Potomac. A mystery has always shrouded his personal history. His swarthy visage (darkened, perchance, by a tinge of baser blood) and destructive arm, however, live in the fireside legends of the West; and many a tale is told of the deeds of the Black Rifle — the Black Hunter — the Wild Hunter of the Juniata, or the Black Hunter of the Forest — under all of which sobriquets he was known. It was a misfortune for Braddock that he neglected to secure the services of such an auxiliary.[1]

Being at last, if not thoroughly prepared, at least sufficiently so to warrant his undertaking the long and tedious journey that was before him, Braddock issued his orders

[1] IV. Haz. Penn. Reg, 389, 390, 416. V. Ibid, 191.

for the army to leave Fort Cumberland. On the 30th of May, Sir John St. Clair, with Major Chapman, of the 44th, and 600 men, set out to clear a road to the Little Meadows on the Youghiogeny, thirty miles distant, where they were to erect a fortified camp. The army followed in three divisions: the first, under Halket, on the 7th of June; the next, under Gage, on the 8th; and the third, under Dunbar, on the 10th; Braddock delayed his own departure until the last man had marched; and the expedition was now fairly on its way to the Ohio. The opposite map will give the reader a perfect idea of its route, and in Captain Orme's text almost every detail of the march is minutely noted down.[1] Owing to the innumerable difficulties of its situation, the progress of the army was painfully slow; five miles being a good day's march, and even half this distance being sometimes barely accomplished. Roads were to be cut through the forests and over the steep mountains; streams were to be bridged, and morasses made passable. The number of wagons and pack-horses struggling through this untravelled land protracted the line to a most dangerous length, and all the difficulties predicted by Franklin were in a fair way to be realized.[2] Accordingly, at the

---

[1] In 1847, Mr. T. C. Atkinson, of Cumberland, Maryland, being employed upon a railroad survey through this region, traced Braddock's route with great accuracy by means of the indications still remaining on the ground; and under his supervision, an excellent map was prepared by Mr. Middleton. This plan was subsequently engraved for the Olden Time (Vol. II, p. 539), where it appears with a very valuable explanatory paper by Mr. Atkinson. It is to the politeness of Mr. Craig that we are indebted for the original plate from which the impression that accompanies this volume is taken.

[2] Entertaining some doubts of the result so confidently anticipated by the General, Franklin had remarked to him, "To be sure, sir, if you arrive

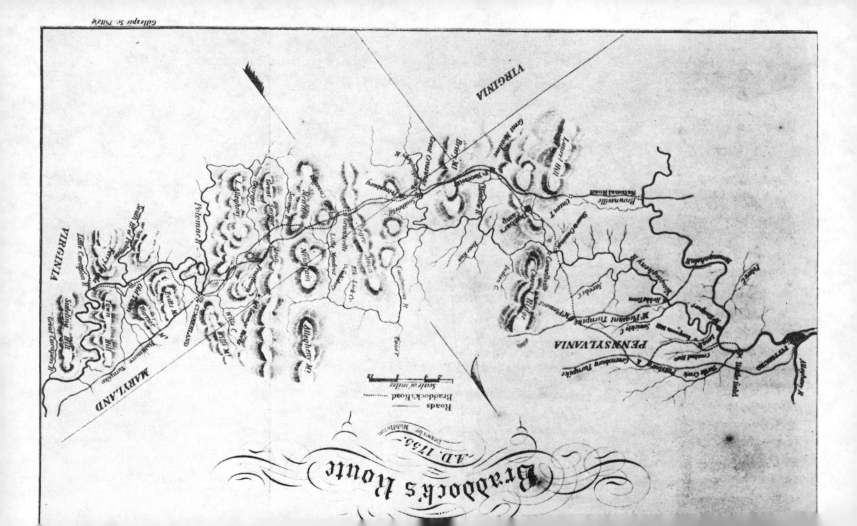

Braddock's Route
A.D. 1755.
Drawn by Middleton

Roads
Braddock's Road
Scale of miles

end of the first day's journey, it was resolved to considerably lighten their numbers and burthens. A part of the artillery and fifty men were sent back to Cumberland; fifty more, under Captain Hogg, were despatched as a covering party to the workmen on the Pennsylvania Road; and twenty-eight of the soldiers' wives were sent on their way to Philadelphia. So far as their names are any indication, they serve to show the Scottish complexion of the two regiments.[1] The officers, who even in the infantry always rode upon a march, returned to Will's Creek all but such luggage as was absolutely essential; and over a hundred of their superfluous horses were freely contributed to the public service; the General and his aides setting the example by giving twenty.

The route pursued by Braddock was in many respects an unwise one. Reference to the Journals will show what difficulties it occasionally presented; and the same pages testify how indifferently, even in the region immediately adjacent to Fort Cumberland, St. Clair had attended to its

well before Du Quesne with these fine troops, so well provided with artillery, the fort, though completely fortified and assisted with a very strong garrison, can probably make but a short resistance. The only danger I apprehend of obstruction to your march is from the ambuscades of the Indians; who, by constant practice, are dexterous in laying and executing them; and the slender line, near four miles long, which your army must make, may expose it to be attacked by surprise in its flanks, and to be cut, like a thread, into several pieces, which, from their distance, cannot come up in time to support each other." He smiled at Franklin's ignorance, and replied, "These savages may indeed be a formidable enemy to your raw American militia; but upon the King's regular and disciplined troops, sir, it is impossible they should make any impression." I. Sparks's Franklin, 190.

[1] II. P. A., 348. VI. C. R., 426, 430.

exploration. Much time and labor had already been exhausted on the road over Will's Mountain, which Major
Chapman had surmounted, with considerable loss, on the
30th of May; and the service was finally indebted to a
naval officer for the easy discovery of the valley path that
leads around its base, subsequently adopted for the United
States' National Road. As it was, marching on a newly-
opened track, Halket, who started three days before, had
got no further on the night of the 10th than the men who
left Will's Creek that morning; a distance of five miles.
The truth is, that Sir John implicitly followed the path
that Nemacolin, a Delaware Indian, had marked out, or
blazed for the Ohio Company some years before, and which,
a very little widened, had served the transient purposes of
that association, and of Washington's party in 1754. To
be sure, with many windings, it led to the Ohio; yet a few
intelligent scouts, sent out betimes, could not have failed
to discover a shorter and a better course. But precautionary steps of this kind were not within the sphere of
Braddock's comprehension.

In addition to every other reason of delay, a general
sickness prevailed among the troops, caused by their long
and continued confinement to a salt diet; from the effects
of which, though few died, few escaped. During a later
period of the march, even Washington's hardy constitution
succumbed; and for many days he was severely, perhaps
dangerously, unwell. Convalescent, at length, through the
personal attention of the General, he was left on the road
with a guard, to rejoin his post as soon as his strength
would permit. Long ere these scenes occurred, however,

an important change had been made in the constitution of affairs. The army had been ten days in reaching the Little Meadows, but twenty-four miles from Cumberland, passing, with a line sometimes four miles long, through numerous spots too well adapted for an ambush or a surprise not to arrest a soldier's eye. Such were those dark forests of enormous white pines that shadow the region beyond the Great Savage Mountain. The loneliness and perfect monotony of such a scene are not readily to be described; it more resembles the utter stillness of the desert than anything beside. No bird chirps among the foliage, or finds its food in these inhospitable boughs; no wild creature has its lair beneath its leafy gloom. Like the dark nave of some endless, dream-born cathedral, the tall columns rise before, behind, on every side, in uncounted and bewildering multiplicity, and are lost in the thick mantle that shuts out the light of heaven. The senses weary of the confusing prospect, and imagination paints a thousand horrid forms to people its recesses. At every step the traveller half looks to find a bloody corse, or the blanched skeleton of some long murdered man, lying across his pathway through these woods, so aptly named the *Shades of Death!*

It was not until the 18th of June that the troops were beyond these inauspicious scenes; and Braddock, as, slowly descending the shaggy steep of Meadow Mountain,

He wound, with toilsome march, his long array,

beheld his whole force in sight of the fortified camp erected by St. Clair at the Little Meadows.[1] Here a council of

---

[1] II. Sp. Wash., 79, 81. Consult, also, Mr. Atkinson's paper in II. O. T., 540.

war was held, which is not noticed by Orme, and which consisted, as usual, of all the field-officers present. A further reduction of baggage was agreed upon, and a dozen more horses given to the service; among them, Washington's best charger, his luggage being retrenched to a single portmanteau, half-filled. Before the council met, Braddock also privately consulted him as to the propriety of pushing more rapidly forward with a light division; leaving the heavy troops, &c., to follow by easy marches. This course Washington warmly approved, urging the present weakness of the garrison at Du Quesne, and the difficulty with which, during the dry season, any supplies could reach them from Venango by the Rivière aux Bœufs, whose waters were then at a very low stage. His rank did not permit him an opportunity of pressing these views at the council-board; but they were brought forward there by the General himself, and it was decided that St. Clair, with Gage and 400 men, should start on the 18th to open a road. On the 19th, Braddock in person followed, with Halket (who acted as brigadier), Burton, and Sparks, and about 800 men, the elite of the army. Inasmuch as in the selection of the troops for this manœuvre he made a point of choosing those he considered the best, without any reference to the wishes of his subordinates, this step gave great and lasting offence to Dunbar, Chapman, and the others left behind.[1] He took with him four howitzers, four twelve-pounders, twelve cohorns, thirteen artillery-wagons, and seventeen of ammunition. The provisions were borne by pack-horses. His expectation was then to strike the

[1] Penn. Gaz., No. 1392.

fort by the 28th of June, at the furthest, ere the garrison should receive its reinforcements; five hundred regulars being reported to be at that moment on their way thither. Four artillery-officers, eighty-four wagons, and all the ordnance-stores and provisions which were not indispensable to the General's march, were left with Dunbar.[1]

From the Little Crossings, on the upper waters of Castleman's River (a tributary of the Youghiogeny), to the Great Crossings on those of the Youghiogeny itself, is but about seventeen miles; yet it was only on the 24th of June that the latter was passed. The advanced party under St. Clair was constantly engaged in cutting the road; but its progression was necessarily slow, and the rest of the army had to encamp at their heels and march within sound of their axes. Steep, rugged hills were to be clomb, to whose summits the artillery and baggage were with cruel labor drawn; headlong declivities to be descended, down which the cannon and wagons were lowered with blocks and tackle; or deep morasses to be threaded, where the troops sunk ankle or knee-deep in the clinging mire. The road, too, was beset with outlying parties of the enemy, who constantly aimed at embarrassing their march. On one occasion, Scarroyaddy was even captured; and his treatment evidently shows that many of the savages in the service of the French were of his old acquaintance in

[1] II. Sp. Wash., 81, 83. Penn. Gaz., No. 1387. VI. C. R., 477. Sharpe (MS. Corresp.) says, "I think the General had with him 52 carriages; the artillery and 18 wagon-loads of amunition included." This nearly tallies with the above statement; the 20 gun-carriages, 13 caissons, and 17 wagons, making just 50.

Pennsylvania.[1] On another, three Mohawk Indians came into camp with intelligence from Du Quesne, for which they were well paid. But disgusted either by the General's indifference to their merits, or by the accounts of his demeanor which they received from their brethren in his ranks, they deserted during the night, and probably returned to the French, whence they came. With them disappeared, too, one of the General's Indians, who had long manifested a disposition to slip off. During the march, he would constantly conceal himself upon the flanks; lying down flat behind a stump or a stone, or creeping into a clump of tall grass. But he was as constantly routed out by the sergeants of the flanking parties, to whose surveillance he had been especially commended; men, trained in Ireland to find a hare squatting in her form beneath a cluster of fern, whose keen eyes, ever on the watch, never failed to discover the refuge of the would-be fugitive. But on the very next night after his flight, three Englishmen, straggling beyond the lines, were shot and scalped upon the very edge of the camp; in which affair he doubtless had a hand.

Not satisfied with the small temporal assistance which his province had afforded the expedition, Governor Morris by proclamation enjoined his people to unite with him in a solemn invocation upon Heaven to preserve and bless the royal arms; and the 19th of June was appointed as a season of public humiliation, of fasting, and of prayer. For that day, all servile labor was discontinued throughout the province: the sound of the mallet and the anvil was not heard; the

[1] See Captain Orme's Journal.

fields were left untilled; the unfettered waters glided idly beneath the motionless wheel; and no smoky columns arose from the cold forge. An unwonted stillness prevailed over the land, save where from the house of prayer was uplifted the preacher's voice in supplication to Almighty God, "that He would be pleased to avert the punishments due to their sins, favor them with a fruitful season, and give success to the measures which His Majesty, ever attentive to the good and welfare of his people, had concerted for the security and preservation of their just rights and commerce."[1]

While thus supernal succor was importuned, the arm of flesh was slowly advanced, and was even now on the borders. Until after it had forded Castleman's river, the course of the army was generally a very little north of west, and lay entirely through Maryland. On the 21st of June, Braddock for the first time entered Pennsylvania. Traversing the high and watery glades of Somerset county and the precipitous region of Fayette, whose mountain-tops attain an altitude of 2500 feet above the sea, with valleys scooped between, 1000 feet below their summits, on the 30th of June he reached Stewart's Crossing on the Youghiogeny, about thirty-five miles from his destination. So far, the efforts of the hostile Indians were less a source of positive danger than of increasing annoyance. That indefatigable foe had by this time got into the rear of the army; their spies environed it on every side, and watched its every motion. As one said to an English captive at Du Quesne: "Their scouts saw him every day from the

[1] VI. C. R., 423.

mountains—that he was advancing in close columns through the woods"—(this he indicated by placing a number of red sticks parallel to each other and pressed closely together)—"and that the Indians would be able to shoot them down 'like one pigeon.'" But so strict was Braddock's police hitherto, that the English loss was very inconsiderable, consisting but of a wagoner, three bat-men, and a horse. Scattering in various directions, the savages threaded the woods in hopes of scalps and plunder. On the night of the 29th, they visited and fired into Dunbar's camp at the Little Meadows, which had been well fortified by St. Clair, and was entirely surrounded by an abattis. They also kept the workmen and convoys on the Pennsylvania road in such a state of alarm that in one day thirty deserted in a body, and the road was soon at a stand.[1]

It was on the evening of the 3d of July at the camp at Jacob's, or Salt Lick Creek,[2] that Sir John St. Clair brought forward his proposition to halt here until Colonel Dunbar and the rest of the forces should come up. The continued remissness in furnishing supplies had compelled these troops to almost forego the use of fresh provisions, and they were afflicted as generally and even more fatally than those with Braddock by the disorders incident to such privations. Many had died; and many more, officers as well

[1] I. O. T., 74. VI. C. R., 467. Penn. Gaz., Nos. 1386, 1387. A *batman* is an officer's servant. IX. Notes and Queries, 530.

[2] Probably a *salt lick* or spring on a branch of Jacob's creek caused this double nomenclature, which has led to some little confusion; there being another stream called Indian Lick falling into the Youghiogeny. Orme styles it Salt Lick Creek; but Scull's large map (Lond. 1775), gives both titles.

as men, were on the sick list. On the 2nd of July, however, Dunbar had moved forward from the Little Meadows; and his van was now not far from the Great Crossings, eleven days' march from Jacob's Creek. Considering this fact, and the disadvantages that would result from the delay, it was wisely resolved by Braddock's council to push forward. They conceived themselves to be (as in fact they were), amply strong enough to conquer the fort should they once sit down before it; and the absence of any organized opposition to their previous progress was well calculated to encourage the belief that, through the enemy's weakness, none would be attempted. "Happy it was," afterwards wrote Captain Orme, "that this disposition was made : otherwise the whole must either have starved or fallen into the hands of the enemy, as numbers would have been of no service to us, and our provision was all lost." And had the General waited for Dunbar, it would have been most probably the middle of August ere he left Jacob's Creek. For so scanty in number were the miserable jades on which he depended, that this officer could only move one-half his wagons at a time. After one day's march, the poor beasts were sent back to bring up the remainder; and it was invariably two day's more ere the detachment could start from the spot of the first night's encampment. Truly said Washington, "there has been vile management in regard to horses."[1]

[1] VI. C. R, 477, 489. II. Sp. Wash., 83. Instead of proper draught-horses, all sorts of broken-down hacks, and spavined, wind-galled ponics, were shamelessly palmed off upon the army by contractors who knew its condition was such that nothing could be rejected. Besides, there were (if not now, at least at a later period), scoundrels base enough to hang

To an army that looked longingly forward to a respite at Fort Du Quesne from the unwonted tasks to which it had been so long subjected, and to whom the exciting perils of the battle-shock offered far greater attractions than a supine existence in the wilderness, where no friend was to be encountered, no enemy to be met in open combat, the orders to advance were welcome tidings. Animated by the confidence of success, it moved onward, regardless of natural difficulties, with all that disciplined courage and tenacity of purpose which have ever characterized the Anglo-Saxon race, eager to behold at length the hostile hold, to tear down the hated banner that so insultingly waved over British soil:—

> Tho' fens and floods possest the middle space,
> That unprovok'd they would have feared to pass;
> Nor fens nor floods can stop Britannia's bands
> When her proud foe rang'd on their border stands.[1]

But the fatal halts which Braddock had already too often been obliged to make, proved in the end the cause of his ruin. It will presently be seen of what importance the saving of three days only would have been; for it was in those three days, the last of his march, that the whole plan of attacking and destroying his army was conceived, organized, and executed. The traditionary repugnance of M. de Contrecœur and his red allies to the hazardous experiment would, in all probability, have prevented its

around Dunbar's camp, stealing every horse that was left to graze in the woods without a guard. Above three hundred were thus made away with. (VI. C. R., 547.)

[1] Addison: The Campaign.

adoption at any other moment, as effectually as it did any previous concerted opposition to the march of the English through passes so admirably fitted by nature for defence, that Braddock himself was amazed at their unoccupation. And, as it happened, every account he received but tended to confirm him in his security. On the 3d of July, he had endeavored to prevail on his few Indians to go out for intelligence; a thing he has always been blamed for neglecting, but which he had constantly solicited at their hands, and which they now declined as resolutely as before. Perhaps it was a sense of their scanty numbers that induced this conduct; perhaps a natural reluctance to encounter their own brethren whom they knew to be with the French; but more probably, it was their extreme discontent with the manners of the General that closed their ears to all his suggestions. On the 4th of July, however, he was more successful. Urged by bribes, and the promise of greater rewards, two Indians were persuaded to depart on a scouting expedition; and no sooner were they gone than Christopher Gist, the General's guide, was privately despatched on the same errand. On the 6th, both Indians and Gist rejoined the army, having penetrated undiscovered to within half a mile of the fort. Their reports were favorable and similar; they found the passes open, and no indications of a heavy force about the works, although there was evidence of outlying parties, and perhaps reinforcements, within a moderate distance. The Indians had even encountered a French officer shooting in the woods hard by Du Quesne, whom without hesitation they killed and scalped. Gist was less fortunate. He, in turn, had

14

been set upon by two hostile savages, and had narrowly succeeded in escaping with his life. Welcome as was this promise of an undisturbed advance, the day was clouded by a fatal event that must have considerably disturbed even savage equanimity. A number of French Indians had beset and scalped a few loiterers, and a general alarm was spread through the line. In the midst of the excitement, Braddock's Indians in advance were met by a party of his rangers, who, regardless of or blind to their signals of friendship, fired upon them, killing the son of Scarroyaddy, their chieftain. The General took what steps suggested themselves to his mind to prevent this misadventure impairing the regard of the dead lad's kindred, and, as it would appear, not without success.

Eager as was the army for the fray, it cannot be denied that at this moment there was much in it to weaken its efficacy. The soldiers complained bitterly of the severe and unusual labors which they were compelled to undergo. The quality of their food was not satisfactory, and the quantity was thought too small; nor was the time allotted them in camp always sufficient to properly dress their victuals. The same necessity which exacted this treatment deprived them also of the hitherto invariable allowance of spirits. They had nothing but water to drink, and that often bad and unwholesome. To add to their discomforts, the sagacious provincials were fully impressed with the dangers of a battle to be fought in the woods and against the savages upon the principles of European tactics; and by their constant predictions of calamity did not a little dishearten the regulars of the two regiments. Nor were matters on a better footing in higher quarters. Disputes and jealousies were rife among the leaders; and by this time the General was not even on speaking terms with Halket and Dunbar. Braddock had already, however, conceived a plan to benefit such of the officers as he looked upon with favoring eyes. It was his intention, when Du Quesne should have been captured, to incorporate the provincials into a royal regiment, the command of which was to be bestowed upon Lieutenant-Colonel Burton of the 48th. His aid-de-camp, Captain Morris, was to have been the Lieutenant-Colonel of the new regiment, and Captain Dobson (the senior captain of the 48th), its major: while Orme was to succeed to Burton's position in the 48th. A number of other promotions would necessarily have followed these changes, in which it is not improbable Braddock would have taken occasion to fulfil his promise of providing for Washington. But his defeat and death scattered all these politic schemes to the winds.[1]

We are now approaching the last dread scene of our tragic story, and events crowd thick and rapidly upon us. On the night of the 4th of July the army halted at Thicketty Run, a petty branch of the Sewickly Creek, where, by some dismal fatality, it seems to have remained until the 6th, awaiting the return of its spies and the arrival of a supply of provisions from Dunbar's camp, under convoy of a captain and a hundred men. In the rear of this party, which appeared on the 6th, came Washington. Debilitated by his recent sickness, he was

---

[1] Sharpe's MS. Corr. Review of Military Operations in North America, &c., (Phil. 1757), p. 51.

unable to endure on horseback the ordinary fatigues of such a road, and journeyed in a covered wagon; but it was not until the 8th that he rejoined the General. It was perhaps to this unhappy delay of twenty-four hours that the destruction of the army is attributable; yet it was such as even a more provident leader than Braddock might well have been excused in making. By it he looked to gain intelligence of his foe and subsistence for himself; both objects of primary importance.

It must be borne in mind that the English were now on the west side of the Monongahela, within the obtuse triangle formed by the forks of the Ohio at whose apex stood Fort Du Quesne; but a glance at the maps will show how far they had diverged from the direct line thither. As Mr. Sparks has well pointed out,[1] it must have been Braddock's original design to continue his march on the same shore, were it possible to have avoided the passage of the Narrows in so doing. His guides had rightly informed him that this was a spot where the road must be made upon a narrow, alluvial formation for some two miles along the bank of the stream, with the river on his left hand and the mountain-side upon his right; and that it would require much labor ere it could be made passable. The perils of such a route were self-evident; therefore abandoning all idea of pursuing it, he started on the morning of the 7th, and leaving the Indian track which he had followed so long, essayed to work his way across Turtle Creek some twelve miles above its confluence with the Monongahela: a step which, had it been carried out, would have ensured his success. He would then undoubtedly have sat down before the fort with little or no opposition on his way. But the fates were against him. On reaching the eastern branch of Turtle Creek, or rather what is now called Rush Creek, the road suddenly terminated in one of those headlong, precipitous descents so common along the edges of the water-courses of Alleghany County; practicable perhaps for footmen, or even sure-footed pack-horses, but utterly impassable to artillery and wagons. A halt was at once commanded, and St. Clair sent forth with a suitable force to explore the country. He soon returned with the pleasing intelligence that he had hit upon the ridge which led directly to Fort Du Quesne. But after reflection upon the labor it would require to construct a road across the hill-environed head-waters of Turtle Creek, it was finally decided to quit that rugged region altogether, and to proceed directly to the Monongahela; and at a place where it makes a considerable bend to the north, to cross at the upper arm of the elbow, to follow the chord which would subtend the arc made by the river's curve, and to recross the stream at a point just below the opposite mouth of Turtle Creek. Two excellent fords with easy banks afforded a strong inducement to pursue this plan: but had he persisted in the movement across Rush Creek, he would have marched through a country presenting comparatively few facilities for an ambuscade or covers for an enemy; whereas in twice crossing the Monongahela he exposed himself to the risk of encountering a determined opposition at either ford. The further and really more fatal hazard of running headlong against a natural entrenchment impregnable to the most determined efforts of one ignorant of its key, cannot be supposed to have entered into his calculations. Nor would the Narrows route have saved him from this danger, since, from the natural formation of the country, it must at the second ford have become identical with that Braddock actually pursued. Thus, in either case, there was no possibility on the Monongahela road of evading the spot where the enemy's ambush was eventually laid.

Having settled upon his course, on the 8th of July Braddock, following the valley of Long Run, marched south-westwardly eight miles towards the Monongahela; and pitched his camp for the night upon an inviting declivity between that stream and another rivulet called Crooked Run, some two miles from the river. He was now within two easy marches of the Ohio, to gain which he looked for no other opposition than what he might encounter in the morrow's fordings; and so far as we can discover, there were in his ranks but two individuals at all diffident of success. William Shirley, the General's secretary, was out of all patience at the manner in which the expedition had been conducted; and was determined to go back to England the moment a campaign was brought to a close, of the success of which he was more than doubtful. It is with a little surprise that we find reason to suppose the second in command was not free from similar forebodings. As though gifted with that mysterious power of "second sight" which is attributed to the seers of his native land, Sir Peter Halket, whose sands of life had but twelve more hours to run, with a melancholy earnestness pressed that night upon the General the propriety of thoroughly examining every foot of ground between his present position and the fort, lest through this neglect he should peril his army's existence, and as it were plunge his head into the lion's jaws. The advice, as will be seen, was not altogether neglected; but its more important feature of beating the forest as hunters of the Highlands would drive their game was set aside by Braddock as unsuitable to the exigencies of his position.[1] With a sad presentiment of undefined evil, Halket withdrew. Did he in sooth possess the fatal power of peering into futurity, and exploring the secrets of unborn Time, what awful visions would have pressed upon his soul! Unconscious of their doom, around him slumbered hundreds of gallant men, sleeping their last sleep on an unbloody couch, nor heeding the tempest gathering fast above, which, overcoming like a summer's cloud, should pour destruction on their devoted heads. Through the long summer's day, the wearied army, anticipating aught rather than defeat, had marched steadily onward. The encircling woods shut out all prospect of the heavens save the serene blue sky directly overhead, bright with meridian splendor: but all around, beyond their narrow ken, a dark curtain hung like a pall upon the skirts of the horizon, and driving clouds and gathering eagles boded the coming storm. Footsore and toilworn, the troops were now steeped in slumber; and in dreams that came from heaven through the ivory gates, they beheld themselves

——— arrived at last
Unto the wished haven.

[1] I. Entick, 145.

They saw their labors crowned with glory, their wanderings rounded with well-earned repose. But, through the narrow passage that lay between them and their promised land rolled darkling the waters of an unseen stream, blacker than night, deeper than the grave: for on its shore, not death alone, but dishonor, and disgrace, and defeat, with welcoming hands, awaited their approach. Behind the western hills their sun had sunk for evermore, incarnadining in his parting rays the bright current of the Monongahela, overhung by stately groves bending to the waters their pensile boughs;

—— lucos, amœnæ

Quos et aquæ subeunt et auræ.

To the prophetic vision of the Scottish *deuteroscopia*, these waters would have curdled with the clotted gore of the morrow's eve; the moaning trees would have sighed responsive to the sad wailings of the winds of night; and along the guilty shores would have flitted in griesly bands the bloody ghosts of the unburied slain.

In the mean time, with a commendable discretion, (the utmost, perhaps, that he was capable of,) Braddock had concluded his arrangements for passing what he regarded as the only perilous place between his army and the fort, which he designed to reach early on the 10th. Had the proposition, started and abandoned by St. Clair, to push forward that very night a strong detachment to invest it before morning, been actually made to him, it is very probable he would have discountenanced it. As, in all human likelihood, it would have been crowned with success, it is as well for the General's reputation that the suggestion aborted.

What precautionary steps his education and capacity could suggest, were here taken by Braddock. Before three o'clock on the morning of the 9th, Gage was sent forth with a chosen band to secure both crossings of the river, and to hold the further shore of the second ford till the rest of the army should come up. At four, St. Clair, with a working-party, followed to make the roads. At six A. M., the General set·out, and having advantageously posted about 400 men upon the adjacent heights, made, with all the wagons and baggage, the first crossing of the Monongahela. Marching thence in order of battle towards the second ford, he received intelligence that Gage had occupied the shore according to orders, and that the route was clear. The only enemy he had seen was a score of savages, who fled without awaiting his approach. By eleven o'clock, the army reached the second ford; but it was not until after one that the declivities of the banks were made ready for the artillery and wagons, when the whole array, by a little before two o'clock, was safely passed over. Not doubting that from some point on the stream the enemy's scouts were observing his operations, Braddock was resolved to strongly impress them with the numbers and condition of his forces; and accordingly the troops were ordered to appear as for a dress-parade. In after life, Washington was accustomed to observe that he had never seen elsewhere so beautiful a sight as was.exhibited during this passage of the Monongahela. Every man was attired in his best uniform; the burnished arms shone bright as silver in the glistening rays of the noonday sun, as, with colours waving proudly above their heads, and amid inspiring bursts of martial music, the steady files, with disciplined precision, and glittering in scarlet and gold, advanced to their position.[1]   While the rear was yet on the other side, and the van was falling into its ordained course, the bulk of the army was drawn up in battle array on the western shore, hard by the spot where one Frazier, a German blacksmith in the interest of the English, had lately had his home.   Two or three hundred yards above the spot where it now stood was the mouth of Turtle Creek (the Tulpewi Sipu of the Lenape), which, flowing in a south-westwardly course to the Monongahela that here has a north-westward direction, embraces, in an obtuse angle of about 125°, the very spot where the brunt of the battle was to be borne.   The scene is familiar to tourists, being, as the crow flies, but eight miles from Pittsburg, and scarce twelve by the course of the river.   For three-quarters of a mile below the entrance of the creek, the Monongahela was unusually shallow; forming a gentle rapid or *ripple*, and easily fordable at almost any point.   Its common level is from three to four hundred feet below that of the surrounding country; and along its upper banks, at

---

[1] "My feelings were heightened by the warm and glowing narration of that day's events by Dr. Walker, who was an eye-witness.   He pointed out the ford where the army crossed the Monongahela (below Turtle Creek 800 yards).   A finer sight could not have been beheld; the shining barrels of the muskets, the excellent order of the men, the cleanliness of their apparel, the joy depicted on every face at being so near Fort Du Quesne—the highest object of their wishes.   The music reechoed through the mountains.   How brilliant the morning; how melancholy the evening!"—Judge Yeates' Visit to Braddock's Field in 1776; VI. Haz. Reg., 104.

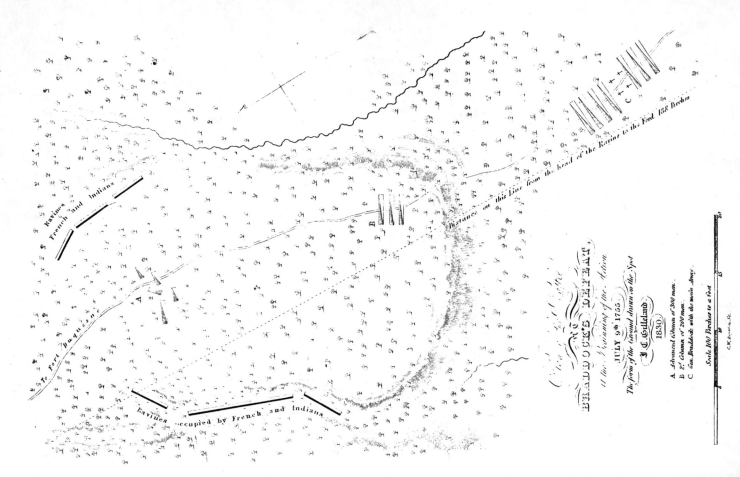

Ravines French and Indians

To Fort Duquesne

A

B

C

Distance on this line from the head of the Ravine to the Ford 156 Perches

Ravines occupied by French and Indians

BRADDOCK'S DEFEAT
at the Beginning of the Action
JULY 9th 1755.
The form of the Ground drawn down on the Spot
by
J. Gilleland
1830.

A. Advanced Column of 300 men.
B. 2d Column of 200 men.
C. Gen. Braddock with the main Army.

Scale 100 Perches to a Foot

C. W. Burton, Sc.

the second crossing, stretches a fertile bottom of a rich pebbled mould, about a fourth of a mile in width, and twenty feet above low-water mark. At this time it was covered by a fair, open walnut-wood, uncumbered with bush or undergrowth.[1]

The ascent from the river, however, is rarely abrupt; but by a succession of gentle alluvial slopes or bottoms the steep hill-sides are approached, as though the waters had gradually subsided from their original glory to a narrow bed at the very bottom of the ancient channel. At this particular place, the rise of the first bottom does not exceed an angle of 3°. Above it again rises a second bottom of the same width and about fifty feet higher than the first, and gradually ascending until its further edge rests upon the bold, rocky face of the mountain-line, climbing at once some two hundred feet to the usual level of the region around.[2] A firm clay, overlaid with mould, forms the soil of the second bottom, which was heavily and more densely timbered than the first; and the underwood began to appear more plentifully where the ground was less exposed to the action of the spring floods. In the bosom of the hill, several springs unite their sources to give birth to a petty rivulet that hurries down the steep to be lost in the river. Its cradle lies in the bed of a broad ravine, forty or fifty feet deep, that rises in the hill-side, and crossing the whole of the second bottom, debouches on the first, where the waters

[1] II. Sp. Wash., 470.   XVI. Haz. Reg., 97.
[2] The frontispiece of this volume gives an exact view of the battle-ground at this day. It is taken from the opposite side of the Monongahela. The crossing is just above the upper part of the stream visible in the engraving. The house and grove in the centre of the piece occupy very nearly the precise spot where was fought the hottest part of the action.

whose current it so far guides, trickle oozily down through a swampy bed. Great trees grew within and along this chasm, and the usual smaller growth peculiar to such a situation ; and a prodigious copse of wild grape-vines (not yet entirely gone) shrouded its termination upon the first bottom and shadowed the birth of the infant brook. About two hundred yards from the line of hills, and three hundred south of the ravine just described, commences another of a more singular nature ; with its steep sides, almost exactly perpendicular, it perfectly resembles a ditch cut for purposes of defence. Rising near the middle of the second bottom, it runs westwardly to the upper edge of the first, with a depth at its head of four or five feet, increasing as it descends, and a width of eight or ten. A century ago, its channel was overhung and completely concealed by a luxurious thicket of pea-vines and trailers, of bramble-bushes and the Indian plum ; its edges closely fringed with the thin, tall wood-grass of summer. But even now, when the forests are gone and the plough long since passed over the scene, the ravine cannot be at all perceived until one is directly upon it ; and hence arose the chief disasters of the day. Parallel with, and about one hundred and fifty yards north of, this second gulley, ran a third ; a dry, open hollow, and rather thinly wooded ; but which afforded a happy protection to the enemy from the English fire. Either of these ravines would have sheltered an army : the second —the most important, though not the largest—would of itself afford concealment to a thousand men.[1]

---

[1] A close personal examination of these localities during the summer of 1854, has confirmed in my mind the conclusion long since arrived at by Mr. Sparks.

There is little reason to doubt that as Braddock drew near, M. de Contrecoeur was almost decided to abandon his position without striking a blow, and, withdrawing his men, as did his successor, in 1758, leave to the English a bloodless victory. He certainly was prepared to surrender on terms of honorable capitulation. A solitary gun was mounted upon a carriage, to enable the garrison to evacuate with the honors of war; it being a point of nice feeling with a defeated soldier that he should retire with drums beating a national march, his own colours flying, and a cannon loaded, with a lighted match. This deprives the proceeding of a compulsory air; and to procure this gratification, Contrecoeur made his arrangements.[1] The British army was so overwhelming in strength, so well appointed and disciplined, that he perhaps deemed any opposition to its advance would be not less fruitless than the defence of the works. However this may be, he had as yet, on the 7th of July, announced no definite conclusion, though possibly his views were perceptible enough to his subordinates. On that day it was known that the enemy, whose numbers were greatly magnified, were at the head-waters of Turtle Creek. On the 8th, when his route was changed, M. de Beaujeu, a captain in the regulars, proposed to the commander that he might be permitted to go forth with a suitable band to prepare an ambuscade for the English on the banks of the Monongahela, and to dispute with them the passage of the second ford. If we may believe tradition, it was with undisguised reluctance that Contrecoeur complied with this request, and even then, it is said,

[1] Mante, 27.

refused to assign troops for the enterprise; bidding him call for volunteers as for a forlorn hope. To that summons the whole garrison responded. If this tale be true, Contrecoeur recanted his determination, and wisely preferred making him a regular detachment, conditioned on his success in obtaining the union of the Indians, who, to the number of nearly a thousand warriors, were gathered at the place.[1] Accordingly, the savages were at once called to a council. These people, consisting of bands assembled from a dozen different nations, listened with unsuppressed discontent to the overtures of the Frenchman. Seated under the palisades that environed the fort, or standing in knots about the speaker, were gathered a motley but a ferocious crew. Alienated from their ancient friends, here were Delawares from the Susquehannah, eager to speed the fatal stroke, and Shawanoes from Grave Creek and the Muskingum; scattered warriors of the Six Nations; Ojibwas and Pottawattanies from the far Michigan; Abenakis and Caughnawagas from Canada; Ottawas from Lake Superior, led on by the royal Pontiac, and Hurons from the falls of Montreal and the mission of Lorette, whose barbarous leader gloried in a name torn from the most famous pages of Christian story.[2]

To these reluctant auditors Beaujeu stated his designs.

[1] XVI. Haz. Penn. Reg., 100.

[2] "Went to Lorette, an English village about eight miles from Quebec. Saw the Indians at mass, and heard them sing psalms tolerably well — a dance. Got well acquainted with Athanase, who was commander of the Indians who defeated General Braddock in 1755 — a very sensible fellow." *MS. Journal of an English Gentleman on a Tour through Canada in 1765;* cited in Parkman, 97.

"How, my father," said they in reply, "are you so bent upon death that you would also sacrifice us? With our eight hundred men do you ask us to attack four thousand English? Truly, this is not the saying of a wise man. But we will lay up what we have heard, and to-morrow you shall know our thoughts." On the morning of the 9th of July, the conference was repeated and the Indians announced their intention of refusing to join in the expedition. At this moment a runner — probably one of those dislodged by Gage in the early dawn — burst in upon the assembly and heralded the advent of the foe. Well versed in the peculiar characteristics of the savages, by whom he was much beloved, and full of tact and energy, Beaujeu took ready advantage of the excitement which these tidings occasioned. "I," said he, "am determined to go out against the enemy. I am certain of victory. What! will you suffer your father to depart alone?" Fired by his language and the reproach it conveyed, they at once resolved by acclamation to follow him to the fray. In a moment, the scene was alive with frantic enthusiasm. Barrels of bullets and flints, and casks of powder, were hastily rolled to the gates: their heads were knocked out, and every warrior left to supply himself at his own discretion. Then, painted for war and armed for the combat, the party moved rapidly away, in numbers nearly 900 strong, of whom 637 were Indians, 146 Canadians, and 72 regular troops.[1] Subordi-

[1] Another French account estimates the French and Canadians as 250, and the savages as 641: a third, at 233 whites and 600 Indians. See Appendix, No. IV. The English rated their numbers from as high as 1500 regulars and 600 Canadians besides savages (XXV. Gent. Mag., 379), to as low as 400 men, all told. (I. Sp. Franklin, 191. Drake's Indian

nate to Beaujeu were MM. Dumas[1] and De Ligneris, both captains in the regular army, four lieutenants, six ensigns,

Captivities, 183); and Washington himself could not have believed they exceeded 300. (II. Sp. Wash., 87).

[1] For his conduct on the 9th of July, M. Dumas was early in the subsequent year promoted to succeed M. de Contrecœur in the command of Fort Du Quesne. Here he proved himself an active and vigilant officer, his war-parties ravaging Pennsylvania, and penetrating to within twenty leagues of its metropolis. A copy of instructions signed by him, on 23d March, 1756, was found in the pocket of the Sieur Douville, who, being sent to surprise the English at Fort Cumberland, got the worst of it and lost his own scalp. This letter concludes in a spirit of humanity honorable to its writer. (II. P. A., 600.) In the spring of 1759, the king created him a major-general and inspector of the troops of the marine, who seem to have constituted the bulk of the usual Canadian army. At the siege of Quebec and during the rest of the war he was actively employed. In July, 1759, he commanded in the unlucky *coup des écoliers*, where 1500 men, partly composed of lads from the schools, in endeavoring to destroy Monckton's battery, became so bewildered in the darkness as to mistake friend for foe, and nearly destroyed each other. We may presume he fought not where Montcalm fell on the Heights of Abraham; since, after the surrender of the capital he held Jacques Cartier with 600 men by order of M. de Levis. And when that general besieged Murray in Quebec, in 1760, Dumas was in command of the lines from Jacques Cartier to Pointe-aux-Trembles. At last, the capitulation of Montreal gave Canada to the English, and Dumas passed with his comrades in arms to France. Here I do not doubt he was visited by the same persecutions that waited alike, on almost every man who had been in a Canadian public employ—on the peculating Bigot and the upright Vaudreuil. Ultimately, however, and after 1763, he was made a brigadier and appointed to the government of the Isles of France and of Bourbon. (I. Pouchot, 41, 84. II. Garneau, liv. ix, x, xi. I. O. T., 75.) Thus much may be positively stated of Dumas. To the romantic story of his persecution by Contrecœur we cannot attach implicit faith. It says that jealousy of his success induced Contrecœur to send Dumas home on a charge of purloining the public stores; that he was tried and cashiered, and retired in disgrace to Provence; that during the revolutionary war Washington informed Lafayette of these circumstances, whose influence speedily brought Dumas in triumph to Paris to receive the grade of a general officer. (XVI. Haz. Reg., 99. II. O. T., 475.) Since Pouchot deliberately insinuates (Vol. I, p. 84), that

and twenty cadets. Though his numbers were thus not so greatly inferior to Braddock's, it is not likely that Beaujeu calculated on doing more than giving the English a severe check, and perhaps delaying for a few days their advance. It is impossible that he should have contemplated the complete victory that was before him.[1]

On the evening of the 8th of July, the ground had been carefully reconnoitred and the proper place for the action selected. The intention was to dispute as long as possible the passage of the second ford, and then to fall back upon the ravines. But long ere they reached the scene, the swell of military music, the crash of falling trees, apprised them that the foe had already crossed the river, and that his pioneers were advanced into the woodlands. Quickening their pace into a run, they managed to reach the broken ground just as the van of the English came in

Dumas was inclined to such practices, we may conclude it not unlikely that on his return to France his conduct was severely scrutinized; but much of the rest of the anecdote is palpably false. It is believed by many that Alexandre Dumas, the famous novelist, is a son of this general; but this view is not confirmed by the Mémoires of the former. He says that his father, Thomas-Alexandre Davy de la Pailleterie, a general of the Republic, was born at St. Domingo in 1762, son of Marie-Alexandre-Antoine Davy, marquis de la Pailleterie (born 1710, died 1786), a colonel of artillery, and Marie Tessette-Dumas of St. Domingo. It is said this last was a quadroon. Independent of the impossibility of the general, and the improbability of the colonel, being the Dumas of Braddock's defeat, it is hardly likely that no reference to the fact, were it so, would be found in the highly-colored pages of our autobiographer. There was a Comte Mathieu Dumas, a French general who served with Rochambeau in America, but he certainly was not this man. Indeed, the name is so common in France that there may well have been several bearing it occupying high ranks in the army at the same time. Had we a series of the Almanach Royale to refer to, the point might be settled.

[1] Pouchot is clear on this point. (Vol. I, p. 38.)

sight. Braddock had turned from the first bottom to the second, and mounting to its brow was about to pass around the head of the ravines to avoid the little morass caused by the water-course before described. His route did not lay parallel with the most dangerous defile, where the banks are so steep and the cover so perfect, but passed its head at an angle of about 45°; thus completely exposing his face and flanks from a point on the second bottom, at a hundred yards distance, to another within thirty, where he would turn the ravine. Of course the further he advanced the nearer he would approach to its brink, till the whole should finally be left behind: thus opening a line of two hundred yards long, at an average distance of sixty, to the enemy's fire. Had he possessed the least knowledge of these defiles, he would undoubtedly have secured them in season, since nothing would have been easier than their occupation by Gage's advanced party. But not a man in his army had ever dreamed of their existence.

The arrangement of the march from the river's bank had been made as follows: The engineers and guides and six light-horsemen proceeded immediately before the advanced detachment under Gage, and the working-party under St. Clair, who had with them two brass six-pounders and as many tumbrils or tool-carts. On either flank, parties to the number of eight were thrown out to guard against surprises. At some distance behind Gage followed the line, preceded by the light-horse, four squads of whom also acted as extreme flankers at either end of the column. Next came the seamen, followed by a subaltern with twenty grenadiers, a twelve-pounder and a company of grenadiers. Then the vanguard succeeded, and the wagon and artillery train, which began and ended with a twelve-pounder: and the rearguard closed the whole. Numerous flanking-parties, however, protected each side; and six subalterns, each with twenty grenadiers, and ten sergeants, with ten men each, were detached for this purpose.

The greater part of Gage's command was actually advanced beyond the spot where the main battle was fought, and was just surmounting the second bottom, when Mr. Gordon, one of the engineers who were in front marking out the road, perceived the enemy bounding forward. Before them, with long leaps, came Beaujeu, the gaily-colored fringes of his hunting-shirt and the silver gorget on his bosom at once bespeaking the chief. Comprehending in a glance the position he had attained, he suddenly halted and waved his hat above his head. At this preconcerted signal, the savages dispersed to the right and left, throwing themselves flat upon the ground, and gliding behind rocks or trees or into the ravines. Had the earth yawned beneath their feet and reclosed above their heads, they could not have more instantaneously vanished. The French (some of whom, according to Garneau, were mounted)[1] held the centre of the semi-circular disposition so instantly assumed; and a tremendous fire was at once opened on the English. For a moment, Gage's troops paused aghast at the furious yells and strangeness of the onset. Rallying immediately, he returned their fire, and halted a moment till St. Clair's working-party came up;[2] when he bade his men advance at once upon the centre of the concentric line. As he drew

[1] This is very improbable, however.   [2] Sharpe's MS. Corresp.

near, he was again greeted with a staggering discharge, and again his ranks were shaken. Then, in return, they opened a fire of grape and musketry, so tremendous as to sweep down every unsheltered foe who was upon his feet, and to utterly fright the savages from their propriety. Beaujeu and a dozen more fell dead upon the spot, and the Indians already began to fly, their courage being unable to endure the unwonted tumult of such a portentous detonation. But reanimated by the clamorous exhortations of Dumas and De Ligneris, and observing that the regulars and militia still preserved a firm front, they returned once more to their posts and resumed the combat. For a time the issue seemed doubtful, and the loud cries of "Vive le Roi" of the French were met by the charging cheers of the English. But precision of aim soon began to prevail over mere mechanical discipline. In vain the 44th continued their fire; in vain their officers, with waving swords, led them to the charge: hidden beneath great trees, or concealed below the level of the earth, the muzzles of their pieces resting on the brink of the ravine, and shooting with a secure and steady aim, the majority of the enemy rested secure and invisible to their gallant foemen.[1]

In the mean time, Braddock, whose extreme rear had not yet left the river's bank, hearing the uproar in advance, ordered Burton to press forward with the vanguard, and the rest of the line to halt; thus leaving Halket with four

---

[1] "None of the English that were engaged saw more than 100, and many of the Officers as well as Men who were the whole time of its Continuance in the Heat of the Action, will not assert that they saw an Enemy." Sharpe's MS. Corresp.

hundred men to protect the baggage while eight hundred engaged the enemy. But just as Burton, under a galling fire, was forming his troops upon the ground, Gage's party gave way and precipitately endeavored to fall into his rear; confusing men who were confused before.[1] The manoeuvre was unsuccessfully executed, and the two regiments became inextricably commingled. Vainly Braddock strove to separate the soldiers, huddling together like frightened sheep. Vainly the regimental colours were advanced in opposite directions as rallying-points.

—

"Ut conspicuum in proelio

Haberent signum quod sequerentur milites."[2]

The officers sought to collect their men together and lead them on in platoons. Nothing could avail. On every hand the officers, distinguished by their horses and their uniforms, were the constant mark of hostile rifles; and it was soon as impossible to find men to give orders as it was to have them obeyed. In a narrow road twelve feet wide, shut up on either side and overpent by the primeval forest, were crowded together the panic-stricken wretches, hastily loading and reloading, and blindly discharging their guns in the air, as though they suspected their mysterious murderers were sheltered in the boughs above their heads; while all around, removed from sight, but making day hideous with their warwhoops and savage cries, lay ensconced a host insatiate for blood.[3] Foaming with rage and indignation, Brad-

[1] Penn. Gaz. No. 1393. [2] Phoed. Fab., liii.

[3] "The yell of the Indians is fresh on my ear, and the terrific sound will haunt me until the hour of my dissolution. I cannot describe the

dock flew from rank to rank, with his own hands endeavoring to force his men into position. Four horses were shot under him, but mounting a fifth, he still strained every nerve to retrieve the ebbing fortunes of the day. His subordinates gallantly seconded his endeavors, throwing themselves from the saddle and advancing by platoons, in the idle hope that their men would follow : but only to rush upon their fate. The regular soldiery, deprived of their immediate commanders, and terrified at the incessant fall of their comrades, could not be brought to the charge; while the provincials, better skilled, sought in vain to cover themselves and to meet the foe upon equal terms : for to the urgent entreaties of Washington and Sir Peter Halket that the men might be permitted to leave the ranks and shelter themselves, the General turned a deaf ear.[1] Wherever he saw a man skulking behind a tree, he flew at once to the spot; and, with curses on his cowardice and blows with the flat of his sword, drove him back into the open road.[2] Wherever the distracted artillerymen saw a smoke arise, thither did they direct their aim; and many of the flankers who had succeeded in obtaining the only position where they could be of any service, were thus shot down. Athwart the

horrors of that scene. No pencil could do it, or no painter delineate it so as to convey to you with accuracy our unhappy situation." Capt. Leslie's Letter, 30th July, 1755. V. Haz. Reg, 191.

[1] VI. Haz. Reg, 104.

[2] "The Enemy kept behind Trees and Loggs of Wood, and cut down our Troops as fast as they cou'd advance. The Soldiers then insisted much to be allowed to take to the Trees, which the General denied and stormed much, calling them Cowards, and even went so far as to strike them with his own Sword for attempting the Trees." Burd to Morris; VI. C. R, 501.

the brow of the hill lay a large log, five feet in diameter, which Captain Waggoner, of the Virginia Levies, resolved to take possession of. With shouldered firelocks he marched a party of eighty men to the spot, losing but three on the way; and at once throwing themselves behind it, the remainder opened a hot fire upon the enemy. But no sooner were the flash and the report of their pieces perceived by the mob behind, than a general discharge was poured upon the little band, by which fifty were slain outright and the rest constrained to fly.

By this time, the afternoon was well advanced, and the whole English line surrounded. The ammunition began to fail, and the artillery to flag; the baggage was warmly attacked; and a runner was despatched to the fort with the tidings that by set of sun not an Englishman would be left alive upon the ground. Still, gathering counsel from despair, Braddock disdained to yield; still, strong in this point only of their discipline, his soldiers died by his side, palsied with fear, yet without one thought of craven flight. At last, when every aide but Washington was struck down; when the lives of the vast majority of the officers had been sacrificed with a reckless intrepidity, a sublime self-devotion, that surpasses the power of language to express; when scarce a third part of the whole army remained unscathed, and these incapable of aught save remaining to die or till the word to retire was given; at last, Braddock abandoned all hope of victory; and, with a mien undaunted as in his proudest hour, ordered the drums to sound a retreat. The instant their faces were turned, the poor regulars lost every trace of the sustaining power of custom; and the retreat became a headlong flight. "Despite of all the efforts of the officers to the contrary," they ran," says Washington, "as sheep pursued by dogs, and it was impossible to rally them."

Beneath a large tree standing between the heads of the northernmost ravines, and while in the act of giving an order, Braddock received a mortal wound; the ball passing through his right arm into the lungs. Falling from his horse, he lay helpless on the ground, surrounded by the dead, abandoned by the living. Not one of his transatlantic soldiery "who had served with the Duke" could be prevailed upon to stay his headlong flight and aid to bear his General from the field. Orme thought to tempt them with a purse containing sixty guineas; but in such a moment even gold could not prevail upon a vulgar soul, and they rushed unheeding on. Disgusted at such pusillanimity, and his heart big with despair, Braddock refused to be removed, and bade the faithful friends who lingered by his side to provide for their own safety. He declared his resolution of leaving his own body on the field: the scene that had witnessed his dishonor he desired should bury his shame. With manly affection, Orme disregarded his injunctions; and Captain Stewart, of Virginia (the commander of the Light-horse which were attached to the General's person), with another American officer, hastening to Orme's relief, his body was placed first in a tumbrel, and afterwards upon a fresh horse, and thus borne away.[1] Stewart seems to have cherished a sense of duty or of friendship towards

[1] III. Walp. Corresp., 144.   II. Garneau, 227.

his chief that did not permit him to desert him for a moment while life remained.

It was about five o'clock in the afternoon when the English abandoned the field. Pursued to the water's edge by about fifty savages, the regular troops cast from them guns, accoutrements, and even clothing, that they might run the faster. Many were overtaken and tomahawked here; but when they had once crossed the river, they were not followed. Soon turning from the chase, the glutted warriors made haste to their unhallowed and unparalleled harvest of scalps and plunder. The provincials, better acquainted with Indian warfare, were less disconcerted; and though their loss was as heavy, their behavior was more composed. In full possession of his courage and military instincts, Braddock still essayed to procure an orderly and soldierlike retreat; but the demoralization of the army now rendered this impossible. With infinite difficulty, a hundred men, after running about half a mile, were persuaded to stop at a favorable spot where Braddock proposed to remain until Dunbar should arrive, to whose camp Washington was sent with suitable orders. It will thus be seen how far was his indomitable soul from succumbing in the discharge of his duties, beneath the unexpected burthen that had been laid upon him. By his directions Burton posted sentries here, and endeavored to form a nucleus around which to gather the shattered remains of the troops, and where the wounded might be provided for. But all was idle. In an hour's time, almost every soldier had stolen away, leaving their officers deserted. These, making the best of their way off, were joined beyond the other ford by

Gage, who had rallied some eighty men; and this was all that remained of that gallant army which scarce six hours before was by friend and foe alike deemed invincible. With little interruption the march was continued through that night and the ensuing day, till at 10 P.M. on the 10th of July, they came to Gist's plantation; where early on the 11th some wagons and hospital-stores arrived from Dunbar for their relief. Despite the intensity of his agonies, Braddock still persisted in the exercise of his authority and the fulfilment of his duties. From Gist's he detailed a party to return towards the Monongahela with a supply of provisions to be left on the road for the benefit of stragglers yet behind, and Dunbar was commanded to send to him the only two remaining old companies of the 44th and 48th, with more wagons to bring off the wounded; and on Friday, the 11th of July, he arrived at Dunbar's camp. Through this and all the preceding day, men half-famished, without arms, and bewildered with terror, had been joining Dunbar; his camp was in the utmost confusion, and his soldiers were deserting without ceremony.

Braddock's strength was now fast ebbing away. Informed of the disorganized condition of the remaining troops, he abandoned all hope of a prosperous termination to the expedition. He saw that not only death, but utter defeat, was inevitable. But conscious of the odium the latter event would excite, he nobly resolved that the sole responsibility of the measure should rest with himself, and consulted with no one upon the steps he pursued. He merely issued his orders, and insisted that they were obeyed.

Thus, after destroying the stores to prevent their falling into the hands of the enemy (of whose pursuit he did not doubt), the march was to be resumed on Saturday, the 12th of July, towards Will's Creek. Ill-judged as these orders were, they met with but too ready acquiescence at the hands of Dunbar, whose advice was neither asked nor tendered on the occasion. Thus, the great mass of those stores which had been so painfully brought thither were destroyed. Of the artillery, but two six-pounders were preserved; the cohorns were broken or buried; and the shells bursted. One hundred and fifty wagons were burned; the powder-casks were staved in, and their contents, to the amount of 50,000 pounds, cast into a spring: and the provisions were scattered abroad upon the ground or thrown into the water. Nothing was saved beyond the actual necessities for a flying march; and when a party of the enemy some time afterward visited the scene, they completed the work of destruction. For this service—the only instance of alacrity that he displayed in the campaign—Dunbar must not be forgiven. It is not perfectly clear that Braddock, intelligently, ever gave the orders; but in any case they were not fit for a British officer to give or to obey. Dunbar's duty was to have maintained here his position, or at the least not to have contemplated falling back beyond Will's Creek. That he had not horses to remove his stores, was, however, his after excuse.[1]

---

[1] Sharpe's MS. Corresp. VI. C. R., 501. Penn. Gaz., No. 1392. The people nick-named this man "Dunbar the tardy." I. Watson's Annals, 100. What provisions belonging to the army remained in Morris's hands were afterwards applied to its uses or sold by him on its account. II. P. A., 469.

It was not until Sunday, July 13th, that all this was finished; and the army with its dying General proceeded to the Great Meadows, where the close was to transpire:

Last scene of all,
That ends this strange, eventful history.

Ever since the retreat commenced, Braddock had preserved a steadfast silence, unbroken save when he issued the necessary commands. That his wound was mortal he knew; but he also knew that his fame had received a not less fatal stab; that his military reputation, dearer than his own life to a veteran or those of a thousand others, was gone forever. These reflections embittered his dying hours; nor were there any means at hand of diverting the current of his thoughts, or ministering to the comfort of his body: even the chaplain of the army was among the wounded. He pronounced the warmest eulogiums upon the conduct of his officers (who indeed had merited all he could say of them), and seems to have entertained some compunctions at not having more scrupulously followed the advice of Washington, or perhaps at the loss of power to provide for that young soldier's interests as thoroughly as he would have done had he returned victorious. At all events, we find him singing out his Virginia aide as his nuncupative legatee, bequeathing to him his favorite charger and his body-servant Bishop, so well known in after years as the faithful attendant of the patriot chief.[1]

[1] So says Mr. Custis, in his Life of Martha Washington. Howe (Hist. Coll. Virg., 184), recites the death in Augusta County, in Feb. 1844, of the slave Gilbert, aged 112 years, whom he represents to have been Washington's attendant not only at Braddock's but at Cornwallis's defeat; and

The only allusions he made to the fate of the battle was to softly repeat once or twice to himself— "Who would have thought it?" Turning to Orme— "We shall better know how to deal with them another time," were his parting words. A few moments later, and he breathed his last.[1] Thus at about eight on the night of Sunday the 13th of July honorably died a brave old soldier, who, if wanting in temper and discretion, was certainly, according to the standard of the school in which he had been educated, an accomplished officer; and whose courage and honesty are not to be discussed. The uttermost penalty that humanity could exact, he paid for his errors : and if his misfortune brought death and woe upon his country, it was through no shrinking on his part from what he conceived to be his duty. He shared the lot of the humblest man who fell by his side.

So terminated the bloody battle of the Monongahela ; a scene of carnage which has been truly described as unexampled in the annals of modern warfare. Of the fourteen hundred and sixty souls, officers and privates, who went into the combat, four hundred and fifty-six were slain outright, and four hundred and twenty-one were wounded ; making a total of eight hundred and seventy-seven men. Of eighty-nine commissioned officers, sixty-three were killed or wounded ; not a solitary field-officer escaping unhurt. The summing up of the whole loss is given as follows :

Washington himself (II. Sparks, 84), seems to refer to one John Alton as his servant on this occasion.
[1] I. Sp. Franklin, 193.

Rank.	Killed.	Wounded.	Safe.
General	1		
Secretary	1		
Colonels and L.-Colonels	1	2	
Major	1		
Captains	7	7	7
Lieutenants	11	15	12
S. Lieutenants or Ensigns	3	5	6
Midshipmen	1		1
Chaplain	1		
Quarter-Master	1		
Surgeon's Mates	1	5	
Sergeants	17	20	21
Corporals and bombardiers	18	22	21
Gunners	6	8	4
Boatswain's Mates	1		1
Drummers	2	6	24
Matrosses and Privates	386	328	486
Total	456	421	583

The number of women and servants killed cannot be ascertained, since they are not entered on the roster of an army: certain it is, however, that but three of the latter were spared. As for the Pennsylvania wagoners, they escaped to a man. At the very first onset each driver cut loose his team, and selecting the best horse, fled with headlong precipitation. In fact, of the whole number which originally set forth, but two never returned to their homes; one of whom had died of disease and the other been scalped on the march. The battle was fought on the afternoon of Wednesday, the 9th of July; yet such was their haste, that at 5 A.M. of Thursday their leader rushed into Dunbar's camp with the dismal tidings that the whole army was destroyed and himself the sole survivor![1] The

[1] Penn. Gaz, Nos. 1381, 1392.

enemy's loss was very inconsiderable, being but three officers killed and two wounded; two cadets wounded; twenty-five soldiers and savages slain; and as many more badly hurt. Beside the artillery abandoned by the English to the victors, they lost everything they had with them save the clothes on their backs and the arms in their hands.[1] One hundred oxen that had just been brought up; all the wagons, provisions, baggage, and stores; the military chest, containing £25,000 in specie; and the General's cabinet with his instructions and private papers fell into the enemy's power. These last were transmitted at once to Canada; and their contents soon made known by the French government to every court in Europe, as eternal monuments of the perfidy of Britain.[2]

Whether we regard the cause, the conduct, or the consequences of this battle, the reflections it gives rise to are alike valuable and impressive. It brought together practically for the first time in our history the disciplined regular of Europe and the rifleman of America; and it taught the lesson to the latter that in his own forests he was the superior man. It was the beginning of a contest in whose revolving years the colonies became a school of arms, and a martial spirit of the people was fostered and trained till they had attained that confidence which naught but custom can afford. Had Braddock been successful, the great pro-

---

[1] "Two 12-pounder cannon," says Burd, "six 4-pounders, four cohorns, and two Hortts, with all the shells, &c." VI. C. R., 501. There is a discrepancy between this statement and that of the park which the General set forth with.

[2] I. Pouchot, 43. VI. C. R., 514. Sharpe's MS. Corresp. II. O. T., 140.

vince of Pennsylvania, and probably those of New Jersey, Maryland, and New York, freed from danger, would have continued in their original ignorance and aversion of military science. His failure left their frontiers open to the enemy, and the spirit of self-preservation soon compelled them to welcome the weapons from which they had once recoiled with loathing. It was there and then that Morgan and Mercer, Gates and Washington, first stood side by side in marshalled array;[1] and in that day's dark torrent of blood was tempered the steel which was to sever the colonies from the parent-stem. "Had an enforced colonial obedience to the omnipotence of Parliament been attempted in 1754, instead of twenty years later," sagaciously observed a soldier of the revolution, himself a captive at Fort Du Quesne when Braddock was defeated, "it would have been undoubtedly successful; for with the partial exception of

[1] Daniel Morgan was born in Pennsylvania, and was serving as an overseer in Virginia shortly before Braddock's arrival. Though then a lawless, dissipated character, he was the possessor of a wagon and a team of horses, with which he engaged in the expedition. Being on an occasion behind time with his wagon, he was sharply reprimanded by an officer. He replied probably with insolence, and the officer drew his sword upon him. Morgan fell on him with his whip, knocked the weapon from his hand, and beat him severely. For this offence he was sentenced to receive 500 lashes, but fainting beneath the cat, 50 were remitted. According to his own story, his adversary subsequently perceived that the original fault was his own, and made the *amende honorable* to the wagoner. In the battle, or on some occasion of the campaign, he was shot in the back of the neck, the ball passing through his mouth and teeth. It is a little odd that Morgan, who afterwards rose to the rank of General in the army of the Revolution was, under the command of Gates, one of the most active opponents of Burgoyne at Saratoga, in 1778. (Howe's Hist. Coll. Virg., 515.) As for Dr. Hugh Mercer (the same that died so gloriously at Princeton, in 1777), he is constantly said to have been engaged in Braddock's campaign. He certainly played an active part in Pennsylvania during the remainder of the war.

the people of New England, the Americans were equally destitute of means of defence or skill to use them."[1] The power and policy of England gave them both; Bouquet and Amherst and Gage himself enured them to the hardy toils of battle; every regiment that was sent to America left skilful soldiers on its shores; and when the final struggle came, it was with the dagger itself had sharpened that the fatal blow was struck; and too late the mother-country realized the fate of Waller's eagle:—

—Which on the shaft that made him die,
Espy'd a feather of his own
Wherewith he wont to soar so high.

But there are other and less satisfying lights in which we must for a moment behold this scene. Never was there an affray, proportionably to the numbers engaged, more awfully destructive of life. Not even at Waterloo, in all the flush and pride of youthful valor and filled with the recent memories of their distant homes, fell on their earliest battle-field a larger share of officers. What terrible tales the tidings of that day of carnage bore to those remote homesteads around which yet lingered the parting echoes of their farewell, cannot be traced here. The fond eyes still filled with the fading image of their youthful heroes, too soon to be dimmed with bitterest tears—the hands that dropped the half-twined chaplet of victorious laurel to pre-pare the cypress-wreath—the hearts whose high triumphal hopes were by one sudden stroke shaken with the throb-bings of despair—all are passed away like the objects they lamented —gone

---

[1] Drake, 262.

Où va la feuille de Rose
Où va la feuille de Laurier.

Early or late, the inevitable fate fell equally upon the peaceful home-dweller beyond the wide-spread fields of barren foam and the warrior upon the rugged banks of occidental streams: the mourned and the mourner have alike disappeared and been forgotten; and they who rest by the murmuring ripple of the Monongahela beneath the brown shades of an American forest, as quietly sleep in their confused and nameless graves as she who lies beneath the church-yard walls of England, above whose mouldered tomb sweep constant sounds of Christian bells.

Of the many melancholy passages of this most melancholy day, some not uninteresting incidents are still recollected. The preservation of Washington is an anecdote of popular currency. With two horses shot under him and four bullets through his coat, and a special mark for the enemy's rifles, not a single stroke told upon his person. In 1770, on the banks of the Great Kanhawa, an aged chief journeyed from his distant lodge to see once more the favorite of the Great Spirit against whom his own gun and those of his young men were fifteen years before so often turned in vain. Well might the eloquent Davies express at the time the public conviction that the signal manner in which Providence had hitherto watched over the heroic youth clearly presaged his future importance to his country.[1]

Nor was the salvation of two other officers less worthy of remark, since the story displays the exercise of some

---

[1] II. Sp. Wash., 91, 476.

of the noblest qualities that can inspire the heart of man to immortal deeds. When the retreat was sounded, Captain Treby of the 44th lay writhing on the ground, so desperately wounded as to be unable even to crawl beneath the shelter of the nearest bush. With death close following at their heels, the human herd rushed by regardless of his fate, when his situation arrested the attention of a gentleman volunteer named Farrel. Uncareful of the peril to which he exposed his safety by such an action, Farrel placed the helpless sufferer upon his own back, and in this wise bore him to such a distance from the field as to be able to procure further assistance and eventually place him beyond the reach of danger.[1] And equally magnanimous was the enthusiastic bravery of the men of Captain John Conyngham's company. At the first fire his horse was shot down and he himself severely wounded. Falling beneath the animal's body, all his efforts to extricate himself would have been in vain had not his soldiers, "for the love they bore him," rushed to his relief; and while many of their number were shot dead in the attempt, succeeded finally in bearing him in triumph from the spot.[2] Such incidents

[1] Mante, 28; where it is said that in 1772 Mr. Farrel was a captain in the 62nd Foot. I take him, however, to be the same Thomas Farrel who, on March 15th, 1763, was appointed to a captaincy in the 65th Foot. (Army Reg. for 1765, p. 120.) In 1763, Captain John Treby still held his rank in the 44th. (Army. Reg. 1763, p. 98.) About the close of the century, we find "a Colonel Treby" apparently a man of fashion in Wiltshire. Chafin's Cranbourne Chase, 18.

[2] Capt. Matthew Leslie's Letter of 30th of July, 1754. V. Haz. Reg., 191, where Conyngham's convalescence is indicated. In 1763 there was no one of this name in either the 44th or 48th regiment; but in 1765 a John Conyngham appears as Lieutenant-Colonel of the 29th Foot (date

as these are enough to brighten a thousand darker shades of character.

Among the most distinguished of the dead was Sir Peter Halket of Pitferran, Colonel of the 44th, and a gallant and sagacious soldier; whose two sons were fighting by his side when he fell. One of these, Lieutenant James Halket of his own regiment, hastened at the moment to his aid, and with open arms bent to raise the dying form. But pierced by an Indian bullet his body dropped heavily across his leader's corpse, and father and son lay in death together.

There is a generally accepted tradition that Braddock was murdered by one of his own men. Thomas Fausett, a subsequent resident of Fayette County, Pennsylvania, is not only commonly believed to have been the perpetrator of the deed, but actually, in later years, avowed the fact. Such an interesting incident — paralleled only by the case of Charles of Sweden — demands in this place a thorough investigation; and this more particularly since the tale, mendacious as we now believe it to be, has been fortified by such constant and positive assertion, and such popular currency, that even Mr. Sparks has not disdained to sanction its naked repetition.[1] A careful summary of the evidence in this matter shall therefore be given; and the result will show what ridiculous forgeries may be foisted off upon the student under the name of History.

---

[1] II. Sp. Wash., 475. Of course Mr. Sparks would not be justified in omitting a mere allusion to a matter so confidently asserted by our local historians. But the occurrence is pointed out here to show how widely error may be diffused.

of commission, 13th Feb., 1762), and a John Conyngham as captain in the 7th Foot: (date of commission, 15th Oct. 1759.) Army Reg. 1765 pp. 60, 82.

It must be premised that not one contemporaneous authority, either in public or in private, even breathed a suspicion of such a circumstance. Washington, who must have participated sooner or later in the secrets of the provincial troops, knew nothing of it. Neither Orme, with all his scorn of colonial morality, nor Sharpe, who hated Braddock, and with his confidential correspondents spared not his memory, once alludes to it. It is not hinted at in Governor Morris's letters, nor in those of Franklin; nor in any of the numerous American and European writings of the period that have been examined. The only original passage that can be at all wrested to bear on this point is to be found in the Gentleman's Magazine for August, 1755. In the first statement of the battle, abounding in pardonable but manifest inaccuracies, it contains this remark: "It is, however, said that the slaughter among our officers was not made by the enemy; but as they ran several fugitives through the body to intimidate the rest when they were attempting in vain to rally them, some others, who expected the same fate, discharged their pieces at them; which, though loaded, they could not be brought to level at the French."[1] This assertion, though unsupported by contemporaneous or other respectable authority, possibly may be true. In 1854, while the writer visited the *locus in quo* in the hope of gaining some hitherto neglected circumstance of the expedition, he received a sufficient number of tales, it is true; but of which all, save two, were so absurdly false as not to merit even remembrance. An aged man who said that he had known Fausett declared that there were three brothers in the action, of whom one

---

[1] XXV. Gent. Mag., 380.

was slain by Braddock, and the other by the captain of
Thomas Fausett's own company; and that in a like manner the death of both was avenged. The importance of
this point will be presently seen.[1]

Let us now take up Fausett's own assertions. In 1781,
(twenty-six years after the defeat,) a subsequent writer in
the National Intelligencer (believed to have been the late
William Darby, Esq.) was cognizant of the common report
in Fayette County that this man had killed the General.
In 1794, he put the plain question to him: "Did you shoot
General Braddock?" and the reply was prompt and explicit: "I did shoot him!" As an apology, he added that for
the preservation of the rest of the army, the instant re-
moval of such an obstinate leader was inevitable. And
this narrative is further confirmed by the testimony of the
Hon. Andrew Stewart, of Uniontown, who often heard
Fausett make the same avowal. It also appears that he
was a man of unusual stature and of rude habits; dwelling alone in a mountain-cabin, earning a precarious subsistence by his rifle, and rarely herding with his kind but
to get drunk. His usual account of the transaction was
this: Joseph, his brother, in defiance of Braddock's injunctions, persisting in sheltering himself behind a tree, was
finally cut down by his infuriated commander; on which
Thomas, who from a little distance witnessed the whole,
instantly levelled his gun and shot Braddock down.[2] So

[1] At the time, I did not believe in the truth of a word of this story.

[2] Day's Hist. Coll. Penn. 335. Here occurs, too, another inconsistency.
In 1794, says the writer in the Intelligencer, Fausett declared himself to
be in his 70th year. In January, 1828, he died at the Laurel Hill, aged
114 years, says a clerical contributor to the Christian Advocate, who has
done much to extend the belief of the truth of the tradition. It is not

much for Fausett's own story. It does not satisfactorily appear that Thomas Fausett had any other brother in the action than Joseph; therefore it may be concluded there is either confusion or a positive falsehood in the various versions of the tradition lately cited. However this may be, it is certain that Thomas Fausett was enlisted at Shippensburg, Pennsylvania, by Captain Polson, into Captain Cholmondeley's company of the 48th regiment; and that, deserting from the same subsequently to the battle, he was not retaken by the 1st of September, 1755.[1] And as Captain Cholmondeley was killed in the fight, it is not impossible that it was he who slew Joseph Fausett and was in turn murdered by his brother. But, in the face of all the negative testimony that has been adduced, it is useless to propose the confessions of an ignorant peasant, uttered in his cups twenty years after, as proof of the manner of death of the chief of the army. Yet, it may be urged, Fausett is not singular in his tale : it is supported by the assertion of other witnesses. This is very true : let us see what their assertions are worth.

The first and most important witness is William Butler; who served throughout the Seven Years' War, under Braddock in 1755, under Forbes in 1758, and under Wolfe in 1759. He states that in Braddock's expedition he was marched, with twenty-five hundred others, from the camp

---

doubted that the reverend annotator believed all that he recited to have been a fact; but it is impossible for a man who was but 70 years old in 1794 to have attained 114 by 1828. The age of 97, as given by Hazard (I. Penn. Reg; 49), is patriarchal enough, and far more probable; but it is equally irreconcilable with Fausett's own statement.

[1] Penn. Gaz., No. 1394.

at Philadelphia, by way of Germantown and Reading, towards Du Quesne; that Dunbar, who had arrived at Baltimore, joined them on the route; and that Washington led four hundred riflemen. "At the time of the action, he was just off duty, near Washington's tent. Near there he saw Generals Braddock, Forbes, and Grant talking; and Braddock calling out to Captain Green to clear the bushes ahead by opening a range with his artillery. Then Washington came out, put his two thumbs into the arm-pits of his vest, made a little circle, and came into their presence and said, 'General, be assured, if you even cut away the bushes, your enemy can make enough of them artificially to answer their purposes of shelter and concealment: it will not answer.' Braddock, upon hearing this, turning to his officers, said sneeringly, 'What think you of this from a young hand,—a beardless boy?'" "He was a great user of snuff," adds Butler, "which he carried loose in his pocket; of middle stature, and thick set." He then goes on to the distinct declaration that the General was slain by "one Fawcett, brother of one whom Braddock had just killed in a passion: this last, who killed Braddock, was in the ranks as a non-commissioned officer: the former was a brave major, or colonel; by birth an Irishman. The soldier shot Braddock in the back; and this man, he said, he saw again in 1830, at or near Carlisle."[1]

Now, we are willing to admit that Butler, being in his 104th year when he put forth this story, may have mistaken its last date; since Fausett was dead and buried at the period when he said he was at Carlisle; but how shall

---

[1] II. Watson's Annals Phil. 140.

we get over the remainder of his chapter of blunders? In the first place, Braddock's army was never at Philadelphia; he never saw that city in his life. Nor did Dunbar join him from Baltimore, where he did not arrive, and probably never visited. There was no Captain Green in the army, nor any General Forbes, or Grant; nor was any such order given or conversation held. Washington had no command whatever in the army; he was merely attached to the staff; and the four hundred riflemen are more like Falstaff's men in green buckram than substantial beings of flesh and blood. Nor were there any tents at all pitched "at the time of the action." The last had been struck six hours before. In short, poor old Butler had so lamentably jumbled together in his mind the two expeditions of Forbes and Braddock (if, indeed, he ever served with the latter), that in repeating the last rhodomontade that imagination or some gasconading gossip had served him with, he could not keep the twain separate. At his age, when an old soldier shoulders his crutch and fights his battles o'er again, he is too apt to repeat, as of his own memory, the last idle tale that has been put into his mouth. But we cannot be expected, after finding every other of his statements unfounded, to place any credence in the most absurd of all.[1]

---

[1] Butler had another story, to the effect that he was sentinel before Braddock's tent one day when Washington approached. Instead of coming to the tent diagonally, as any one else would have done, he came marching down in a decided and — according to Butler's representation of the performance — in an exaggerated military step, and perfectly straight line. When parallel with the tent, he suddenly faced about, marched to its door, and informed Braddock that unless he procured a greater number of Indians and threw them out as scouts, the army would certainly be cut to pieces. This advice Braddock disdainfully repulsed.

The evidence of Billy Brown, a negro living at Frankford, Pennsylvania, taken in 1826, when he was ninetythree years old, is next adduced to confirm Fausett's story. But though he speaks with much hesitation and uncertainty as to the important fact, he gives us a sufficient number of other anecdotes to test the veracity of his recollections. He, too, is alleged to have been at the deaths of Braddock and Wolfe. Born in Africa, and brought a slave to this country at an early age, he loved to tell his hearers of the elephants of his native land, so prodigious as to make "quite a fog with their breath!" "He was present in that memorable fight as servant to Colonel Brown, of the Irish regiment, and was most of the time near the person of General Braddock. He confirmed the idea that he was shot by an American because he had killed his brother. He said that none seemed to care for it: on the contrary, they thought Braddock had some sinister design; for no balls were aimed at him! He kept on foot, and had all the time his hat bound across the top and under his chin with his white handkerchief. They suspected that the white emblem was a token of his understanding with the French. He told me," continues the relator of this conversation, "that Washington came up to him in the fight, and fell upon his knees to beseech him to allow him to use

Now, setting aside the improbability of this dramatic tale, let us simply point out the fact that the sentries for the General's tent were taken exclusively from the two regiments. Therefore Butler could not have been in the position he alleges. But the anecdote may be worthy of preservation, as showing a possible sentiment in the ranks that Braddock held Washington's advice as naught.

three hundred of his men in tree-fighting; and that the General cursed him, and said, 'I've a mind to run you through the body'; and swearing out, 'we'll sup to-day in Fort Du Quesne, or else in hell!'"[1]

Now, there was no Colonel Brown in the army. A Colonel Burton, indeed, there was; and the negro may have confounded their names; though, since he continued to serve the same master for eight years, it seems a little strange that he should stumble so on this point. Nor did Braddock fight unaimed at or on foot. He was continually mounted, and had four horses shot under him. The idea of putting Washington on his knees is too palpably false for comment.

The third and last account that remains to be examined is fathered by Daniel Adams, of Newburyport, Massachusetts, and may be shortly dealt with. In 1842, he proclaims what he had been told by one who had it from another, who was present at the occurrence. "He stated that the principal officers had previously advised a retreat, which the General pertinaciously refused; that after nearly all the principal officers were shot down, he was approached by a captain to renew the advice, whom he forthwith shot down. Upon seeing this, a lieutenant, brother of the cap-

---

[1] I. Watson's Ann., 602. II. *ib*., 141. Watson's MSS. in Penn. Hist. Soc., 63. It is not pleasant to thus doubt the genuineness of some of the stores garnered up by this worthy and laborious collector; but to ignore them entirely, or to admit them as true, would be equally repugnant to our convictions. It may be noted here, that as Braddock had no notion of reaching Du Quesne before the 11th, his alleged invocation was, to say the least, an oath of supererogation. It is odd that Ormsby puts the same expression into Forbes's mouth : "he would sleep the next night in the Fort or in hell!" II. O. T., 2.

tain, immediately shot Braddock. Several of the soldiers saw the act, but said nothing. Braddock wore a coat of mail in front, which turned balls in front; but he was shot in the back, and the ball was found stopped in front by the coat of mail." [1]

The reader is now in possession, *totidem verbis*, of all the evidence in the case; and may deduce his own conclusions. He will bear in mind the character and circumstances of the principal witness, and the inducements which a man who had deserted from his colours may find in a moment of intoxication to magnify his crime. Supposing he had killed his captain, it was a simple murder, calculated to excite disgust perhaps, but nothing further. But by substituting the commander's name, he became at once the pot-house hero; the cynosure of their neighboring eyes to whom the slaughter of a British general was become to be regarded as a praiseworthy achievement. He will likewise consider the credibility of the remaining witnesses, not one of whom could have known the fact of his own knowledge, since they unite in making poor Fausett a colonel, a major, or at least a captain, when he was but a private at sixpence *per diem*; and will notice the manifold errors with which dotage or ignorance had embroidered the tissue of their memory. No two unite on the same facts. If there be any force in the good old law maxim — Qui falsus in singulis, falsus est in omnibus — he will not be long in coming to a conclusion; but if he should still hold to the Fausett story, we can only commend him to the pages of Mandeville or Pinto; if any "historian" since the days of

Herodotus can pretend to appease such an appetite for the marvellous.

In considering the conduct of this battle, it is easy to perceive how readily victory might have been lured to perch upon an opposite banner. Had the American method of Indian-fighting been followed from the outset, the whole plan of the campaign must have been altered. But, pursuing the instructions under which he acted, there were several occasions when malicious fate would seem to have dashed the chalice from Braddock's lips. Thus, when he abandoned the design of passing to Fort Du Quesne by the head-waters of Turtle Creek, he lost a golden opportunity. And as it was, had his advanced party been but half an hour sooner in reaching the ravines, all might have been well. The invisibility of their foe was the chief feature in that contest which disconcerted the English. An enemy sheltered by trees only could never have so surprised them; the dusky forms, flitting from cover to cover, would soon have familiarized their eyes with the tactics of the foe; and though perhaps with heavy loss, they would probably have got the better of their adversaries. Instead of this, while men were dropping by scores on every side, not more than half a dozen Indians were seen by the majority of the troops at any one time during the fight; and the fire appeared to issue from the very bowels of the earth itself. So ignorant were all of the existence of the ravines, that when convinced by subsequent reflection that some such shelter must have been, it was the belief of the survivors that the French had prepared elaborate and artful entrenchments here, in which the army was involved.[1] Nothing was more easy than, as the column approached a part of the defile hitherto undefended, for a hundred warriors to glide unperceived under the cover to the spot, and at their very feet to open an instantaneous and murderous fire upon the bewildered troops. In vain the artillery swept the scene. The harmless balls passed ten feet above the heads of the savages, who lay concealed beneath the surface of the earth. A more astute or experienced leader would have had out his rangers beating the forest on every side, peering into every thicket and tangled dell, and would never have been left unacquainted with the precise topography of such a dangerous spot. Even after the slaughter had commenced, it would have been easy to have cleared the ravines, by bringing a field-piece to their mouths and with grape and cannister sweeping their channels from bottom to top, sending their naked inhabitants scattered and howling like wolves through the forest. Following this manœuvre, a column of grenadiers at the bayonet's point and properly supported on the upper plains, would have completed the business. The Indian has not that moral courage—the child of discipline—which will enable him to stand a charge. He dreads the cold steel. And though the front ranks of the storming party would perhaps have fallen to a man, the very nature of the passage would have protected the remainder; and few of the enemy would have had an opportunity of giving more than one fire. But it is too plain why these methods were not pursued.

[1] II. P. A., 383.   VI. C. R., 496.

It is ever an invidious task to point out how a lost field might have been won; but it was reserved for another leader in the same war to give a practical exemplification of the stratagem which turned the battle of Hastings, and of which Braddock might well have availed himself. Had he been as sagacious as Bouquet at Bloody Run, he would have exercised a manoeuvre so difficult and dangerous that nothing but the last necessity can justify its use; so ingenious that no Indians can ever hold out against it, if properly carried out.

So soon as the fortune of the day seemed perilous, had the rear-guard and wagons been quietly moved back to the river-side, and at least a portion of the pack-horses reconveyed across the stream, it would greatly have facilitated a retreat, without withdrawing any strength from the forces at the time engaged. This being done, the army might have countermarched in three divisions, as though retiring. The two wings should have proceeded in opposite diagonal directions towards the Monongahela, encouraging the enemy with an appearance of haste; while the centre slowly retraced its own steps, falling as it were in a perpendicular line upon the base of the triangle whose subtense was occupied by the rear-guard and whose sides were the courses of the wings. The Indians would inevitably have pursued, though at first with caution; and beyond a doubt a number of lives, particularly of the centre, would have been sacrificed. But when both factions reached the open woods of the first bottom, and the savages beheld the water dotted with wagons and crossing horses, their exultation would have known no limit, and hatchet in hand they would rush on the flight. Then would have been the moment to annihilate them. The rear-guard, widening its ranks to receive the thinned centre and to enable the artillery posted for the emergency to open on the foe, should attack him in front while the wings, in like wise facing about, fell upon his either flank. One discharge the troops might have poured in, and then given him the bayonet. The result would have been instant and inevitable. Enclosed between three crashing walls of steel, all converging to a common centre, the enemy would have been utterly and instantly crushed; and before that evening's sun was set, Fort Du Quesne would have been in flames and abandoned. These are no idle speculations; and though a manoeuvre like this requires a steady obedience and abundant nerve, yet its efficacy has been amply tested. And surely no men were more capable of its execution than Braddock's soldiers, whose discipline was perfect until three hours of unceasing disaster had thrown their souls back into a chaotic confusion where self-preservation was the only surviving thought.

The die was cast, however, and the victory was with those who could only abuse it. In the exuberance of their joy, the Indians had not bestirred themselves to make prisoners. Scalps were the first object of their search; and not only from the dead, but from the throbbing temples of the yet living, the bloody trophy was torn, and weltering in his gore the wretch was left to die of his wounds, or, more horrid still, to perish beneath the fangs of the wild creatures of the forest or the obscene beak of the bird of prey. Then the enraptured warriors turned to a harvest of spoil such as never before or since gladdened a savage eye. What share of the booty fell to the French or Canadians, we know not; probably, however, they managed to secure the money and the more valuable stores, while the ignorant native was busy in stripping the gaudy clothing from the corpses on the plain, and, frantic with joy, parading in the scarlet sash, brilliant gorget, and gold-laced coat of a murdered officer. The artillery was claimed by the garrison as the spoil of Louis XV.; but such were the difficulty of transporting the pieces and the apprehension of Dunbar's vicinity, that the howitzers and twelve-pounders were spiked and dismounted and left on the field, and the shells bursted. The brass six-pounders only were taken to the fort, where that very night a division of the plunder was made.[1]

Since nearly every Englishman with strength left to run had fled from the field, few but the wounded fell into the enemy's hands; and it not being their use to cumber themselves with infirm captives, these were speedily put to death. By an Indian report there were thirty prisoners, men and women, carried off by the Chesagechroanus.[2] But the evidence of William Johnson, a Pennsylvania resident during all this period at Venango, at Du Quesne, and among the Ohio Indians, is positive that there were but three of

---

[1] In March, 1756, the artillery (including the howitzers and mortars), captured here was sent to Niagara, and afterwards to Frontenac; and served the French a useful part in the war. In August, 1756, Montcalm opened his lines against Fort Ontario with a part of it. I. Pouchot, 43, 67. Penn. Gaz., Nos. 1389, 1393. I. Entick, 475. VI. C. R., 603.

[2] VI. C. R., 615. These may have been the Chaounaons or Shawanoes.

17

the English saved alive, and these women; one of whom was retained by the French commander at Venango, and the other two sent slaves to Canada.[1] A score of regulars, however, ignorant perchance of savage customs and not dreaming of other treatment than that of prisoners of war, being cut off from flight threw down their arms and surrendered. A Virginian, too, was captured;[2] and these are the only English that so far as can be ascertained remained in life when the victors left the field; yet of even this little band one-half were tomahawked ere they reached the Ohio. A darker departure was reserved for their fellows.

During all that anxious day, James Smith, an American captive languishing within the walls of Fort Du Quesne, listened with careful ear for the roll of the English drums, or explored with seeking eye the forest paths whence he looked for the coming of his deliverers.

An hour before sunset the French and Indians returning to the fort halted within a mile's distance and announced their success by a joyful uproar; discharging all their pieces and giving the scalp-halloo. Instantly the great guns responded, and the hills around re-echoed to their roar. Pushing hastily on, the majority of the savages soon appeared, blood-stained and laden with scalps, and uncouthly arrayed in the spoils of the army. Tall grenadier's caps surmounted their painted faces, and the regimental colors trailed disgracefully at their heels. With less disordered pace the French succeeded, escorting a long train of pack-horses borne down with plunder. Last of all, and while the parting light of day lingered on the

---

[1] VII. C. R., 342.

[2] Penn. Gaz., No. 1389.

beautiful bosom of the Ohio, appeared a small party who had dallied behind to make the needful preparations for the crowning scene of horror. Before them, stripped perfectly naked, their faces blackened and their hands bound behind their backs, with reluctant steps were driven twelve British regulars on whom God's sun had shone for the last time. Delirious with excitement, their barbarous conquerors could hardly wait for the tardy night to consummate their unhallowed joy. A stake was at once sunk on the opposite bank of the Alleghany, whither the crew repaired; the prisoners lost in dumb sorrow at the surprising fate which they now began to comprehend. Here one by one they were given to the most cruel and lingering of deaths. Bound to the post under the eyes of their remaining comrades and of the French garrison, who crowded the ramparts to behold the scene, they were slowly roasted alive. Coals from an adjacent fire were first applied to various parts of the victim's person. Sharp splinters of light dry pine wood were thrust into his flesh, and ignited to consume and crackle beneath the skin, causing the most exquisite tortures. His trunk was seared with red-hot gunbarrels; blazing brands were thrust into his mouth and nostrils; boiling whiskey was poured in flames down his throat, and deep gashes made in his body to receive burning coals. His eye-balls were gradually consumed by the thrusts of pointed sticks or the application of a heated ramrod; and the warrior was prized the most highly who could furthest prolong sensibility in his prey, and extract a renewed cry of anguish from the wretch who had almost ceased to suffer: "his weary soul hanging upon his trembling lips—

willing to take its leave, but not suffered to depart!" The last expedient was generally to scalp the poor creature, and on his bare, palpitating brain, flash gunpowder or throw a handful of live embers. Terrible as it may seem, the human frame will endure such torment for an hour or more ere vitality ceases ; consequently the horrors of this night endured till dawn, affording a scene unmatched by any other out of Pandemonium. The dark back-ground of the deep woods ; the river flickering in the glare of a score of huge fires kindled on its shore ; the shrieking soldier bound to the stake, and mingling his dolorous cries with those of his companions, foretasting their own woe ; and, to complete the picture, a thousand savages, their naked ghastliness made more hideous by paint, yelling like famished wolves, and waving aloft red torches or dripping tomahawks blood-encrusted to the heft, as with maniac bounds they danced like lubbar fiends around the prisoner. "It seemed," said an eye-witness, "as if Hell had given a holiday and turned loose its inhabitants upon the upper world." And, shame to tell, there on the opposite shore frowned the gloomy bastions of Fort Du Quesne, from whose ramparts, with the fair flag of France (never more sullied than on this occasion), heavily drooping above their heads, Contrecœur and his brave garrison beheld unmoved to remonstrance the terrific spectacle.[1]

[1] Smith's Narrative, in Drake, 184. When we contrast the excesses permitted to the savages in this war by Frenchmen of all ranks, from Contrecœur to St. Véran, with the conduct of the English leaders, humanity rejoices with national pride. Of 870 Indians in Amherst's army, 700 withdrew in one body at the capture of Fort Levi in 1760. They insisted on their right to massacre the captured Frenchmen ; but Sir Jeffrey sternly

Return we now to the army and its dead general. On the morning of July 14th he was buried, "decently but privately," in a spot purposely selected in the middle of the road; nor was care spared to close evenly the mouth of his grave, and to pass the troops and the train over the place, in order to efface any guide-marks by which sacrilegious and hostile hands might be enabled to disinter and insult his remains.[1] But this disgusting feat was reserved for other days and other men.[2] So soon as Braddock was beneath the sod, the march was resumed under Dunbar,

[1] Mr. Headley (XLIV. Graham's Mag., 255), gives a picturesque sketch of Braddock's interment by torch-light, and adds that the services for the burial of the dead were read by Washington; but the Journal is distinct that he was buried the next morning. It is probable, however, that the services of the church were recited; and since the chaplain was wounded, it is not improbable that Washington, the only active member of his family, paid this sad duty to his chief.

[2] Until the opening of the National Road, Braddock's was a thoroughfare between Baltimore and the Ohio. About 1823, while working on it, some laborers exposed his remains, still distinguishable by their "military trappings." "One and another took several of the most prominent bones, and the others were reinterred under the tree on the hill, near the National Road. Mr. Stewart of Uniontown (father of the Hon. Andrew Stewart), afterwards collected the scattered bones from the individuals who had taken them, and sent them, it is believed, to Peale's Museum in Philadelphia." Day's Penn., 334. I have essayed without success to trace further particulars of this disgraceful tale.

warned them that the first blow struck in this design should be the signal for his falling on them with his whole army. Even victory was too dear a purchase to a man of honor at such a rate. (Mante, 306.) But though no punishment in kind was inflicted by Amherst, the French Indians escaped not unscathed during the war. The destruction of Kittaning; the invasion of the Muskingum; the fall of Pontiac;—involved not only the loss of much life, but of national pride; and other scourges than the sword wasted their borders. Within a year the Abenakis, so active against Braddock, were visited with the small-pox, and nearly entirely extirpated. (II. Garn., 252.)

who, with 300 wounded in his ranks, arrived at Fort Cumberland on Tuesday, July 22nd, at two in the afternoon.[1] By his position in the rear and the sluggishness of his motions, this officer had already acquired the unflattering sobriquet of "Dunbar the Tardy;" and his conduct now encountered the censure of his superiors, the disgust of his equals, and even the criticism of his inferiors. At headquarters, his retreat was estimated as more disastrous than the defeat itself.[2]

During all this time, there was no thought in the colonies but of Braddock's certain triumph. In Philadelphia the warmer spirits, eager to echo back the first jubilant shout from the western mountains, were already taking about subscription papers, and preparing to kindle the staid city with festal fires. But the cooler counsels of Franklin tempered their zeal.[3] Upon the adherents of the Assembly, in particular, the disastrous intelligence came with a double sting, when they reflected how it would sharpen the Governor's invectives on their obstinacy and neglect.

---

[1] VI. C. R., 502.

[2] II. P. A., 387.   "What Dishonor," writes Shirley, "is thereby reflected on the British Army! Mr. Dunbar has ever been esteem'd an exceeding good Officer, but nobody here can guess at yᵉ Reason of his Retreat in the Circumstances he was in, and some severe Reflections are thrown out upon his Conduct; Some would have him sent with 500 Men to bring back what he bury'd with 1500."

[3] "I looked grave," he writes, "and said it would, I thought, be time enough to prepare the rejoicing when we knew we should have occasion to rejoice. They seemed surprised that I did not immediately comply with their proposal. 'Why, the d—l!' said one of them, 'you surely don't suppose that the fort will not be taken?' 'I don't know that it will not be taken; but I know that the events of war are subject to great uncertainty.'" I. Sp. Fr., 194.

At first, they would not confide in a syllable of the intelligence; and men even insulted Mr. Morris in the public streets, "for giving out that General Braddock was defeated;"[1] nor, indeed, did he in turn omit any occasion of blaming this matter on his opponents.

On July 11th, Col. Innes at Cumberland received the first uncertain news, and hurried away expresses to the neighboring provinces. Close at the heels of his flying posts came the runaway wagoners seeking their Pennsylvanian homes. Morris was in the interior at the moment, superintending the construction of the new road, and the transmission of supplies; and at Carlisle he satisfied himself of the miserable fact. The wagoners, examined under oath by him, in their confused accounts all united on the main point—that the army was annihilated. To confirm all the rest, moreover, came an open letter from one of Braddock's messengers, sent from post to post, and spreading terror as it passed; for it was marked to be read as it went at every hostel on the road; "by Mr. Bingham at the Sign of the Whip, and from that to be told at the Indian Queen." On the 16th, the Governor gave his Assembly a week's notice to meet him at Philadelphia, and urged the instant organization of such a force as should enable Dunbar to resume the offensive, ere yet the defenceless borders were overrun by the foe.[2] This too he warmly pressed on Shirley, to whom the chief command of all the King's American armies was now fallen. Meanwhile Dunbar announced his intention to abandon everything, and to put his troops, in the month of July, in winter-

[1] VI. C. R.. 480.

[2] Ibid, 481.

quarters at Philadelphia. Against this Morris remonstrated, and effectively pleaded to have at least a few men left in the posts west of the Susquehannah. Dunbar called a council, whose report shows conclusively what cowardly or stultified infatuation must have governed the destruction near the Meadows; since it appears that the troops being now half-naked and the munitions naught, the army had become more demoralized than ever. Leaving then a considerable part of his still remaining stores with the Virginia and Maryland troops at Fort Cumberland (of which place Col. Innes had been appointed Governor), on the 2nd of August he started, 1200 strong, for Philadelphia. Much to Dinwiddie's indignation, who considered that these at least had been ordered by the King for the especial service of the Ohio campaign, he took with him too the three Independent Companies. It may be noticed here that beside those who had recovered, and the small proportion that had succumbed after reaching it, there were still 300 of Braddock's army left at the fort wounded and unable to travel.[1]

General Shirley's first orders (6th August) were that Dunbar should march the 44th and 48th, by Philadelphia and Jersey, direct to Albany; leaving the three Independent Companies at Cumberland. But by Morris's influence on the 12th he issued supplementary orders that those of the 6th should be followed only in case it were found impossible to carry out a renewed design against Du Quesne. The army was to be put in the best order possible, and, when united with the expected Pennsylvania, Maryland,

and Virginia provincials, to fall on Du Quesne or Presqu' Isle. Failing success in this, he was to cover the English frontiers.[1]

This scheme was never undertaken. The Assembly and the governor still persevered in their opposite stand-grounds; and no troops were raised in Pennsylvania. The three colonies came into no concurrent measures; and, to crown all, Dunbar and his men had no notion to repeat the horrors of the 9th of July.[2] In truth, he made a very reasonable explanation of the impropriety of reattacking the French, which was approved by every field-officer and the five oldest captains of his command. He pleaded the advanced season (it was now near the end of August) to begin provincial preparations; the fact that all his artillery was but four six-pounders, the balance being destroyed or strengthening the walls of the French Fort; and the destitution of the troops. There were not half enough tents, and all sorts of clothing and camp equipage was absolutely required. Defections, too, were incessant. By September, there were no less than one hundred and seventy-five deserters from his immediate command.[3] In short, as Morris wrote at the time to Shirley, "they are in a very bad order; the officers disagreeing with one another, and

---

[1] VI. C. R., 559.   [2] II. P. A., 530.   VI. C. R., 602.

[3] See Gov. Morris's proclamation of 6th Sept., 1755 (Penn. Gaz., No. 1394), where a guinea a head is offered for their capture. In the long list of names, it may be noticed that of the 74 deserters from the 44th, seventy-one were American recruits; three only having come with it from Ireland. So of the 48th, whose 46 deserters consisted of forty-three enlistments and but three Irish drafts. The three Independents had fifty-five deserters. In the same journal (No. 193) we find Capt. Adam Stephen advertising four deserters from his command at Cumberland.

most of them having a contempt for the Colonel that commands them, while the men are in a poor and ragged condition, and don't relish another campaign, as it is called." [1]

With a persistive aversion to the scene of danger, unusual, to say the least, in the history of British arms, the troops, with their backs ever to the distant foe, attempted nothing more. With all his faults, certainly Braddock could never have counselled such a course. Moving languidly through Shippensburg and Lancaster, the army, like a scotched snake, "dragged its slow length along," till at last, on August 29th, it reached Philadelphia and encamped on Society Hill; the city having refused to provide quarters. [2] Here, with tender solicitude, the suffering troops were cared for. The naked were clothed, the hungry fed, the sick and wounded hospitably treated. Churchman and Quaker united with cha-

[1] VI. C. R., 596. "I find, also," continues Morris, "that the scheme is to loiter as much time and make as many difficulties as possible, that these troops may not move from this place (Philadelphia), or, if that cannot be done, then, that they may go no further than Albany this season."

[2] VI. C. R., 533, 604. Society Hill was mainly comprehended within Second and Front, and Union and Pine Streets; but its slopes probably extended to Fourth and to Cedar Streets. It was then a considerable elevation, mostly unoccupied and unenclosed, and used for public purposes by the citizens. Here was the provincial flag-staff, when, so early as 1730, the Assembly ordered the royal standard to be displayed on Sundays and holidays; and here Whitfield, with an eloquent vociferation, discovered to the rapt multitude that Tillotson was no "Christian believer." A water-battery (perhaps the earliest fortification here) was erected beneath its bank by Franklin's famous "Association;" and whenever a salute was to be fired, this hill was the chosen spot. The erection of the market-house in Second Street at last caused this district to be built up and the hill to be cut down and graded; and probably there are now comparatively few residents of Southwark who dream of its ancient elevation. Dunbar's troops were encamped on the west of Fourth, between Pine and Cedar Streets. I. Watson, 329, &c.

racteristic zeal in the fulfilment of duties alike recommended by Religion and Loyalty. In fine, the troops had scarce been here three weeks ere the officers took occasion to testify their gratitude or their gallantry by a ball to the ladies; which was given in the State House on Monday, the 22d of September.[1] On October 1st, fifteen hundred strong, the army marched for New York and Albany by Perth Amboy.[2]

Dunbar's pusillanimous retreat before no foe (for their own accounts show that the enemy, fearful of his advance, scampered as quickly back to Du Quesne lest he should fall on them, as he, dreading their attack, did from the Great Meadow), if dictated by a cold valor, was surely not executed in sound discretion.[3] In every quarter the colonies for whose protection he was sent were disconcerted by his conduct. All who could, fled to the closer settlements;

[1] I. Watson, 285. When, during the revolution, each other religious society in Philadelphia had given to the Whigs the use of a church for their quarters or hospitals, the late Col. Biddle (father of Thomas Biddle, Esq.,) was deputed to select a Quaker meeting-house for the like purpose. Col. Biddle was himself a Friend, though, in girding on the sword and becoming a man of war, he had greatly scandalized his brethren. He could therefore say to his ancient associates, "We only ask you to treat the Continentals as you did Braddock's soldiers after their defeat: give them a flannel jacket apiece and an apple-pie dinner!"

[2] Penn. Gaz., Nos. 1397, 1399.

[3] Thomas Dunbar had been Lieutenant-Colonel of the 18th (Royal Irish) Foot; and, 29th April, 1752, was named Colonel of the 48th. In Nov. 1755, his regiment was given to another; he being sent into honorable retiracy as Lieutenant-Governor of the city and garrison of Gibraltar, with a salary of £730, which post he filled so late as 1765. Though he was never again actively, or even independently, employed, he was made a major-general Jan. 18th, 1758; and a Lieutenant-General December 18th, 1760. He was dead before 1778.

and by early autumn, the borders were ravaged with fire and sword.[1] The history of the steps that ensued in defence of the middle provinces; of the savage and desolating war that laid their confines in ruins, and swept, almost unopposed, over the greater part of Pennsylvania; or of the subsequent career of Dunbar's soldiery, now withdrawn from this portion of the stage, do not come within the compass of our story. A brief glance at the fate of Fort Du Quesne subsequent to the battle must conclude the narrative.

Immediately on their victory, many of the French troops seem to have been sent to the more northern posts; whence, probably, they had, for this urgency, been withdrawn. The greater number of the Indians, too, were speedily dispersed; seeking their homes ere yet the fresh lustre of victory began to dim. Nor did they all part from their allies on friendly terms. The Ottawas, who are said to have been five hundred strong in the battle, already provoked by the conduct of the French on the field, now fell into hot dispute with them in the division of the spoil. Casting scornfully back the hatchet they had received from Contrecoeur, they vowed henceforward to ally themselves with his enemies. As they left the fort, and under the very eye of its garrison, they encountered two Frenchmen, whom they unhesitatingly killed and scalped. This done, they disappeared in the forest gloom.[2] The troops, hastening to Frontenac, uncertain if it had not already fallen before Braddock's arms, on the 1st of August encountered other savage bands, gay in the spoils they had stripped from the slain; who, by the waters of Erie, gave them the first advices of the rout of the Monongahela.[1]

For several months longer M. de Contrecœur continued in command at Fort Du Quesne. It does not appear that he was considered to possess all the requisite talents for the maintenance of his difficult and precarious position; but it was not until after Montcalm's arrival in May, 1756, and his conference with Vaudreuil at Montreal, that he was superseded by the more energetic Dumas. In anticipation of the nine thousand men which the English were expected to bring to bear upon this post and Niagara, thirty-five hundred Canadians and savages were at this time posted along the lines from Lake Erie, by the Ohio, to the Illinois; but the fall of Oswego, and the disarrangement of the English plans, prevented, for a season, the threatened attack. The expense to France of its Ohio defences during the year 1756 did not fall far short of three millions of francs.[2]

Meanwhile, the English, though they effected nothing, were not idle. Instantly on Dunbar's retreat, Dinwiddie proposed to Pennsylvania and Maryland to unite with his government in building a fort at the Great Crossing or the Meadow in the ensuing October. His notion was to furnish it with six guns from Cumberland, and, burning the woods for a mile about to prevent covert for an enemy, to garrison it during the winter of 1755–6 with eight hundred men.[3] Unfortunately, this plan fell through. Had it been adopted, it would have been a mighty protection to the English set-

[1] I. Pouchot, 37. [2] Ibid, 84. II. Garneau, 240, 253.
[3] VI. C. R., 602.

tlements. For two years, the French position on the Ohio was as a floodgate to open ruin and woe upon the adjacent colonies; and though its destruction was ever a main object, yet opinions differed as to the wisdom of attacking it directly or through its connections on the Lakes. In December, 1755, Shirley held a council at New York; where the plans of the ensuing campaign, including the reduction of all the Ohio establishments, were resolved on; but, as has just been noticed, they were not destined to any result. In the early autumn of 1757, (or perhaps sooner,) M. de Ligneris relieved Dumas in his command; and about the same time, reinforcements were furnished from Canada to the number of four hundred men.[1] In the summer of 1758, however, Brigadier-General John Forbes had undertaken its reduction. With three hundred and fifty men of the Royal Americans, twelve hundred of Montgomery's Highlanders, and sixteen hundred Virginia and twenty-seven hundred Pennsylvania provincials (making a total of fifty-eight hundred and fifty men, beside one thousand wagoners), he set out from Philadelphia. At Raystown, he halted and sent forward Bouquet, with two thousand men, to occupy the Loyalhanna. Conceiving himself able to its capture, this officer imprudently detached Major Grant, with eight hundred men, to make the necessary observations; but the party was surprised and dreadfully cut up by M. Aubry, with seven or eight hundred Frenchmen and an unknown number of savages. Following up their victory, they soon advanced against Bouquet himself, who was entrenched in a position to which, in honor of a favorite general, was

[1] VII. C. R., 28.　II. Garneau, 259.

given the title of Fort Ligonier. It was with difficulty that they were repulsed. At this juncture, Forbes was almost tempted to abandon the enterprise; but the good news he presently received persuaded him to resume his route.

Their triumph at Grant's Hill had wrought the ruin of the foe. The Ottawas, Ojibwas, Pottawattamies, and Wyandots gathered thither, since July, from the distant lakes, believing that the English were now entirely discomfited, had returned to their deserted families and homes. The troops from Detroit and the Illinois had likewise retired; and the utmost strength of De Ligneris, who was still in command, did not exceed five hundred men. English emissaries, too, among the neighboring Indians, and the conciliating gifts and promises of the Quakers, had not been working in vain. The Ohio tribes were inclined to a peace. No persuasion could tempt them to come to the relief of the French; and as the overwhelming army of Forbes drew near, De Ligneris, after firing the buildings, and destroying the stores and all that he could of the works, retired with the garrison to Fort Machault, on Lake Erie, embarking his artillery for the Illinois, and, without a blow, abandoned the long-desired and dearly-bought prize to the English. On the 25th of November, 1758, the standard of Great Britain was unopposedly displayed upon the dismantled fortress.[1]

During the 24th, Forbes had encamped at Turtle Creek, twelve miles' distance from the Ohio, where his council advised him that the provisions and forage were so nearly

[1] Garneau, 287. Smith's Narr., 233. Mante, 157.

exhausted as to render a retreat a question of grave propriety. With a furious oath he spurned their monitions, resolved to carry the fort the next day, or to leave his body beneath its walls; and orders were issued for an early march. That very evening his scouts reported that in the distance they had discovered the smoke of a wide conflagration; and at midnight the camp was startled by the dull, heavy sound of a remote explosion; and it was rightly conjectured that the enemy, with purpose or by accident, had destroyed their magazine. Encouraged by this view, the army pushed eagerly on; the provincials in their fringed hunting-shirts and modest uniform leading the way.[1] Next, with solid tread and disciplined array, came the Royal Americans, their dark scarlet coats faced with blue, and their drums beating a lively march. In a litter in their midst reclined the wasted form of their dying old general, known among the savages for his indomitable obstinacy by the title of the Head of Iron. Last of all, in a long and picturesque line, followed the 77th Highlanders in kilts and belted plaids, the "petticoat warriors" of Indian sarcasm.[2]   Apprehensive of an ambush, the troops moved on in wary step; for Forbes alone was aware of the rumored evacuation, and he was too cautious to be thrown off his guard by placing implicit reliance on its truth. As they

[1] Wm. Butler (before cited), says it was green turned up with buff. II. Watson, 139.

[2] Nothing could surpass the horror of the Highlanders at the barbarous customs of Indian battle, or their rage at the well-comprehended insults which were offered to themselves. At Grant's defeat, a flying Scot reported the fate of his comrades. "They were a' beaten," he said, "and he had seen Donald M'Donald up to his hunkers in mud, and a' the skeen aff his head!" (Howe's Virg., 205.)

approached the fort the route fell into a long, open race-path, where the savage was wont to pass his prisoners through the ordeal of the gauntlet; and here a dismal prospect met their eyes. On either side a long row of naked stakes were planted in the ground, on each of which grinned in decaying ghastliness the severed head of a High-lander killed or captured under Grant; while beneath was insultingly displayed the wretch's kilt. Disgusted and provoked at the scene, the Americans quickened their pace and hastened on. The next moment the 77th came suddenly upon the ground.

One who was present among the advanced provincials relates, that the first intimation given by the Scots of their discovery of the insulted remains of their butchered bro-thers, was a subdued, threatening murmur, like the angry buzzing of a swarm of bees. Rapidly swelling in violence, it increased to a fierce, continuous, low shriek of rage and grief, that none who listened to would willingly hear again. In this moment, officers as well as men seem to have aban-doned every sentiment but of quick and bloody vengeance, and, inspired by a common fury, cast all discipline to the winds. Their muskets were dashed upon the ground, and bursting from the ranks, the infuriated Gael, with bran-dished claymore, rushed madly forth with hope to find an enemy on whom to accomplish retribution. Startled at the sudden sound of swiftly-tramping feet, the amazed provincial looked round to see the headlong torrent sweep by, burthening the air with imprecations, and foaming, said he, "like mad boars engaged in battle." When we consider the provocation that had so excited their noble rage, it is almost a matter of regret that of all the cruel band there remained not one behind. The fort was in flames, and the last boat of the flying Frenchmen was disappearing in the evening mist that hung around Smoky Island. The coronach sung by the waters of fair Loch Lomond or in the gloomy pass of Glencoe was not yet to awake a responsive sorrow in the breast of the widows of the foe.[1]

Since 1755 a smaller work had been added to the fortifications of Du Quesne; built about two hundred yards distant from the first, so as to more effectually command the Alleghany, by which their connection with Canada was preserved. The scientific Bouquet pays a suitable testimony to their strength. But now they were a heap of smoking ruins, and the stacks of thirty chimnies alone remained to point out the place of the houses. The enemy had departed in such haste as to leave unsprung the mine which was to explode the magazine of Du Quesne; and here the victors gathered the only *spolia optima* of the expedition; sixteen barrels of powder and ball and "a cartload of scalping-knives." A tenable post was speedily erected from the ruins of the old, to which was now given the name of FORT PITT; and leaving two hundred men to garrison it through the winter, Forbes soon wended his way back to Philadelphia, where he died early in March, 1759.

---

[1] I. O. T, 181 ; II. ib , 2. It is sad to relate that after Grant's defeat M. de Ligneris was so base as to deliver up five of the prisoners to be burned at the stake on the parade-ground of the fort by his confederate savages. The remainder were tomahawked in cold blood. What countless scenes of like barbarity were enacted here during the war cannot be computed. The narrative would defile a full page in History : but happily for human nature, the memory of these infamies lies buried with their perpetrators.

His body rests in the chancel of Christ Church in that city.[1]

Before marching from Fort Pitt, however, Forbes took care to perform a sacred duty. It was well known that the unburied bones of Braddock's army lay bleaching on the ground, and he was resolved to pay this last, late tribute to their memory. Himself not only a Scot but a native of Halket's own shire, his affectionate zeal was prompted by the presence of a son and brother. The then Sir Peter Halket, a major of the 42nd, had come to America and accompanied Forbes for no other end than to ascertain, with what certainty he might, the fate of his father. A lingering hope haunted his soul that his kindred might not have been slain outright, and were possibly even yet captives among the foe. Accordingly, with other officers of the Highland regiment, Sir Peter set forth with a company of Pennsylvania Rifles under Captain West, an elder brother of Benjamin West the painter. With him as guides went a few Indians from the neighborhood, who had fought for the French on that fatal day.

"Captain West and his companions proceeded through the woods, and along the banks of the river, towards the scene of the battle. The Indians regarded the expedition as a religious rite, and guided the troops with awe and in profound silence. The soldiers were affected with sentiments not less serious, and as they explored the bewildering labyrinths of those vast forests, their hearts were often melted with inexpressible sorrow; for they frequently found skeletons lying across the trunks of fallen trees — a

[1] I. O. T., 183, 189.

mournful proof to their imaginations, that the men who sat there had perished of hunger, in vainly attempting to find their way to the plantations. Sometimes their feelings were raised to the utmost pitch of horror by the sight of bones and skulls scattered on the ground—a certain indication that the bodies had been devoured by wild beasts; and in other places they saw the blackness of ashes among the relics—the tremendous evidence of atrocious rites."[1]

In reply to his anxious questions, one of his tawny guides had already told Halket, that he recollected during the combat to have seen an officer fall beneath such a remarkable tree as he should have no difficulty in recognizing; and that at the same moment another rushing to his side was instantly shot down, and fell across his comrade's body. As they drew near the spot, the detachment was halted, and the Indians peered about through the trees to recall their memories of the scene. With speaking gesture, they briefly discoursed in their own tongue. Suddenly and with a shrill cry, the Indian of whom we have spoken sprang to the well-remembered tree. While the troops rested on their arms in a circle around, he and his companions searched among the thick-fallen leaves. In a moment two gaunt skeletons were exposed lying together, the one upon the other, as they had died. The hand that tore away their scalps had not disturbed their position; but no sign remained to distinguish the relics from the

[1] Galt's Life of West, p. 65. The unknown and innumerable cruelties of the French savages, as has already been mentioned, can never be demonstrated; and imagination itself can but faintly picture their horrors.

hundred others that strewed the ground. At the moment Sir Peter remembered him of a peculiar artificial tooth which his father bore. The bones were then separated, and an examination of those which lay undermost at once solved all doubts. "It is my father!" exclaimed the unhappy youth, as he sunk into the arms of his scarce less affected friends.

Brief and stern, as befits a soldier buried upon the battle-field, were the rites that followed. Wrapped in a Highland plaid, the twain who "in death were not divided," were interred in a common grave. In lieu of solemn dirges and the passing bell, the rattling sounds of musketry awoke the long-slumbering echoes of the mountains as the customary volleys were fired above their breasts. As the chasm was being closed, a stone was brought from the hill-side and placed within its mouth. Overgrown now with tall grass, this and the waning memories of a few old men alone point out the spot where for nine-and-ninety years have slept well the brave, the accomplished, the unfortunate representatives of a chivalrous line.

Thus, remote from the dust of their fathers, in unmoted, unhonored graves, rest the bones of Braddock and of his scarce less unfortunate subordinate. A forest oak appropriately points out the sepulture of the first; but this memorial will not long serve to fulfil its task, since its system is already touched by the finger of decay, and its blasted crest seems to relate with a melancholy significance to not only his fate to whom it owes a name, but to its own prospective doom.[1] Less perishable than the productions of

---

[1] The wood-cut upon page 280 of this volume gives a very accurate representation of this tree. The original drawing was made, during the

nature, the handiworks of art have remained to link the interest of later times with the associations of the past. The sash in which the body of the General was carried from the field, is said to be yet preserved in the family of the late President Taylor, to whom it was presented during the Mexican campaign through the intervention of General Gaines. Of its history during the interim, nothing is said; but a detailed description of its present appearance and the circumstances under which it came into General Taylor's hands are given us.[1] The reader will recollect that for a long period it was the custom of officers to wear with their uniform a sash of scarlet silken net-work, the use of which was to bear them, if wounded, from the ground. On that of Braddock the date of its manufacture (1707) is wrought in the woof; and the dark stains upon its texture still exist, mute but unfailing witnesses of the fatal stroke.

After the burial of the Halkets, in a large shallow pit hard by were cast what remained of about four hundred soldiers; this done, the troops returned to Fort Pitt, satisfied with having at least removed from sight so many of the most melancholy testimonials of their misfortunes. But the work was incomplete: twenty-one years after, when Jasper (subsequently Mr. Justice) Yeates visited the field, he found it strewed with skulls and bones, and the trees around, to the height of twenty feet from the earth, scarred with musket bullets and cannon balls.[2] When

[1] De Hass : Hist. Western Virg. 129.

[2] Galt's West. VI. Haz. Reg., 104. In 1854 I was accompanied to this spot by a garrulous old man alleging himself the son of one of the

summer of 1854, by that skilful artist, Mr. Weber : by whom it was presented to the Historical Society of Pennsylvania.

peace returned and the farmer's plough was passed over the spot, the scene of the thickest of the fight became known as the Bullet Field. But fifty years of cultivation have wrought their customary effect; and where once the hill-sides ran red with blood down to the stream below, now

Peaceful smiles the harvest,
And stainless flows the tide.

A more tranquil, rural landscape than that at this day presented by the battle-ground of the Monongahela cannot well be imagined. The ploughman no longer turns up in his labors the evidences of war; and it is difficult, at first blush, to recognize the features of the scene. As yet, how-

party who buried the Halkets. He was possessed with the vulgar idea that there was considerable treasure upon the bodies, and only needed a little countenancing to explore the ground. It is hoped that the discouragement he received will preserve this grave from such an unhallowed violation as attended Braddock's. It is singular what an infatuation on this subject obtains in the common mind. The accidental discovery by an Irish laborer on a railway cutting of twenty golden guineas among a mass of bones sufficed to set in a ferment the souls of many of the lower classes about Braddock's Field. If these may be relied on, it would seem that a little harvest of dollars was once fished from the river where they had laid since his defeat, by a neighboring farmer. But probably the tale is entirely the creature of a clumsy imagination. There have, however, been found other and more interesting relics of the French occupation of Du Quesne. Some of their artillery they appear to have sunk in the Ohio, when they evacuated the fort: and M'Kee's Rocks, just below the mouth of Chartier's Creek, is pointed out as the particular spot. One of their gun-carriages was not long since discovered here; and in the siege of Fort Henry (Wheeling), in 1782, by the British and Indians, the defendants found their account in the possession of a cannon similarly obtained. De Hass, 47, 266.

ever, swale and valley and ravine remain to mark the various courses of the fray ; but ere long these too will be obliterated or concealed by the growing hamlet that lies hard by ; and the physical traces of the event we have sought to chronicle will be lost to sight forever.

Braddock's Grave.

Captain Orme's Journal.

[BRITISH MUSEUM: KING'S MSS., No. 212. PRESENTED
BY KING GEORGE IV.]

Sir:

I am ordered to send this packet to you to be deliver'd to his Royal Highness. I am sorry the plans are not finished, but I am to have them to-morrow night.

Thursday morning.

Sir

Y^r most hum^{ble} and obed^t servant,

Rob^T. Orme.

[This letter was doubtless addressed to Col. Napier, the Duke of Cumberland's aid-de-camp.]

(282)

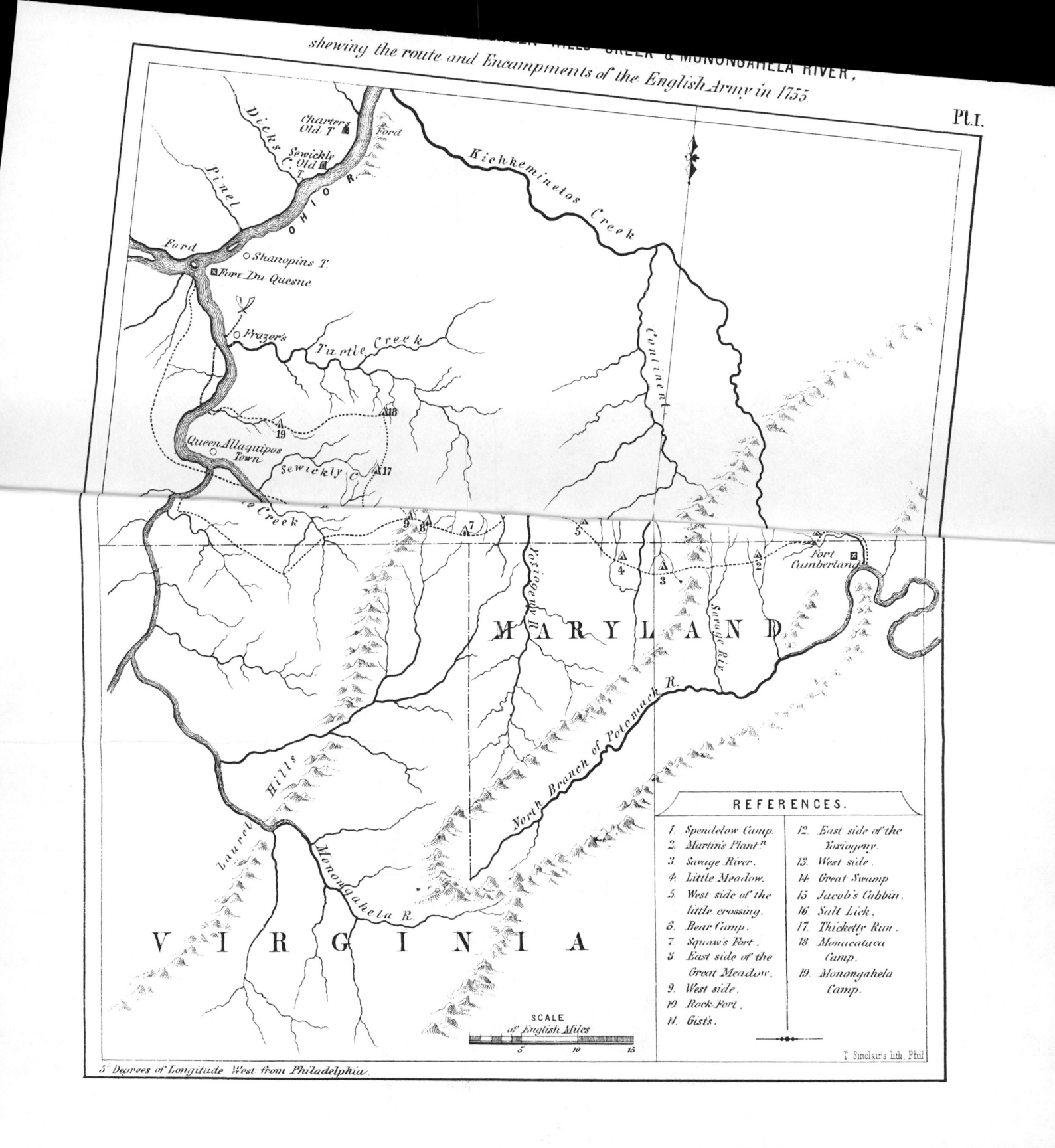

shewing the route and Encampments of the English Army in 1755.

Pl. I.

REFERENCES.

1. Spendelow Camp.
2. Martin's Plant.ⁿ
3. Savage River.
4. Little Meadow.
5. West side of the little crossing.
6. Bear Camp.
7. Squaw's Fort.
8. East side of the Great Meadow.
9. West side.
10. Rock Fort.
11. Gist's.
12. East side of the Yoxiogeny.
13. West side.
14. Great Swamp.
15. Jacob's Cabbin.
16. Salt Lick.
17. Thicketty Run.
18. Monacatuca Camp.
19. Monongahela Camp.

SCALE
of English Miles

5   10   15

5° Degrees of Longitude West from Philadelphia.

T. Sinclair's lith. Phil.

JOURNALS.

THE General arrived at Hampton in Virginia, the 20th of February, 1755, and set out immediately for Williamsburgh, where Commodore Keppel agreed to meet him, to settle the properest place for the disembarkment of the Troops. Orders were left on board the Centurion to be delivered to each Transport as she arrived, directing the commanding officer to send the sick on shore to the hospitals provided for them by Sʳ John Sᵗ Clair; and orders were given to Mr. Hunter, the Agent at Hampton, to supply the sick and well with fresh provisions at the fullest allowance.[1]

---

[1] Robert Orme, the author of this Journal, entered the army as an ensign in the 35th Foot. On 16th Sept. 1745, he exchanged into the Coldstreams, of which he became a lieutenant, April 24, 1751. He was never raised to a captaincy, though always spoken of as such. (II. MacKinnon, 484.) He probably obtained leave of absence to accompany General Braddock, with whom he was a great favorite. He was an honest and capable man, says Shirley (VI. C. R., 404), and it was fortunate that the General was so much under his influence. He brought letters of introduction from Thomas Penn to Gov. Morris (II. P. A., 195), and seems to have made a most favorable impression on all whom he encountered. Two months after the battle we find him a guest of Morris's, and nearly recovered of his wound. "Cap-

(283)

The General acquainted Governor Dinwiddie with his Majesty's pleasure, that the several assemblies should raise a sum of money to be employed towards defraying the expences of the Expedition, And desired he would propose it

tain Orme is going to England," writes he to Gen. Shirley on Sept. 5th, 1755 (II. P. A., 400), "and will put the affair of the western campaign in a true light, and greatly different from what it has been represented to be; and you know his situation and abilities gave him great opportunities of knowing everything that passed in the army or in the colony, relative to military matters, and I am sure he will be of great use to the Ministry in the measures that may be concerted for the future safety and defence of these provinces." * * "The opportunities which Mr. Orme will have with the Duke, and all the King's ministers, upon his return, of explaining American affairs, makes it quite necessary that you should agree in general in your representations, that both may have the greater weight; and my friendship for you obliges me to hint this matter for your consideration, that you may in your letters to the Ministry refer to him, and give him an opportunity of enforcing what you may write; the substance of which you will, I believe, think it necessary to communicate to him." Orme went from Philadelphia to New York, whence, or from Boston, he embarked for England. In Oct. 1756, he resigned his commission in the Guards (probably on occasion of his marriage), and retired into a private life. It seems that Orme was as bold in the boudoir as on the battle-field, and had already before going to America, "made some noise in London by an affair of gallantry." On his return, a mutual attachment sprung up between himself and the Hon. Audrey Townshend, only daughter of Charles, 3d Viscount and the celebrated Audrey (Harrison), Lady Townshend. The lady had no little motive of interest in one who had gone through an American campaign; for of her brothers, one, Lieut.-Col. Roger Townshend, was slain in this very war at Ticonderoga (July 25, 1759); and another, George (the first Marquess), succeeded to Wolfe's command at the capture of Quebec. However, much to the displeasure of her family, who had destined her for Lord George Lenox, she was married to Capt. Orme, and went to reside at Hartford, Eng. Nothing further can be traced of Captain Orme, save that he died in Feb. 1781. It is more than likely, however, that he belonged to the family of that Robert Orme whose name seems through continued generations to be identified with that of the East India Company. (III. Walp. Corr., 115, 144 II. Collins' Peerage, 473.)

to his Assembly; And that his Majesty also expected the Provinces to furnish the Troops with provisions and carriages. The General desired the Governor would use all imaginable dispatch in raising and convening the Levies to augment the two Battalions to 700 each. He also proposed to the Governor to make an establishment for some provincials, amongst which he recommended a Troop of light horse.

The Governor told the General his Assembly had voted twenty thousand pounds, which sum was to be employed in the purchasing provisions, and the payment of their own troops. That many men were already raised, and that Sr John St Clair had promised him to select the best for the two Regiments, and that the others should be formed into Companies; accordingly two of Hatchet men or carpenters, six of Rangers, and one troop of light Horse were raised, and their pay fixed at the same, in the Currency of that Country, as our Officers of the same rank in sterling. Alexandria was named as the head Quarters, as the most convenient place for forming and cloathing them.

Sr John St Clair[1] came to Williamsburgh and informed the General of his having draughted the best men of the Virginia Levies for the two Battalions; and that about three hundred which were not of proper size remained for the Provincial Companies. Sr John St Clair laid before the

---

[1] St. Clair remained for a long time in service in America. On the 20th March, 1756, he was made a Lieut.-Col. of the 60th; in Jan. 1758, the local rank of Colonel in America was bestowed on him; and on Feb. 19th, 1762, he was made a full Colonel. He is said to have dwelt near Tarbet, in Argyleshire. At the defeat he "was shot through the body, under the right pap," (Sharpe's MS. Corr.), but soon recovered.

General a Roll of the Independent Companies, upon which were several men from sixty to seventy years of age, lame and everyway disabled; many were inlisted, only for a term of one, two, or three years; some were without discipline and very ill-appointed; in short, they were Invalids with the ignorance of militia. These were all to be recruited with men who would otherwise have served in the Regiments or Virginia Companies.

Sr John St Clair gave General Braddock a plan for cantoning the two Regiments; one, with part of the Artillery, was to disembark at Alexandria, where five Companies were to remain; two and a half were to canton at Frederick in Maryland, half a one at Conegogee, one at Marlborough and one at Bladensburgh. The other Regiment and the rest of the Artillery were to disembark about twenty miles from Fredericksburg upon the Potomack, at which place and Falmouth five Companies were to be cantoned, and the other five at Winchester. As these Cantonments, of only a thousand men, took in a circuit of more than three hundred miles, the General thought it advisable to encamp them on their arrival; especially as the severity of the weather was then over. He knew that much confusion must arise in disembarking at different places: That it would be impossible to cloath, arm and discipline the Levies when so much dispersed, and that soldiers are sooner and better formed in Camps than in Quarters. He therefore, in conjunction with Mr. Keppel, fixed upon Alexandria to disembark and encamp at; and the Levies for the two Regiments were ordered to that place.

The General desired Governor Dinwiddie would inform him of the present disposition of the Indians towards the English; what Nations and number he might expect, and what steps were already taken to obtain them.

The Governor said he had sent a proper person [1] to bring with him the Cherokee and Catawber nations, the latter being about one hundred and twenty fighting-men, and much the bravest of all the Indians; He added a peace was to be concluded at Winchester in April, between the Catawbers and the Six Nations through the mediation of his Government: That he had intended to be present at the Congress; but that he should be prevented by the meeting of his Assembly. However, he would take care, at the Ratification of the Peace, that they should take up the hatchet, and act under the General. [2]

Mr Dinwiddie laid before the General contracts made for eleven hundred head of cattle, eight hundred of which were to be delivered in June and July, and three hundred in August; he said that he had also written to Governor Shirley, for a large quantity of salt fish, that a great deal of flour was already at Fort Cumberland, and that the assembly of Pensylvania had promised to deliver flour, to the amount of five thousand pounds of their currency, at the mouth of Conegogee, in April, which was to be carried up the Potomack to Fort Cumberland: He had also ordered a great quantity of bacon to be made at the Fort. There

---

[1] Mr. Gist, son of Washington's guide in 1753.

[2] The Six Nations, who were not on friendly terms with these Southern Indians, alleged that their refusal to assist Braddock was based on their reluctance to be brought in contact with the Catawbas and Cherokees. II. Doc. Hist. N. Y., 393.

were on board the transports one thousand barrels of beef, for which the General applied to Mr Keppel and they were landed at Alexandria. Upon making a calculation on these Estimates, there was found to be six months provisions for four thousand men.

General Braddock apprehended the greatest difficulty in procuring waggons and horses, sufficient to attend him upon his march, as the assembly had not passed an Act for the supplying them, but Sr John St Clair assured the General that inconveniency would be easily removed, for, in going to Fort Cumberland, he had been informed of a great number of Dutch settlers, at the foot of a mountain called the Blue Ridge, who would undertake to carry by the hundred the provisions and stores, and that he believed he could provide otherwise two hundred waggons and fifteen hundred carrying horses to be at Fort Cumberland by the first of May. The General desired him to secure the former of these, upon his return to the Fort. At Williamsburgh the General wrote circular letters to all the Governors upon the Continent, informing them of his Commission, and recommending to them the constituting of a common fund, and desiring them to assist and forward as much as possible the general service, that it might answer the end, for which his Majesty had sent troops to their assistance. And, in the letters to Governors Shirley, Delancey, Morris and Sharpe, he desired they would meet him at Annapolis the beginning of April, that he might confer with them on some matters of the greatest importance to the Colonies, and settle with them a general plan of operation for the approaching Campaign.[1]

Two transports being arrived at Hampton, the General and Commodore went thither immediately; and orders were given to the Commanding Officer of each ship to sail as soon as they had received their fresh provisions, and to disembark their men at Alexandria. The soldiers were to take their beds ashore, and Lieutenant Colonel Burton was ordered to Quarter the troops in the town till the arrival of more ships, in case the weather should prove severe. The General waited here three days, but no more ships arriving, he, and the Commodore, returned to Williamsburgh.

The General applied to Mr Keppel for some Blocks, Cordage, and other stores, and also for thirty seamen, who he thought would be very serviceable on the march, if it should be found necessary to pass the rivers in floats or in boats. He also desired a carpenter to direct the construction of them; with which the Commodore complied very readily, constantly expressing an ardent desire to forward the success of the expedition, and never, I believe, two men placed at the head of different Commands co-operated

---

[1] Robert-Hunter, second son of Governor Lewis Morris of Morrisania, after twenty years of public service in the council and as Chief Justice of New Jersey, was appointed Deputy Governor of Pennsylvania: a post he filled during two stormy years. I do not learn that he left any descendants; but the line was continued through those of his elder brother, Lewis; one of whom married the celebrated Duchess Dowager of Gordon; and others established some of the more distinguished families in America. A character of Mr. Delancy is given in the "Review of Military Operations in North America," and of Shirley, in I. Entick, 371.

with more spirit, integrity and harmony for the publick service.

In about ten days, all the transports being arrived, orders were given for all the ships to proceed immediately to Alexandria; but so little care had been taken at Corke, in the stowage of the cloathing, Arms, and camp necessaries belonging to the Regiments of Shirley and Pepperell,[1] that some was put on board almost every ship; they were removed into one Vessel, and dispatched immediately to New York and Boston, which caused a delay of four or five days.[2]

Every thing seemed to promise so far the greatest success. The Transports were all arrived safe, and the men in health. Provisions, Indians, carriages and horses were already provided; at least were to be esteemed so; considering the authorities on which they were promised to the General.

The 22ᵈ of March the General set out for Alexandria,

---

[1] "The Conduct of Major General Shirley," &c., (Lond., 1758,) which was perhaps prepared from materials furnished by himself, states that these two regiments were the 50th and 51st. But the Army lists do not indicate that Shirley or Pepperell were ever colonels of these regiments. Shirley was indeed of the rank of a colonel in the line since August 31, 1745; but I cannot learn of what regiment he was an actual leader. On 26th February, 1755, he was made a major-general; and on 30th January, 1759, a lieutenant-general. The uniform of the 50th, hereabove alluded to, was red faced with red, with white linings and white lace, which soiled so readily as to give the regiment the sobriquet of "the dirty half-hundred." That of the 51st differed but in having white buttons in lieu of white linings.

[2] Under convoy of the Syren, Captain Proby, a transport, with the clothing, &c., of Shirley's regiment on board, sailed from Hampton Roads about March 10th; arriving at Boston in four days. Pepperell's clothing did not follow till about the 20th. Penn. Gaz., No. 1371.

accompanied by the Governor and Mr Keppel, where they arrived the 26th. The next day the General named his Aid de Camps, and the Major of Brigade and Provost Mareschal, and gave out the following Orders, for the better regulation of the camp.

ORDERS GIVEN OUT AT ALEXANDRIA.

As the two Regiments now employed have served under his Royal Highness the Duke,[1] they are consequently very well acquainted with Military Discipline. The General therefore expects their behaviour should be so conformable to good Order, as to set the most soldierlike example to the new Levies of this country.

As an encouragement to the men, they shall be supplied with a daily allowance of provision gratis; but if any man be found negligent or disorderly, besides corporal punishment, this gratuity shall be stopped.

The articles of war are to be immediately and frequently read, and all orders relating to the men are to be read to them by an Officer of a Company.

Any soldier that deserts, though he return again, shall be hanged without mercy.

The Commanding Officers of companies are to be answerable that their men's Arms are kept in constant good order. Every man is to be provided with a brush, picker and two

---

[1] In the Scottish campaign of 1746. It may be noticed that these regiments were of the youngest in the service : only dating from 1741. The 49th was at this time the single regiment junior to the 48th. The uniform of the 44th was red faced with yellow; that of the 48th, red faced with buff.

good spare flints, and kept always completed with twenty four rounds.

The Roll of each Company is to be called over, by an Officer, every morning, Noon and night, and a return of the absent and disorderly men is to be given to the Commanding Officer of the Regiment, who is to see them properly punished.

Each Regiment is to have Divine Service performed at the head of their respective Colours every Sunday.

The two Regiments are to find the General's Guard Alternately, which is to consist of a Lieutenant and thirty men, and the Regiment which finds the General's Guard is to find also the Adjutant of the day.

All Guards are to be relieved in the morning at eight of the Clock. Guards, though ever so small, to be told off into two divisions.

All reports and returns to be made at nine of the clock. Guards, ordered at orderly time, are to remain for that day; and a new detachment is to be made for any ordered afterwards.

All returns are to be signed by the Commanding Officers of the Regiments.

Each Regiment, Troop, or Company, is to make a daily return to the Major of Brigade, specifying their Numbers wanting to complete, who is to make a General return for his Excellency.

A daily return of the sick is to be made to the General, through an Aid de Camp.

In case of any Alarum, the Virginia troops are to parade before the Church.

The line is to find daily one field-Officer, who is to be relieved at nine of the clock. This duty is to be done by the two Lieutenant Colonels and the two Majors. The field Officer of the day is to visit all Guards and out-parties, except the General's, and to go the rounds of the Picket, which as well as the other Guards and out-parties, are to report to him. He is to make his report of the whole at nine of the clock to the General, and in case of any Alarum, the field Officer is to repair with all expedition to the place where it is, and to send for any necessary Assistance to the two Regiments which are immediately to comply with his Orders.

The eldest Battalion company is to act as a second Grenadier company, and to be posted upon the left of the Battalion, leaving the same interval as the Grenadiers upon the right.

This company is to be kept complete of Officers, and two of them, as well as of the other Grenadier companies are to be posted in the front, and the other in the rear.

The eight Battalion companies are each of them to be told off into two divisions, that they may either form eight firings, or sixteen platoons, and are alwayes to be commanded by their own Officers, who are to be posted in the same manner as the Grenadier Officers, and that every Company might be complete of Officers, the General made three Ensigns to each Regiment, without pay.

Each Regiment is to mount a Picket guard, consisting of one Captain, two Subalterns and fifty Men which are to report to the field Officer of the day.

Upon any application from Sᵗ John Sᵗ Clair to either of

the Regiments for men, they are immediately to furnish them.

Sr Peter Halket is to regulate all affairs relative to the provisions.[1]

The Commissary of Provisions is to make two weekly

[1] Sir Peter Halkett of Pitferran, Fifeshire, a baronet of Nova Scotia, was the son of Sir Peter Wedderburne of Gosford, who, marrying the heiress of the ancient family of Halkett, assumed her name. In 1734, he sate in the Commons for Dunfermline, and was Lieutenant-Colonel of the 44th at Sir John Cope's defeat in 1745. Being released on his parole by Charles Edward, he was ordered by Cumberland to rejoin his regiment and serve again against the Jacobites. With great propriety, he refused such a dishonorable duty, saying that "His Royal Highness was master of his commission, but not of his honor." The King approved of Sir Peter's course, and he retained his rank. On the 26th Feb., 1751, he succeeded to the colonelcy of his regiment. He was married to the Lady Amelia Stewart, second daughter of Francis, 8th Earl of Moray, by whom he had three sons: Sir Peter, his successor, who would also appear to have been in the army; Francis, major in the Black Watch; and James, a subaltern in his own regiment, who died with him on the 9th July, 1755. (Burke's Peerage, &c.) High and generous talents seem to have been hereditary in Sir Peter's family. His father's sister, Mrs. Elizabeth Wardlaw (whom Dr. Percy thought he had sufficiently introduced to the public when he announced her as the aunt of the officer "killed in America, along with General Braddock"), was the authoress of what Coleridge would have styled "the grand old ballad" of Hardiknute.

"Let Scots, while Scots, praise Hardiknute."

What little we know of the good and noble hero who died on the banks of the Monongahela, irresistibly leads us to the conclusion that in painting her sketches of character Mrs. Wardlaw need not have gone (and perhaps did not go), beyond the circle of her own fireside. It is discouraging to reflect upon the fate of such a man: loyal, honorable, and sagacious, an experienced soldier and a worthy gentleman, he died in the arms of defeat, and the traditions of a foreign land alone preserve the memory of his virtues. In another place we have recorded the horrid circumstances of his death and the tardy burial of his bones. We would that we could here do justice to the spirit which animated his living frame. Notices of Mrs. Wardlaw will be found in II. Percy's Reliques, 105; and I. Blackwood's Mag., 380.

returns; one for the General, the other for Sr Peter Halket.

When any man is sent to the General Hospital, he is to carry with him a Certificate, signed by an Officer of his Company, setting forth his name, Regiment, and Company, to what day he is subsisted, and what Arms and Accoutrements he carries with him, which are to be bundled up and marked with the man's name, regiment, and company.

Each regiment is to send to the Artillery for twenty five thousand flints, out of which they are to choose five thousand and send the remainder back; and where any of the troops have occasion for ammunition, or any military stores, the commanding officers are to send to the train for them, giving proper receipts.

The Captains of the two Regiments are to account with their men for their sea pay, giving them credit for their subsistence to the first of April, and for their Arrears to the 24th of February; and they are to stop for the watchcoats, blankets, and flannel waistcoats.

The men enlisted or incorporated into the 44th and 48th regiments are to have credit for twenty shillings, and are to be charged with the above necessaries.

All casualties, or remarkable occurrences in Camp, are to be reported, immediately, to the General, through an Aid de Camp.

Whenever Sr John St Clair has occasion for tools, the commissary of the train is to supply them on proper receipts.

Those officers of Companies, who call the evening roll, are to inspect the ammunition of their respective companies, and report the deficiencies to the commanding officer.

No man, upon a March, is on any account to fasten his tent pole, to his firelock, or by any means encumber it.

The quarter-masters of each regiment are to apply to the assistant quarter master-general, who will show them their store-houses, in which their regimental stores are immediately to be lodged.

The soldiers are to leave in the store, their shoulder-belts, waist-belts and swords, the sergeants their halberts, and those officers that can provide themselves with fusils, their espontons.[1]

The General enquired of Sr John St Clair the nature and condition of the roads through which the troops and artillery were to march, and also if he had provided the waggons for the Ohio. Sr John informed the General that a new road was near completed from Winchester to Fort Cumberland, the old one being impassable, and that another was cutting from Conegogee to the same place, and that if the General approved of making two divisions of the troops and train, he might reach Will's Creek with more ease and expedition. He proposed that one regiment with all the powder and ordnance should go by Winchester, and the other regiment with the ammunition, military and hospital stores by Frederick in Maryland. That these should be carried ten miles up the Potomack to Rock Creek, and then up the Potomack to Fort Cumberland.

Sr John assured the General that boats, batteaux, canoes and waggons were prepared for the service, and also that provisions were laid in at Frederick for the troops. A return was called for of the waggons and teams wanted to

---

[1] Spontoons; or a sort of half-pikes, carried by infantry officers.

remove the train from Alexandria, which Sr John went up the country to provide.

He told the General two men had undertaken to furnish two hundred waggons and fifteen hundred carrying horses at Fort Cumberland early in May.

Before the General reached Alexandria, the troops were all disembarked, but, very little of the Ordnance stores or provisions were[1] yet on shore, the properest places and methods of unlading them were settled, and they were landed with the utmost dispatch.

On the 3d of April, the General, Governor and Commodore went to Annapolis to meet the eastern Governors.[2] The General found no waggons were provided for the Maryland side of the Potomack. He applied to Governor Sharpe, who promised above one hundred, which he said should attend at Rock Creek to carry away the stores as fast as they could be landed.

The General was very impatient to remove the troops from Alexandria, as the greatest care and severest punishments could not prevent the immediate[3] use of spirituous liquors, and as he was likewise informed the water of that place was very unwholsome: Therefore as the Governors were not arrived, the General returned the 7th to Alexandria for the Congress.[4]

The Virginia troops being cloathed were ordered to march immediately to Winchester, to be armed, and the

---

[1] Being (?).

[2] They arrived there the afternoon of April 3d. (Penn. Gaz., No. 1373.)

[3] Immoderate (?).

[4] With him, on Monday morning, went Dinwiddie and Keppel, Orme and W. Shirley. (Penn. Gaz., No. 1373.)

General appointed ensign Allen of the 44th to make them as like soldiers as it was possible.

Captain Lewis was ordered with his company of Rangers to Green Briar River, there to build two stockade Forts, in one of which he was to remain himself, and to detach to the other a subaltern and fifteen men.[1] These forts were to cover the western settlers of Virginia from any inroads of Indians.

The soldiers were ordered to be furnished with one new spare shirt, one new pair of stockings, and one new pair of shoes; and Osnabrig waistcoats and breeches were provided for them, as the excessive heat would have made the others insupportable, and the commanding officers of companies were desired to provide leather or bladders for the men's hats.

Sr Peter Halket with six companies of the 44th marched on the 9th to Winchester, and was to remain there till the roads were completed from thence to Fort Cumberland, and Lieutenant Colonel Gage[2] was left with the other four companies to escort the artillery.

[1] Probably Andrew Lewis of Augusta Co, appointed Captain of the Virginia troops, March 18th, 1754, whose five brothers were enlisted in his company. It would seem that he rejoined the main army and was with the working-party at the opening of the action. This was the respectable Brigadier General Lewis, whom Washington at the commencement of the Revolution had fixed upon as the foremost soldier in all America. (Howe's Virg., 204. Sharpe's MS. Corr.)

[2] Thomas Gage was the 2nd son of Thomas, 8th Baronet and 1st Viscount Gage. His family, though noble, was poor. His father once remarking in a political dispute that he always gave his sons their own way:— "Yes," said Winnington, "but that is the only thing you ever do give them!" Gage rose to high rank in the army, and was long employed and conspicuous in American affairs. He married Margaret, daughter of

As boats were not provided for the conveying of the stores to Rock Creek, the General was obliged to press Vessels, and to apply to the Commodore for seamen to navigate them. At length with the greatest difficulty they were all sent up to Rock Creek, and an Officer with thirty men of the 48th was sent thither with orders to load and dispatch all the waggons as fast as they came in, and to report every morning and evening to the General the number he had forwarded. He was directed to send a party with every division, and to apply for more men as the others marched: and all the boats upon that part of the river were ordered to assist in transporting over the Potomack the 48th Regiment.

On the 18th, the 48th Regiment marched to Frederick in Maryland. Colonel Dunbar was ordered to send one company to Conegogee to assist in forwarding the stores from thence to Fort Cumberland, and to remain with the Corps at Frederick till further orders. Thirty more men were ordered to be left with the Officer at Rock Creek.

The sick men of the two regiments, Artillery, and Virginia Companies, were left in the Hospital at Alexandria, and an Officer and twenty men were ordered for its guard and escort. At this place a General Court Martial was held, of which Lieutenant Colonel Gage was president; the prisoner was ordered one thousand lashes, part of which was remitted, and at this place the troops were also mustered.

Peter Kemble, Esq., of the Coldspring (N. Y.), family of that name, and their son subsequently succeeded his uncle in the peerage. Gen. Gage died in 1788.

On the 13th of April, the Governors arrived at Alexandria, and with them Colonel Johnston; and on the 14th a Councell was held at which was present General Braddock, Commodore Keppel, Governor Shirley, Lieut. Govr Delancy, Lieut. Govr Dinwiddie, Lieut. Govr Sharpe, Lieut. Govr Morris.[1]

At this Council the General declared to them his Majesty's pleasure that the several assemblies should constitute a common fund for defraying in part the expences of the expedition.

He showed them the necessity of cultivating a friendship and alliance with the Six Nations of Indians, and asked their opinion if Colonel Johnson was not a proper person to be employed as negotiator, also what presents they judged proper, and how they should be furnished.

The General also acquainted them with his intention of attacking Crown Point and Niagara at the same time with Fort Du Quesne, and desired they would inform him if they thought it advisable to attempt the reduction of Crown Point with the forces agreed to be supplied by the Provinces of New York, New Jersey, Connecticut, Rhode Island, Massachusetts, and New Hampshire, amounting to four thousand four hundred men; and whether, as they were all Irregulars, they did not think Colonel Johnson a proper man to command this expedition.

The General told the Council his intention to reinforce the fort at Oswego with two companies of Sr William Pepperell's and one independant company of New York, as

[1] The minutes of this Council are in II. Doc. Hist. N. Y, 376. VI. C. R, 365.

this fort commanded the south east side of the lake Ontario, and was a post of great consequence to facilitate the attack, or to secure the retreat of the troops destined to Niagara, and as the entire command of the Lake was of the greatest consequence to cutt off the French communication with the western countries, and could only be obtained by Vessels, he was of opinion two or more should be built for that purpose, and desired their advice as to the burthen and force of them.

The Governors said, they had severally applied to their respective assemblies to establish a common fund, but could not prevail.

They were of opinion it was necessary to make a treaty with the Six Nations. That Mr Johnson was the properest man to negotiate it, and that eight hundred pounds should be furnished by the several governments to be laid out in presents for them.[1]

They approved of the attack of Crown Point by the Irregulars, and also of Colonel Johnson's having the command of that expedition.

It was agreed two vessels of sixty tons should be built upon the Lake Ontario, of which Commodore Keppel undertook to furnish draughts, and to defray the expence and the direction thereof was given to Governor Shirley.[2]

---

[1] For the details of Johnson's employments, see the Johnson MSS., II. Doc. Hist. N. Y.

[2] "The scheme for a naval armament at Oswego was first proposed by the Honorable Thomas Pownall to the Congress of Commissioners of the several colonies, met at Albany in June, 1754. Copies were sent to England, and taken by the Commissioners for the perusal of their respective governments." Lewis Evans' Essays, No. II. (Phil. 1756), 17. The vessels were not finished till Sept. 1755, and cost £22,000.

The three Governments of Virginia, Maryland, and Pennsylvania were to bear the expence of any additional works at Fort Du Quesne, they were to maintain the Garrison, and also to pay for any vessels that it should be found necessary to construct upon the Lake Erie.[1]

Orders were immediately sent to the commanding officer of Sr William Pepperell's regiment to detach two complete companies with all dispatch to Oswego, and also Capt. King's Independent Company[2] was ordered to that Fort, and the commanding officer was instructed to put the works into the best repair the nature of them would admit of, and Governor Delancey gave four thousand pounds out of the money that was voted by the Assembly of New York to be employed in the victualling of Oswego; directions were sent to New York to prepare ship carpenters and proper persons of all sorts for constructing and completing the

---

[1] When he had captured Du Quesne, Braddock proposed to march thence to Niagara, reducing all the French posts on his way. A garrison of at least 200 of the Maryland and Virginia provincials was to be left at the fort, and anticipating that should the enemy evacuate it at his approach, they would destroy as much as they could of its defences, he designed that the provinces most concerned in the business should furnish its provisions and artillery. He certainly would not be able to spare any from his own train. Morris anticipated from the first that the furnishing of cannon and stores of war would be repugnant to 'the non-resisting principles of his Quaking Assembly;' and he came to no understanding with them on this point. Virginia sent ten ship-cannon, mounted on trucks, with all the appurtenances, by way of Rock Creek and Conococheague, to Will's Creek; thence, when the time arrived, to be transported to Fort Du Quesne. (VI. C. R., 400, 409, 413, 405, 465. II. P. A., 347.) The general anticipated an easy though an important capture, and already looked forward after all his victories, to spending a merry Christmas with Morris at Philadelphia. (VI. C. R., 400.)

[2] This was the remaining Independent Company of New York.

Vessels intended for the Lake, and directions were given to fell with all diligence proper timber for that purpose, and circular letters were written to the several Eastern Governments to raise and assemble as fast as possible the troops designed for the Crown Point expedition.

It was proposed to Mr. Johnson to employ him as Plenipotentiary to the Six Nations, which he at first declined, as the promises made in the year 1746 in regard to these Indians were not fulfilled, by which means he was then laid under the disagreeable necessity of deceiving them. And the French had made use of this neglect very much to our disadvantage and their own Interest; However, the universal and deserved opinion of the General's integrity prevailed upon him to undertake their negotiation.[1]

A speech was prepared for Mr Johnson to deliver to the Indians in the General's name, setting forth that his Majesty had sent a very considerable body of troops to drive the French from the Encroachments they had from time to time made on his Dominions, and on their lands and hunting-grounds, which in the treaty of 1726, between the English and them, they had given us in trust to be guarantied to them for their use and benefit. And that his Majesty had invested him with the supreme command upon the Continent, with orders to strengthen and confirm the Amity which had so long subsisted between the English and them. And that his Majesty had also ordered him to fulfil the spirit of that treaty by building proper fortresses and

[1] This is but one of the many testimonials to Braddock's character for public honesty and truthfulness borne by the records of the time.

securing to them those lands and hunting-grounds which were given in trust by the said treaty.

The General also told them, that as his distance from them made it impossible for him to meet them himself, and finding their uneasiness at the improper appointment and ill-treatment from the Commissioners of the Indian affairs at Albany, and being also informed that they had expressed a great desire to have Colonel Johnson, one of their own sachems, intrusted with that business, he had therefore given him a Commission appointing him whole and sole director and manager of Indian affairs; That he had also impowered Colonel Johnson to call them together, to give them presents and to confirm, treat and conclude with them the strictest and most lasting Treaty of Friendship and alliance; and the General engaged to confirm and ratify all such promises as should be made to them by Mr Johnson, and desired they would confirm and conclude with him, as if the General himself was present.

A commission was given to Colonel Johnson appointing him whole and sole manager and director of Indian affairs, and also empowering him to convene, confer and conclude any treaties with the Six Nations and their allies, at such times, and in such places, as he should think proper for the good of his Majesty's service and interest in America.

Colonel Johnson was also instructed to call them immediately together to give them presents, and prevail upon them to declare against the french, and also to prevail upon the Six Nations to send Messengers forthwith to the Southern and Western Indians to forbid them acting with the french and to order them immediately to take up the hatchet and join the General upon his march or before. He was to take especial care that in all meetings, conferences, agreements, or treaties with the Indians, he was always to have in view his Majesty's honour, service and Interest.

And he was by the most early and frequent opportunities to remit to the General copies of all transactions of every kind with the Indians, and also of the progress, situation, and success relating to the expedition in which he was employed.

Governor Shirley had orders to supply him with a sum of two thousand pounds at such times, and in such proportions, as he should choose to draw for it; of which sum, as well as all others, he might hereafter be entrusted with, he was to dispose in the best manner for the most effectual gaining and preserving the Indians to his Majesty's Interest, and he was to keep regular and exact Accounts of the nature of the disbursements; as it was apprehended it might more readily induce the Six Nations to take up arms in our favour if they were employed upon a service immediately under him, he was permitted to take with him such as would declare upon the expedition against Crown point. This commission and instructions bearing throughout the whole a regard to the integrity of Colonel Johnson's character engaged him to undertake and to proceed upon this negotiation with the greatest spirit and zeal for the service.

Colonel Shirley having much interest in, and being extremely well acquainted in the Eastern Governments was supposed most capable of removing the principal difficulties attending the expedition to Niagara, which would arise from procuring provision and artillery, and from transporting them and the troops. And Mʳ Shirley expressing the greatest desire to be employed upon that service, he was appointed by the General to that command.

Letters of credit were accordingly given to him, and instructions for that service, whereby he was directed to take his own and Sʳ William Pepperell's regiments and the companies of New York under his command; and to proceed with the greatest diligence and dispatch to Niagara; taking care to see the Vessels designed for the lake Ontario built and equipt. He was also to order the works of Oswego to be put in the best repair, and to leave a proper garrison for its defence.

He was directed to give frequent accounts to the General of his situation, and proper marks were agreed between them to render any letters useless which might be intercepted by the enemy.

As the General judged the success of the several expeditions would very much depend upon their being carried into execution at or near the same time, and as the very great distance at which they were to act, made it impossible to be agreed by letter, he desired Colonel Shirley and Colonel Johnson would fix the time in which they would be able to appear before Niagara and Crown point. They both agreed upon the end of June, nearly in July, and the General assured them he would use his utmost endeavours to be at Fort Du Quesne by that time.

The General dispatched a Courier to Lieutenant Colonel Monkton to take upon him the Command of the troops destined for the attack of Beau Sejour upon the Isthmus of Nova Scotia.

The business of the Congress being now over, the General would have set out for Frederick, but few waggons or teams were yet come to remove the Artillery; He then sent an Express to St John St Clair informing him of it, and in a few days set out for Frederick in Maryland leaving Lieutenant Colonel Gage with four Companies of the 44th regiment, who was ordered to dispatch the powder and artillery as fast as any horses or waggons should arrive, taking care to send proper escorts with them.

The General at Rock Creek called for a return of the stores, and gave orders for such as were most necessary to be first transported, and for some of the provisions, ordnance, and hospital stores to be left there, the waggons coming in so slow as to render it impossible to convey the whole to Fort Cumberland in proper time.

Upon the General's arrival at Frederick, he found the troops in great want of provision; no cattle was laid in there; The General applied to Governor Sharpe, who was then present, for provision and waggons, but so little is the Authority of a Governor in that Province, that he afforded the General no Assistance; Upon which the General was obliged to send round the country to buy cattle for the subsistence of the troops.

It was above a month before the necessary Ammunition and stores could be transported from Rock Creek to Conegogee, and as the Patomack was not then navigable, even by the smallest Canoes, new difficulties arose in providing Waggons to send them to Fort Cumberland; proper persons were sent to the justices of peace of those Counties, and at last by intreaties, threats, and money, the stores were removed.

As the General had met with frequent disappointments, he took the opportunity of Mr Franklin's being at Frederick to desire he would contract in Pensylvania for one hundred and fifty waggons and fifteen hundred carrying horses upon the easiest terms, to join him at Fort Cumberland by the 10th of May, if possible; Mr Franklin procured the number of waggons, and about five hundred horses.[1] As those carriages were to pass through Conegogee in their way to Fort Cumberland, the General sent orders to Cressop the Agent at that place to make use of that opportunity of conveying to Fort-Cumberland the flour which the Government of Pensylvania had delivered there, it being much wanted at the Fort.

As no road had been made to Will's Creek on the Maryland side of the Patomack, the 48th Regiment was obliged to cross that river at Conegogee, and to fall into the Virginia road near Winchester. The General ordered a bridge to be built over the Antietum, which being furnished, and provision laid in on the road, Colonel Dunbar marched with his regiment from Frederick on the 28th of April,

[1] In Jan. 1756, Governor Morris, under the instructions of General Shirley, appointed a commission to audit, settle and adjust the claims of Franklin and others upon the Crown for the hire of these waggons and horses. In conjunction with Robert Leake, Esq., the King's Commissary General, the board sate ten days in Lancaster to decide upon the accounts of the Pennsylvania creditors, and then met in Philadelphia and passed upon those from Maryland and Virginia. By their action, a saving of seven thousand pounds accrued to the Government. II. P. A., 583, 598, 638.

and about this time the bridge over the Opeccon was finished for the passage of the Artillery, and floats were built on all the rivers and creeks.

The 31 of April the General set out for Winchester hoping to meet the Indians, but as none were, or had been there, he proceeded to Fort Cumberland, where he arrived the 10th of May, and also the 48th Regiment. Sir Peter Halket with six companies of the 44th, two independant companies and the Virginia troops were already encamped at this place.

The General had applied to Governor Morris for some Indians who lived upon the Susque hannah; about thirty of them met him at this place.[1] The General shewed them the greatest Marks of attention and esteem, and the next day called them to his tent, and conferred with them agreeably to their forms and customs.

The General told them of the troops and Artillery his Majesty had sent to their Assistance, and made use of every argument to persuade them to take up the hatchet

[1] These were the Aughquick Indians brought by George Croghan, whom Braddock formally commissioned their captain for the campaign. Having been long settled as a trader among the savages, he had acquired the languages of several of their nations, and possessed great influence over them. By occasion of the war, he was unable to collect a great number of debts due to him by the Indians, and became bankrupt. But the Pennsylvania Assembly considering his value on the frontier, passed an act granting him a freedom from arrest for ten years; and he was soon made a captain in the service of the colony. In 1756, he went to Onondaga, and probably died in New York, as his will (dated 12th June, 1782) is recorded in the Court of Appeals at Albany. He is styled as "late of Passyunk, Pa.," and appears to have left but one child, Susannah, who married Lieutenant Augustine Prevost. (II. P. A., 689. IV. Doc. Hist, N. Y. 420.)

against the French, and to act with spirit and fidelity under him.

A few days after, at another Congress, they informed him of their resolutions to serve with him, and declared war against the French according to their own ceremonies. They desired leave to return to the Susquehannah with their wives and children (to whom the General made considerable presents) and promised to rejoin him in a few days, only eight of them remaining with him, who were immediately employed in getting intelligence.[1] The others

---

[1] None who left ever returned. Of the eight who remained one was Scarroyaddy (or Monacatootha), already noticed; another was his son, killed on the march. The names of the remainder we find in the proceedings of a Council at Philadelphia on the 15th of August, 1755, where, after condoling with Scarroyaddy on his loss, Morris thanks individually and by name all the savages who fought with Braddock : viz., Cashuwayon, Froson, Kahuktodon, Attscheehokatha, Kash-wugh-daniunto, and Dyoquario.; all Iroquois. (VI. C. R., 524. Du Simitiere MSS.) Doubtless these were their formal and genuine names ; but they were known to the whites by other titles, and nothing was more usual than for an Indian to have two names ; so that it is now perhaps impossible to identify them all. I take it, however, that Kash-wughdanionto was the Belt of Wampum (VII. C. R., 6) ; a Seneca, who had contended with Scarroyaddy for the succession to the Half-King. Cashuwayon, we are fortunately able to say with certainty, was the well-known Captain Newcastle. In January 1756, one Thomas Greene being adopted by the Indians, he received Newcastle's old name ; the warrior thenceforth being called Ah Knoyis (VII. C. R., 6). He died at Philadelphia, of small-pox, during the same year. Perhaps Aroas (or Silver-Heels), a Seneca ; Iagrea, Scarroyaddy's son-in-law ; and the Mohawks Esras and Moses (or the Song), his wife's brothers, may have been of the others. This last was one of Stobo's messengers from Du Quesne. An inventory of the morrice-bells, tobacco, knives, cloths, powder, &c., presented to these savages by Morris in August, 1755, may be found in VI. C. R., 566. They were all constant and active allies of the English ; but it is not within the compass of this design to dilate upon their exploits.

never returned to the General, but about sixteen of them advanced as far as Colonel Dunbar's Camp. The General sent Messengers to the Delawar and Shawnoe Indians to invite them to join him.

We had been promised the greatest plenty of all kinds of provisions at this place, but none fresh could be procured. The General was greatly concerned to see the want of all refreshments begin so early, fearing it would disable the men from undergoing the fatigues and hardships they were to meet with on their March to the Ohio. They had already marched two hundred miles through an uninhabited wilderness without any other but the salt provision that they had carried with them, or that had been laid in for them upon the road. The General offered large rewards, and lent several people his own money to enable them to provide the camp, and gave all manner of encouragement to such as would bring provision. Everything brought to camp was to be sold at a particular place, and any person was to suffer death who should dare to interupt or molest anybody bringing provision, or should offer to buy of them before it was carried to the publick market, which was put under the care and inspection of the Captains of the Picket, and a Sergeant with a small Guard of the Picket attended the market to prevent all quarrels or confusion.

As a further encouragement, the price of provisions was raised a penny in the pound, and no good meat was to be sold at less than the fixed price, lest the Peasants should be distress'd when they had brought it many miles. These regulations and encouragements produced some supplies, tho' by the nature of the country inadequate to the wants of the camp.

About the 20th of May, the Artillery, which marched in two divisions, arrived. They had remained at Alexandria a fortnight after the General had left it, through the want of waggons and horses, nor could they at last have marched without press parties, which Lieutenant Colonel Gage sent for many miles round, and he was obliged to continue this method the whole march, having neither pasture nor forage on the road, not even at those places where it had been said to have been provided. This march was over a prodigious chain of mountains, and through deep and rocky roads. The troops were now joined, except a North Carolina company, commanded by Capt[n] Dobbs,[1] which was daily expected.

The General had now frequent opportunities of seeing and hearing of the appearance and disposition of the Virginia Recruits and companies. Mr Allen had taken the greatest pains with them, and they performed their evolutions and firings as well as could be expected, but their languid, spiritless, and unsoldierlike appearance considered with the lowness and ignorance of most of their Officers, gave little hopes of their future good behaviour.

Guards were posted upon the Patomack and Will's Creek, and two other guards were ordered for the security of the horses that were grazing in the woods ; and Detachments of the Picket lay advanced from retreat beating till daylight, having been informed some Indians had been seen near the Camp.

About the latter end of May, the Pensylvania waggons came up to us, but brought very little flour from Conego-

---

[1] Son of the Governor of the colony.

gee, occasioned by the infamous neglect of Cressop the Agent at that place, who suffered almost all the waggons to pass without giving them the Order before mentioned. Much about the same time this man's father was employed by Governor Sharpe to salt a quantity of beef for the use of the Maryland troops; which beef had been reckoned in the estimate of those provisions designed for the March; it was no sooner brought to Camp but it was condemned to be buried by a survey. The Surveyors reported that it had no pickle, and that it was put into dry casks, which could never have contained any.[1]

Being thus disappointed in flour and beef, the General sent away that night thirty waggons with a Captain's detachment to Winchester for provisions over sixty miles of Mountainous and rocky country; and also three hundred carrying horses for flour, with part of the troop of light horse, to Conegogee, ninety miles distance, with orders to bring up Cressop, another commissary being appointed.

Most of the horses which brought up the train were either lost, or carried home by their owners, the nature of the country making it impossible to avoid this fatal inconvenience, the whole being a continued forrest for several hundred miles without inclosures or bounds by which horses can be secured: they must be turned into the woods for their subsistance, and feed upon leaves and young shoots of trees. Many projects, such as belts, hobles, &c., were tried, but none of these were a security against the wildness of the country and the knavery of the people we

[1] These men were Colonel Thomas and Captain Michael Cresap. See Mr. Brantz Mayer's paper, read before Md. Hist. Soc, May, 1851.

were obliged to employ: by these means we lost our horses almost as fast as we could collect them, and those which remained grew very weak, so we found ourselves every day less able to undertake the extraordinary march we were to perform.

The General, to obviate as much as possible these difficulties, appointed a waggon Master General, and under him waggon masters over every forty waggons; and horse Masters over every hundred horses, and also a drover to every seven horses; the waggon and horse masters with the drovers were to go into the woods with their respective divisions, to muster their horses every night and morning, and to make a daily report to the waggon master General, who was to report to the General.

These regulations remedied in a great measure that evil. Some Indians arrived from the Delawars, with whom the General conferred, and to whom he made presents. They promised to join him with their Nation upon the march, which they never performed.

Of all the Indians promised by Governor Dinwiddie, none had joined the General; and a few days before we marched the person sent to the Catawbers and Cherokees returned; He informed the General that three hundred of their warriors had marched three or four days with him in their way to the Camp; but one Pearus[1] an Indian Trader had by means of a quantity of liquor diverted them from their undertaking; advising them to call upon Gist (who was the person employed) to shew some written and sealed authority by which he acted; who not being provided with

---

[1] Perhaps Paris, who commanded at the defeat of Donville in 1756.

any instrument of this nature from the Government of Virginia, they judged him an imposter, and returned to their towns.

The General wond'red that the Governments of Carolina had not been applied to for obtaining these Indians, as being their natural allies.

While these disappointments were still fresh, one Hile a Virginian, with whom the commissaries appointed by Governor Dinwiddie had made a contract for five hundred Beeves to be delivered at Fort Cumberland, came to the Camp and informed the General, the Committee of the Virginia Assembly would not confirm the contract, and that it was consequently void. He had already received a part of the money, and the General offered to pay him the ballance, but he said he had recalled his Factors from Carolina, and would not make another contract without an advanced price; and even then would not engage to perform 'till September. The General therefore resolved to supply himself elsewhere.

General Braddock had applied to the Governor of Pensylvania, soon after his arrival in America, to open a road from that country towards the Ohio, to fall into his road to that place from Fort Cumberland, either at the great meadows, or at the Yoxhio Geni, that he might keep open a communication with Pensylvania either for reinforcements, or convoys. The Governor had laid this before his Assembly, and had represented to them in the strongest terms the use, and indeed necessity, of such a measure; but they would pay no regard to it. Upon a farther acquaintance with the nature and state of Virginia, and the frequent disappointments the General experienced from that Province, he thought it would be imprudent to depend entirely upon contracts made with, or promises received from them; he therefore wrote again to Governor Morris to desire he would once more apply to his Assembly to open a road, and as he was every day the more convinced of the necessity of such a communication, he desired that it might immediately be begun and carried on with all possible expedition, and that he would undertake to defray the expence of it, in case they should again refuse it. The Governor through his Zeal for his Majesty's service, had it carried into great forwardness in a very short time.

Mr Peters the Secretary of Pensylvania, who had been to inspect the road, waited upon the General at Fort Cumberland to inform him of its progress; The General desired Mr Peters would in conjunction with Governor Morris make a contract in his name for a magazine of provisions to be formed at Shippensburgh, sufficient to subsist three thousand men for three months, and to be completed by the beginning of July; he desired they would appoint some proper person to forward the whole or part with all expedition when demanded. This contract was concluded, and the deposit made agreeable to the time mentioned. The General also fixed with Mr Peters that the junction of the two roads should be at the Crow foot of the Yoxhio Geni.[1]

---

[1] The union of the Youghiogeny proper, the Laurel Hill Creek, and Castleman's River, in Somerset County, is commonly called the Turkey Foot, or the Crow Foot of the Youghiogeny.

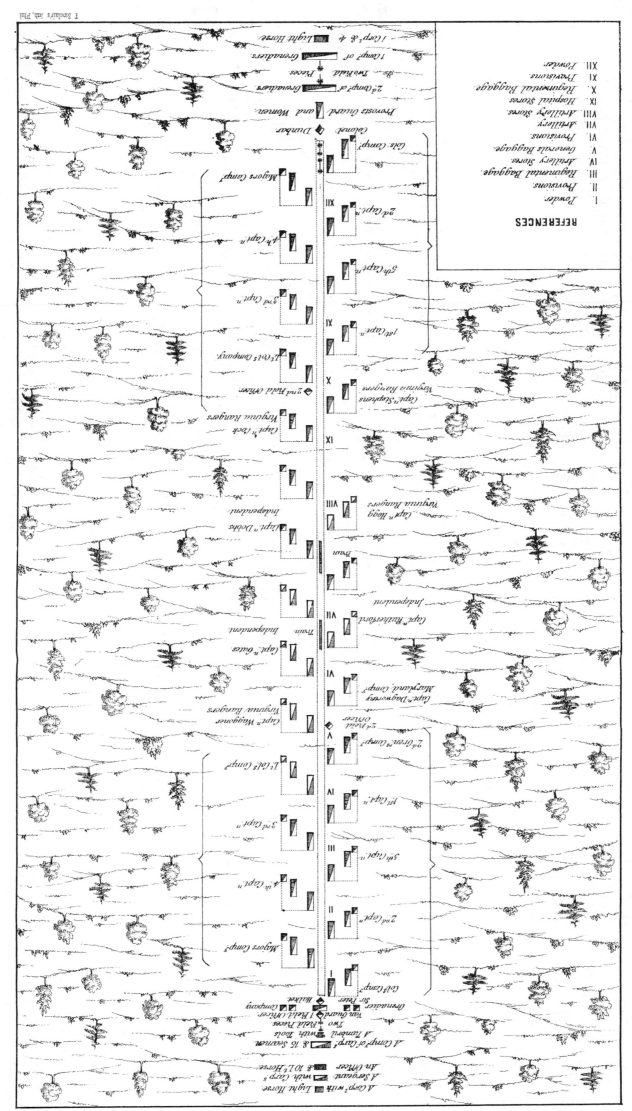

Line of March with the whole Baggage.

Pl. V.

REFERENCES

I. Powder.
II. Provisions.
III. Regimental Baggage.
IV. Artillery Stores.
V. Generals Baggage.
VI. Provisions.
VII. Artillery.
VIII. Artillery Stores.
IX. Hospital Stores.
X. Regimental Baggage.
XI. Provisions.
XII. Powder.

T. Sinclair's lith. Phil.

The General called a Council of War consisting of

Colonel Sr Peter Halket.   Colonel Dunbar.
Lieut. Colonel Gage.   Lieut. Col° Burton.[1]
Major Chapman.[2]   Major Sparks.[3]
  Major Sr John St Clair, D. Q. G.

The General acquainted the Council he had formed a plan of March and encampment upon the Nature of the service, Country, and Enemy he was engaged in and expected to be opposed by; That he offered it to them for their opinions, in which he desired they would be very explicit, and make such objections, and offer such amendments, as they should judge proper, by which some general plan might be formed which would effectually answer the end proposed, of marching and encamping with the greater security. He said he should be very much encumbered with a vast number of carriages and horses, which it was absolutely necessary to secure from the insults of the Indians from whom he apprehended frequent annoyance. It would be therefore necessary to divide the troops into small parties

[1] Ralph Burton, lieutenant-colonel of the 48th, seems to have been a favorite of Braddock's. In January, 1748, he received the local rank of a colonel in North America, and commanded the right wing at the capture of Quebec. After its fall, he was made governor of the department of Trois-Rivières. (II. Garneau, 374, 380.) He was a colonel in the line, December 10, 1760, and of the 3d Foot (Buffs), 22d Nov., 1764. He was created major-general 10th July, 1762.

[2] On 7th March, 1751, Russel Chapman was appointed major of the 44th, and on 20th March, 1756, was gazetted lieutenant-colonel of the 62d regiment.

[3] All I can learn of this officer is that he marched with Dunbar to Philadelphia, and that his name was William Sparkes. (VI. C. R., 594.)

to cover as much as possible the baggage, which would be obliged to march in one line through a road about twelve foot wide, and that it appeared to him also necessary to extend small parties very well upon the flanks, in the front, and in the rear, to prevent any surprise which the nature of the country made them very liable to; and he proposed, as it would be impracticable to have a regular parade, that every commanding officer of a company should regulate that company's duty by detaching always upon his flanks a third of the effectives with a Sergeant, which Sergeant was to detach a third of his men upon his flanks with a Corporal; these out parties were to be relieved every night at retreat beating, and to form the advanced pickets.

Each regiment was to find one Captain and three subalterns for the picket of each flank; and the independent companies, Virginia, Maryland, and Carolina rangers, One Captain and two Subalterns for each of the flanks of their division; and the field Officer of the day was to command the whole. The officers of the pickets were to march upon their respective flanks. The waggons, Artillery, and carrying horses were formed into three divisions, and the provisions disposed of in such a manner as that each division was to be victualled from that part of the line it covered, and a commissary was appointed to each. The waggon masters were to attend their respective divisions to proportion the goodness of teams, and to assist at every steep ascent by adding any number of horses from other waggons, till their respective divisions had passed.

The waggons were subdivided again into smaller divisions, every company having a certain number which they were to endeavour to keep together, however the line might be broke : The Companies were to march two deep that they might extend the more, be more at liberty to act, and less liable to confusion.

A field officer was to march with a van, and another with a rear guard. Sʳ Peter Halket was to lead the column, and Colonel Dunbar to bring up the Rear. The field officer of the Picket had no fixed posts. There was also an advanced party of three hundred men to precede the line to cut and make the roads, commanded by a field officer or the quarter master general. This detachment was to be either a day's march before the line or to move earlier every morning, according to the country we were to pass through, or the intelligence we could get of the enemy.

The form of the encampment differed very little from that of the march. Upon coming to the ground, the waggons were to draw up in close order in one line, the road not admitting more, care being taken to leave an interval in the front of every company. When this was done the whole was to halt and face outward. The serjeants' flank parties were to divide, facing to the right and left, and to open a free communication by cutting down saplings and underwood, till they met the divisions of the other serjeants' parties : they were then to open a communication with the corporal in front, who was to keep his men under arms. The serjeant was then to advance half of his party, which was to remain under arms whilst the corporal opened his communications to the right and left. All this was carried on under the inspection of the Picket Officers of the respective flanks. Whilst this was executing, half of each Company remained under arms, whilst the other half opened the communication to the right and left, and to the serjeants in front, and also cleared ground for the tents, which were pitched by them, and placed in a single row along the line of baggage, facing outwards. These parties were then to be relieved, and the corporal's party was all posted in centinels, which made a chain of centinels round the camp. The grenadiers were to encamp across the road, and each company to advance a serjeant's party.

Upon beating the General, the men were to turn out, but not to strike their tents till they received orders; upon the Assembly the horses were to be loaded; and upon beating the March the Corporals were to join their parties, and the whole was to face upon the right and left.

When the waggons were all closed up, the waggon and horse-masters were to assemble in some particular place their respective divisions, and to give their orders to the waggoners and drovers. The horses were then to be turned out within the centinels, every centinel having orders not to suffer any horse to pass him.

It was the opinion of the Council this line of march and plan of encampment would answer extremely well for the service we were engaged in; every field officer was to have a copy of it, and they were desired to assemble the Captains and explain to them fully the duty they were to perform.

Some Indians returned from a reconnoitring party, and informed the General about a hundred soldiers were then in Garrison at Fort Du Quesne, but that they soon expected greater reinforcements from Montreal and Quebec.

Two days after, the General called another Council of War. He informed them of the present state of the Garrison, and read to them some letters of intelligence, that he had received from the Governors of New York and Pennsylvania.

The General told the Council, that he found by his returns, that he had not above forty waggons over and above the hundred and fifty he had got from Pensylvania, and that the number of carrying horses did not exceed six hundred, which were insufficient to carry seventy days flour and fifty days meat, which he was of opinion was the least he could march with without running great risques of being reduced to the utmost distress before the Convoy could be brought to him if he should meet with any opposition at the Fort. And he desired to know their opinions of a measure he had formed for carrying eight days more provision and for saving some days in the march.

The General reminded the Council of the Waggons sent to Winchester for provisions, which could not return in less than seven days, and this time would absolutely be lost if the march of the whole was delayed for their return. The General therefore proposed the sending forwards of a party of six hundred men, workers and coverers, with a field officer, and the Quarter-master-General; that they should take with them two six-pounders, with a full proportion of ammunition; that they should also take with them eight days provision for three thousand two hundred men; that they should make the road as good as possible, and march five days towards the first crossing of the Yoxhio Geni, which was about thirty miles from the camp, at which place they

were to make a deposit of the provisions, building proper
sheds for its security, and also a place of arms for its defence
and the security of the men. If they could not in five days
advance so far, they were at the expiration of that time to
choose an advantageous spot and to secure the provisions
and men as before.   When the waggons were unloaded,
the field officer with three hundred men was to return to
camp, and S⟨r⟩ John S⟨t⟩ Clair with the first engineer was to
remain and carry on the works with the other three hundred.   The General proposed marching from Fort Cumberland to the first camp in three divisions, as it would be
impossible for the whole line with the baggage to move off
the ground in one day.

S⟨r⟩ Peter Halket with the 44ᵗʰ Regiment was to march
with the first division, taking with him about a hundred
waggons of provisions, stores and powder.

Lieutenant Colonel Burton with the independent Companies, Virginia, Maryland, and Carolina rangers, was to
march with the artillery, ammunition, some stores and
provision, and to form the second division.

Colonel Dunbar, with the 48ᵗʰ, was to make the third
division, and to take with him the provision waggons from
Winchester, the returned waggons from the advanced
party, and all the carrying horses.

The whole of the General's plan was universally
approved of, and agreed to; and the Resolutions of the
first, and of this Council of War were signed by the
members.[1]

This detachment of six hundred men commanded by Major Chapman marched the 30th of May at daybreak, and it was night before the whole baggage had got over a mountain about two miles from the camp. The ascent and descent were almost a perpendicular rock; three waggons were entirely destroyed, which were replaced from the camp; and many more were extremely shattered. Three hundred men, with the miners (of whom the General had

to Gov. Morris, dated at Fort Cumberland, 23rd May, 1755. (VI. C. R., 404.) "It is a joke to suppose that secondary Officers can make amends for the defects of the First. The main spring must be the mover; others in many cases can do no more than follow and correct a little its motions. As to them, I don't think we have much to boast. Some are insolent and ignorant; others capable, but rather aiming at showing their own abilities than making a proper use of them. I have a very great love for my friend Orme, and think it uncommonly fortunate for our Leader that he is under the influence of so honest and capable a man, but I wish, for the sake of the Publick, he had some more experience of business, particularly in America. As to myself, I came out of England expecting that I might be taught the business of a military secretary, but I am already convinced of my mistake. I would willingly hope my time may not be quite lost to me. You will think me out of humor. I own I am so. I am greatly disgusted at seeing an Expedition (as it is called), so ill-concerted originally in England and so ill-appointed, so improperly conducted in America; and so much fatigue and expense incurred for a purpose which, if attended with success, might better have been left alone. I speak with regard to our particular share. However, so much experience I have had of the injudiciousness of public opinion, that I have no little expectation, when we return to England, of being received with great applause. I am likewise further chagrined at seeing the prospect of affairs in America which, when we were at Alexandria I looked upon to be very great and promising, through delays and disappointments which might have been prevented, grown cloudy and in danger of ending in little or nothing." The writer was destined never to enjoy his country's predicted applause. He was shot through the head at the first fire on the fatal 9th of July, just six weeks after the date of this letter.

formed a company), had already been employed several days upon that hill.

The General reconnoitred this mountain, and determined to set the engineers and three hundred more men at work upon it, as he thought it impassable by Howitzers.[1] He did not imagine any other road could be made, as a reconnoitring party had already been to explore the country; nevertheless, Mr. Spendelow, Lieutenant of the Seamen, a young man of great discernment and abilities, acquainted the General, that, in passing that mountain, he had discovered a Valley which led quite round the foot of it. A party of a hundred men, with an engineer, was ordered to cut a road there, and an extreme good one was made in two days, which fell into the other road about a mile on the other side of the mountain.

From this place the General wrote to Colonel Shirley and Colonel Johnson, desiring them to use all possible dispatch in the carrying their expeditions into execution, and he wrote also to the Governor of New York, to desire he would afford them all possible assistance in his Government, as they must necessarily depend entirely upon it for their subsistance.

Mr. Shirley represented to the General the weakness of Sir William Pepperell's regiment, and applied for the five hundred men under the command of Colonel Schyler, who were raised in New Jersey for the Crown Point expedition; which men the Governor, Assembly, and Colonel Schyler,

---

[1] A howitzer is a short gun for throwing shells, and is mounted on a field carriage. It differs from a mortar mainly in having its trunnions in the middle.

were willing should join Mr. Shirley. The General therefore acquiesced, and wrote to that purpose to Governor Belchier.[1]

The Governor of South Carolina sent the General bills for four thousand pounds, being part of six thousand which was voted by that Assembly towards a common fund. These bills were remitted to Governor Morris to pay in part for the magazine at Shippensburgh.[2] This was the only money raised by the Provinces which ever passed through the General's hands.

The General wrote to the Governors of Virginia, Maryland, and Pensylvania, desiring the two former to have their Militia ready to escort his convoys, if he should not be able to detach a sufficient number of men from his own body; and also desired the three Governments to provide Artillery for the Fort, in case he should make himself master of it, as he could not leave any of his Ordnance in that place. He also informed them that the French had threatned to fall with their Indians upon the back Inhabitants as soon as the Army should march, and the General desired they would make the best use of that information.[3]

A proper Commissary was appointed at Conegogee, with

[1] Pepperell's regiment was not more than half-filled when, on the 26th May, he wrote from New York to his old friend Gov. Morris, asking permission for his recruiting officers to 'raise a hundred or two of brave men' in Pennsylvania. (II. P. A., 329.) It has already been observed how many hundreds from this province were enlisted in the northern campaigns of the war. The New Jersey troops alluded to in the text were commanded by Colonel Peter Schuyler, of whose family was Philip Schuyler of the Revolution. John Belcher was governor of this latter colony.

[2] See VI. C. R., 426, 429.

[3] See VI. C. R., 400, 413. This threat was considered a mere bravado.

orders to send up all the flour to Fort Cumberland, and directions were given for gathering to that place all the provision which had been left for want of carriages at Alexandria, Rock Creek, Frederick, and Winchester. Thus two Magazines were formed in different parts of the country, from either of which the General might supply himself as he should find most convenient.

It appearing to the General absolutely necessary to leave some proper person to superintend the commissaries, and to dispatch the convoys, and also to command at the Fort, Colonel Innys was appointed Governor of it. Instructions were given to him, and money was left with him for contingent expences, lest the service should for want of it meet with any checks. The General fixed with the several Governors of Virginia, Maryland, and Pensylvania proper places for laying horses for the more ready conveyance of their expresses : men were also employed with proper badges ; and orders were given in the several Governments to supply them with horses upon a proper application.

A company of guides were established under two Chiefs ; each regiment had three guides. The General had one, and the Quarter-master General three.

An Hospital was left at this place, and the most infirm Officers and men remained in Garrison.

Every thing being now settled, Sr Peter Halket with the 44th regiment marched the 7th of June.

Lieutenant Colonel Burton with the independent Companies and Rangers on the 8th, and Colonel Dunbar with the 48th regiment on the 10th, with the proportions of baggage, as was settled by the Council of War.

The same day the General left Fort Cumberland, and joined the whole at Spendelow camp, about five miles from the Fort.

ORDERS GIVEN AT FORT CUMBERLAND.

None of the men that came with the Regiments from Ireland to be suffered to act as Bat-man.

All the troops to be under arms, and to have the Articles of War read to them, at which time the servants and followers are to attend.

A return to be made of such men as understand mining, to whom proper encouragement shall be given.

The troops to begin immediately their field days, each man to have twelve rounds of powder.

The troops are to be immediately brigaded in the following manner:

The first Brigade, Commanded by Sir Peter Halket.

	Compliment.	Effective.
44th Regiment of Foot.......	700 ...	700
Captn Rutherford's[1] ...... Independant Compy of New York	100 ...	95
Captn Gates		
Capt. Polson's[2] ...... Carpenters	50 ...	48

[1] Capt. John Rutherford was stationed at Will's Creek in March, 1755; an interesting letter from him will be found in II. P. A., 277. At the end of the year, he held the rank of major under Shirley at New York. (VII. C. R., 23.)

[2] William Polson was probably a Scot who had been concerned in the rebellion of 1745; since, early in 1755, he writes to James Burd complaining bitterly of a report that assigned him in that affair "such a low station as I detest as much as the author of such a falsehood." (I. Shippen MSS. 18.) In 1754, he served under Washington, and received the thanks of the Virginia Burgesses and Governor for his good conduct. His captaincy in the Virginia services dated from 21st July, 1754. (Sharpe's

		Compliment.	Effective.
Capt. Peronee's[1] }			
Capt. Wagner's[2] }	Virginia Rangers...........	50 ...	47
	Virginia Rangers...........	50 ...	45
Capt. Dagworthy's[3]	Maryland Rangers..........	50 ...	49

Second Brigade, Commanded by Colonel Dunbar.

48th Regiment of Foot	.....	700 ...	650
Capt. Demerie's[4]	South Carolina Detach[1]	100 ...	97

MS. Corr.) Being killed in 1755, an annual pension of £26 was bestowed by Virginia upon his widow. (VII. Sp. Wash, 87.) I believe, too, a lieutenant's commission in the 60th, of which Gage was commandant and Gates major, was given to his son John on 5th May, 1756. (II. Sp. Wash., 127.) He was made captain June 16th, 1773, which rank he held in 1778.

[1] William, Chevalier de Peyronie, was a French Protestant, settled in Virginia, and highly esteemed. At Fort Necessity he was an ensign under Washington, whose warm favor he enjoyed. Being desperately wounded in that action, he obtained leave to wait upon the Assembly to petition for some recompense for his personal losses of clothes, &c. On 30th Aug., 1754, the Burgesses voted him their thanks, and especially desired the Governor to promote him; and he accordingly received a captain's commission to date from 25th August, 1754. He died unmarried. (II. Sp. Wash. Sharpe's MS. Corr.)

[2] Thomas Waggener (Capt. Virg. troops, July 20th, 1754), was a lieutenant in the campaign of 1754, and was slightly wounded at Jumonville's defeat. He had previously served under Gov. Shirley, in the projected Canada expedition of 1746. At Fort Necessity he was a lieutenant, and was one of those thanked by the Virginia legislature. His gallant conduct in Braddock's campaign has been noticed: it may be added, that so late as 1757, he continued actively engaged in the war. (II. Sp. Wash. II Belknap's Hist. N. H. Sharpe's MS. Corr.)

[3] Ely Dagworthy had held the King's commission in the previous French war, and was engaged in Shirley's Canada design. For this reason, he esteemed himself superior to any mere provincial officer, though he was himself considered in that very light by Braddock, insomuch as he had no other command than that of a Maryland company. In the fall of 1756, his impudent assumptions of superiority to Washington were summarily put down by Gen. Shirley (II. Sp. Wash.); and not long after he seems to have obtained one of the lieutenancies in the 44th, made vacant by the action of 9th July. His commission dated from 15th July, 1755. In 1765, he had risen no higher.

[4] Paul Demerie, who was killed by the Cherokees in 1760, during the Indian war of South Carolina. I. Ramsay's S. C, 182.

		Compliment.	Effective.
Capt. Dobb's	North Carolina Rangers ...	100 ...	80
Capt. Mercer's [1]	Company of Carpenters	50 ...	35
Capt. Stevens's [2]	Virginia Rangers............	50 ...	48
Capt. Hogg's [3]	Virginia Rangers............	50 ...	40
Capt. Cox's [4]	Virginia Rangers............	50 ...	43

The Detachment of Seamen to encamp with the Second Brigade and the Troop of light horse separately.

The General is to be acquainted through an aid de Camp the night before the regiments are to exercise.

Prohibitory Orders were given against spirituous liquors being sold to the Indians, or any soldiers going into their camp.

Proper Victualling returns were ordered to be given in to the Commissary General of the stores, signed by the commanding officers of the Regiments and Artillery, the several Companies, Detachment of Seamen and Troop of light horse, the Director of the Hospital, Waggon-Master General, and Indian manager, specifying the names and qualifications of those persons, who drew provisions under their command or directions.

[1] I do not know if this was George or John Mercer. Both were at Fort Necessity, and thanked by the Burgesses : the former was a Virginia captain, June 4th, 1754, and in 1760, agent of the Ohio Company at London. The latter was a lieutenant, 21st July, 1754, and Washington's aid in 1756; in which year he was killed by the enemy.

[2] Adam Stephen was, in 1754, perhaps the senior captain in Frey's regiment. He rose to be colonel of the Virginia troops, and was a general officer in the Revolution.

[3] Peter Hogg was a captain, March 9th, 1754; and so late as the end of 1757 was still in the Virginia service. Being detached on the march, he and his command escaped the dangers of the 9th of July.

[4] Probably Thomas Cocke, commissioned as captain in the Virginia troops, Dec. 13th, 1754.

All the troops were to account to the director of the hospital once in three months for stoppages at the rate of four pence sterling per day for every man that was admitted into the General Hospital.

It was also ordered, that no suttler should dare to sell any more spirits to the men than one gill a day to each, which an Officer of the Picket was to see delivered out at eleven of the clock and mixed with three gills of water; and any suttler offending against this order was to be sent to the Provost.

If any non-commissioned Officer or soldier shall be found gaming, he shall immediately receive three hundred lashes, and the standers by shall be deemed principals and punished as such.

If any Soldier is seen drunk in Camp, he is to be sent immediately to the Quarter Guard, and to receive two hundred lashes the next morning.

Agreeably to a resolution of a Council of War, it was ordered that every Subaltern superintending the work upon the road should receive three shillings per day; each serjeant one shilling; each corporal nine pence; and every drum or private man six pence. But as it was thought this would weaken too much the Military Chest, and there being no publick markets, the General promised to settle with them in their winter quarters.

Any soldier or follower of the Army that shall be detected in stealing or purloyning any of the provisions, shall suffer death.

SPENDELOW CAMP.

Lieutenant Colonel Burton represented to the General that he had been two days in marching about five miles on a better road than we were to expect afterwards, occasioned by the extreme faintness and deficiency of the horses.

The General thereupon called together all the Officers, and told them, that through this inconvenience it would be impossible to continue the March without some alterations, which he was convinced they would readily assist in, as they had hitherto expressed the greatest spirit and inclination for the service. He recommended to them to send to Fort Cumberland all such baggage as was not absolutely necessary, and told them, if any of them had able horses, which they could spare to the publick cause, he would take care that such testimonies of their regard to it should not be forgotten, and excited them to it by his example; he and his family contributed twenty horses. This had such an effect, that most of the Officers sent back their own, and made use of Soldiers tents the rest of the Campaign, and near a hundred able horses were given to the publick service.

June 11th. The General called a council of war, consisting of

Colonel Sr Peter Halket,   Colonel Dunbar,
Lieut. Colo. Gage,   Lieut. Colo. Burton,
Major Chapman,   Major Sparks.

In which it was agreed to send back two six-pounders, four cohorns, some powder and stores, which cleared near twenty waggons. All the King's waggons were also sent back to the Fort, they being too heavy, and requiring large horses for the shafts, which could not be procured; and country waggons were fitted for the powder in their stead.

This day was employed in shifting the powder, fitting the waggons, and making a proper assortment of the stores.

The loads of all the waggons were to be reduced to fourteen hundred weight; seven of the most able horses were chose for the Howitzers, and five to each twelve-pounder, and four to each waggon. The other horses were all to carry flour and bacon. Every horse was by the contract to have carried two hundred weight, but the contractors were so well acquainted with our situation, (which did not permit us to reject anything), that most of the horses furnished by them were the offcasts of Indian traders, and scarce able to stand under one hundred weight.

A detachment of a Captain, two subalterns, and fifty men, were sent as a covering party to the workers upon the Pensylvania road; and fifty of the worst men from the Independents and Rangers were ordered to reinforce the Garrison at Fort Cumberland; and only two women per company were allowed to be victualled upon the March, but proper provision was made for them at the Fort, to which place they were sent back.[1]

Some orders were found necessary for the farther regulation and security of the Camp.

We were now encamped according to the plan approved of by the Council of War. When the carriages were closed up, leaving proper intervals of communications, the extent of the Camp, from the front to the rear guard, was less than half a mile.

---

[1] They were, however, sent to Philadelphia. II. P. A., 348.

ORDERS GIVEN AT SPENDELOW CAMP.

The captains of the picket are to be at the field officer of the day's tent to receive the countersign, which they are to give to the subalterns, the subalterns to the serjeants, the serjeants to the centinels, who are not to suffer any person to come within ten paces without receiving the countersign; and all advanced corporals and centinels are to have their bayonets fixed.

The field officer of the picket is to be received as grand rounds, whenever he goes his rounds either night or day.

No person whatever to fire a piece within a mile of the Camp.

No hutts or bowers to be built by the advanced pickets or centinels.

One tumbril with tools is to march in the front and another in the center of the carriages, and one engineer with part of the pioneers is to march in the front, and another with the rest of the pioneers in the center.

It required two days to new load the waggons, and put everything in order, which being settled we marched on the 13th to Martin's plantation, being about five miles from Spendelow Camp. The first brigade got to their ground that night, but the second could not get up before the next day at eleven of the clock, the road being excessively mountainous and rocky. This obliged the General to halt one day for the refreshment of the men and horses.

ORDERS GIVEN AT THE CAMP AT MARTIN'S PLANTATION.

Upon the beating of the General, which is to be taken from the 44th Regiment, all the troops are to turn out, accoutre and form two deep at the head of their encampments upon all halts, tho' ever so small; the pickets and companies are to face outwards. The officers of the pickets are to take care that their pickets keep at a proper distance upon their flanks. Upon the firing of a cannon, either in front, centre or rear, the whole line is to form, to face outwards, and to wait for orders.

The field officers, excepting him that commands the Van Guard, are to take no particular post, but to see that the men assist in getting up the waggons at any steep ascent, or difficult pass.

In case any waggon should break down, it is immediately to be drawn out on one side of the road, and a report of it with its lading to be sent to the Waggon Master-General, who is to order it to be repaired and fall in the rear, or the load to be divided among the other waggons, as he shall think proper.

The carrying horses having suffered very much by bearing their loads so long the day before, they were ordered with an escort of two companies upon the right of the 44th to proceed to the little meadows, at which place Sr John St Clair was encamped with the three hundred men, not having been able to proceed further in the five days.

June 15th. The line began to move from this place at five of the clock; it was twelve before all the carriages had got upon a hill which is about a quarter of a mile from the front of the Camp, and it was found necessary to make one-half of the men ground their arms and assist the carriages while the others remained advantageously posted for their security.

We this day passed the Aligany Mountain, which is a

rocky ascent of more than two miles, in many places extremely steep; its descent is very rugged and almost perpendicular; in passing which we intirely demolished three waggons and shattered several.[1] At the bottom of the mountain runs Savage river, which, when we passed was an insignificant stream; but the Indians assured us that in the winter it is very deep, broad and rapid. This is the last water that empties itself into the Potomack.

The first Brigade encamped about three miles to the westward of this river. Near this place was another steep ascent, which the waggons were six hours in passing.

In this day's march, though all possible care was taken, the line was sometimes extended to a length of four or five miles.

June 16th. We marched from the Camp near Savage river to the little meadows, which is about ten miles from Martins' Plantations, where the first brigade arrived that evening, but the second did not all arrive till the 18th. A great part of this day's march was over a bogg which had been very well repaired by Sr John St Clair's advanced party with infinite labour.[2]

By these four days' marches it was found impossible to proceed with such a number of carriages. The horses grew every day fainter, and many died: and the men would not have been able to have undergone the constant and necessary fatigue, by remaining so many hours under arms; and

---

[1] Mr. Atkinson (II. O. T, 542) very justly points out the error of not passing this mountain by the spur since adopted for the National Road.

[2] The route this day lay through the region of dense pine forests called the Shades of Death.

by the great extent of the baggage the line was extremely weak'ned.

The General was therefore determined to move forward with a detachment of the best men, and as little incumbrance as possible.

Therefore a detachment of one field-officer with four hundred men and the deputy quarter master general marched on the 18th to cut and make the road to the little crossing of the Yoxhio Geni—taking with them two sixpounders with their ammunition, three waggons of tools, and thirty five days provision—all on carrying horses. And on the 19th the General marched with a detachment of one Colonel, one Lieutenant Colonel, one Major, the two eldest Grenadier Companies, and five hundred rank and file. The party of Seamen and eighteen light horse, and four howitzers with fifty rounds each, and four twelve pounders with eighty rounds each, and one hundred rounds of ammunition for each man, and one waggon of Indian presents; the whole number of carriages being about thirty. The Howitzers had each nine horses, the twelve pounders seven, and the waggons six. There was also thirty five days provision carried on horses.

This detachment marched and encamped according to the annexed plan.

The Indians were ordered to march with the advanced party; this day Monocatuca the Indian chief being at a small distance from the party was surrounded and taken by some French and Indians. The former were desirous of killing him, but the Indians refused, declaring they would abandon them and join with us if they persisted in

Line of Ma[rch]

Light Horse

Serjt. & 10 Grenadiers

Serjt. & 10 Men

Sub.

Serjt. & 10 Men

Sub.n

Serjt. & 10 Men

Sub.n

Serjt. & 10 Men

Light Horse

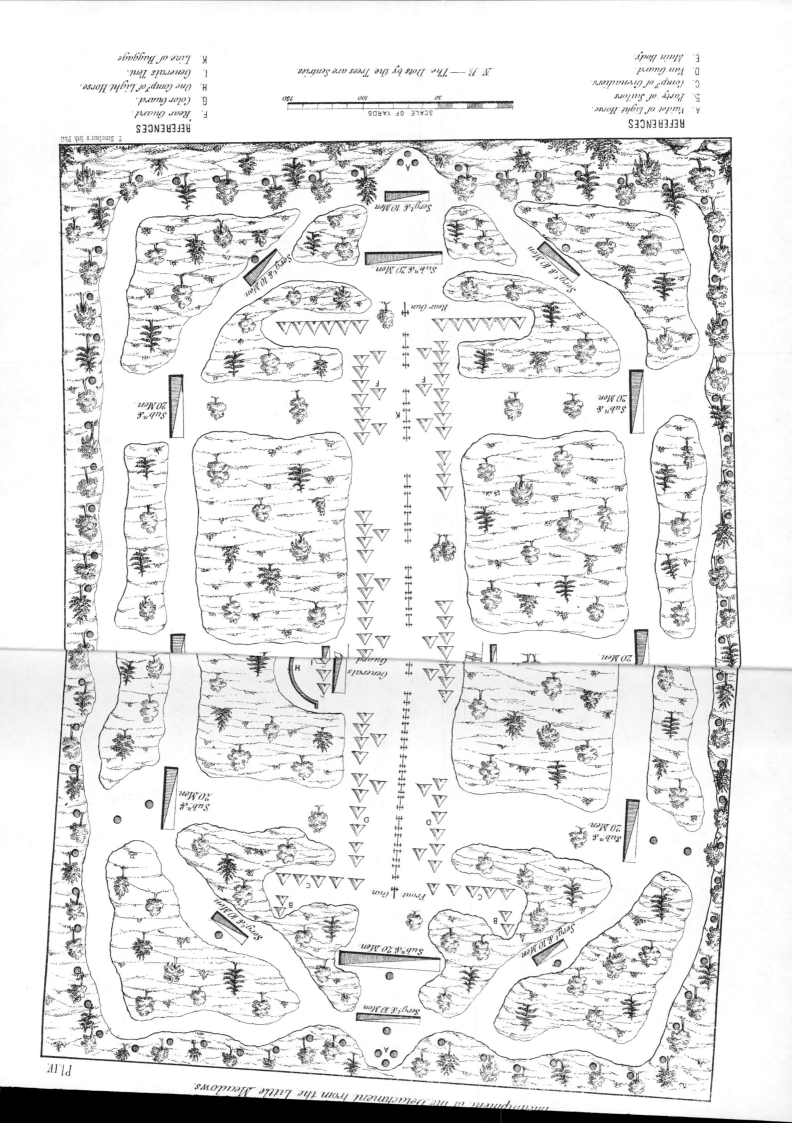

Encampment of the Detachment from the Little Meadows.

PL IV.

T. Sinclair's lith Phil.

Serg^t & 10 Men

Sub^n & 20 Men

Serj^t & 10 Men

Rear Gun

Sub^n & 20 Men

Sub^n & 20 Men

20 Men

Generals Guard

Sub^n & 20 Men

Sub^n & 20 Men

Serg^t & 10 Men

Sub^n & 20 Men

Front Gun

Serg^t & 10 Men

Serg^t & 10 Men

their design. They agreed at last to tye him to a tree, and leave him: But his son who was with him escaped, and informed our Indians, who went soon after and brought him off.

We this day crossed the first branch[1] of the Yoxio Geni, which is about four score yards over and knee deep. After having marched four miles from the little meadows we came up with the rear of the advanced party, and were obliged to encamp, as they were then at work in cutting a travers-road over an immense mountain, which could not be finished till the next day. Immediately upon coming to our ground, some guides ran into us, extremely frightened, and told us a great body of the enemy were marching to attack our advanced guard. The General sent forward an aid de camp to know the truth of this report, who found Lieutenant Colonel Gage in possession of the top of the mountain, and his men very advantageously posted. Our Indians had discovered the tracks of several men very near the advanced party, which had given rise to this alarm. Lieutenant Colonel Gage remained about two hours under arms, but no enemy appearing he sent parties to scour the neighboring woods, and upon their return proceeded with the work, leaving proper parties to secure the heights, and encamped there that night.

As the advanced party was to move forward early in the morning, the General ordered a detachm[t]. of a Captain and one hundred men to march at daybreak, and to occupy that eminence till he should pass it with the Artillery and baggage.

[1] Castleman's River: the ford is called the Little Crossings.

22

Every field-officer had an orderly light horseman by whom they were to inform the General of all accidents, stops or delays in their respective parts of the line; by which means, the extent of the carriages, upon the march, was very seldom above half a mile; and the encampments was but three hundred yards from the front to the rear.

ORDERS AT THE CAMP ON THE WEST SIDE THE LITTLE CROSSING OF THE YOXHIO GENI.

June 19. The quarter masters are constantly to see the communications opened.

The pickets of the detachment to consist of two captains and the subaltern officers parties that are advanced upon the flanks in the front and in the rear.

The eldest captain of the picket is to command and visit the pickets of the front Grenadiers and the left flank, and the youngest captain the picket and the rear Grenadiers and the right flank. The retreat is to beat an hour before sunset, at which time the picket is to be relieved, that the officers may have light to reconnoitre the ground and to post their centinels.

From thence we marched about nine miles to Bear Camp over a chain of very rocky mountains and difficult passes. We could not reach our ground 'till about 7 of the clock, which was three hours later than common, as there was no water, nor even earth enough to fix a tent, between the great Mountain and this place.

We halted here two days, having a road to cut in the side of a mountain, and some swamps to make passable.

ORDERS AT BEAR CAMP; *June 20th.*

The men of the pickets are always to load afresh when they go on duty, and to take particular care to save the ball, which the commanding officers of companies are to see returned to the train.

The troops that are encamped here are to be formed into Companies according to the number of Captains present.

The Articles of War are to be read to the men, and that article relating to the alarming of camps to be particularly explained to them.

The General having observed upon the March some neglects upon the out detachments, orders that for the future the subalterns' parties, when the ground will possibly admit of it, keep at least one hundred yards distance from the line, and that the serjeants keep their parties within sight of the subaltern's from which they are detached; and upon every halt, though ever so small, the men are to form two deep, face outwards, and stand shouldered.

The Officers and serjeants are to be very attentive to the beat of the drum, taking care always to halt when they hear the long roll beat at that part of the line from which they are detached, and to march upon beating the long march.

The field officers and all officers commanding any part of the line are to be particularly careful to beat the long roll and long march upon their halting and marching.

Exact victualling returns are to be given in to the commissaries, signed by the commanding officer.

The quarter masters of the two regiments are always to

attend at the delivery of provisions, and to receive from the commissary the full quantity for their respective corps, which they are to distribute to the serjeants of the companies, who are to issue it to the men. The Artillery, seamen, and light horse, and waggon masters, are to do the same.

On the 23rd of June we marched from this Camp to the Squaw's fort, making about six miles of very bad road.

Three Mohawk Indians pretending friendship came to the General and told him they were just come from the French fort. They said that some reinforcement[s] were arrived from Montreal, and that they were in expectation of many more: that they had very little provision at the fort, and that they had been disappointed of their supplies by the dryness of the season having stopped the navigation of Buffler river.[1]

The General caressed them, and gave them presents, but they nevertheless went off that night, and with them one of our Indians, whom we had very long suspected. This fellow had frequently endeavored to conceal himself upon the flanks on the March, but was always discovered by the flank parties. Notwithstanding this, we could not punish him, as the Indians are so extremely jealous that we feared it would produce a general disaffection.

The 24th of June we marched at five in the morning, and passed the second branch of the Yoxhio Geni, which is about one hundred yards wide, about three feet deep, with a very strong current.[2]

---

[1] The Rivière aux Bœufs, or French Creek, is here signified.

[2] This was at the Great Crossings. "The route thence to the Great Meadows or Fort Necessity was well chosen, though over a mountainous

In the day's march, we discovered an Indian Camp, which they had just abandoned: our Indians informed us that, by their hutts, their number was about one hundred and seventy. They had stripped and painted some trees, upon which they and the French had written many threats and bravados with all kinds of scurrilous language.

We marched this day about six miles, and at night joined the two detachments.

ORDERS AT THE CAMP ON THE EAST SIDE THE GREAT MEADOWS.

At daybreak the men of the advanced pickets are to examine their panns and to put in fresh priming.

The subalterns upon the advanced parties are to keep one of their men within sight of the line, whom they are to have always in view; and the serjeants are to do the same by the subalterns.

The General is determined to put the first officer under arrest whom he shall find any ways negligent in any of these duties.

On the 25th, at daybreak, three men who went without the centinels, were shot and scalped. Parties were immediately sent out to scour the woods on all sides, and to drive in the stray horses.

This day we passed the Great Meadows, and encamped

tract, conforming very nearly to the ground now occupied by the National Road, and keeping on the dividing ridge between the waters flowing into the Youghiogeny on the one hand, and the Cheat River on the other." II. O. T., 543.

about two miles on the other side.[1] We this day saw several Indians in the woods; the General sent the light horse, our Indians, and some volunteers, to endeavour to surround them, but they returned without seeing them.

About a quarter of a mile from this camp, we were obliged to let our carriages down a hill with tackles, which made it later than usual before we got to our ground.

The soldiers were now so accustomed to open the communications, and understood so well the reason and method of our encampment, that they performed this work with great alacrity and dispatch; and the marching through the woods, which they at first looked upon as unnecessary fatigue, they were now convinced to be their only security, and went through it with the greatest cheerfulness.

Some French and Indians endeavoured to reconnoitre the camp, but wherever they advanced, they were discovered and fired upon by the advanced Centinels.

Two Captain's Detachments of 50 men each, were ordered to march at 10 o'clock in the morning with guides. One party was to march out at the front and the other in the rear. They were to divide the detachments into small parties, and to lie upon their arms about half a mile wide upon each flank of the encampment. At break of day the pickets were to advance, and at the same time these small parties were to move forward towards the camp. By this

---

[1] A mile west of the Great Meadows 'Braddock must have passed over the very spot destined for his grave. The Mount Braddock farm occupies a portion of the route.

measure, any Indians who had concealed themselves near the camp must have been taken; but these parties returned without having seen any of the enemy.

ORDERS AT THE CAMP ON THE WEST SIDE OF THE GREAT
MEADOWS, *June the 25th*.

The advanced pickets are to take no more blankets than will be sufficient to cover their centinels.

The line is never to turn out upon any account but by order from the General, or the field officer of the picket.

Every soldier or Indian shall receive five pounds for each Indian scalp.

June the 26th. We marched at five o'clock, but by the extreme badness of the road could make but four miles. At our halting place we found another Indian camp, which they had abandoned at our approach, their fires being yet burning. They had marked in triumph upon trees, the scalps they had taken two days before, and a great many French had also written on them their names and many insolent expressions. We picked up a commission on the march, which mentioned the party being under the command of the Sieur Normanville. This Indian camp was in a strong situation, being upon a high rock with a very narrow and steep ascent to the top; it had a spring in the middle, and stood at the termination of the Indian path to the Monongehela, at the confluence of Red-stone creek. By this pass the party came which attacked Mr. Washington the year before, and also this which attended us. By their tracks, they seemed to have divided here, the one part going straight forward to fort du Quesne, and the other returning by Red-stone Creek to the Monongohela. A Captain, four subalterns, and ninety volunteers, marched from this camp with proper guides to fall in the night upon that party which we imagined had returned by the Monongohela. They found a small quantity of provisions, and a very large Batteau, which they destroyed, and the Captain according to orders joined the General at Gist's plantation, but saw no men.

June 27th. We marched from the camp of Rock fort to Gist's plantation, which was about six miles ; the road still mountainous and rocky. Here the advanced party was relieved, and all the waggons and carrying horses with provision belonging to that detachment joined us, and the men were to be victualled from us.

June the 28th. The troops marched about five miles to a camp on the east side of the Yoxhio Geni.[1]

ORDERS AT THE CAMP ON THE EAST SIDE OF THE YOXHIO

GENI, *June the* 29th.

Whereas by the connivance of some officers several of the men have fired their pieces in a very irregular and unmilitary manner ; The General declares that, for the future, if any officer, of whatever rank, shall suffer the men to fire their pieces, he shall be put under arrest. And it is ordered, that whenever it is found necessary to fire any of the men's pieces, that cannot be drawn, the commanding officers of the several troops are to apply to the General for leave, through an Aid de Camp.

[1] From the Great Meadows, the route had diverged in a north-westwardly direction, to gain a pass through Laurel Hill ; it then struck the river at Stewart's Crossing, half a mile below Connellsville. See II. O. T, 543.

The commanding officers of regiments, troops, and companies, are to send to the train all their damaged cartridges, and to apply to the commanding officer of the Artillery for fresh ones in the lieu of them.

June the 30th. We crossed the main body of the Yoxhio Geni, which was about two hundred yards broad and about three feet deep. The advanced guard passed, and took post on the other side, till our Artillery and baggage got over; which was followed by four hundred men who remained on the east side 'till all the baggage had passed.

We were obliged to encamp about a mile on the west side, where we halted a day to cut a passage over a mountain. This day's march did not exceed two miles.

Part of the flour having been unavoidably damaged by severe rains, the General sent an order to Colonel Dunbar to forward to him with the utmost diligence one hundred carrying horses with flour, and some beeves, with an escort of a Captain and one hundred men.

Upon this day's halt the men's arms were all drawn and cleaned, and four days provision served to the men that they might prepare a quantity of bread, and dress victuals to carry with them.

ORDERS ON THE WEST SIDE OF THE YOXHIO GENI.

The men's tents are to be pitched in a single line facing outwards, and no officer is to pitch his tent or have his picket of horses in front of the soldiers tents. And that there may be sufficient room for this, it is the General's order that as soon as the troops come to their ground and the carriages close up, that the commanding officers of each regiment order their several detachments to advance twenty five paces from that part of the line of carriages which they covered, and there to pitch their tents. No fire upon any account to be lighted in front of the pickets.

On the first of July, we marched about five miles, but could advance no further by reason of a great swamp which required much work to make it passable.

On the 2ⁿᵈ July, we marched to Jacob's cabin, about 6 miles from the camp. A field officer was sent from the line to take the command of the advanced guard, and the disposition thereof was settled according to the annexed plan.

ORDERS AT JACOB'S CABIN.

No more bell tents are to be fixed : the men are to take their arms into their tents with them ; and an officer of a company is to see at retreat beating that the men fix on their thumb stalls.

July 3ʳᵈ. The swamp being repaired, we marched about six miles to the Salt Lick Creek.[1] Sʳ John Sᵗ Clair proposed to the General to halt at this Camp, and to send back all our horses to bring up Colonel Dunbar's detachment.

The General upon this called a council of war consisting of

Colonel Sʳ Peter Halket,
Lieuᵗ Colonel Gage,   Lieuᵗ Colonel Burton,
Major Sparks,   Major Sʳ John Sᵗ Clair, D. Q. G.,

---

[1] Now known as Jacob's Creek.

And informed them of the proposition made to him by Sr John, and desired their opinions thereof. Then the following circumstances were considered:

That the most advanced party of Colonel Dunbar's detachment was then at Squawse fort, and the other part a day's march in the rear, from which place with our light detachment we had been eleven days. And tho' we had met with some delays while the roads were making, yet, when the badness of them was considered, and the number of carriages Colonel Dunbar had with him, it was judged he could not perform the march in less time:

That the horses could not join him in less than two days:

That no advantage seemed to accrue from this junction, as the whole, afterwards, could not move together:

That Colonel Dunbar was unable to spare many men:

That, besides, he would be more liable to be attacked than at his present distance:

That the horses through their weak situation were not judged capable of performing it:

That by the loss of so many days the provision brought with us from Fort Cumberland would have been so near expended, as to have laid us under the necessity of bringing up a convoy, had we met with any opposition at the fort:

That by these delays the French would have time to receive their reinforcements and provisions, and to entrench themselves, or strengthen the fort, or to avail themselves of the strongest passes to interrupt our march:

That it was conjectured they had not many Indians or great strength at the fort, as they had already permitted us to make many passes which might have been defended by a very few men:

Upon these considerations, the council were unanimously of opinion not to halt there for Colonel Dunbar; but to proceed the next morning.

The General sent for the Indian manager, and ordered him to endeavor to prevail with the Indians to go towards the fort for intelligence, which the General had often assayed, but could never prevail upon them since the camp at the great Meadows. They now likewise refused, notwithstanding the presents and promises which he constantly made them.

ORDERS AT SALT LICK CAMP.

The commanding officers of companies are to view their men's arms this evening before retreat beating, and to see them put in the best order.

At the beating of the assembly to-morrow, all the troops are to load with fresh cartridges. The centinels upon the advanced pickets for the future to be doubled at night, by placing two centinels at every post.

The officers upon the advanced pickets during the night time are to have half their men constantly under arms with fixed bayonets and to relieve them every two hours; and the half that is relieved may lye down by their arms, but are not to be suffered to quit their pickets.

When the captains of the pickets are not going their rounds, they are to remain at the head of the center picket of that flank which they are appointed to visit.

Whenever any advanced centinel fires his piece in the

night, the captain of the picket of that flank from which the shot is fired is immediately to go a visiting round to that part of the picket, and to send word to the field officer of the occasion of the shot being fired.

July 4th. We marched about six miles to Thicketty-run; the country was now less mountainous and rocky, and the woods rather more open, consisting chiefly of white oak.[1]

From this place two of our Indians were prevailed upon to go for intelligence towards the French fort; and also (unknown to them), Gist, the General's guide:

The Indians returned on the 6th, and brought in a French officer's scalp, who was shooting within half a mile of the fort. They informed the General that they saw very few men there, or tracks; nor any additional works. That no pass was possest by them between us and the fort, and that they believed very few men were out upon observation. They saw some boats under the fort, and one with a white flag coming down the Ohio.

Gist returned a little after the same day, whose account corresponded with their's, except he saw smoke in a valley between our camp and Du Quesne. He had concealed himself with an intent of getting close under the fort in the night, but was discovered and pursued by two Indians, who had very near taken him.

[1] "From the crossing of Jacob's Creek, which was at the point where Welchhanse's Mill now stands, about 1½ miles below Mount Pleasant, the route stretched off to the north, crossing the Mount Pleasant turnpike near the village of the same name, and thence, by a more westerly course, passing the Great Sewickley near Painter's Salt Works, thence south and west of the post-office of Madison and Jacksonville, it reached the Brush Fork of Turtle Creek." II. O. T., 544.

At this camp the provisions from Colonel Dunbar with a detachment of a Captain and one hundred men joined us, and we halted here one day.

On the 6th July we marched about six miles to Monaka-tuca Camp, which was called so from an unhappy accident that happened upon the march.

Three or four people loitering in the rear of the Grenadiers were killed by a party of Indians and scalped. Upon hearing the firing, the General sent back the Grenadier company, on whose arrival the Indians fled. They were discovered again a little after by our Indians in the front, who were going to fire upon them, but were prevented by some of our out-rangers, who mistaking these our Indians for the enemy, fired upon them and killed Monakatuca's son, notwithstanding they made the agreed countersign, which was holding up a bough and grounding their arms. When we came to our ground, the General sent for the father and the other Indians, condoled with and made them the usual presents, and desired the officers to attend the funeral; and gave an order to fire over the body.

This behaviour of the General was so agreeable to the Indians, that they afterwards were more attached to us, quite contrary to our expectations.

The line of carrying horses extending very often a prodigious length, it was almost impossible to secure them from insults, tho' they had yet marched without any interruption, every Bat-man having been ordered to carry his firelock, and small parties having kept constantly upon the flanks. The disposition of march for these horses had varied almost every day, according to the nature of the country; but the most common was to let them remain upon the ground an hour after the march of the line, under the guard of a Captain and one hundred men : by which means there was no confusion in leaving the ground, and the horses were much eased. They were now order'd, when the woods would permit, to march upon the flanks between the subalterns' picket and the line; but whenever the country was close or rocky, they were then to fall in the rear, and a strong guard marched thither for their security, which was directed to advance or fall back in proportion to the length of the line of carrying horses, taking particular care always to have parties on the flanks.

ORDERS AT MONAKATUCA CAMP.

If it should be ordered to advance the van or send back the rear guard, the advanced parties detached from them are to remain at their posts, facing outwards.

Whenever there is a general halt, half of each of the subalterns' advanced parties are to remain under arms with fixed bayonets, facing outwards, and the other half may sit down by their arms.

On the 7th July we marched from hence, and quitting the Indian path, endeavored to pass the Turtle Creek about 12 miles from the mouth, to avoid the dangerous pass of the narrows. We were led to a precipice which it was impossible to descend. The General ordered Sr John St Clair to take a captain and one hundred men, with the Indians, guides, and some light horse, to reconnoitre very well the country. In about two hours he returned and informed the General that he had found the ridge which led the whole way to fort Du Quesne, and avoided the narrows and Frazier's, but that some work which was to be done would make it impossible to move further that day. We therefore encamped here, and marched the next morning about eight miles to the camp near the Monongahela.[1]

When we arrived here, Sr John St Clair mentioned (but not to the General), the sending a detachment that night to invest the fort; but being asked whether the distance was not too great to reinforce that detachment in case of an attack, and whether it would not be more advisable to make the pass of the Monongahela, or the narrows, whichever was resolved upon, with our whole force, and then to send the detachment from the next camp, which would be six or seven miles from the fort, Sr John immediately acquiesced, and was of opinion that that would be a much more prudent measure.

The guides were sent for, who described the Narrows to be a narrow pass of about two miles, with a river on the left and a very high mountain on the right, and that it would require much repair to make it passable by carriages. They said the Monongahela had two extreme good fords, which were very shallow, and the banks not steep. It was therefore resolved to pass this river the next morning; and Lieutenant Colonel Gage was ordered to march before break of day with the two companies of Grenadiers, one hundred

[1] Abandoning thus the passage of the Brush Fork of Turtle Creek, Braddock here turned into the valley of Long Run, near where now is Stewartsville, and encamped on the 8th July at two miles distance from the Monongahela. On the 9th, he followed the valley of Crooked Run to the river.

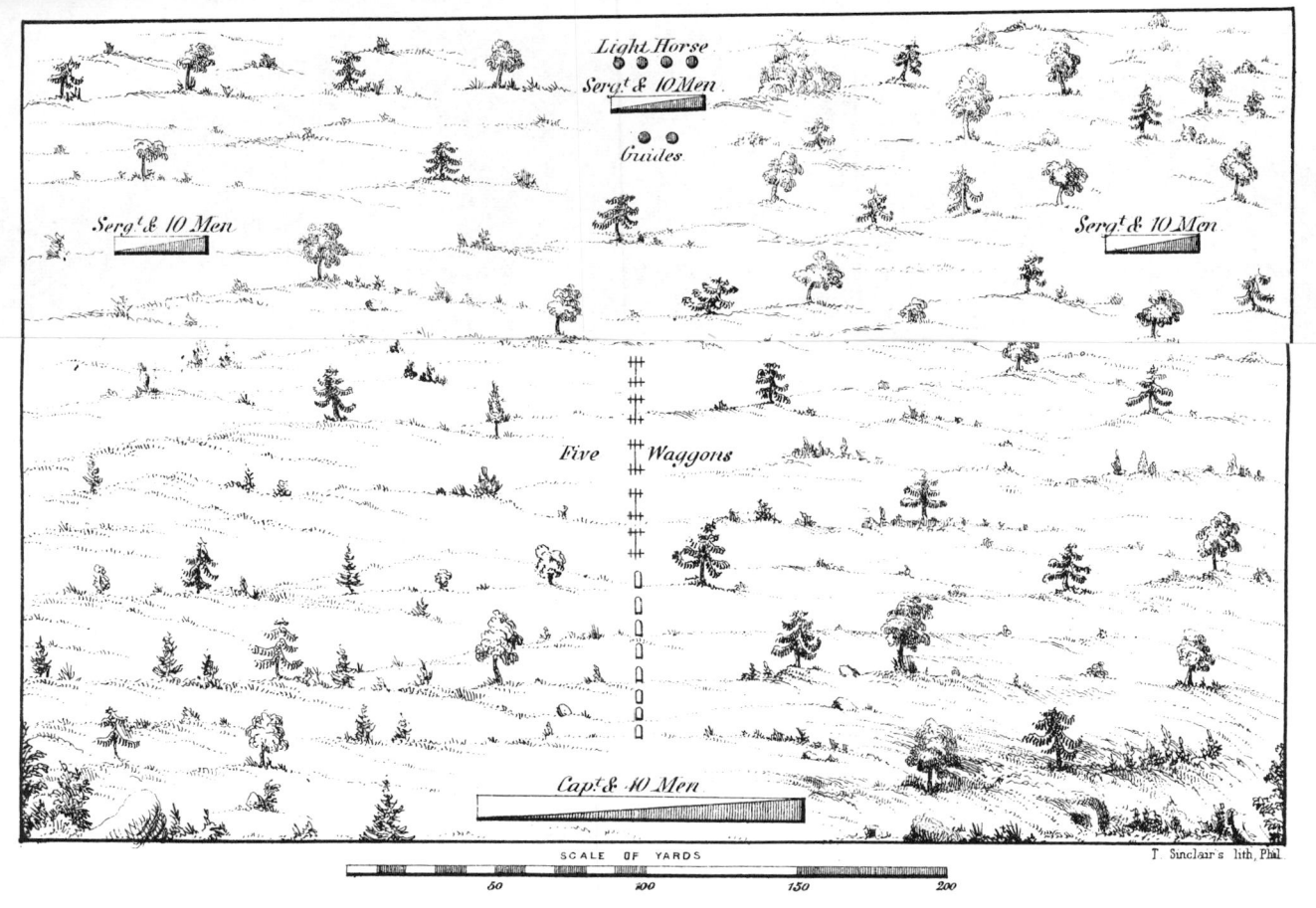

Light Horse

Serg.t & 10 Men

Guides.

Serg.t & 10 Men

Serg.t & 10 Men

Five Waggons

Cap.t & 10 Men

SCALE OF YARDS

50   100   150   200

T. Sinclair's lith, Phil.

and sixty rank and file of the 44th and 48th, Captain Gates's independent company, and two six-pounders, with proper guides; and he was instructed to pass the fords of the Monongehela and to take post after the second crossing, to secure the passage of that river.

Sr John St Clair was ordered to march at 4 of the clock with a detachment of two hundred and fifty men to make the roads for the artillery and baggage, which was to march with the remainder of the troops at five.

Orders at the Camp near the Monongahela.

All the men are to draw and clean their pieces, and the whole are to load to-morrow on the beating of the General with fresh cartridges.

No tents or baggage are to be taken with Lieutenant Colonel Gage's party.

July 9th. The whole marched agreeably to the Orders before mentioned, and about 8 in the morning the General made the first crossing of the Monongahela by passing over about one hundred and fifty men in the front, to whom followed half the carriages. Another party of one hundred and fifty men headed the second division; the horses and cattle then passed, and after all the baggage was over, the remaining troops, which till then possessed the heights, marched over in good order.

The General ordered a halt, and the whole formed in their proper line of march.

When we had moved about a mile, the General received a note from Lieutenant Colonel Gage acquainting him with his having passed the river without any interruption, and having posted himself agreeably to his orders.

When we got to the other crossing, the bank on the opposite side not being yet made passable, the artillery and baggage drew up along the beach, and halted 'till one, when the General passed over the detachment of the 44th, with the pickets of the right. The artillery waggons and carrying horses followed; and then the detachment of the 48th, with the left pickets, which had been posted during the halt upon the heights.

When the whole had passed, the General again halted, till they formed according to the annexed plan.

It was now near two o'clock, and the advanced party under Lieutenant Colonel Gage and the working party under Sr John St Clair were ordered to march on 'till three. No sooner were the pickets upon their respective flanks, and the word given to march, but we heard an excessive quick and heavy firing in the front. The General imagining the advanced parties were very warmly attacked, and being willing to free himself from the incumbrance of the baggage, order'd Lieutenant Colonel Burton to reinforce them with the vanguard, and the line to halt. According to this disposition, eight hundred men were detached from the line, free from all embarrassments, and four hundred were left for the defence of the Artillery and baggage, posted in such a manner as to secure them from any attack or insults.

The General sent forward an Aid de Camp to bring him an account of the nature of attack, but the fire continuing, he moved forward himself, leaving Sr Peter Halket with the command of the baggage. The advanced detachments soon gave way and fell back upon Lieutenant Colonel Burton's detachment, who was forming his men to face a rising ground upon the right. The whole were now got together in great confusion. The colours were advanced in different places, to separate the men of the two regiments. The General ordered the officers to endeavour to form the men, and to tell them off into small divisions and to advance with them; but neither entreaties nor threats could prevail.

The advanced flank parties, which were left for the security of the baggage, all but one ran in. The baggage was then warmly attacked; a great many horses, and some drivers were killed; the rest escaped by flight. Two of the cannon flanked the baggage, and for some time kept the Indians off: the other cannon, which were disposed of in the best manner and fired away most of their ammunition, were of some service, but the spot being so woody, they could do little or no execution.

The enemy had spread themselves in such a manner, that they extended from front to rear, and fired upon every part.

The place of action was covered with large trees, and much underwood upon the left, without any opening but the road, which was about twelve foot wide. At the distance of about two hundred yards in front and upon the right were two rising grounds covered with trees.

When the General found it impossible to persuade them to advance, and no enemy appeared in view; and nevertheless a vast number of officers were killed, by exposing themselves before the men; he endeavored to retreat them in good order; but the panick was so great that he could not succeed. During this time they were loading as fast as possible and firing in the air. At last Lieutenant Colonel Burton got together about one hundred of the 48th regiment, and prevailed upon them, by the General's order, to follow him towards the rising ground on the right, but he being disabled by his wounds, they faced about to the right, and returned.

When the men had fired away all their ammunition and the General and most of the officers were wounded, they by one common consent left the field, running off with the greatest precipitation. About fifty Indians pursued us to the river, and killed several men in the passage. The officers used all possible endeavours to stop the men, and to prevail upon them to rally; but a great number of them threw away their arms and ammunition, and even their cloaths, to escape the faster.

About a quarter of a mile on the other side the river, we prevailed upon near one hundred of them to take post upon a very advantageous spot, about two hundred yards from the road. Lieutenant Colonel Burton posted some small parties and centinels. We intended to have kept possession of that ground, 'till we could have been reinforced. The General and some wounded officers remained there about an hour, till most of the men run off. From that place, the General sent Mr Washington to Colonel Dunbar with orders to send waggons for the wounded, some provision, and hospital stores; to be escorted by two youngest Grenadier companies, to meet him at Gist's plantation, or nearer, if possible.   It was found impracticable to remain here, as the General and officers were left almost alone; we therefore retreated in the best manner we were able.   After we had passed the Monongahela the second time, we were joined by Lieutenant Colonel Gage, who had rallied near 80 men.   We marched all that night, and the next day, and about ten o'clock that night we got to Gist's plantation.

GIST'S PLANTATION.

July 11th.   Some waggons, provisions, and hospital stores arrived.   As soon as the wounded were dressed, and the men had refreshed themselves, we retreated to Colonel Dunbar's Camp, which was near Rock Fort.   The General sent a serjeant's party back with provision to be left on the road on the other side of the Yoxhio Geni for the refreshment of any men who might have lost their way in the woods. Upon our arrival at Colonel Dunbar's camp, we found it in the greatest confusion.   Some of his men had gone off upon hearing of our defeat, and the rest seemed to have forgot all discipline.   Several of our detachment had not stopped 'till they had reached this camp.

It was found necessary to clear some waggons for the wounded, many of whom were in a desperate situation; and as it was impossible to remove the stores, the Howitzer shells, some twelve pound shot, powder, and provision, were destroyed or buried.

July 13th.   We marched from hence to the Camp, near the great Meadows, where the General died.

GENERAL COURT MARTIALS.

ALEXANDRIA.

Lieutenant Colonel Gage, President.

The prisoner ordered one thousand lashes, but part of punishment remitted.

FORT CUMBERLAND.

12th May. Major Sparks, President.

Luke Woodward, of the 48th regiment, condemned to dye, but pardoned.[1]

Several other prisoners sentenced to corporal punishment, but part of them remitted.

24th May. Lieutenant Colonel Gage, President.

The punishments put in execution, all corporal ones.

26th May. Sᵣ Peter Halket, President.

To try Lieutenant MᶜLeod, of the Artillery.[2]

Part of the sentence remitted.

3d June. Major Sparks, President.

The punishments put in execution, all corporal ones.

[END OF ORME'S JOURNAL.]

---

[1] The pardon seems to have made little impression on this fellow. He had been enlisted by Captain Polson, at Shippensburg, and was drafted into Captain Mercer's company of the 48th. Deserting a second time from Dunbar's camp, he was not retaken on 6th Sept., 1755. Penn. Gaz., No. 1394.

[2] William McLeod was made a captain of the Royal Regiment of Artillery, Oct. 21st, 1758, which position he held in 1763. In 1765, his name does not appear on the register.

COPY OF A DOCUMENT

GIVEN BY CAPTAIN HEWITT, R. N., TO HIS FRIEND CAPTAIN HENRY GAGE MORRIS, R. N., WHOSE FATHER WAS AN AIDE DE CAMP WITH WASHINGTON TO MAJOR GENERAL BRADDOCK IN THE EXPEDITION.

Winchester, 9th July, 1827.

FROM Alexandria to the Little Meadows by this Journal 216 miles.

[I do not know who was the author of this Journal: possibly he may have been of the family of Capt. Hewitt. He was clearly one of the naval officers detached for this service by Com. Keppel, whom sickness detained at Fort Cumberland during the expedition. There are two documents from which the ensuing pages are printed. The first, which is the text followed here, appears to have been a revised copy of the second. It is in the possession of the Rev. Francis-Orpen Morris, Nunburnholme Rectory, Yorkshire, to whose father it was given by Capt. Hewitt. The other and perhaps the original journal is written in a looser and less particular style, and in point of extent is inferior to its companion. It is preserved in the library at Woolwich. What passages of this latter document have seemed to the Editor to differ from the former in any degree save of a clerical error, are appended by way of notes; which are distinguished from his own by alphabetical instead of numeral references, and by being enclosed within brackets. For the rest, so far as the lesser MS. goes, its language is so similar to that

(359)

General Braddock was 22 days marching from the little Meadows to the fatal Monongahela river, which appears to be within eight miles of the French fort Du Quesne, without a single Indian in his Army, or the least suspicion of falling into an ambush, although he was in a country, of all the Globe, the most adapted for one to encounter an enemy whose mode of fighting is confined to that method.

List of those Officers that were present and of them that was killed and wounded in the action on the banks of y° Monongohela River, y° 9th July, 1755.

Officers' Names.	Rank.	Killed or Wounded.
His Excellency Edward Braddock, Esqr.....	General and commr in chief.	Died of his wounds on the 12th.
Robert Orme, Esqr	Aid de Camps.	Wounded.
Roger Morris, Esqr		"
George Washington, Esqr		"
William Shirley, Esqr	Secretary.	"
Sir John Sinclair, Bart.	Dr. Qr. Mr. Gl.	Killed.
M. Leslie, Esqr¹........	Gl. Assist. do.	Wounded.
Fras. Halkett, Esqr...	Major Brigade.	"

of the greater as would render its publication here a mere repetition. It is proper to add that in the summer of 1854 (and since the advertisement of this volume), the Journal in the possession of the Rev. Mr. Morris was published in pamphlet form by him for a charitable end: (Lond. Groombridge & Sons, 8vo, pp. 10).]

¹ Lieut. Matthew Leslie of the 44th: promoted to a captaincy, 29 Sept. 1760.

LIST OF OFFICERS—*Continued.*
44th *Regiment.*

Officers' Names.	Rank.	Killed or Wounded.
Sir Peter Halkett	Colonel.	Killed.
Gage, Esqr	Lieut. Colonel.	Slightly wounded.
Tatton	Captain.	Killed.
Hobson [1]	"	
Beckworth [2]	"	"
Githius..............	"	
Falconer [3]	Lieutenant.	
Sittler	"	Wounded.
Bailey	"	
Dunbar [4]	"	"
Potenger.............	"	
Halkott..............	"	Killed.
Treby................	"	Wounded.
Allen [5]	"	Died of his wounds.
Simpson	"	Wounded.
Lock [6]	"	"
Disney [7]...........	Ensign.	"
Kennedy [8]..........	"	"
Townsend............	"	Killed.
Preston..............	"	
Clarke...............	"	
Nortlow..............	"	"
Pennington [9]	"	

[1] In the Army Register for 1765, Thomas Hobson ranks as a lieutenant of the 44th from 5 Nov. 1755. This and other instances authorize us to suppose that the above list was made rather from memory than authentic records.

[2] John Beckwith: major of the 54th, 18 July, 1758: lieut.-col. in the line, 13 Jan. 1762.

[3] Thomas Falconer: captain of the 44th, 5 Nov. 1755.

[4] For an anecdote of Capt. Dunbar, see XVIII. Sparks's Am. Biog, 11.

[5] This may be a mistake. In 1765, James Allen was a lieut. of the 44th; and though his commission dates but from 9 Nov. 1755, it is as old as those of many others who were in the action.

[6] Robert Lock: lieut. of 44th, 27 June, 1755, which rank he held ten years after.

[7] Daniel Disney: capt. in the line, 4 Oct. 1760; of the 44th, 22 Sept. 1764; major in the line, 7 Aug. 1776; of the 38th (which regiment he accompanied to America), 10 March, 1777.

[8] Primrose Kennedy: lieut. of the 44th, 6th June, 1757; capt. 15 May, 1772. In 1778, he seems to have been with his regiment in America.

[9] George Pennington: a lieut. of the 44th, 6 June, 1755. When he

LIST OF OFFICERS—Continued.

48th Regiment.

Officers' Names.	Rank.	Killed or Wounded.
Burton, Esqr	Lieut. Col.	Slightly wounded.
Sparks, Esqr	Major.	
Dobson, Esqr	Captain.	
Cholmondeley	"	
Bowyer, Esqr	"	Killed.
Ross, Esqr[1]	"	Wounded.
Barbutt, Esqr	Lieut.	"
Walsham, Esqr	"	
Crymble, Esqr	"	
Widman, Esqr	"	Killed.
Hansard, Esqr	"	"
Gladwin, Esqr[2]	"	"
Hotham, Esqr	"	Wounded.
Edmonstone, Esqr[3]	"	
Cope, Esqr	"	"
Brereton, Esqr	"	Killed.
Stuart, Esqr[4]	"	"
Montresore[4]	Ensign.	
Dunbar	"	Wounded.
Harrison	"	
Colebatt	"	
Macmullen	"	"
Crowe	"	"
Stirling[5]	"	"

arrived at Philadelphia, after the fight, he sought out the residence of Edward Penington, a leading merchant there, with whom he claimed kindred and resided until his regiment marched for Albany. He was probably of the Dysart family.

[1] Robert Ross: lieut-col. in the line, 6 Jan. 1762; of 48th, 2 Sept. 1762.

[2] Henry Gladwyn, who achieved great distinction in the remainder of the war, was made lt.-col. 17 Sept. 1763, and Deputy Adjutant General in America. His gallant defence of Detroit against Pontiac and his leaguering hordes is familiar to the reader in the pages of Parkman. He was made a colonel, 49 Aug. 1777; and maj.-gen. Nov. 26, 1782.

[3] William Edmestone: capt. in the 48th, 23 March, 1758; lt.-col. in the line, 29 Aug. 1777; and in Oct. 1777, was major of the 48th, and a prisoner of war at Easton, Pa.

[4] John Montresor: lt. in the 48th, 4 July, 1755.

[5] Among the officers of the 48th who were left with Dunbar, and there-

LIST OF OFFICERS—*Continued.*

48th *Regiment.*

INDEPENDENTS.

Officers' Names.	Rank.	Killed or Wounded.
Gates	Captain.	Wounded.
Sumain	Lieutenant.	Killed.
Miller	"	
Haworth	"	Wounded.
Grey	"	"

VIRGINIA OFFICERS.

Stevens	Captain.	Wounded.
Waggoner	"	
Polson	"	Killed.
Perinie	"	
Stewart[1]	"	
Hamilton[2]	Lieutenant.	"
Woodward[3]	"	
Wright[4]	"	"
Spidolf[5]	"	
Stewart[6]	"	Wounded.
Waggoner[7]	"	Killed.
M'Neal[8]	"	

fore do not find a place in this list, were Capts. Gabriel Christie (afterwards lt.-col. of the 60th in 1775), Mercer, Morris, and Boyer; Capt. Lieut. Morris, and Lts. Savage, Caulder, and Hart. (Penn. Gaz., No. 1394.)

[1] Robert Stewart; commissioned 1 Nov. 1754. Of his 29 light horse, 25 were killed in the action. See Penn. Gaz., No. 1391: where it is justly observed that "the Virginia officers and troops behaved like men and died like soldiers!"

[2] John Hamilton: commissioned Nov. 2, 1754.

[3] Henry Woodward: commissioned Dec. 13, 1754.

[4] John Wright: commissioned Nov. 18, 1754.

[5] Ensign Carolus Gustavus de Spiltdorph: commissioned July 21, 1754. I follow Washington's orthography, under whom he served in 1754. He was the officer selected to escort to Virginia the prisoners captured in Jumonville's affair.

[6] Ensign Walter Stewart: commissioned Aug. 25, 1754. I apprehend him to have been the same who was an additional lieutenant in the 44th during the war, retiring on half-pay in 1763; and who afterwards was conspicuous in our Army of the Revolution.

[7] Ensign Edmond Waggoner: commissioned Jan. 1, 1755.

[8] If this was Lt. John M'Neill (Nov. 1, 1754), or Ensign Hector M'Neill (Dec. 12, 1754), I do not know.

LIST OF OFFICERS—*Continued.*

48th *Regiment.*

ARTILLERY.

Officers' Names.	Rank.	Killed or Wounded.
Orde [1]	Captain.	Killed.
Smith	Capt. Lieut.	Wounded.
Buchanan [2]	Lieutenant.	Wounded.
M'Cloud	"	"
M'Culler	"	"

ENGINEERS.

Officers' Names.	Rank.	Killed or Wounded.
M'Keller, Esqr [3]	} Engineers.	Wounded.
Williamson, Esqr [4]		"
Gordon, Esqr [5]		"

[1] Thomas Orde in 1759 became lt.-col. of the R. R. of Artillery. He was an excellent officer, and stood high in Cumberland's esteem, by whom he was especially selected for this service. Landing in Newfoundland, he hastened to take command of Braddock's artillery, arriving from New York at Philadelphia, June 7, 1755. (II. P. A., 346.) He was accompanied by 13 non-commissioned officers; and was in such an enfeebled condition as to render his joining the army a work of much difficulty. The Assembly's committee not feeling themselves called upon to provide conveniences for his journey, Mr. Morris was compelled to procure him a horse and chaise at his own cost; at the same time issuing a warrant of impressment for waggons for the rest of the party. (Ib. 356, 358. VI. C. R., 417.) Capt. Orde took a conspicuous part in his line of service during the rest of the war.

[2] Sir Fr. Ja. Buchanan: capt. 1 Jan. 1759.

[3] Patrick Mackellar: Sub-Director and Major of Engineers, 4 Jan. 1758; Director and lt.-col. 2 Feb. 1775; col. in the line, 29 Aug. 1777.

[4] Adam Williamson: Engineer Extraordinary and capt. lieut. 4 Jan. 1758.

[5] Harry Gordon: Engineer in Ordinary and captain, 4 Jan. 1758; lt.-col. in the line, 29 Aug. 1777.

LIST OF OFFICERS—*Continued.*

48th *Regiment.*

NAVAL OFFICERS.

Officers' Names.	Rank.	Killed or Wounded.
Spendelowe.............	Lieutenant.	Killed.
Haynes	Mid.	"
Talbot...................		"

VOLUNTEERS.

Stone....................	Captain.	Killed.
Hayer[1]..................	"	Wounded.

Captain Stone was a captain in Lascelle's, and Hayer in Warburton's Regiment.[2]

[2] Mr. Morris prints this name Flayer.

[1] These were the 45th and 47th reg'ts. The late venerable Bishop White well remembered the corpse of one of Braddock's officers being brought to Philadelphia after the battle, where it lay in state for some days at the old Norris or Penn House at the corner of Second St. and Norris's Alley.

(a.) *A Journal of the proceedings of the Seamen (a detachment), ordered by Commodore Keppel to assist on a late
expedition to the Ohio, from the 10th of April, 1755, when
they received their first orders from the Army at Alexandria in Virginia, to the 18th day of August following,
when the remaining part of the Detachment arrived on
board His Majesty's ship "Garland" at Hampton : with
an impartial account of the action that happened on the
banks of the Monongohela, and defeat of Major General
Braddock on the 9th of July, 1755. (b.)*

April 10th, 1755. Moderate and fair but sultry weather ;
to-day we received orders to march tomorrow morning, and
6 Companies of Sir Peter Halket's Regiment to march in
their way to Wills's Creek.

(a.) Here begins the lesser MS., previously referred to, as follows :
[Journal of M. General Braddock's March, &c., towards Fort Du Quesne,
1755.

Names of the Principal French and Canadian Officers.

Monsr. Beaujeu   Captain Commanding the French and Canadians.
Monsr. Dumas   Captain and Second in command.
Monsr. Derliguiris   Captain.
Monsr. Montigny   Captain.
Messieurs Montesamble, Normanville, &c., &c., subalterns.

The Canadians say, 600 savages joined the French and Canadians after
the Attack began two hours.

F. M., Montreal, 1769.]

(b.) [Extracts from a Journal of the Proceedings of the Detachment of
Seamen, ordered by Commodore Kepple, to assist on the late Expedition
to the Ohio, with an impartial Account of the late Action on the Banks
of the Monongohela the 9th of July, 1755 ; as related by some of the
Principal Officers that day in the Field, from the 10th April, 1755, to
the 18th August, when the Detachment of Seamen embarked on board His
Majesty's ship Guarland at Hampton in Virginia.]

April 11th. Our orders were countermanded, and to provide ourselves with 8 days provisions, and to proceed to Rock Creek, 8 miles from Alexandria, in the Sea Horse and Nightingale's boats tomorrow.

On the 12th, agreeably to our orders we proceeded and arrived at Rock Creek at 10 o'clock. This place is 5 miles from the lower falls of Potomack, and 4 from the eastern branch of it. Here our men got quarters, and we pitched our tents: found here Colonel Dunbar, whose orders we put ourselves under.

On the 13th:—We were employed in getting the Regimental Stores into Waggons, in order to march tomorrow: This is a pleasant situation, but provisions and everything dear.

On the 14th:—We began our march at 6, and were ordered with our Detachment to go in front, and about 2 o'clock at one Lawrence Owens, 15 miles from Rock Creek, and 8 miles from the upper falls of Potomack; and encamped upon good ground.

On the 15th:—Marched at 5 in our way to one Dowden's a Public-house 15 miles from Owen's, and encamped upon very bad ground on the side of a hill. We got our tents pitched by dark, when the wind shifted from the South to the North—from a sultry hot day it became excessively cold, and rained with thunder and lightning till about 5 in the morning, when in 10 minutes it changed to snow, which in 2 hours covered the ground a foot and a half.

On the 16th :—On account of the bad weather, we halted to-day, though a terrible place, for we could neither get provisions for ourselves, nor fodder for our horses, and as it was wet in the Camp it was very disagreeable, and no house to go into.

On the 17th :—Marched at 6 on our way to Frederick's Town, 15 miles from Dowden's ; the roads this day were very mountainous. After going 11 miles, we came to a river called Mouskiso, which empties itself into the Potomack ; it runs very rapid, and after hard rain is 13 feet deep : we ferried the Army over here in a flatt for that purpose, and at 3 o'clock arrived at the town, and put our men and ourselves into quarters, which were very indifferent. This town has not been settled above 7 years, and there are about 200 houses and 2 churches, one English, one Dutch ; the inhabitants, chiefly Dutch, are industrious but imposing people : here we got plenty of provisions and forage.

On the 18th :—At 10 the drums beat to arms, when the Army encamped at the North end of the town, upon good ground : we got our tents pitched and lay in the camp, and the Sutler dieted us here : orders came for us to buy horses to carry our baggage, as there will be no more waggons allowed us. We found here an Independent Vessel belonging to New York under the command of Captain Goss.

On the 19th :—The weather here is very hot in the day, but the nights are very unwholesome, occasioned by heavy dews.

On the 20th:—A guard turned out to receive the General.

On the 21st:—At noon the General arrived here attended by Captains Orme and Morris¹ his Aids de Camp, and Secretary Shirley, and went to the Head Quarters, a house provided for him; and Sir John St. Clair arrived here.

¹ Roger Morris, descended from one of the most ancient families in Britain, was born 28 Jan, 1727. At an early age adopting the profession of arms, he obtained a captaincy in the 17th Foot when but 17 years old. After Braddock's defeat, he continued to serve with reputation in America; and married, 19 Jan, 1758, Mary, daughter of Frederick Philipse, of New York; a great heiress, who is said to have been unsuccessfully wooed by Washington, and whose character is beautifully drawn by Cooper in the heroine of "The Spy." It affords a curious speculation to consider how circumstances might have moulded the future career of the Father of his Country had his lot been linked with that of Mary Philipse instead of Martha Custis. The landed possessions of the Philipse family were enormous, embracing much of the site of the city of New York, and covering an area twice as great as all Yorkshire. Morris continued to reside in New York, where he occupied a seat in the Council, till the breaking out of the Revolution. Adhering to the Crown, his estates and those of his wife were confiscated, and he returned to England. By a marriage contract, however, Mrs. Morris's property had been settled on her children, and these being omitted in the act of confiscation, the ministry conceived their rights remained unaffected. Therefore but £17,000 were granted from the treasury to Mr. Morris in satisfaction of his life-interest. After the peace, it was found impracticable to reinstate the children in their possessions, and in 1809 their claims were purchased by the late Mr. John Jacob Astor for £20,000. The estimated value of the property in question was then nearly £1,000,000; at this day, the sum would be incalculable. On 19 May, 1760, Morris was made Lieutenant-Colonel of the 47th Foot, and died 13 Sept., 1794. His widow, who was born 5 July, 1730, survived to 18 July, 1825. Their only surviving son was the late Admiral Henry Gage Morris, R. N., of Keldgate House, Yorkshire. Colonel Morris is sometimes confounded with his cousin, Lieutenant-Colonel Roger Morris, of the Coldstreams, an intimate of the Duke of York, under whose command he fell in Holland.

On the 24ᵗʰ:—Very hard showers of rain, and from being very hot became excessively cold and blew hard.

On the 25th:—Received orders to be ready to march on Tuesday next. Arrived here 80 recruits and some ordnance stores.

On the 27th:—We sent 3 of our men to the hospital, vizᵗ., John Philips, Edwᵈ Knowles and James Connor. Employed in getting ready to march.

On the 29ᵗʰ:—We began our march at 6, but found much difficulty in loading our baggage, so that we left several things behind us, particularly the men's hammocks. We arrived at 3 o'clock at one Walker's, 18 miles from Frederick, and encamped there on good ground; this day we passed the South Ridge or Shannandah Mountains, very easy in the ascent. We saw plenty of Hares, Deer, and Partridges: This place is wanting of all refreshments.

On the 30ᵗʰ:—At 6, marched in our way to Conneco-chieg, where we arrived at 2 o'clock, 16 miles from Walker's: this is a fine situation, close by the Potomack. We found the Artillery Stores going by water to Wills's Creek, and left 2 of our men here.

May 1ˢᵗ, 1755. At 5, we went with our people, and began ferrying the Army &c. into Virginia, which we completed by 10 o'clock, and marched in our way to one John Evans, where we arrived at 3 o'clock—17 miles from Connecochieg, and 20 from Winchester. We got some provisions and forage here. The roads now begin to be very indifferent.

On the 2nd :—As it is customary in the Army to halt a day after 3 days march, we halted to-day to rest the Army.[c]

On the 3rd :—Marched at 5 on our way to one Widow Barringer's, 18 miles from Evans : this day was so excessively hot that several officers and many men could not get on till the evening, but the body got to their ground at 3 o'clock. This is 5 miles from Winchester, a fine station if properly cleared.

On the 4th :—Marched at 5 in our way to one Potts — 9 miles from the Widow's—where we arrived at 10 o'clock. The road this day very bad : we got some wild turkeys here : in the night it came to blow hard at N. W.

On the 5th :—Marched at 5 in our way to one Henry Enock's, being 16 miles from Potts, where we arrived at 2 o'clock. The road this day over prodigious mountains, and between the same we crossed over a run of water 20 times in 3 miles distance. After going 15 miles we came to a river called Kahapetin, where our men ferried the Army over and got to our ground, where we found a company of Peter Halket's encamped.

On the 6th :—We halted this day to refresh the Army.[d]

---

[c] [May 2nd :—Halted, and sent the horses to grass.]

[d] [May 5th :—Marched to Mr. Henry Enock's, a place called the *forks of Cape Capon.* * * *

May 6th. Halted, as was the Custom to do so every third day. The Officers, for passing away the time, made Horse Races, and agreed that no Horse should run over 11 Hands and to carry 14 Stone.]

7th :— We marched at 5 in our way to one Cox's,[1] 12 miles from Enock's. This morning was very cold but by 10 o'clock it was prodigiously hot. We crossed another run of water 19 times in 2 miles, and got to our ground at 2 o'clock, and encamped close to the Potomack.

On the 8th :— We began to ferry the Army over the river into Maryland, which was completed at 10, and then we marched on our way to one Jackson's, 8 miles from Cox's. At noon it rained very hard and continued so till 2 o'clock, when we got to our ground, and encamped on the banks of the Potomack. A fine situation, with a good deal of clear ground about it. Here lives one Colonel Cressop, a Rattle Snake Colonel, and a vile Rascal;[e] calls himself a Frontier man, as he thinks he is situated nearest the Ohio of any inhabitants of the country, and is one of the Ohio Company. He had a summons some time ago to retire from the Settlement, as they said it belonged to

---

[1] I take this person to be the same alluded to in the following paragraph : "There has a strange affair happened in Virginia : one Cox, which, you may remember by the Gazettes, behaved gallantly against the Indians some time ago, and another person, thinking their services not taken proper notice of, dressed themselves up like Indians and attacked a house a few miles from Winchester. The in-dwellers were so fortunate as to escape, altho' Cox and his partner fired on them several times. An Officer, being informed that the house was attacked by the Indians, sent a detachment to pursue the Enemy, who, finding tracks, pursued by them until they came near the place where the fellows, Cox and the other, were sitting by a fire ; fired on them — killed Cox on the spot and wounded the other so mortally that he had scarce time before his departure to disclose who they were." David Jameson to Lieutenant-Colonel Burd. Philadelphia, April 25, 1758. (Shippen MSS.)

[e] [There lives Colonel Cressop, a Rattle Snake Colonel and a D——d Rascal.]

them, but he refused, as he dont want resolution; and for his defence has built a log fort round his house. This place is the track of the Indians and Warriors when they go to war, either to the Northward or Southward. There we got plenty of provisions, &c., and at 6, the General arrived here with his Attendants, and a Company of Light Horse for his guard, and lay at Cressop's. As this was a wet day, the General ordered the Army to halt tomorrow.

On the 10th:—Marched at 5 on our way to Will's Creek, 16 miles from Cressop's; the road this day very pleasant by the water side. At 12 the General passed by, the drums beating the Grenadier March. At 1 we halted and formed a circle, when Colonel Dunbar told the Army that as there were a number of Indians at Will's Creek, our Friends, it was the General's positive orders that they do not molest them, or have anything to say to them, directly or indirectly, for fear of affronting them. We marched again, and heard 17 guns fired at the Fort to salute the General. At 2 we arrived at Will's Creek, and encamped to the Westward of the Fort on a hill, and found here 6 Companies of Sir Peter Halket's Regt., 9 Companies of Virginians, and a Maryland Company. Fort Cumberland is situated within 200 yards of Will's Creek, on a hill, and about 400 from the Potomack; its length from east to west is about 200 yards, and breadth 46 yards, and is built by logs driven into the ground, and about 12 feet above it, with embrasures for 12 guns, and 10 mounted, 4 pounders, besides stocks for swivels, and loop holes for small arms. We found here Indian men, women and children, to the number of about 100, who were greatly surprised at the regular way of our soldiers marching, and the numbers. I would willingly say something of the customs and manners of the Indians, but they are hardly to be described. The men are tall, well made, and active, but not strong, but very dexterous with a rifle barrelled gun, and their tomahawk, which they will throw with great certainty at any mark and at a great distance. The women are not so tall as the men, but well made and have many children, but had many more before spirits were introduced to them. They paint themselves in an odd manner, red, yellow, and black intermixed. And the men have the outer rim of their ears cut, which only hangs by a bit top and bottom, and have a tuft of hair left at the top of their heads, which is dressed with feathers. Their watch coat is their chief clothing, which is a thick blanket thrown all round them, and wear moccasins instead of shoes, which are Deer skin, thrown round the ankle and foot. Their manner of carrying their infants is odd. They are laid on a board, and tied on with a broad bandage, with a place to rest their feet on, and a board over their head to keep the sun off, and are slung to the women's backs. These people have no notion of religion, or any sort of Superior being, as I take them to be the most ignorant people as to the knowledge of the world and other things. In the day they were in our Camp, and in the night they go into their own, where they dance and make a most horrible noise.

On the 11th :—Orders that the General's Levee be always in his tent from 10 to 11 every day.

On the 12th:—Orders this morning that there will be a congress at the General's tent at 11 o'clock, at which time all the officers attended the General, and the Indians were brought; the Guard received them with their Firelocks rested. The Interpreter was ordered to tell them that their Brothers, the English, who were their old friends, were come to assure them that every misunderstanding that had been in former times should now be buried under that great mountain (a mountain close by). Then a string of wampum was given them; then a belt of wampum was held forth with the following speech, vizt.: that this wampum was to assure them of our friendship; that everybody who were their enemies were ours; and that it was not the small force only that we had here, but numbers to the northward under our great War Captains, Shirley, Pepperell, Johnston and others that were going to war, and that we would settle them happy in their country, and make the French both ashamed and hungry: But that whatever Indians after this declaration did not come in, would be deemed by us as our enemies, and treated as such. The General then told them he should have presents for them in a few days, when he should have another speech to make to them, so took their leaves after the ceremony of Drams round. In the afternoon Mr. Spendlowe and self surveyed 20 casks of beef by order of the General and condemned it, which we reported to the General. This evening we had a gust of wind, with lightning, thunder and rain, which drove several tents down, and made the camp very uncomfortable.

On the 13th:—The weather is now extremely hot. This day as the Corporal came to exercise our men in the evening, I went to see the Indian camp, ¼ mile from ours, in the woods. Their houses are 2 stakes driven into the ground, with a Ridge pole, and bark of trees laid up and down the sides, but they generally have a fire in them. This is all the shelter they have from the weather when they are from home.[r] As soon as it was dark they began to dance, which they do round a fire in a ring. Their music is a tub with a sheep skin over it, and a hollow thing with peas to rattle.[1] It is a custom with them, once or twice a year, for the women to dance and all the men sit by. Each woman takes out her man that she likes, dances with him and lies with him for a week, and then return to their former husbands, and live as they did before.

On the 14th:—This day 2 of our men arrived from Frederick hospital, and our men from Connecockieg that were left to assist the Artillery. Orders to send the returns of our people to the Brigade major every morning.

[r] This day's journal in the lesser MS. concludes here thus: [The Americans and Seamen exercising.]

[1] The TAY WA' EGUN (struck-sound-instrument) is a tambourine, or one-headed drum, and is made by adjusting a skin to one end of the section of a moderate sized hollow tree. When a heavier sound is required, a tree of larger circumference is chosen, and both ends covered with skins.—The SHESHEGWON, or Rattle, is constructed in various ways, according to the purpose or means of the maker. Sometimes it is made of animal bladder, from which the name is derived; sometimes of a wild gourd; in others, by attaching the dried hoofs of the deer to a stick. This instrument is employed both to mark time, and to produce variety in sound." (Schoolcraft; Red Race of America, 223.)

On the 15th:—Mr. Spendlowe and self surveyed 22 casks of beef, and condemned it, which we reported to the General.

On the 16th:—Arrived here Lieut. Col. Gage, with 2 Companies of Sir Peter Halket's, and the last division of the train, consisting of 3 field pieces, 4 howitzers, a number of cohorns, and 42 waggons with stores. Departed this life Captain Bromley of Sir Peter Halket's.

On the 17th:—Had a survey of our men's arms, and found several of them unserviceable. All the officers are desired to attend Captain Bromley's funeral tomorrow morning, and at the General's tent at 12.

On the 18th:—Excessively hot. At 10 o'clock we all attended the funeral, and the ceremony was a Captain's guard marched before the corpse, with the Captain of it in the rear, and the fire locks reversed, the drums beating the dead march. When we came near the grave, the guard formed 2 lines facing each other; rested on their arms, muzzles downwards; and leaned their faces on the butts: the Corpse was carried between them, the sword and sash on the coffin, and the officers following two and two. After the Clergyman[1] had read the service, the guard fired 3 vollies over him and returned. At 12 we attended the General's tent, when all the Indians came, and the General made a speech to them to this purpose. He desired they would immediately send their wives and children into Pen-

[1] The chaplain of the 44th was Mr. Philip Hughes: that of the 48th I do not know. One of these gentlemen marched with the expedition, and was wounded at the defeat.

sylvania, and take up the Hatchet against the French : that the great King of England, their Father, had sent them the presents now before them for their families, and that he had ordered arms &c. to be given to their Warriors ; and expressed concern for the loss of the Half-King killed last year. The presents consisted of strouds, rings, beads, linen, knives, wire, and paint. They received their presents with 3 belts and a string of wampum, and promised their answer next day. And to show they were pleased, they made a most horrible noise, dancing all night.

On the 19th :—Captain Gate's New York Company arrived here. This evening the Indians met at the General's tent to give their answer, which was, that they were greatly obliged to the Great King their Father, who had been so good as to send us all here to fight for them, and that they would all give their attendance, and do what was in their power of reconnoitring the country and bringing intelligence. That they were obliged to the General for his expressing concern for the loss of the Half-King our Brother, and for the presents he had given them. Their chief men's names are as follows : Monicotoha, their wise man who always speaks for them ; g—Belt of Wampum or White Thunder, who has a daughter called Bright Lightning—he keeps the wampum : the next is the great Tree and Silver Heels,h with many others belonging to the Six Nations. The General told them he was their Friend, and never would deceive them, after which they sung the war song, which is shouting and making a terrible noise, declaring the French their

g [Monicatoha their Mentor.]   h [Jerry Smith and Charles.]

perpetual enemies, which they never did before. After this the General carried them to the Artillery, and ordered 3 Howitzers, 3 12-Pounders, and 3 Cohorns to be fired, all the drums and fifes playing, and beating the point of war, which astonished and pleased the Indians greatly. They then retired to their own Camp, where they ate a bullock, and danced their war dance, which is droll and odd, shewing how they scalp and fight, expressing in their dance the exploits of their ancestors, and warlike actions of themselves.

On the 20th:—Arrived here 80 waggons from Pennsylvania, to assist in the expedition, and eleven waggons from Philadelphia, with presents for the officers of the Army.[i] An Indian arrived from the French fort in 6 days, and said they have only 50 men in the fort, but expect 900 more; that when our Army appears they will blow it up. I believe this fellow is a villain, as he is a Delaware, who never were our friends.

On the 21st:—There are 100 Carpenters employed, under the Carpenter of the "Sea-horse," in building a Magazine, completing a Flatt, and squaring timber to make a bridge over Will's Creek; the Smiths in making tools; the Bakers baking biscuits; and Commissaries getting the provisions ready for marching. Arrived here a troop of light Horse, and 2 companies of Sir Peter Halket's.[j] On the 22nd, the Indians had arms and clothes given them.

---

[i] [Arrived 80 Waggons from Pennsylvania with Stores; and 11 likewise from Philadelphia, with Liquors, Tea, Sugar, Coffee, &c., to the Amount of £400, with 20 Horses, as presents to the Officers of the 2 Regiments.]

[j] [A Troop of Light-Horse and 2 Companies of Sir P. Halket's Regiment, under the command of Major Chapman, came in from Winchester.]

On the 23rd : — Both the Regiments exercised and went through their firings.k Sent 3 of our men to the Provost for neglect of duty and disobedience of orders.

On the 24th : — Our Force here now consists of 2 Regiments of 700 men each ; 9 companies (Virginia) of 50 men each ; 3 Independent Companies of 100 men each ; one Maryland Company of 50 men ; 60 of the train[1] and 30 seamen. This day 2 men were drummed out of Sir Peter Halket's Regiment for theft, after receiving 1000 lashes, and preparations making for marching.

On the 27th : — We have now here 100 waggons, which the Commissaries are loading with provisions. In the evening a Captain's Guard marched for Winchester, to escort the provisions to the Camp. Some Indians came in here belonging to the Delawares.

On the 28th : — At 11, the Delawares met at the General's tent, and told him that they were come to know his intentions, that they might assist the Army. The General thanked them, and said he should march in a few days towards Fort De Quesne. The Indians told him they would return home and collect their warriors together, and meet him on his march. These people are villains, and always side with the strongest. At noon it blowed and rained hard.

On the 29th : — A detachment of 600 men marched towards Fort de Quesne, under the command of Major Chapman, with 2 field pieces, and 50 waggons with provi-

k [—formings.]
1 2 New York, 1 Independant *Carolina* Companies of 100 men, * * *
1 Company of Artillery of 60.]

sions. Sir John St. Clair, 2 Engineers, Mr. Spendlowe, & 6 of our people to cut the road, and some Indians went away likewise.[m]

On the 30th:—Arrived here a Company from North Carolina, under the command of Captain Dobbs.

June 1st:—We hear the Detachment is got 15 miles: Mr. Spendlowe and our people returned.

On the 2nd:—Col. Burton, Capt. Orme, Mr. Spendlowe and self went out to reconnoitre the road. Mr. Spendlowe left us, and returned to Camp at 2 o'clock, and reported he had found a road to avoid a great mountain. In the afternoon we went out to look at it, and found it would be much better than the old road, and not above 2 miles about.

On the 3rd:—This morning an Engineer[n] and 100 men began working on the new road from Camp, and Mr. Spendlowe and self with 20 of our men went to the place where the new road comes into the old one, and began to clear away, and completed a mile to-day.

On the 4th:—Went out to-day, and cleared another mile.[o]

On the 5th:—We went out as before, and at noon, Mr. Spendlowe and I went to the other party to mark the road

---

[m] [—and 6 seamen with some Indians were ordered to clear the Roads for them.]

[n] [—Mr. Engineer Gordon.]

[o] [1 Midshipman and 20 men cleared ¾ of a Mile.]

for them, but at 1, it came to blow, rain, thunder, and lighten so much, that it split several tents, & continued so till night, when we returned to the Camp.

On the 6th:—We went out as usual, and at 2 o'clock completed the road, & returned to Camp. This Evening I was taken ill.

On the 7th:—A rainy day, with thunder and lightning. Sir Peter Halket and his Brigade marched with 2 field pieces, and some waggons with provisions. A midshipman & 12 of our people went to assist the train.

On the 9th:—Orders for Col. Dunbar's Brigade to march tomorrow morning.

On the 10th:—The Director of the Hospital came to see me in Camp, and found me so ill of a fever and flux, that he desired me to stay behind, so I went into the Hospital, & the Army marched with the Train &c., and as I was in hopes of being able to follow them in a few days, I sent all my baggage with the Army, and in the afternoon the General, his Aids de Camp &c., with a company of Light-Horse, marched.[1]

---

[1] The long and fatal delay of the English at Fort Cumberland was undoubtedly produced, in great part, by the necessities of the case: but a different view of the matter was taken by some of the subordinates of the army. Thus Captain Rutherford, after pointing out the success which crowned Halket's command of the encampment at that place, pictures Braddock arriving there to waste the precious moments like a second Hannibal at Capua. According to his letter (Philadelphia Evening Bulletin, Sept 19th, 1849), the General there "spent a month idly with his women and feasting." It will be noticed that the writer was a professed supporter of the inefficient Dunbar, and that the whole burthen of his strain is the

On the 24th:—A man came into the Fort, and reported that a party of Indians of about 20 had surprised, killed & scalped two families to the number of about 14 or 15 people, and not above 3 miles from this place.

On the 26th:—An account came in of 2 more families being scalped within 2 miles of us. The Governor sent out a party to bury the dead, as well as to scour the woods for the Indians. They found a child of about 7 years old, standing in the water scalped & crying; they brought it into the Fort and the Doctors dressed it: it had 2 holes in its skull, besides being scalped, but was in spirits, and had its skull not been wounded might have lived, but as it was it died in a week. It would be too tedious to recount every little incident here in the Fort, therefore will return to the Army, and give an account of their proceedings from the time they left us.

June 10th, 1755. The last division of His Majesty's Forces marched from Will's Creek or Fort Cumberland, with General Braddock and his Aides de Camp, &c.

The 15th.—The General and all the Army arrived at the little Meadows, which is 22 miles from the Fort. He found here that the number of carriages, &c., that he had with him occasioned his marches to be very short, and that in all probability if they continued to do so, the French fort would be reinforced before he got before it. He therefore thought proper to take 1200 of the choicest men,

laudation of that incompetent man and depreciation of Braddock. The measures adopted by the General upon the suggestion of Washington appear to have elicited his warmest indignation besides Artillery and Sailors, with the most necessary stores that would be wanted to attack the Fort, making up in all 51 carriages, and left all the heavy baggage, &c. with Col. Dunbar, and the rest of the forces to follow him as fast as possible, and marched accordingly, and continued so to do without being molested (except now and then losing a scalp, which in the whole amounted to 8 or 9, a number far less than expected), till the 8th of July, when he encamped within 8 miles of the French Fort, and there held a Council of War, which agreed that as they were to pass over the Mongohela river twice (this river is a ¼ mile broad, and 6 miles from the French Fort), that the Advance party should parade at 2 o'clock to secure that pass, as on the contrary if the Enemy should have possession of it, they would not be able to get over without a great loss. They likewise agreed that the Army should march over the river in the greatest order, with their bayonets fixed, Colors flying, and Drums and Fifes beating and playing, as they supposed the Enemy would take a view of them in the crossing.

On the 9th July, 1755.—The advance party consisted of 400 men and upward, under the command of Lieut. Col. Gage, and marched accordingly; and about 7 o'clock started a party of about 30 Indians, but they got off.[p] They marched on and secured both crossings of the river without interview of them in the crossing.

P [About 7 o'clock, some Indians Rushed out of the Bushes, but did no Execution. The party went on and secured both Passes of the River; and at 11 the Main Body began to cross, with Colours flying, Drums beating, and Fifes playing the Grenadiers' March, and soon formed: when they thought that the French would not Attack them, as they might have done it with such Advantage in crossing the Monongohela.]

ruption. The main body marched about 6 o'clock and about 11 began to cross over as proposed in the Council of War, and got over both passes, when they began to think the French would not attack them, as they might have done with so many advantages a little time before.

The Advance Party was now about ¼ of a mile before the Main Body, the rear of which was just over the river when the front was attacked. The 2 Grenadier Companies formed the 2 flank advance Picquets, 2 Companies of Carpenters cutting the Roads, and the rest covering them. The first fire our men received was in front, and on the flank of the flank Picquets, which in a few minutes nearly cut off the most part of the Grenadiers and a Company of Carpenters.[a] As soon as the General with the Main Body heard the Front was attacked, they hastened to succour them, but found the Remains retreating. Immediately the General ordered the cannon to draw up and the Batallion to form. By this time the Enemy began to fire on the Main Body, who faced to the right and left and returned it, and the Cannon began to play, but could not see at what, for our men were formed in the open road they had just cut, and the Enemy kept the Trees in front and on the flanks. On the right they had possession of a hill, which we could never get possession of, though our Officers made many attempts to do it: but if the Officers dropped, which was generally the case, or that the Enemy gave a

[a] [The first fire the Enemy gave was in front, and they likewise galled the Picquets in flank, so that in a few minutes the Grenadiers were nearly cut in pieces, and drove into the greatest confusion, as was Captain Polson's company of Carpenters.]

25

platoon of ours advancing up the hill a smart fire, they immediately retreated down again. As numbers of our Officers declared they never saw above 4 of the Enemy at a time the whole day, it struck a panic through our men to see numbers daily falling by them, and even their comrades scalped in their sight. As soon as the General saw this was the case, he ordered that our men should divide into small parties and endeavour to surround the Enemy, but by this time the greatest part of the Officers were either killed or wounded, and in short the Soldiers deaf to the commands of those few that were left alive.ʳ By this time, too, the greatest part of the Train were cut off, having fired between 20 and 30 rounds each cannon, for the Enemy made a mark of them and the officers.

The General had 4 horses shot under him before he was wounded, which was towards the latter end of the Action,

ʳ [It was in an open Road that the Main Body were drawn up, but the Trees were excessive thick around them, and the Enemy had possession of a Hill to the Right, which consequently was of great advantage to them. Many officers declare that they never saw above 5 of the Enemy at one time during the whole affair. Our soldiers were encouraged to make many attempts by the Officers (who behaved Gloriously), to take the Hill, but they had been so intimidated before by seeing their comrades scalped in their sight, and such numbers falling, that as they advanced up towards the Hill, and their Officers being pict off, which was generally the case; they turned to the Right About, and retired down the Hill. When the General perceived and was convinced that the soldiers would not fight in a regular manner without Officers, he divided them into small parties and endeavoured to surround the Enemy, but by this time the major part of the Officers were either killed or wounded, and in short the soldiers were totally deaf to the commands and persuasions of the few Officers that were left unhurt. The General had 4 Horses shot under him before he was wounded, which was towards the latter part of the Action, when he was put into a Waggon with great difficulty, as he was very solicitous for being left in the Field.]

for when the General was put in a Waggon the men soon dropped out of the field, and in a little time became too general after standing three hours, and with much difficulty got the General out of the Field (for he had desired to be left.) [1] It was the opinion of most of the Officers there, that had greater numbers there, it would have been the same, as our people had never any hopes of getting the field, for they never got possession of the ground the front was attacked on. But very luckily for us they pursued us no further than the Water, and there killed and scalped many. One of our Engineers, who was in the front of the Carpenters marking the road, saw the Enemy first, who were then on the run, which plainly shews they were just come from the Fort, and their intention certainly was to secure the pass of the Monongahela, but as soon as they discovered our Army, an Officer at the head of them dressed as an Indian, with his gorget on, waved his hat, and they immediately dispersed to the right and left, forming a half-moon. [s] It was impossible to judge of their numbers, but it was believed they had at least man for man.

---

[1] According to Geo. Croghan, the grenadiers delivered their fire at 200 yards distance, completely throwing it away. (Chas. Swayne's letter in Phila. Evening Bulletin, Sept. 19th, 1849.) The same authority estimates the French in the action at 300, 'clad in stuffs;' besides the naked Indians. 400 Onondagos, he says, came into the fort the day before; and there were also '100 Delawares, 60 Wiandots, 40 Puywaws, 300 Pawwaws, the Shaw-nees who lived about Logtown, and some of all other tribes.' In conclu-sion, a curious anecdote of Braddock is given: when Croghan approached him, after he was wounded, the General sought to possess himself of the former's pistols, with a view to self-destruction. The story is given here for what it is worth.

[s] [Mr. Engineer Gordon was the first Man that saw the Enemy, being in the Front of the Carpenters, marking and picketing the Roads for them,

Our remains retreated all night, and got to Col. Dunbar's Camp the next day, which was near 50 miles from the field of action, and then the General ordered Col. Dunbar to prepare for a retreat, in order to which they were obliged to destroy all the Ammunition and provisions they could not possibly carry, and the reason of so much was the absolute necessity there was for a number of waggons to carry the wounded officers and men: The General's pains increased in such a manner—for he was shot through the arm into the body—together with the great uneasiness he was under, that on the 12ᵗʰ, at 8 at night, he departed this life, much lamented by the whole Army, and was decently, though privately, buried next morning. The number killed, wounded, and left on the Field, as appeared by the returns from the different companies, was 896, besides Officers, but cannot say any particular Company suffered more than another, except the Grenadier Companies and Carpenters; for out of Colonel Dunbar's Grenadiers, who were 79 complete that day, only 9 returned untouched, and out of 70 of Halket's, only 13.[t] Amongst the rest, I believe I may say the Seamen did their duty, for out of 33, only 15 escaped untouched:[u] and every Grenadier Officer either killed or wounded. Our loss that day consisted of 4 field-

and he declared when he first discovered them, that they were on the Run, which plainly shows they were just come from *Fort Du Quesne*, and that their principle Intention was to secure the pass of *Monongohela River*, but the Officer who was their leader, dressed like an Indian, with a gorget on, waved his hat by way of signal to disperse to the Right and Left, forming a half Moon.

[t] [Sir P. Halket's were 69, and only 13 came out of the Field.]

[u] [The Seamen had 11 killed and wounded out of 33.]

pieces, 3 Howitzers, and 2 Waggons, with Cohorns,[v] together with the 51 carriages of provisions and Ammunition, &c., and Hospital stores, and the General's private chest with £1000 in it,[1] and about 200 horses with officers' baggage.

Col. Dunbar with the remains of the Army continued their retreat, and returned to Will's Creek, or Fort Cumberland, the 20th of July.[w]

August 1st, 1755.—Colonel Dunbar received a letter from Commodore Keppel, desiring the Remains of the Detachment of Seamen might be sent to Hampton in Virginia. Colonel Dunbar gave us our orders, and on the 3rd we left the Army, marched down through Virginia, and on the 18th we arrived on board His Majesty's ship "Garland" at Hampton.[x]

August 5th.   Arrived at Winchester.

August 11th.   Marched into *Fredericksburgh*, and hired a Vessel to carry the Seamen to *Hampton* where they embarked on board His Majesty's ship Guarland the 18th August, 1755.]

---

[v] [4 six pounders, 2 twelve-pounders, 3 howitzers, 8 cohorns.]

[1] Probably a clerical error for £10,000.

[w] [On the 21st, the wounded officers and soldiers were brought in.]

[x] [30th July.   Orders were given for the Army to march the 2nd August.

1st August.   Colonel Dunbar received a letter from Commodore Kepple to send the Seamen to *Hampton*, and accordingly the 2nd, they marched with the Army, and on the 3rd August left them.

Appendices.

APPENDIX No. I.

BRADDOCK'S INSTRUCTIONS, ETC.

[THE first paper that ensues is printed from a contemporaneous copy in II. Penn. Arch. 203, which more than probably was given to Gov. Morris, if not by the general himself, at least by one of his family; by Shirley or Orme. It naturally differs materially from the copy translated from English into French and back again into English, published in the American version of the French *Mémoire*. (II. Olden Time, 217.) The second document is that taken from the Mémoire as above, collated with the garbled fragments in XXVI. Gent. Mag., 269.]

G. R. *Instructions for our Trusty & well beloved Edw'd Braddock, Esq'r. Major General of all our Forces*, and whom We have appointed Gen¹ & Commander of all & singular our Troops & Forces y'r are now in North America, & y't shall be sent or rais'd there to vindicate our just Rights &-Possessions in those Parts. Given at our Court, at S't James, y'e 25th day of Nov'r, 1754, in the 28th Year of our Reign.

Whereas, We have by our Commission, bearing date the 24th day of Sept'r last past, appointed you to be Gen¹ & Commander of all & singular our Forces, y't are or shall be in North America. For your better direction in discharge of y'e Trust thereby reposed in You, We have judged it proper to give You the following Instructions.

1st. We having taken under our Royal & serious Consideration the Representations of our Subjects in North America, & y'e present State of our Colonies, in order to vindicate our just Rights and Possessions from all Encroachments, & to secure y'e Commerce of our Subjects, We have given

(393)

direction y^t Two of our Regiments of Foot now in Ireland, commanded by
Sr Peter Halket & Col. Dunbar, & likewise a suitable Train of Artillery,
Transports & Store Ships, together with a certain Number of our Ships of
War, to convey the same, shall forthwith repair to North America.

2^d. You shall immediately, upon ye Receit of these our Instructions,
embark on board one of our Ships of War, and you shall proceed to North
America, where you will take our said Force under your Command. And
We having appointed Aug: Keppel, Esqr., to command ye Squadron of our
Ships of War on ye American Station, We do hereby require & enjoin you
to cultivate a good understanding & correspondence with ye s^d Commander
of our Squadron during your continuance upon ye Service, with which you
are now entrusted. We having given directions of ye like nature to ye s^d
Commander of our Squadron, with Regard to his conduct & correspondence
with you.

3^d. And Whereas, there will be wanting a number of men to make up
ye designed complements of our said Regiments, from 500 to 700 each:
And Whereas, it is our Intention y^t Two other Regiments of Foot, to consist of 1000 men each, shall be forthwith raised & comanded by Govr
Shirley and S^r W^m. Pepperell, whom We have appointed Col^s of ye same
in our Provinces & Colonies, in North America, and have given directions
y^t ye Regiment under ye command of ye former should rendezvous at
Boston, & y^t under ye command of ye latter at New York and Philadelphia ; and We having given orders to our several Governors to be taking
the previous steps toward contributing, as far as they can, to have about
3000 men in readiness to be enlisted for these Purposes, & to be put in
Proportion as they shall be raised under your command, & be subject to
your distribution into the corps above mentioned. And We having thought
proper to dispatch Sir John St. Clair, our deputy Quarter Master Genl &
Ja^s. Pitcher, Esqr., our Commissary of ye musters, in North America, to
prepare every thing necessary for ye arrival of ye Two Regiments from
Europe, and for ye raising of ye Forces above mentioned, in America. You
will inform yourself of such of our Governors as you can most conveniently
upon your arrival, & of all of them in due time, & likewise of our s^d deputy
Quarter Master Genl & Commissary of ye musters, concerning ye Progress
they shall respectively have made in ye Execution of our commands above
mentioned, in order y^t you may be enabled without delay to act accordingly.

4th. Whereas, it has been represented to Us y^t ye Forces, which are to
go from Cork under your command, may be in want of Provisions upon y^r
arrival in America, We have caused in consideration thereof 1000 Barrels
of Beef and 10 Tons of Butter, to be put on board the Transport Vessels,

& to be delivered to you upon your arrival in America, in case you shall find yᵉ same to be necessary in order to be distributed among yᵉ officers & Troops, & yᵉ several Persons belonging to yᵉ Train of Artillery. But it is our Royal Will & Pleasure, yᵗ in case yᵉ Govrˢ of our Colonies shall have provided a proper Quantity of Provisions for our Troops upon their arrival, you will then signify yᵉ same to yᵉ Commander in Chief of our Fleet in those Parts, yᵗ yᵉ sᵈ 1000 Barrels of Beef and 10 Tons of Butter, or such Part thereof as shall not be expended may be applied to yᵉ Use of our Royal Navy.

5ᵗʰ. Whereas, We have given Orders to our said Govrˢ to provide carefully a sufficient Quantity of fresh victuals for yᵉ use of our Troops at their arrival, & yᵗ they should also furnish all our officers who may have occasion to go from Place to Place, with all necessaries for travelling by Land, in case there are no means of going by Sea; & likewise, to observe & obey all such orders as shall be given by You or Persons appointed by you from time to time for quartering the Troops, impressing Carriages, & providing all necessaries for such Forces as shall arrive or be raised in America, and yᵗ the sᵈ several Services shall be performed at the charge of yᵉ respective Governments, wherein the same shall happen. It is our Will & Pleasure yᵗ you should, pursuant thereto, apply to our sᵈ Governors, or any of them, upon all such Exigencies.

6ᵗʰ. And Whereas, We have further directed our said Govrˢ to endeavour to prevail upon yᵉ Assemblies of their respective Provinces to raise forthwith as large a sum as can be afforded as their contribution to a common Fund, to be employed provisionally for yᵉ general Service in North America, particularly for paying the charge of levying yᵉ Troops to make up yᵉ complements of yᵉ Regiments above-mentioned. It is our Will & Pleasure yᵗ you shou'd give them all yᵉ advice & assistance you can towards effectuating these good Purposes, by establishing such a common Fund as may fully supply yᵉ intended Service; But you will take particular Care to prevent yᵉ Payment of any money whatever to yᵉ Troops under your command, except such as shall be, pursuant to yᵉ Returns, made to you of effective men.

7ᵗʰ. We having likewise directed our sᵈ Govrˢ to correspond, advise & confer with you about all such matters as may tend to yᵉ promoting the said Levies in their respective Provinces, you are hereby required to be aiding & assisting to them in yᵉ Execution of our sᵈ Instructions, for which purpose you will not only keep a constant & frequent correspondence in writing with them, but will likewise visit the sᵈ Provinces, or any one of them yᵗ you shall think it necessary for our Service so to do. And you will remind our said Governors to use all possible dispatch, that yᵉ Execution of our design may not be retarded by yᵉ Slowness of Levies to be made in their respective Provinces, or for yᵉ Want of Transports, Victuals, or any other necessaries, at such times & Places as you shall think fit to appoint for their General Rendezvous. And if any Preparation should be necessary for carrying on our Service, which is not contained in these our Instructions, you shall, with yᵉ concurrence of the Governors who are to assist in any such Service, make any such Preparations, provided yᵗ yᵉ same shall appear to you absolutely necessary for yᵉ Defence of our just Rights and Dominions; and you will, in all such Emergencies & occurences yᵗ may happen, whether herein mentioned or not provided for by these Instructions, not only use your best Circumspection, but shall likewise call to your assistance a Council of War when necessary, which We have thought fit to appoint upon this occasion, consisting of yourself, yᵉ Commander in Chief of our Ships in those Parts, such Governors of our Colonies or Provinces, & such Colonels & other of our Field officers as shall happen to be at a convenient distance from our sᵈ Genˡ & Commander of our Forces, and you shall with yᵉ advice of them or a majority of them, determine all Operations to be performed by our said Forces under your command, and all other important points relating thereto, in a manner yᵗ shall be most conducive to yᵉ Ends for which yᵉ sᵈ Forces are intended, & for yᵉ faithful discharge of yᵉ great Trust hereby committed to you.

8ᵗʰ. You will not only cultivate yᵉ best Harmony & Friendship possible with yᵉ several Governors of our Colonies & Provinces, but likewise with yᵉ Chiefs of yᵉ Indian Tribes, & for yᵉ better Improvement of our good Correspondence with yᵉ sᵈ Indian Tribes, you will find out some fit & proper Person agreeable to the Southern Indians to be sent to them for this purpose, in like manner as we have orderd Col. Johnson to repair to yᵉ Northern Indians, as yᵉ person thought to be most acceptable to them, to endeavour to engage them to take part & act with our Forces, in such operations as you shall think most expedient.

9ᵗʰ. You will inform yourself from time to time, of yᵉ Nature & Value of yᵉ Presents yᵗ shall be voted or orderd by yᵉ Assemblies of our different Colonies & Provinces, in yᵉ accustomed manner of the inviting & engaging yᵉ Indian Tribes to our Alliance & Interest, and you will be very watchful yᵗ a just & faithful distribution be made of yᵉ same, by all such Persons who shall be entrusted therewith, and you shall assist yᵉ sᵈ Persons with your best advice in yᵉ sᵈ distribution. You will likewise give a particular attention to yᵉ prudent disposal of such Presents as shall be made upon any Occasion, or such as shall have been prepared by Lieut. Governor Dinwiddie, for yᵉ said Indians, out of yᵉ money already vested in his Hands or otherwise.

10ᵗʰ. Whereas, it has been represented to Us, yᵗ an illegal Correspondence & Trade is frequently carried on between the French & our Subjects in yᵉ several Colonies, you will diligently take all possible measures to prevent the continuance of all such dangerous Practices, particularly that the French should not, upon any account whatever, be supplied with Provisions, &cᵃ.

11ᵗʰ. Whereas, We have thought it necessary upon this occasion to establish & ascertain the Rank that shall be observed between the officers bearing our immediate Commission, & those who act under the Commissions of our Governors, Lieutᵗ or Deputy Governors, or yᵉ Presidents of our Colonies, for the Time being. We have orderd several printed Copies thereof to be put into your Hands, to be affix'd or dispersd as you shall judge proper in America.

12ᵗʰ. You will herewith receive a Copy of yᵉ early directions that were sent by our Order on yᵉ 28ᵗʰ August, 1753, to our several Governors, enjoining & exhorting our Colonies & Provinces, in North America, to unite together for their common & mutual defence, & you will see by our directions of 5ᵗʰ July, Copies whereof are now also delivered to you our repeated commands, for enforcing the Observance of our said orders of yᵉ 28ᵗʰ August, 1753, and yᵗ We were graciously pleased to order the Sum of £10,000 to be remitted in Specie to Lieuᵗ Govᵣ Dinwiddie, to draw Bills for a farther Sum of £10,000, upon yᵉ conditions mentioned in our Warrant of the 3ᵈ July last, & transmitted to yᵉ sᵈ Lᵗ Govᵣ Dinwiddie, on yᵉ 27ᵗʰ Septᵣ following, by our Order for yᵉ general Service & Protection of North America, and yᵉ several other Letters of October yᵉ 25 & 26, & of Novᵣ yᵉ 4ᵗʰ, to our Govᵣˢ, to Sir Wᵐ. Pepperell & Col. Shirley, Copies of which will be delivered to you herewith, will fully acquaint you with our Orders & Instructions which have been signified to our officers & Governors upon this Subject, at those respective Times, will enable you to inform yourself what Progress has been made in the Execution thereof; And as Extracts of Lieuᵗ Govᵣ Dinwiddie's Letters of May 10ᵗʰ, June 18ᵗʰ, & July 24ᵗʰ, relating to the Summons of the Fort which was erecting on yᵉ Forks of yᵉ Monongahela, and yᵉ Skirmish yᵗ followed soon after, & likewise of yᵉ action in the Great Meadows, near the River Ohio, are herewith delivered to you, you will be fully acquainted with what has hitherto happened of a hostile Nature upon the Banks of that River.

13ᵗʰ. You will not fail to send Us by the first, & every occasion that may offer, a full and clear account of your Proceedings, & of all material Points relating to our Service, by Letter, to one of our Principal Secretaries of State, from whom you shall receive, from time to time, such farther Orders as may be necessary for your Guidance and Direction.

G. R.

A LETTER WRITTEN BY COLONEL NAPIER AND SENT TO GENERAL BRADDOCK BY ORDER OF THE DUKE OF CUMBERLAND.

LONDON, *November 25th*, 1754.

SIR,

His Royal Highness the Duke, in the several audiences he has given you, entered into a particular explanation of every part of the service you are about to be employed in; and as a better rule for the execution of His Majesty's instructions, he last Saturday communicated to you his own sentiments of this affair, and since you were desirous of forgetting no part thereof, he has ordered me to deliver them to you in writing. His Royal Highness has this service very much at heart, as it is of the highest importance to his majesty's American dominions, and to the honour of his troops employed in those parts. His Royal Highness likewise takes a particular interest in it, as it concerns you, whom he recommended to his majesty to be nominated to the chief command.

His Royal Highness's opinion is, that immediately after your landing, you consider what artillery and other implements of war it will be necessary to transport to Will's Creek for your first operation on the Ohio, that it may not fail you in the service; and that you form a second field train, with good officers and soldiers, which shall be sent to Albany and be ready to march for the second operation at Niagara. You are to take under your command as many as you think necessary of the two companies of artillery that are in Nova Scotia and Newfoundland as soon as the season will allow, taking care to leave enough to defend the Island. Captain Ord, a very experienced officer, of whom his Royal Highness has a great opinion, will join you as soon as possible.

As soon as Shirley's and Pepperel's regiments are near complete, his Royal Highness is of opinion you should cause them to encamp, not only that they may sooner be disciplined, but also to draw the attention of the French and keep them in suspense about the place you really design to attack. His Royal Highness does not doubt that the officers and captains of the several companies will answer his expectation in forming and disciplining their respective troops. The most strict discipline is always necessary, but more particularly so in the service you are engaged in. Wherefore his Royal Highness recommends to you that it be constantly observed among the troops under your command, and to be particularly careful that they be not thrown into a panic by the Indians, with whom they are yet unacquainted, whom the French will certainly employ to frighten them. His Royal Highness recommends to you the visiting your posts night and day; that your Colonels and other officers be careful to do it; and that you yourself frequently set them the example; and give all your troops plainly to understand that no excuse will be admitted for any surprise whatsoever.

Should the Ohio expedition continue any considerable time, and Pepperell's and Shirley's regiments be found sufficient to undertake in the mean while the reduction of Niagara, his Royal Highness would have you consider whether you could go there in person, leaving the command of the troops on the Ohio to some officer on whom you might depend, unless you shall think it better for the service to send to those troops some person whom you had designed to command on the Ohio; but this is a nice affair, and claims your particular attention. Colonel Shirley is the next commander after you, wherefore if you should send such an officer he must conduct himself so as to appear only in quality of a friend or counsellor in the presence of Colonel Shirley: and his Royal Highness is of opinion that the officer must not produce or make mention of the commission you give him to command except in a case of absolute necessity.

The ordering of these matters may be depended on, if the expedition at Crown Point can take place at the same time that Niagara is besieged.

If after the Ohio expedition is ended it should be necessary for you to go with your whole force to Niagara it is the opinion of his Royal Highness that you should carefully endeavour to find a shorter way from the Ohio thither than that of the Lake; which however you are not to attempt under any pretence whatever without a moral certainty of being supplied with provisions, &c. As to your design of making yourself master of Niagara, which is of the greatest consequence, his Royal Highness recommends to you to leave nothing to chance in the prosecution of that enterprize.

With regard to the reducing of Crown Point, the provincial troops being best acquainted with the country, will be of the most service.

After the taking of this fort his Royal Highness advises you to consult with the Governors of the neighboring provinces, where it will be most proper to build a fort to cover the frontiers of those provinces.

As to the forts which you think ought to be built (and of which they are perhaps too fond in that country), his Royal Highness recommends the building of them in such manner, that they may not require a strong garrison. He is of opinion that you ought not to build considerable forts, cased with stone, till the plans and estimates thereof have been sent to England and approved of by the Government here. His Royal Highness thinks that stockaded forts, with pallisadoes and a good ditch, capable of containing 200 men or 400 upon an emergency, will be sufficient for the present.

As Lieutenant Colonel Lawrence, who commands at Nova Scotia, hath long protracted the taking of Beau-Sejour, his Royal Highness advises you to consult with him, both with regard to the time and the manner of executing that design. In this enterprize his Royal Highness foresees that his majesty's ships may be of great service, as well by transporting the troops and warlike implements, as intercepting the stores and succours that might be sent to the French either by the Baye Françoise, or from Cape Breton by the Baye Verte on the other side of the Isthmus.

With regard to your winter quarters after the operations of the campaign are finished, his Royal Highness recommends it to you to examine whether the French will not endeavor to make some attempts next season and in what parts they will most probably make them. In this case it will be most proper to canton your troops on that side, at such distances, that they may easily be assembled for the common defence. But you will be determined in this matter by appearances, and the intelligence, which it hath been recommended to you to procure by every method immediately after your landing. It is unnecessary to put you in mind how careful you must be to prevent being surprised. His Royal Highness imagines that your greatest difficulty will be the subsisting of your troops. He therefore recommends it to you to give your chief attention to this matter, and to take proper measures relative thereto with the Governors and with your quarter-masters and commissaries.

I hope that the extraordinary supply put on board the fleet, and the 1000 barrels of beef destined for your use, will facilitate and secure the supplying of your troops with provisions.

I think I have omitted nothing of all the points wherein you desired to be informed : if there should be any intricate point unthought of, I desire you would represent it to me now, or at any other time ; and I shall readily take it upon me to acquaint his Royal Highness thereof, and shall let you know his opinion on the subject.

I wish you much success with all my heart ; and as this success will infinitely rejoice all your friends, I desire you would be fully persuaded that no body will take greater pleasure in acquainting them thereof, than him, who is, &c.

(Signed.)

ROBERT NAPIER.

(A. D. C. to the Duke.)

APPENDIX No. II.

FANNY BRADDOCK.

Goldsmith's Miscellaneous Works (London, 1837), Vol. III., p. 294.
(*Life of Richard Nash.*)

"MISS SYLVIA S—— was descended from one of the best families in the kingdom, and was left a large fortune upon her sister's decease. She had early in life been introduced into the best company, and contracted a passion for elegance and expense. It is usual to make the heroine of a story very witty and very beautiful, and such circumstances are so surely expected, that they are scarce attended to. But whatever the finest poet could conceive of wit, or the most celebrated painter imagine of beauty, were excelled in the perfections of this young lady. Her superiority in both was allowed by all who either heard or had seen her. She was naturally gay, generous to a fault, good-natured to the highest degree, affable in conversation, and some of her letters and other writings, as well in verse as prose, would have shone amongst those of the most celebrated wits of this, or any other age, had they been published.

"But these qualifications were marked by another, which lessened the value of them all. She was imprudent. But let it not be imagined that her reputation or honour suffered by her imprudence : I only mean, she had no knowledge of the use of money; she relieved distress by putting herself into the circumstances of the object whose wants she supplied.

"She was arrived at the age of nineteen, when the crowd of her lovers and the continued repetition of new flattery had taught her to think she could never be forsaken, and never poor. Young ladies are apt to expect

(401)

26

a certainty of success from a number of lovers; and yet I have seldom seen a girl courted by a hundred lovers that found a husband in any. Before the choice is fixed, she has either lost her reputation or her good sense; and the loss of either is sufficient to consign her to perpetual virginity.

"Among the number of this young lady's lovers was the celebrated S——, who, at that time, went by the name of 'the good-natured man.' This gentleman, with talents that might have done honour to humanity, suffered himself to fall at length into the lowest state of debasement. He followed the dictates of every newest passion; his love, his pity, his generosity, and even his friendships were all in excess; but they were in general head against any of his sensations or desires; he was unable to make worthy wishes and desires, for he was constitutionally virtuous. This gentleman, who at last died in a gaol, was at that time this lady's envied favourite.

"It is probable that he, thoughtless creature, had no other prospect from this amour but that of passing the present moments agreeably. He only courted dissipation, but the lady's thoughts were fixed on happiness. At length, however, his debts amounting to a considerable sum, he was arrested and thrown into prison. He endeavoured at first to conceal his situation from his beautiful mistress; but she soon came to a knowledge of his distress, and took the fatal resolution of freeing him from confinement by discharging all the demands of his creditors.

"Nash was at that time in London, and represented to the thoughtless young lady, that such a measure would effectually ruin both; that so warm a concern for the interests of Mr. S—— would in the first place quite impair her fortune in the eyes of our sex, and what was worse, lessen her reputation in those of her own. He added, that this bringing Mr. S—— from prison would be only a temporary relief; that a mind so generous as his would become bankrupt under the load of gratitude; and instead of improving in friendship or affection, he would only study to avoid a creditor he could never repay; that though small favours produce good-will, great ones destroy friendship. These admonitions, however, were disregarded; and she found, too late, the prudence and truth of her adviser. In short, her fortune was by this means exhausted; and, with all her attractions, she found her acquaintance began to disesteem her in proportion as she became poor.

"In this situation she accepted Nash's invitation of returning to Bath. He promised to introduce her to the best company there, and he was assured that her merit would do the rest. Upon her very first appearance, ladies of the highest distinction courted her friendship and esteem; but a settled melancholy had taken possession of her mind, and no amusements that they could propose were sufficient to divert it. Yet still, as if from habit, she followed the crowd in its levities, and frequented those places where all persons endeavour to forget themselves in the bustle of ceremony and show.

"Her beauty, her simplicity, and her unguarded situation soon drew the attention of a designing wretch, who at that time kept one of the rooms at Bath, and who thought that this lady's merit, properly managed, might turn to good account. This woman's name was Lindsey, a creature who, though vicious, was in appearance sanctified, and, though designing, had some wit and humour. She began by the humblest assiduity to ingratiate herself with Miss S——; shewed that she could be amusing as a companion, and, by frequent offers of money, proved that she could be useful as a friend. Thus by degrees she gained an entire ascendency over this poor, thoughtless, deserted girl; and in less than one year, namely, about 1727, Miss S——, without ever transgressing the laws of virtue, had entirely lost her reputation. Whenever a person was wanting to make up a party for play at dame Lindsey's, Sylvia, as she was then familiarly called, was sent for; and was obliged to suffer all those slights which the rich but too often let fall upon their inferiors in point of fortune.

"In most, even the greatest minds, the heart at last becomes level with the meanness of its condition; but in this charming girl, it struggled hard with adversity, and yielded to every encroachment of contempt with sullen reluctance. But though in the course of three years she was in the very eye of public inspection, yet Mr. Wood, the architect, avers, that he could never, by the strictest observations, perceive her to be tainted with any other vice than that of suffering herself to be decoyed to the gaming-table, and at her own hazard playing for the amusement and advantage of others. Her friend Nash, therefore, thought proper to induce her to break off all connections with dame Lindsey, and to rent part of Mr. Wood's house, in Queen's square, where she behaved with the utmost complaisance, regularity, and virtue.

"In this situation, her detestation of life still continued. She found that time would infallibly deprive her of a part of her attractions, and that continual solicitude would impair the rest. With these reflections she would frequently entertain herself and an old faithful maid in the vales of Bath, whenever the weather would permit them to walk out. She would even sometimes start questions in company, with seeming unconcern, in order to know what act of suicide was easiest, and which was attended with the smallest pain. When tired with exercise, she generally retired to meditation, and she became habituated to early hours of sleep and rest;

but when the weather prevented her usual exercise, and her sleep was thus more difficult, she made it a rule to rise from her bed, and walk about her chamber, till she began to find an inclination for repose.

"This custom made it necessary for her to order a candle to be kept burning all night in her room; and the maid usually, when she withdrew, locked the chamber door, and pushing the key under it beyond reach, her mistress, by that constant method, lay undisturbed till seven o'clock in the morning, when she arose, unlocked the door, and rang the bell as a signal for the maid to return.

"This state of seeming piety, regularity, and prudence continued for some time, till the gay, celebrated, toasted Miss Sylvia was sunk into a housekeeper to the gentleman at whose house she lived. She was unable to keep company, for want of the elegancies of dress, which are the usual passports among the polite; and was too haughty to seem to want them. The fashionable, the amusing, and the polite in society now seldom visited her; and from being once the object of every eye, she was now deserted by all, and preyed upon by the bitter reflections of her own imprudence.

"Mr. Wood and part of his family were gone to London, and Miss Sylvia was left with the rest as governess at Bath. She sometimes saw Mr. Nash, and acknowledged the friendship of his admonitions, though she refused to accept any other marks of his generosity than that of advice. Upon the close of the day upon which Mr. Wood was expected to return from London, she expressed some uneasiness at the disappointment of not seeing him, took particular care to settle the affairs of his family, and then as usual sat down to meditation. She now cast a retrospect over her past misconduct, and her approaching misery; she saw that even affluence gave her no real happiness, and from indigence she thought that nothing could be hoped but lingering calamity. She at length conceived the fatal resolution of leaving a life in which she could see no corner for comfort, and terminating a scene of imprudence in suicide.

"Thus resolved, she sat down at her dining-room window, and with cool intrepidity wrote the following lines on one of the panes of the window:

'O Death! thou pleasing end of human woe!
Thou cure for life, thou greatest good below!
Still mayst thou fly the coward and the slave
And thy soft slumbers only bless the brave.'

"She then went into company with the most cheerful serenity, talked of indifferent subjects till supper, which she ordered to be got ready in a little library belonging to the family. There she spent the remaining hours preceding bed-time, in dandling two of Mr. Wood's children on her knees.

In retiring from thence to her chamber, she went into the nursery to take her leave of another child, as it lay sleeping in the cradle. Struck with the innocence of the little babe's looks, and the consciousness of her meditated guilt, she could not avoid bursting into tears, and hugging it in her arms; she then bid her old servant a good-night, for the first time she had ever done so, and went to bed as usual.

"It is probable she soon quitted her bed, and was seized with an alternation of passions, before she yielded to the impulse of despair. She then dressed herself in clean linen and white garments of every kind, like a bride-maid. Her gown was pinned over her breast, just as a nurse pins the swaddling clothes of an infant. A pink silk girdle was the instrument with which she resolved to terminate her misery, and this was lengthened by another made of gold thread. The end of the former was tied with a noose, and the latter with three knots, at a small distance from one another.

"Thus prepared, she sat down again and read; for she left the book open at that place, in the story of Olympia, in the Orlando Furioso of Ariosto, where, by the perfidy and ingratitude of her bosom friend, she was ruined and left to the mercy of an unpitying world. This fatal event gave her fresh spirits to go through her tragical purpose; so, standing upon a stool, and flinging the girdle, which was tied round her neck, over a closet-door that opened into her chamber, she remained suspended. Her weight, however, broke the girdle, and the poor despairer fell on the floor with such violence, that her fall awakened a workman that lay in the house, about half an hour after two o'clock. Recovering herself, she began to walk about the room, as her usual custom was when she wanted sleep; and the workman imagining it to be only some ordinary accident, again went to sleep. She once more, therefore, had recourse to a stronger girdle, made of silver thread, and this kept her suspended till she died. Her old maid continued in the morning to wait as usual for the ringing of the bell, and protracted her patience, hour after hour, till two o'clock in the afternoon; when the workmen at length entering the room through the window, found their unfortunate mistress still hanging and quite cold. The coroner's jury being impanelled, brought in their verdict lunacy; and her corpse was next night decently buried in her father's grave.

"Thus ended a female wit, a toast, and a gamester; loved, admired, and forsaken; formed for the delight of society, fallen by imprudence into an object of pity. Hundreds in high life lamented her fate, and wished, when too late, to redress her injuries. They who once had helped to impair her fortune, now regretted that they had assisted in so mean a pursuit. The little effects she had left behind were bought up with the greatest avidity, by those who desired to preserve some token of a companion that had once given them such delight. The remembrance of every virtue she was possessed of was now improved by pity. Her former follies were few, but the last swelled them to a large amount; and she remains the strongest instance to posterity, that want of prudence alone almost cancels every other virtue.

"In all this unfortunate lady's affairs Nash took a peculiar concern : he directed her when they played, advised her when she deviated from the rules of caution, and performed the last offices of friendship after her decease, by raising the auction of her little effects."

APPENDIX No. III.

GEORGE CROGHAN'S STATEMENT.

"THE Government continued to maintain the Indians that lived at my house till the Spring, when General Braddock arrived. They then desired Governor Morris to let me know that they would not maintain them any longer, at which time Governor Morris desired me to take them at Fort Cumberland to meet General Braddock, which I did. On my arrival at Fort Cumberland, General Braddock asked me where the rest of yᵉ Indians were? I told him I did not know: I had brought with me about 50 men which was all which was at that time under my care and which I had brought there under direction of Gov. Morris. He replied 'Governor Dinwiddie told me at Alexandria that he had sent for 400 which would be here before me.' I answered I knew nothing of that, but that Capt. Montour the Virginia Interpreter was in camp and could inform his Excellency; on which Montour was sent for, who informed the General that Mr. Gist's son was sent off some time ago for some *Cheroquees Indians*, but whether they would come he could n't tell: on which the General asked me whether I could not send for some of yᵉ Delawares and Shawnese to Ohio. I told him I could; on which I sent a messenger to Ohio who returned in eight days and brought with him three chiefs of the Delawares. The General had a conference with these chiefs in company with those 50 I had brought with me, and made them a handsome present, and behaved as kindly to them as he possibly could during their stay, ordering me to let them want for nothing. The Delawares promised in council to meet yᵉ General on the road, as he marched out, with a number of their warriors, but whether the former breaches of faith on the side of the English prevented them,

(407)

or that they had before engaged to assist the French, I cannot tell : but they disappointed the General and did not meet him.

Two days after the Delaware Chiefs had left the camp at Fort Cumberland, Mr. Gist's son returned from the Southern Indians where he had been sent by Governor Dinwiddie, but brought no Indians with him. Soon after the General was preparing for y[e] march with no more Indians than those I had with me, when Col. Innis told the General that the women and children of the Indians which was to remain at Fort Cumberland would be very troublesome, and that the General need not take above ten men out with him, for if he took more, he would find them very troublesome on the march, and of no service : on which the General ordered me to send all the men, women and children back to my house in Pennsylvania, except eight or ten which I should keep as scouts : which I accordingly did.

But I am yet of opinion that had we had fifty Indians instead of eight, that we might in a great measure have prevented the surprise, that day of our unhappy defeat." (George Croghan's Journal to the Ohio during Mr. Hamilton's and part of Mr. Morris's administration, taken from the original delivered by himself to Mr. Peters. August 18th, 1757.— Du Simitiere MSS., Library Co. of Philadelphia.)

APPENDIX No. IV.

THE FRENCH REPORTS OF THE ACTION OF THE 9TH JULY, 1755.

THE ensuing three papers are taken from copies procured by Mr. Sparks from the originals in the Archives of the War Department at Paris : and it is to his kindness that they are now for the first time published *en bloc.* Their gist has indeed been given in the second volume of his Washington.

I.

RÉLATION DU COMBAT DU 9 JUILLET, 1755.

Monsieur de Contre-cœur Capitaine d' Infanterie commandant au fort Duquesne sur la belle riviere, ayant été informé que les Anglois armoient dans la Virginie pour le venir attaquer, fût averti peu de temps àprès qu'ils étoient en marche, il mit des découvreurs en campagne que s'informèrent fidellement de leur routte. Le Sept du courant il fût averti que leur armée composée de 3000 hommes de troupes de la vieille Angleterre étoient à Six lieux de ce fort : Cet officier employa le landemain a faire ses dispositions, et le neuf il détache Monsieur de Beaujeu et lui donna pour second Monsieur Dumas et de Lignery, tous trois Capitaines, avec quatres Lieutenants, 6 Enseignes, 20 Cadets, 100 Soldats, 100 Canadiens et 600 Sauvages, avec ordre de s'aller embarquer[1] dans un lieu favorable qu'il avoit fait reconnoitre la vieille. Le détachement se trouva en presance de

---

[1] Embusquer ?

(409)

l'ennemi a trois lieux de ce fort avant d'avoir pû gagner son poste. Monsieur de Beaujeu voyant son embuscade manquée prit le parti d'attaquer:
il le fît avec tant de vivacité que les ennemis qui nous attendoient dans le
meilleur ordre du monde en parurent étonnées, mais leur artillerie chargée
a cartouche ayent commencé à faire feû, notre trouppe fût ébranlée a son
tour. Les Sauvages aussi, épouvantés[1] par le bruit du canon plutôt que
par le mal qu'il pouvoit faire, commencoient à perdre leur terrain. Lorsque
Monsieur de Beaujeu fût tué, Monsieur Dumas s'appliqûa aussitôt a rani-
mer son détachement: il ordonna aux officiers qui conduisoient les Sauvages de s'étandre sur les aisles pour prendre l'ennemi en flanc, dans le temps
que lui, Monsieur de Ligneri, et les autres officiers qui etoient a la tête
des françois attaquoient de front. Cet ordre fût executé si promptement
que les ennemis qui poussoient deja leurs cris de Vive le Roi ne furent
plus occuppés que de bien deffendre. Le combat fût opiniatre de part et
d'autre, et le succés longtemps douteux, mais enfin l'ennemi pliat. Il
chorcha inutilement de mettre quelques ordres dans sa retraite: les cris
des Sauvages, dont les bois rétantissoient, portérent l'épouvante dans tous
les cœurs des ennemis. La deroutte fût complette: le champ de bataille
nous rosta avec six pieces de canons de fonte de douze et de Six, quatre
affûts a bomb de 50, 11 petite Mortiere à grenade Royale, toutes leur munitions et generalement tous leurs bagages. Quelques déserteurs qui nous
sont venus depuis nous ont dit que nous avions eû affaire qu'a 2000
hommes, le reste de l'armée étant à quatre lieux plus loin. Ces mêmes déserteurs nous ont dit que les ennemis se retiroient en Virginie, et des découvreurs qu'on à envoyé presqu'a la hauteur des terres nous l'ont confirmées
en nous rapportant que les milles hommes qui n'avoient point combatû
avoient également pris l'épouvante, et abandonnes vivres et munitions en
chemin, sur cette nouvelle l'on a envoyé un détachement sur la routte qui
a détruit ou brulé tout ce qui pouvoit rester en nature. Les ennemis ont
laissés plus de 1000 hommes sur les champs de bataille. Ils ont perdu vué[2]
grande partie d'artillerie et de munitions de vivres, ainsi que leur général
nommé Monsieur Bradork et presques tous les officiers. Nous avons eus
3 officiers de tués et 2 de blessés; 2 Cadets blessés. Un tel succés que
l'on avoit pas lieu de se promettre, vu l'inégalité des forces, est le fruit de
l'experiance de Monsieur Dumas et de l'activité et de la valeur des officiers qu'il avoit sous ses ordres.

---

[1] Epouvantés?   [2] Une?

II.

RÉLATION DEPUIS LE DÉPART DES TROUPPES DE QUEBEC, JUSQU' AU 30 DU MOIS DE SEPTEMBRE, 1755.

Les regimans partagés par division de quatre et cinq compagnies etoient partis pour se rendre en partie au fort frontenac ou nous devions former un camp et dela aller faire le siege de chozen; ce projet n'a pu avoir son exécution, ayant été obligé de les faire marcher pour empecher les ennemis de faire se lui du fort St. frédéric, et on fut dans l'obligation de faire redescendre le régiment de la Regne et notre première division qui étoit deja fort avancée. Les ennemis avoient trois corps d'armée, l'une étoit destinée pour les trois Riviéres, ou ils ont échoués. Le corp étoit de trois mils hommes commandés par le Général *Braudolk*; Leurs intentions étoit de faire le Siege du fort *du Quesne*. Ils avoient beaucoup d'artillerie, beaucoup plus qu'il nén faut pour faire le Siege des forts de ce pais, la plus part ne valent rien, quoiqu'il ayent beaucoup couté au Roi. Monsieur *de Beaujeu* qui commandoit dans ce fort prevenu de leurs marche et fort embarassé de pouvoir, avec le peu de monde qu'il avoit, empecher ce Siège, se détermina à aller au devant de l'ennemi. Il le proposa aux Sauvages qui etoient avec lui, qui dabord rejetterent son avis, et lui dire quoi, mon père, tu veux donc mourir et nous sacrifier, les Anglois sont plus de quatres Mils hommes et nous autres nous ne Sommes que huit cent, et veux les aller attaquer; tu vois bien que tu n'a pas d'esprit: Nous te demandons jusqu'a demains pour nous déterminer. Ils tinrent conseil entre eux ils ne marchent jamais qu'il ne fassent de même. Le landemain matin Monsieur de Beaujeu sorti de son fort avec le peu de troupes qu'il avoit et demanda aux Sauvages qu'elles avoient été leurs déliberations. Ils lui répondirent qu'ils ne pouvoient marcher. Monsieur de Beaujeu, qui etoit bon, affable et qui avoit de l'esprit, leur dit: Je suis déterminé à aller au devant des ennemis: quoi — laisserez-vous aller notre[1] pere seul? Je suis sur de les viancre. Ce détachement étoit composé de 72 hommes de trouppes, de 146 Canadians et 637 Sauvages: La rencontre s'est faite à 4 lieux du fort le 9 du Juillet à une heure apres midi; la faire[2] a duré jusqu'a cinq. Monsieur de Beaujeu à été tué a la première discharge. Les Sauvages qui l'amoient beaucoup vangerent sa mort avec toutte sa[3] bravoure imaginable. Ils obligerent l'ennemi a prandre la fuitte après un perte considerable. Cela n'est pas extraordinaire; leur façon de se battre est bien différente de celle de nous autres Européens, la quelle ne vaut rien en ce pais. Ils se mirent en bataille, présanterent un front, a qui, a des hommes cachés derrière des armes[4] qui chaque coup

[1] Votre?   [2] L'affaire?   [3] La?   [4] Arbres?

de fusil en culbutoient un ou deux : c'est ainsi qu'ils défirent presque entièrement les Anglois et cela presque tous ces vieilles troupes qui avrient passé l'hiver dernier. On fait monter la perte des ennemis à 1500 hommes. Monsieur de Braudolk leur général y a été tué et quantité d'officiers. On leur a pris 13 pièces d'artillerie, beaucoup de boulets et de bombes, cartouches et poudres, et farines, 100 bœufs, 400 chevaux tués, ou pris, tous leur chariots pris ou cassés. Si nos Sauvages ne s'étoient pas amusés a piller, il ne s'en seroit pas retourné un. Il y a grande aparence qu'ils ne tanteront plus rien pour cette partie, puis qu' on se retirant ils ont brulé un fort qu'ils avoient établis pour leurs retraites. Nous avons perdus trois officiers, dont Monsieur de Beaujeu, 25 Soldats, Canadiens, ou Savages, environ autant de blessé. Nous n'avons pas été aussi heureux dans nôtre partie : revenons à nous autres.

III.

DE MONSIEUR LOTBINIERE A MONSIEUR LE COMTE D'ARGENSON.

Au camp de Carillon, le 24 Octobre, 1755.

Des l'automne dernière comme j'eus l'honneur de vous le marquer, l'Anglois commença un fort au pied des montagnes d'Aliganai qu'il nomma fort de *Comberland* : le fort est éloigné du nôtre sur la Belle rivière de 110 miles suivant leur estime. Its ont fait partir d'Europe dans l'hiver deux régimens de troupes réglés de 500 hommes chacun sous le commandement de Monsiur Braddock qui est arrivé à Alexandrie en Virginie le 24 fevrier. Ce roi lui avoit donné la commission de général de toutes les forces du nord de l'Amérique et c'est lui qui devoit présider aux opérations préparées à la Cour de Londres tandis qu'on amusoit la cour de france de Mile propositions de paix pour être un état d'Envahir plus surement ce pays. Le général Braddok, sitot son arrivée en Virginie, fit ses préparatifs pour se mettre en campagne dans le premiers jours d'Avril. Il se réserva la réduction du fort de l'Ohio, et assemblé prendre toutes ses précautions pour s'assurer de la réussite. Cependant comme il n'a pas été servi par les provinces de la nouvelle Angleterre suivant ses désirs et qu'on la fait attendre un temps infini pour les chariots et autres choses qui devoient lui être fourni par les provinces il n'a pû laisser le fort de Comberland que dans les premiers jours de juin. Nos sauvages nous ont rapporté dans l'hiver qu'il se fasoit de grands préparatifs chez l'Anglois, mais Monsieur Duquesne, a qui cette nouvelle fut raporté, bien des fois traita ce la de fanfaronade et dit que ce n'étoit qu'un feu de paille. En consequence, il ne prit aucun des précautions nécessaires pour un mouvement si général.

Monsieur de Vaudreuil arriva dans le mois de Juin, a qui l'on dit que le gouvernement étoit dans un état mervillieux. Monsieur Duquesne, arriva dans les derniers jours de juin qui confirma à son successeur ce qu'il lui avoit déja écrit et deux jours après on sut la prise de Beauséjour. Monsieur Duquesne, qui avoit sû son fort ménacé, avoit envoyé a son secours, négligeant totalement les autres cotés. Secours arriva a point nommé et le Général de Guillet sachant que l'ennemi n'étoit qu'a trois lieux du fort Duquesne, on fit partir 891 hommes dont 250 français le reste sauvage sous le commandement de Monsieur de Beaujeu, Capitaine de nos troupes, qui se trouva vis-a-vis de l'ennemi a 11 heures du matin. Il l'attaqua avec beaucoup de chaleur et après 5 heures de combat notre detachment réussit a mettre totalement en déroute un avant-garde de 13 cents et quelques hommes, non compris les voituriers, on se trouva le général Braddock. Son arriere-garde de 700 hommes étoit a environ huit lieux et ne fut point attaqué. Il se trouva dans cet avant-garde le régiment d'halke, completté depuis son arrivée en Virginie à 700 hommes, 3 compagnies franches de 100 hommes chacune, le reste étoit troupe de province. Il resta sur la place plus de 600 morts, un nombre tres grand de blessés qui sont mort au retour: le général lui même y fut blessé et mourut à quelques lieux du Champs de Bataille. En un mot il n'a rétourné de ces 1300 hommes qu'- environ 300 hommes dont 11 officiers de plus de 150 qu'ils étoient. Nous n'y perdimes que le commandant avec deux autres officiers, 30 et quelques Canadiens et sauvages, et a peu près même nombre de blessé. Toute l'Artillerie de l'ennemi, ces chariots et tous ses équipages resterent au champs de bataille: ce qui fit un pillage considerable qui arreta notre troupe. On eut les papiers du Général Braddock parmi lesquelles se retrouverent les instructions du Roi donné avec réserve, qui se trouverent plus étendu par une lettre de Colonel Napier adjutant Général ecrite par ordre du Duc de Comberland pour lui servir de conduite dans toutes ses opérations.

APPENDIX No. V.

THE poetical sensibilities of the nation do not seem to have been very strongly affected by the inception or by the failure of Braddock's Expedition. A few copies of contemporaneous verses having fallen in my way, however, they are preserved here, as part of the *res gestæ*.

I.

[This jingling provincial ballad was composed in Chester County, Pennsylvania, while the army was on its march in the spring or early summer of 1755. During the Revolution it was still a favourite song there, the name of Lee being substituted for Braddock's. It has never, I believe, appeared in print before. There is no doubt of its authenticity.]

To arms, to arms! my jolly grenadiers!
Hark, how the drums do roll it along!
To horse, to horse, with valiant good cheer;
We'll meet our proud foe, before it is long.

Let not your courage fail you:
Be valiant, stout and bold;
And it will soon avail you,
My loyal hearts of gold.
Huzzah, my valiant countrymen!—again I say huzzah!
'Tis nobly done—the day's our own—huzzah, huzzah!

(414)

March on, march on, brave Braddock leads the foremost;
The battle is begun as you may fairly see.
Stand firm, be bold, and it will soon be over;
We'll soon gain the field from our proud enemy.
  A squadron now appears, my boys;
  If that they do but stand!
  Boys, never fear, be sure you mind
    The word of command!
Huzzah, my valiant countrymen! again I say huzzah!
'Tis nobly done—the day's our own—huzzah, huzzah!

See how, see how, they break and fly before us!
See how they are scattered all over the plain!
Now, now—now, now, our country will adore us!
In peace and in triumph, boys, when we return again!
  Then laurels shall our glory crown
  For all our actions told:
  The hills shall echo all around,
    My loyal hearts of gold.
Huzzah, my valiant countrymen!—again I say huzzah!
'Tis nobly done—the day's our own—huzzah, huzzah!

II.

[The following lines are from the Gentleman's Magazine, Vol. XXV., p.
383 (Aug. 1755). It would seem that they were first published as a
broadside and sold through the streets.]

*On the Death of Gen. Braddock, said to be slain in an Ambuscade by the
French and Indians, on the Banks of the Ohio, July 9, 1755.*

  Beneath some *Indian* shrub, if chance you spy
  The brave remains of murder'd *Braddock* lie,
  Soldiers, with shame the guilty place survey,
  And weep, that here your comrades fled away.
  Then, with his brother-chiefs[1] encircled round,
  Possess the hero's bones of *hostile* ground,
  And plant the *English Oak;*[2] that gave his name,
  Fit emblem of his *valour* and his *fame!*
  Broad o'er this *stream*[3] shall thus his honours grow,
  And last as long as e'er its waters flow!

---

[1] *His officers.*
[2] *Brad in old Saxon-English is the same as Broad, and Brad-oke the same as Broad-oak.*
[3] *The Ohio.*

[From XXV. Gent. Mag. (Sept. 1755), p. 421.]

III.

Apology for the Men who deserted Gen. Braddock when surpriz'd by the ambuscade.

Ah! *Braddock*, why did you persuade
To stand and fight each recreant blade,
    That left thee in the wood?
They knew that those who run away,
Might live to fight another day,
    But all must die that stood.

APPENDIX No. VI.

BRADDOCK'S LAST NIGHT IN LONDON.

SINCE the preceding pages were in press, the editor has been referred to a passage in the "Apology for the Life of George Anne Bellamy" of too interesting a character to be entirely omitted; though, unfortunately, it is now impossible to introduce it in its proper connection. It seems that from her earliest youth Braddock had been the constant friend of this beautiful and accomplished, although sometimes frail, actress. He had, at her request, given the agency of his regiment to her putative husband, Mr. Calcraft; and on the eve of his departure he came, with Colonel Burton and Captain Orme, to take a last farewell. Miss Bellamy was at this time living, under a contract of marriage, with Mr. John Calcraft, as his "domesticated wife," and the mistress of an establishment in Brewer Street. "Before we parted," continues she, "the General told me he should never see me more; for he was going with a handful of men to conquer whole nations; and to do this they must cut their way through unknown woods. He produced a map of the country, saying, at the same time, 'Dear Pop, we are sent like sacrifices to the altar.' The event of the expedition too fatally verified the General's expectations. On going away, he put into my hands a paper, which proved to be his will. As he did not doubt my being married to Mr. Calcraft * * * he made *him* his sole executor; leaving me only the plate which he had received as the usual perquisite from government on his nomination." (Vol. I. p. 194, Vol. V., p. 155.) This plate, which had, "besides the royal arms, a greyhound for the crest," the Treasury officers were so mean as to endeavor afterwards to recover, but were cast in the courts. What were the grounds of their demand is

27

(417)

not known. The value of Braddock's estate was £7000 (Vol. V., p. 192). Certainly, the fate of "her second father" would appear to have brought no common shock to the mind of the fair Apologist; and we are indebted to her memoirs for a further anecdote:

"This great man having been often reproached with brutality, I am induced to recite the following little anecdote, which evidently shows the contrary. As we were walking in the Park one day, we heard a poor fellow was to be chastised; when I requested the General to beg off the offender. Upon his application to the general officer, whose name was Dury, he asked Braddock, How long since he had divested himself of brutality and the insolence of his manners? To which the other replied, 'You never knew me insolent to my inferiors. It is only to such rude men as yourself that I behave with the spirit which I think they deserve.' " (Vol. III., p. 55.)

In the same work (Vol. II., p. 129, Vol. III., pp. 116, 153), may be found some notices of Colonel Burton's first wife (Miss St. Leger, of Ireland) and her family. After her death, and while yet in this country, he became enamored of an Indian beauty; but he seems to have subsequently married an American lady.

INDEX.

(419)

INDEX.

THE END.

The First American Frontier

AN ARNO PRESS/NEW YORK TIMES COLLECTION

Agnew, Daniel.
A History of the Region of Pennsylvania North of the Allegheny River. 1887.

Alden, George H.
New Government West of the Alleghenies Before 1780. 1897.

Barrett, Jay Amos.
Evolution of the Ordinance of 1787. 1891.

Billon, Frederick.
Annals of St. Louis in its Early Days Under the French and Spanish Dominations. 1886.

Billon, Frederick.
Annals of St. Louis in its Territorial Days, 1804-1821. 1888.

Littel, William.
Political Transactions in and Concerning Kentucky. 1926.

Bowles, William Augustus.
Authentic Memoirs of William Augustus Bowles. 1916.

Bradley, A. G.
The Fight with France for North America. 1900.

Brannan, John, ed.
Official Letters of the Military and Naval Officers of the War, 1812-1815. 1823.

Brown, John P.
Old Frontiers. 1938.

Brown, Samuel R.
The Western Gazetteer. 1817.

Cist, Charles.
**Cincinnati Miscellany of Antiquities of the West and Pioneer
History.** (2 volumes in one). 1845-6.

Claiborne, Nathaniel Herbert.
**Notes on the War in the South with Biographical Sketches
of the Lives of Montgomery, Jackson, Sevier, and Others.**
1819.

Clark, Daniel.
Proofs of the Corruption of Gen. James Wilkinson. 1809.

Clark, George Rogers.
**Colonel George Rogers Clark's Sketch of His Campaign in
the Illinois in 1778-9.** 1869.

Collins, Lewis.
Historical Sketches of Kentucky. 1847.

Cruikshank, Ernest, ed,
**Documents Relating to Invasion of Canada and the
Surrender of Detroit.** 1912.

Cruikshank, Ernest, ed,
**The Documentary History of the Campaign on the Niagara
Frontier, 1812-1814.** (4 volumes). 1896-1909.

Cutler, Jervis.
**A Topographical Description of the State of Ohio, Indian
Territory, and Louisiana.** 1812.

Cutler, Julia P.
The Life and Times of Ephraim Cutler. 1890.

Darlington, Mary C.
**History of Col. Henry Bouquet and the Western Frontiers
of Pennsylvania.** 1920.

Darlington, Mary C.
Fort Pitt and Letters From the Frontier. 1892.

De Schweinitz, Edmund.
The Life and Times of David Zeisberger. 1870.

Dillon, John B.
History of Indiana. 1859.

Eaton, John Henry.
Life of Andrew Jackson. 1824.

English, William Hayden.
Conquest of the Country Northwest of the Ohio. (2 volumes in one). 1896.

Flint, Timothy.
Indian Wars of the West. 1833.

Forbes, John.
Writings of General John Forbes Relating to His Service in North America. 1938.

Forman, Samuel S.
Narrative of a Journey Down the Ohio and Mississippi in 1789-90. 1888.

Haywood, John.
Civil and Political History of the State of Tennessee to 1796. 1823.

Heckewelder, John.
History, Manners and Customs of the Indian Nations. 1876.

Heckewelder, John.
Narrative of the Mission of the United Brethren. 1820.

Hildreth, Samuel P.
Pioneer History. 1848.

Houck, Louis.
The Boundaries of the Louisiana Purchase: A Historical Study. 1901.

Houck, Louis.
History of Missouri. (3 volumes in one). 1908.

Houck, Louis.
The Spanish Regime in Missouri. (2 volumes in one). 1909.

Jacob, John J.
A Biographical Sketch of the Life of the Late Capt. Michael Cresap. 1826.

Jones, David.
A Journal of Two Visits Made to Some Nations of Indians on the West Side of the River Ohio, in the Years 1772 and 1773. 1774.

Kenton, Edna.
Simon Kenton. 1930.

Loudon, Archibald.
Selection of Some of the Most Interesting Narratives of Outrages. (2 volumes in one). 1846.

Monette, J. W.
History, Discovery and Settlement of the Mississippi Valley. (2 volumes in one). 1808-1811.

Morse, Jedediah.
American Gazetteer. 1797.

Pickett, Albert James.
History of Alabama. (2 volumes in one). 1851.

Pope, John.
A Tour Through the Southern and Western Territories. 1792.

Putnam, Albigence Waldo.
History of Middle Tennessee. 1859.

Ramsey, James G. M.
Annals of Tennessee. 1853.

Ranck, George W.
Boonesborough. 1901.

Robertson, James Rood, ed.
Petitions of the Early Inhabitants of Kentucky to the Gen. Assembly of Virginia. 1914.

Royce, Charles.
Indian Land Cessions. 1899.

Rupp, I. Daniel.
History of Northampton, Lehigh, Monroe, Carbon and Schuykill Counties. 1845.

Safford, William H.
The Blennerhasset Papers. 1864.

St. Clair, Arthur.
A Narrative of the Manner in which the Campaign Against the Indians, in the Year 1791 was Conducted. 1812.

Sargent, Winthrop, ed.
A History of an Expedition Against Fort DuQuesne in 1755. 1855.

Severance, Frank H.
An Old Frontier of France. (2 volumes in one). 1917.

Sipe, C. Hale.
Fort Ligonier and Its Times. 1932.

Stevens, Henry N.
Lewis Evans: His Map of the Middle British Colonies in America. 1920.

Timberlake, Henry.
The Memoirs of Lieut. Henry Timberlake. 1927.

Tome, Philip.
Pioneer Life: Or Thirty Years a Hunter. 1854.

Trent, William.
Journal of Captain William Trent From Logstown to Pickawillany. 1871.

Walton, Joseph S.
Conrad Weiser and the Indian Policy of Colonial Pennsylvania. 1900.

Withers, Alexander Scott.
Chronicles of Border Warfare. 1895.